Sports Wagering in America

Policies, Economics, and Regulation

Anthony Cabot
Keith Miller

UNLV Gaming Press
4505 Maryland Parkway Box 457010
Las Vegas, NV 89154-7010
gamingpress.unlv.edu

Sports Wagering in America:
Policies, Economics, and Regulation

Library of Congress call number GV717 .C32 2018
Paperback ISBN 978-1-939546-12-8

Layout by David G. Schwartz
Cover photography Aaron Mayes

Set in Minion Pro and Noto Sans

Keith Miller dedicates this book to Liz and Dori. For fourteen years I have been blessed by the inspiration, comfort, and love they have given me.

Anthony Cabot dedicates this book to the late Bob Hannum. The world lost a great mathematician, an even better human being and friend.

Contents

Editors' Note

The momentum to expand regulated sports betting has accelerated considerably over the past few years. Indeed, we are likely at a point where one can accurately say it is no longer a matter of *if*, but a matter of *when*, sports betting as a legal form of gambling will spread across the U.S.

The court litigation challenging the federal law, the Professional and Amateur Sports Protection Act (PASPA), which has limited single-game sports betting to Nevada, has been the topic of a great deal of discussion and writing. Missing from the scholarship of sports betting, however, is a comprehensive analysis of the "how" of sports wagering regulation. That is, assuming that sports betting will become part of the fabric of gambling in the U.S., how will this activity be regulated?

Our goal in writing this book is to explore these "how" issues. We believe this is important because uninformed and misguided regulation of sports betting can undermine many of the objectives of establishing regulated sports betting markets. The book examines the issues that legislators and regulators must consider as they construct sports betting systems, and offers some guidance on the difficult choices they will be required to make.

We welcome comments about the materials and are happy to discuss the use of the materials in classrooms or otherwise. Our contact information is Professor Keith C. Miller, Drake University Law School, (515) 271-2071, keith.miller@drake.edu, and Anthony Cabot, Distinguished Fellow, UNLV Boyd School of Law, anthony.cabot@unlv.edu.

Author Miller wishes to thank his research assistant Matthew Engelstad for his reliable and substantial contributions to the book. The Dean of his law school, Jerry Anderson, has also been a source of support and guidance throughout the work on this and other projects. Author Cabot has equally high regard for the Dean of his law school, Daniel Hamilton, who had the foresight to create the only LL.M. program for gaming law and supports a broad range of initiatives related to gaming law and regulation. Special thanks go to legendary sports book operators Art Manteris of Red Rock Casinos, and Vic Salerno and sports industry veterans Pete Korner and Bob Kocienski, for reviewing and contributing to chapter 1. Finally, this book would not have been possible without the steady support of Dr. David G. Schwartz, Director of the UNLV Center for Gaming Research.

Sports Wagering in America

Policies, Economics, and Regulation

1

Sports Wagering in America

This chapter explains the sports wagering industry in America with a focus on the regulated market in Nevada, the only state currently with legal full-service sportsbooks. An understanding of the sports wagering industry is necessary to regulate the sector properly and to achieve the goals of protecting wagering and sports competition integrity. Knowledge of the various types of wagers, for example, is essential because some are especially vulnerable to manipulation by match-fixers. Also, understanding the economics of sports betting is important when establishing taxes and allocating sports wagering revenue. Finally, an awareness of who the key persons are in the sports wagering process informs the establishment of regulatory standards and licensing requirements.

WHAT SPORTS DO AMERICANS BET ON?

A person can place wagers on almost any event today. In December 2016, Ladbrokes, a British bookmaker who does not offer wagering in the United States, posted odds of 6/4 that Donald Trump would resign as President.[1] While Nevada law allows Nevada books to accept wagers on non-sporting events, few books have sought approvals to do so. Nevada sportsbooks offer wagering (called "action") on most sports, including: (1) professional football; (2) college football; (3) professional basketball; (4) college basketball; (5) professional baseball; (6) professional hockey; (7) professional soccer; (8) boxing; (9) mixed martial arts (MMA); (10) auto racing; (11) professional tennis; (12) professional golf; (13) horse racing; and (14) Australian rules football. Besides these sports, some Nevada books have offered non-sports wagering on eSports and the NFL draft, virtual horse

---

1 Browne, Amy, *11 Strange Things You Can Bet on Happening in 2017*, Liverpool Echo, Dec. 31, 2016, http://www.liverpoolecho.co.uk/news/11-things-you-can-bet-12389237.

racing, and major events like the World Series of Poker.[2]

While Nevada sportsbooks can provide wagering on virtually any sporting event, they typically limit wagering to professional and amateur sporting events that will generate significant betting action. The following chart shows which sports Nevada books offer wagering and the sanctioning body for each of these sports. For example, with professional baseball, a sportsbook could offer wagering on the Frontier League, an independent minor professional baseball league unaffiliated with Major League Baseball. Because a sportsbook would expect minimal action on the Traverse City Beach Bums (a real team), wagering on professional baseball is limited to Major League Baseball and some international competitions. [3]

Major Sports for Wagering and Sanctioning Bodies				
Football	Basketball	Baseball	Hockey	Soccer
National Football League (NFL)	National Basketball Association (NBA)	Major League Baseball (MLB)	National Hockey League (NHL)	UEFA Champions Euro Europa Supercup
AFL (Arena Football)	Women's National Basketball Association (WNBA)	National Collegiate Athletic Association (NCAA) (usually only major tournaments if offered)	NCAA College Hockey (futures on national championship and games during the NCAA tournament)	English Premier
Canadian Football League (CFL)	Men's National Collegiate Athletic Association (NCAA) Basketball			Major league Soccer (MLS)
NCAA Football Divisions 1-A and I-AA	Women's (NCAA) Basketball			Fédération Internationale de Football Association (FIFA) World Cup and Confederations Cup, Others[3]

2 In Nevada, the Nevada Gaming Commission must approve wagering on non-sports events. Nev. Gaming Comm. Reg. 22.120(2). Whether they would approve wagering on competitions where voters determine the outcome, like elections or the Oscars, has not been determined.

3 Others - Argentina Primera, Brazil Serie A League, French Ligue 1, German Bundesliga,

Major Sports for Wagering and Sanctioning Bodies				
Auto Racing	Boxing (although they are somewhat obsolete and lacking relevance)	Mixed Martial Arts	Tennis	Golf
National Association for Stock Car Auto Racing (NASCAR)	World Boxing Organization (WBO)	Ultimate Fighting Championship (UFC)	Association of Tennis Professionals (ATP)	Professional Golfers' Association (PGA)
Fédération Internationale de l'Automobile (FIA) Formula One	World Boxing Association (WBA)	Bellator MMA	Women's Tennis Association (WTA)	
INDYCAR	World Boxing Council (WBC)			
	International Boxing Hall of Fame (IBHOF)			
	International Boxing Federation (IBF)			

Despite the variety of wagering opportunities, the three leading sports for wagering are football, baseball, and basketball. Excluding pari-mutuel horse racing, Nevada bettors only made about 7% of all wagers on sports other than football, basketball, and baseball. Football is the most popular with about 40% of all sports wagering, followed by basketball with about 32% and baseball with about 22%.[4]

The following chart shows the number of Nevada locations that offer each type of sports wagering, the amount bet (called the "handle"), the amount retained after paying all wagers (called the

Holland Eredivisie, Italian Series A, Mexico Primera, Spanish La Liga League.

4 Actual breakdown for each sport in Nevada as a percentage of handle is as follows:

	Football	Basketball	Baseball
2010	42.92%	30.06%	14.98%
2011	46.6	25.62	19.39
2012	45.41	28.27	20.11
2013	44.80	29.08	18.80
2014	44.85	28.43	18.50

"win") and the gross margin (called the win %) for 2016.

Calendar Year 2016	# of locations	Handle ($US in 1000s)	Win ($US in 1000s)	Win %
Pari-Mutuel Horse Race	82	291,613	46,279	15.87
Football	190	1,692,820	91,243	5.39
Basketball	190	1,402,778	66,632	4.75
Baseball	190	1,046,753	32,204	3.08
Sports Parlay Cards	189	60,254	10,412	17.28
All Others		304,215	18,648	6.07
Sports Pari-Mutuel	56	332	35	10.54

This chart shows amounts wagered on each sport over the past 22 calendar years.

Nevada Handle by Sport[5]						
	Football	Basketball	Baseball	Other	Parlay	Total
1995	1,039,936	679,704	533,023	96,031	71,088	2,428,593
1996	999,964	680,739	608,373	114,385	78,324	2,483,312
1997	949,086	637,477	566,172	132,166	66,882	2,431,382
1998	915,937	557,723	600,513	134,433	68,280	2,269,062
1999	980,276	610,333	678,254	129,433	63,510	2,470,407
2000	914,212	638,993	567,537	137,822	65,301	2,323,377
2001	806,319	567,179	495,657	112,780	58,004	2,042,855
2002	860,000	513,503	386,783	109,444	66,431	1,936,544
2003	826,244	489,167	378,875	106,634	63,984	1,863,678
2004	969,129	543,661	426,479	86,813	59,943	2,087,273
2005	1,051,198	579,396	464,067	100,176	62,864	2,257,174
2006	1,136,397	635,365	457,541	131,147	68,265	2,427,605
2007	1,176,512	687,193	528,792	134,000	68,616	2,594,191
2008	1,122,229	738,268	522,013	131,486	64,614	2,579,225
2009	1,093,596	803,529	488,630	126,848	58,981	2,568,362
2010	1,185,462	830,422	528,668	158,563	56,707	2,762,267
2011	1,341,788	737,432	558,011	179,465	62,633	2,877,935
2012	1,566,499	975,153	693,687	157,692	58,178	3,449,533
2013	1,622,791	1,053,132	681,007	204,889	57,658	3,622,107
2014	1,749,723	1,109,182	721,831	266,990	57,782	3,901,117
2015	1,698,477	1,251,732	897,312	333,174	54,070	4,237,422
2016	1,692,820	1,402,779	1,045,584	307,216	60,255	4,509,753
2017	1,755,616	1,481,881	1,139,783	427,579	62,923	4,868,434

5 David G. Schwartz. *Nevada Sports Betting Totals: 1984-2016*. Las Vegas: Center for Gaming Research, University Libraries, University of Nevada Las Vegas, 2017.

The Nevada government does not release statistics on the handle broken down between professional and amateur sports. Based on interviews with various sportsbook managers, it appears the handle skews slightly in favor of professional football compared to amateur games. In basketball betting, the handle is roughly the same for NCAA and professional games. Virtually all betting on baseball is on MLB, except for the College World Series which generates some action.[6] Of course, the amount wagered on an average professional game in football is much higher (5 or 6 times) than an NCAA game. However, this is because on any given week the NFL has 12 to 16 games while the books will post about 75 NCAA games.

WAGERING SYSTEMS AND BET TYPES

The three dominant systems of gambling on sporting events are (1) pari-mutuel wagering, (2) fixed odds, and (3) exchange wagering. Most sports wagers in the United States are fixed odds wagers where the odds and the payouts are fixed and not subject to change once the bettor makes the wager. Legally, a fixed odds bet is a contract; the price (amount won or lost) is honored according to the terms of the contract when the bettor and a bookmaker enter it. The distinctive part of a wagering contract is that the promise of performance is based on a future contingent event (the outcome of the sports competition) not under the control of the sportsbook or the bettor. With fixed odds wagers, the terms of the contract are agreed to in advance, including the odds and payouts. After that, whether the sportsbook must fulfill its promise to pay the bettor is dependent on the terms of the bet and the outcome of the game. Pari-mutual wagers are different because the sportsbook and the bettor do not agree on the odds or payouts, but only on the formula for making the payout. Whether the sportsbook must fulfill its promise to pay is still determined by a future contingent event.

While other types of wagers exist, common types of fixed odds wagers on American sports are (1) fractional odds including money line wagering, (2) point-spread wagering, (3) parlay wagers, (4) proposition bets, and (5) in-game betting.

Fractional Odds Including Money Line Wagering

Among the oldest type of fixed odds wagers is fractional odds. In

6 Interview of Vic Salerno, July 28, 2017.

the United States, sportsbooks offer fractional odds on some events, particularly futures, where, as an example, the Cleveland Cavaliers may have 5/1 odds to win the next NBA championship. Bookmakers in the UK and Ireland feature fractional wagers, such as odds of 2/1 or 1/2 on a game. On 2/1 odds, if a person bets a dollar, he would win $2 and collect $3 (the bet and the winnings). In the 1/2 situation, the bettor would win 50 cents on a $1 bet. Many betting sites in Europe, and in Australia, New Zealand, and Canada, use decimal odds. A bettor can use the decimal posted by the bookmaker to determine the total payout. If bettor wagered $10 and the decimal odds posted is 3, then he would receive a total of $30 on his winning wager (his original wager of $10 plus $20).

In the United States, "money line" bets are popular fixed odds wagers on low scoring events, like baseball and hockey, where bettors find the use of point spreads less appealing.[7] A money line wager is a fractional odds wager expressed differently than in Europe, Australia, New Zealand and Canada. For example, a money line wager where both teams are evenly handicapped, and there is no house commission, would be +100 on a money line, 2.0 in decimal odds and 1/1 in fractional odds. The following chart gives examples of how different probabilities are expressed as odds under each system:

Probability	Fractional	Money line	Decimal
66.67	1/2	-200	1.50
50	1/1	+100	2.00
33.33	2/1	+200	3.00

The book makes its profit on money line wagers by including its commission (vig) in setting the money line. For example, a money line wager on the 2017 MLB All-Star Game may look like the following:

American League +106

@ National League -116

7 Sportsbook may offer baseball (run line) and hockey (goal line) using a spread of 1 ½ points where this does act as a point spread, but the volume of these types of wagers pales in comparison to regular game wagers. Interview of Pete Korner, July 27, 2017.

The "minus" (-) before the number for the National League indicates that it is the favorite. The "plus" (+) before the number for the American League means that it is the underdog. The National League odds are -116, meaning a winning bet of $11.60 would produce a $10 return and a total take with the return of the wager of $21.60. The American League odds are +106, meaning a $10 bet would win $10.60, for a return of $20.60, if the bettor won.[8]

A dime line is a betting line with a 10-cent straddle, which is the difference between the payout on the underdog and the favorite. With a dime line, if the favorite is minus -120, the underdog is plus +110. Here the book makes its commission on the difference in the line between the favorite and the underdog. If both teams were equally handicapped and the book offered a dime line, the money line on each team would be -105, meaning a $1.05 wager on either team would win a dollar. If the book had equal wagers of $100 on both teams, it would collect $105 and pay $100, for a total commission of $5 on $200 in wagers (handle). A dime line thus gives the books a lower commission rate and house advantage than on point spread wagers on football and basketball.

The chart on page 4 shows that the win percentage on baseball for Nevada books is consistently lower than on football or basketball. Almost all bets in baseball (and hockey) use the money line and not a point spread.[9] Without a point spread, the result, no matter what the odds were, is always the same as the score. A book manager can increase or decrease the size of the odds (the money line) on a given game, but the number does not affect the final score. Bettors do not have to handicap the games in any way other than deciding who is going to win. In short, a Nevada sportsbook director knows that a considerable percentage of their baseball bets are on the teams with winning records and against the teams losing records. According to Pete Korner:

> In 1990, bettors had different personalities. A sizeable baseball price on a pitcher and team could scare away money. But that is not the case anymore. Today's bettors have no fear in betting high odds for smaller gains. Today's market in the gambling industry demands instantaneous results. Sports bettors traditionally sought the value in wagering $110 for a profit of $100. But today, bettors see they can bet $100 on a huge favorite for an immediate return of a $40 profit in a three-hour game. A 40% profit in that short of a time span sure beats

8 Allen Moody, *How a Moneyline Works in Sports Betting*, THOUGHTCO., Aug. 2, 2017, https://www.thoughtco.com/sports-betting-understanding-money-lines-3116852.
9 www.docsports.com/current/sports-betting-how-wager-baseball-16.html

what the stock market can do in one day.[10]

Moreover, although the average person thinks he is playing a dime line in football because he bets $11 to win $10, in fact, it is the equivalent to a 20-cent money line.[11] The house advantage on that football point spread bet is 4.545% while the house advantage on a dime line money line wager in baseball is 2.77%. Typically, Nevada sportsbooks will offer a dime line on baseball games until the favored team gets up to about a 2 to 1 favorite.

According to some experienced sportsbook managers, baseball has a higher percentage of "wise guy" bettors, who are experienced sports bettors with greater skill than casual bettors. While baseball features significantly more games than either football or basketball, individual regular season games rarely attract a high level of attention or passion from casual or square bettors, although there is greater interest during the playoffs. Moreover, the hot summer months tend to bring fewer visitors to the desert climate of Las Vegas. Therefore, the audience for baseball tends to be the more sophisticated daily bettor. These professional bettors make it even more dangerous if book managers make pricing mistakes.

An example of the sportsbook's exposure in this situation is the summer of 2017 where there was considerable betting action on the LA Dodgers and Houston Astros, and against the San Francisco Giants and Philadelphia Phillies. For the sportsbook to make a profit from straight bets and parlays, they needed one, and maybe, two upsets.[12]

MLB Money Line							
Pro Baseball	Open	Consensus	Westgate	MGM	William Hill	Stations	Pinnacle
6/23 7:10 903 Chi Cubs 904 Miami	9u-10 -133 +123	91/2u-20 -113 +103	91/2u-20 -113 +103	9o-20 +100 -120	9o-20 -115 +105	91/2-15 -116 +106	91/2u-23 -110 +102
Pitchers (CHC) John Lackey (R) (MIA) Jose (R)							
Nevada licensed books are in gray; Pinnacle is an Internet book on the island of Curaçao of the Kingdom of the Netherlands The first line above is a totals bet. For example, 9u-10 means the total points is 9 and the -10 means the under is offered at -110.							

The chart above compares the baseball money lines on a game

10 Korner, *supra* note 7.

11 Salerno, *supra* note 6.

12 Korner, *supra* note 7.

between the Chicago Cubs and the Miami Marlins of four Nevada licensed operators and one Internet operator, Pinnacle, which has its headquarters in Curaçao. Notably, Pinnacle offers an 8-cent line, while three of the four Nevada books offer a dime line. Thus, Pinnacle has a lower house advantage because it offers better odds to the bettor.

Most book operations use a graduated line. It may start as a 10 cent line on an evenly handicapped game, but increase as the divide between the favorite and the underdog widens. Some Nevada books will offer a dime line until the favored team gets to a 2-1 advantage.[13] For example, if the teams are even, with a dime line, the money line would be -105 on both teams. If the book has the favorite as -265, it may post the underdog at +235 whereas the dime line book would have it at +255.

MLB Money Line							
Pro Baseball	Open	Consensus	Westgate	MGM	William Hill	Stations	Sportsbk.ag
901 Cinn 902 Wash	+229 -250	+230 -270	+235 -265	+230 -270	+230 -270	+235 -290	+230 -280
Pitchers (CIN) Luis Castillo (R) (Wash) Stephen Strasburg (R)							
Nevada licensed books are in gray, Sportsbook.ag is an Internet book.							

The chart above shows a typical game. At this point in the baseball season, Washington was 43-29 and was starting one of the better MLB pitchers, Stephen Strasburg, who had a season record of 8 wins and 2 losses. He was pitching at home. Cincinnati, on the other hand, was 30-41 and starting a rookie, Luis Castillo, in his first major league game. Hence, Washington was a solid favorite to win. Depending on where he placed his wager, a bettor had to lay between $250 and $290 on Washington to win $100. At the start of the day, if he bet the opening line (the first line posted by the book operator), he would have only had to bet $250 to win $100. The line, however, changed because the bettors wagered more on Washington and the books adjusted the payouts to encourage wagering on Cincinnati. The next section explains the reasons and process for when books move

MGM-Mirage Line Movements			
		Money Line	
Date	Time	Fav	Dog
6/22	9:53pm	Was-250	Cin+210
6/23	11:33am	Was-**270**	Cin+**230**
Line movement in bold.			

13 Salerno, *supra* note 6.

the line. The chart on page 9 shows the line changes at the MGM-Mirage, a licensed Nevada book.

A book also can offer money line wagering on partial game and totals. A partial game wager is merely a money line or point spread wager on the results of a portion of a contest, for example, the first half of a football game, the first five innings of a baseball game, the first quarter of a basketball game or the first period of a hockey game. In a totals wager, the bettor is wagering whether the combined number of points scored by the teams including overtime is over or under the line posted by the sportsbook. This is frequently a 20-cent line at Nevada sportsbooks. The chart above shows an example of a totals line.

Point Spread Wagering

Historians attribute the invention of point spread wagering to a former Chicago teacher, and securities analyst turned bookmaker named Charles McNeil.[14] In the 1940s, McNeil was looking for a system that would make betting on lopsided games more attractive to his clients and help his bookmaking operation generate equal amounts of action on both sides of a game that had an overwhelming favorite.[15] Offering fractional odds on lopsided games, such as 10/1, was less attractive because the bookmaker had to limit wagering on underdogs to manage their risk of substantial losses if an upset occurred. Refusing or limiting bets on the favorite angered persons that could not wager ("get a bet down") on their favorite teams. McNeil's solution was to establish a point system that would "handicap"[16] the favorite so that betting on a handicapped game would be an almost even money proposition. When odds makers set a point spread on a football or basketball game, the bettors now must handicap not only who wins, but by how much. McNeil's system, called point-spread wagering, proved hugely popular with the betting public and bookmakers across the United States quickly copied it.[17] It is the most popular form of wagering on football and basketball games. The point spread is the great equalizer.

---

14 Richard O. Davies & Richard G. Abram. BETTING THE LINE: SPORTS WAGERING IN AMERICAN LIFE 52 (Ohio State University Press, 2001).

15 *Id.* at 53

16 The word "handicap" came from a failed system in the mid-1800s where faster horses had to carry extra weight to make the horse race more competitive.

17 Davies & Abram, *supra* note 14, at 55.

Understanding House Advantage and Win Percentage

House advantage is the most commonly used indicator of the value of a game or bet. From the book's perspective, the house advantage represents how much, in terms of percentage of the money wagered, the book can expect to retain in the long run if all bets were placed randomly. In contrast to house advantage, win percentage represents actual results. That is, win percentage is based on how much the book accepted in wagers (handle) and the amount retained after paying all winning bets. Win percentage is represented by win divided by handle.

Because sports wagering involves skill, both on behalf of the bettor and the bookmaker, house advantage is only the starting point for understanding how much the book ultimately wins (or loses). For example, the house advantage on a dime line money line wager in baseball is 2.77%, assuming all bets are random. If there were a purely random event, like a coin toss at the start of a football game, and the sportsbook book offered this as a -105 bet on both sides, the book has a 2.77% house advantage and should, over time, expect to win $2.77 on every $100 wagered.

But bookmaking is not based on random events. Therefore, the player's skill or lack thereof and the bookmaker's skill or lack thereof can impact how close the actual win percentage is to the house advantage. If the bookmaker is not skilled, and makes a strong favorite an even money bet, it is likely that bettors will bet heavily on the favorite. In this case, the bettors will have a higher expectation of winning than if they bet randomly. Depending on the extent of the bookmaker's error in setting the money line, his mistake could eliminate the entire house advantage, or shift the advantage to the player.

How Point Spread Wagering Works

Single game point-spread wagering is a bet based on the differences in the total amount scored by each competitor of a game or competition. The economics of point spread wagering can take much of the risk out of being a bookmaker. In point-spread wagering, the bettor wagers against the sportsbook, but unlike house-banked casino games (such as blackjack, roulette, or craps), the book usually will attempt to accept an equal amount of wagers on both sides of each event by offering two equally attractive betting options. The bookmaker then makes money by charging a commission for this service. The commission is referred to as the "*vigorish*," "*vig*," or "*juice*."

If the total amount wagered on each side of a contest is the same, the book makes its profit from the commission. If bettors wager more money on the winning side, the sportsbook may incur a loss in paying off the winning wagers. The sportsbook uses a betting line to minimize the risk of suffering such a loss. This method of handicapping makes the underdog in the sporting contest as attractive to bet on as the favorite, also called the "chalk." In point-spread betting, the sportsbook assigns a certain number of points – called the point spread, the line, the number, the price, or the spread – to the favorite and underdog for purposes of deciding the bet. A wager on the favorite wins only if the favorite wins the game by more than the point-spread (i.e., they cover the spread).[18] A bet on the underdog, or dog, wins if either the underdog wins the game outright or if the favorite wins by less than the point-spread. If the favorite wins by precisely the spread amount, the game is a tie for betting purposes, and the sportsbook returns the wagers to the bettors. The favorite is said to be laying points; the underdog is getting points.

A person making a point spread bet usually must pay $11 to win $10.[19] If he wins the wager, he receives $21--the $11 wagered plus the $10 won. If he loses, he loses the $11 wagered.[20] The formula below calculates the expected value and house edge, assuming a 50% chance of picking the correct team with a point-spread bet. The expected value of a $110 bet assuming a 50% probability of success is:

$$EV = (+100)(.5) + (-\$110)(.5) = -\$5.00$$ [21]

This negative $5.00 expectation on a $110 wager equates to a house advantage, sometimes called the "edge," of 0.04545, or about 4.55%.[22] For example, if a patron were to make a wager of equal amounts, $110, on each of the two teams, his total wager amount

18 Robert C. Hannum & Anthony N. Cabot, CASINO MATH (Institute for the Study of Gambling & Commercial Gaming, University of Nevada, Reno, 2nd ed. 2005).

19 Some books allow the bettor to buy a half-point. For example, if the book posts New England at a 9-point favorite, a bettor can take New England at 8.5 by risking $120 to win $100. In effect, the book is willing to give up ½ point in the spread for twice the commission or "vig". *See* James Jeffries, THE BOOK ON BOOKIES, AN INSIDE LOOK AT SUCCESSFUL SPORTS GAMBLING OPERATIONS, 9-10 (Paladin Press 1st ed. 2000).

20 Hannum & Cabot, *supra* note 18.

21 *Id.*

22 *Id.*

would be $220.[23] Assuming no tie, he would win one bet and lose one bet. He would receive $210 back for the winning wager ($110 from the wager plus $100 he won) for a net loss of $10 – which means he is guaranteed to lose $10 or 4.55% of the $220 put at risk.[24] Sportsbooks typically do not require bets to be made in multiples of $11 (or $5.50), but doing so makes payoffs easier and experienced players do so. If the bet amount is not a multiple of $11, the payoff is typically rounded down. For example, the payoff on a winning $50 bet is $45 instead of the 10:11 payoff of $45.45. The difference is called breakage.

The 4.545% house advantage is the primary source of sportsbook profits.[25]

Making and Moving the Line

The sportsbook can employ different strategies when offering point-spread wagering. Most common is to balance the action, the total amount wagered on both teams, so that the expected return is equal to the house advantage. In most circumstances, Nevada sportsbook managers prefer to manage risk by attempting to balance the dollar amount of wagers accepted on each team.[26] Here, the book manager (or an independent odds maker) tries to set the opening line or the odds based on a prediction of what number will attract an equal amount of bets on both teams. This may not equate to a prediction of the outcome of the contest. The odds maker considers how the people are likely to bet on a game by looking at past betting patterns for similar games. The line setter also studies available information regarding the contestants,[27] and other situations that could affect performance. This could include things such as schedules, starting times, injuries, personnel changes, coaching status, past performances, and weather.[28] Finally, this skilled analysis must consider the sophistication, feedback, perception, and biases of the bettors that the odds maker believes will bet on the competition[29]

By balancing the sides, the book manager can assure a profit to the book based on the house advantage built into each single game wager

23 *Id.*

24 *Id.*

25 *Id.*

26 Art Manteris & Rick Talley, SUPERBOOKIE: INSIDE LAS VEGAS SPORTS GAMBLING 37 (Contemporary Books, 1st ed. 1991).

27 Michael Roxborough & Mike Rhoden, SPORTSBOOK MANAGEMENT: A GUIDE FOR THE LEGAL BOOKMAKER (Las Vegas Sports Consultants 1998).

28 Manteris & Talley, *supra* note 26.

29 Roxborough & Rhoden, *supra* note 27.

whether it is a point spread or money line wager. To accomplish this, however, the book typically sets betting limits that assist in assuring that the wagers do not become too heavy on one side of a contest. Where the amounts bet on each side become significantly unbalanced, this places the book at a risk of loss, which is called "exposure."

Books often set both a wager limit and a game limit to guard against being too exposed. A wager limit is the maximum wager that the book will accept on a game from a bettor. Sportsbooks strictly enforce such limits against professional bettors, also known as wise guys, sharps, or sharks. For example, a book may set its maximum exposure at $20,000. In other words, regardless of the outcome, the book's downside on that game will not exceed the game limit of $20,000. This limit varies based on the type of wager and the event on which the bettor is placing the wager. Game limits are much lower in low liquidity games like those in the WNBA, as compared to an NFL game where the amounts wagered are substantial. Moreover, the book may raise the limits for high liquidity games like the NFL Super Bowl. A game bet limit is how much risk (exposure) the book is willing to assume on one side of a wager before it moves the line.[30] These limits protect against errors in setting the lines, actions of professional gamblers, being the victim of competition manipulation,[31] or those having beneficial insider information regarding a sporting event—such as the extent of a player's injury[32] or a coach's decision on starting lineups.[33] Insider trading is covered extensively in Chapter 5.

A major factor impacting the profitability of the sportsbook is that, despite the book manager's best efforts, balanced action on a game is the exception rather than the rule.[34] When patrons wager more money on one team, the sportsbook may change or move the

30 *Id.*

31 *Id.*

32 This last category of professional bettors, i.e., the ones who seek to obtain inside information and profit from it, are the ones most commonly cited as presenting a danger to a game's integrity. In its simplest terms, a "bad guy" can pay money (bribes) to athletic support personnel or a player, in exchange for material inside information, or even pay money to affect the outcome of a game or its components. The first two categories, i.e., professional gamblers who use statistical analyses to inform a betting decision, and those who use arbitrage, are analogous to stock traders, who also use statistical analyses to inform a buy-sell decision and arbitrage to take advantage of spreads in the markets. These types of professional gamblers are much less reliant on "inside information" and therefore may be of less concern to sports leagues and franchises.

33 Roxborough & Rhoden, *supra* note 27.

34 Manteris & Talley, *supra* note 26.

line to encourage bettors to wager on the other team and help balance its book. This effort to balance the money bet is why the line may move up or down from its original spread and may continue moving until game time. If the line changes, however, it does not affect bets that bettors have already placed. Books typically use a "ladder" approach in moving the point spreads. If the wagering becomes unbalanced on one team, the book will look at its exposure, and if it reaches a certain percentage of the game limit, then it will change the line in small increments, perhaps ½ point in a football game. If the action on both sides equalizes, then that point spread will hold. If the action continues to be unbalanced, then the book may make additional moves either up or down the ladder.

Moving the line, however, puts the book at financial risk because if the game ends on precisely the closing point spread, the book may be "sided," that is, the book ties the bettors on one wager (and returns the amount wagered) and loses the wager to bettors who bet earlier with a more favorable line.[35] "Getting middled" is worse. In this case, the book loses the wagers on both sides. For example, if the opening line is 2½ and a majority of the action is on the favorite, the book may move the line to 3½. If the final score is 10-7, the book loses the bets on the favorite at -2½, and on the underdog at +3 ½. Books get middled in perhaps in only 2% of the games,[36] but these occurrences reduce the long-term house advantage to less than 4.55%.[37] Book managers must be especially careful when moving point spreads in football games off the numbers 3, 4, 6, 7, and 10. Because of the way points are scored in football, game results frequently land on these point spreads. Consequently, this presents the greatest threat for the book to be middled and to suffer a negative financial impact.[38]

Sportsbooks can use other strategies to manage risk. The opening line is simply the best estimate of the number that will result in a balanced book. Ultimately, however, the bettors decide the real number by making actual wagers. Some books may accept higher bets after releasing the opening line and attempt to balance their books through the course of this early wagering and once balanced reduce the wager limits to preserve that balance. [39] Other books may limit the amount of wagers after the opening line to allow the market

35 Roxborough & Rhoden, *supra* note 27.

36 Manteris & Talley, *supra* note 26.

37 Roxborough & Rhoden, *supra* note 27.

38 *Id.*

39 Manteris & Talley, *supra* note 26.

to stabilize around a point spread, and then accept larger wagers after that until game time.[40]

A book may deviate from having balanced books for several reasons. First, it may have miscalculated the bettors' interest in the game and set the odds or line incorrectly, with the result being that more money is bet on one side of a contest. Subsequent efforts to balance the book by changing the odds or moving the line to draw more wagers on the other side may not be successful.

Second, some books will "shade" the line to take advantage of irrational bettor behavior. For example, bettors may irrationally wager on strong favorites or unsophisticated bettors may irrationally wager on their hometown or favorite teams regardless of the point spread.[41] A sportsbook may take advantage of these biases by intentionally inflating the line on favorites or against hometown teams.[42] While this strategy may be effective with casual bettors, who are wagering based on favorite teams, natural bias or folklore, this does not influence professional bettors whose actions are driven by data analysis. These sophisticated bettors will take advantage of deviations between the actual line and their calculated result. Book operators prefer unsophisticated bettors to professional bettors because the latter can exploit incorrect lines and have the financial resources to cause the book to be unbalanced on games.[43] The book operation, therefore, may take a wager from an unsophisticated bettor at a shaded line but refuse that same wager from a sophisticated bettor.

Third, a book could, in theory, attempt to earn more than the built-in house advantage on each wager by abandoning efforts to balance games and setting odds based on anticipated results. Bookmakers can use their forecasting ability and knowledge of the biases of bettors to maximize profits.[44] The problem with this approach is the assumption that sportsbooks can consistently forecast outcomes better than the increasing number of well-financed professional bettors who take advantage of advanced analytics.[45] Internet casinos that have a dedicated bookmaking business may devote greater resources to

---

40 *Id.*

41 Steven D. Levitt, *Why are Gambling Markets Organized So Differently from Financial Markets?*, 114 THE ECONOMIC JOURNAL 223 (2004).

42 Richard Borghesi, *Widespread Corruption in Sports Gambling: Fact or Fiction?*, 74 SOUTHERN ECONOMIC JOURNAL 1063 (2008).

43 Levitt, *supra* note 41.

44 *Id.*

45 *Id.*

analytics that diminish the advantage enjoyed by professional bettors. As a result, these sportsbooks may be more willing to take risks.

In Nevada, sportsbooks can only be in licensed casinos. On average, the sportsbooks are less profitable than the casino's slot machines and, despite assertions to the contrary, have not been empirically proven to make significant, indirect contributions to casino products.[46] Most casinos are unwilling to assume significant additional risk by consistently trying to beat the market. Nevada books, therefore, will rarely abandon risk management practices. Still, some books may tolerate greater imbalance to improve handle by accepting higher bet limits, though they will still manage risk by moving their lines to encourage balanced wagers.

Some exceptions to these principles exist. For example, after entering the Nevada market in 2007, Cantor Gaming accepted very high limit bets,[47] often five times the average betting limits of other books. This would naturally increase their exposure on games where the money came in heavily on one team. Federal and state authorities, however, later accused Cantor Gaming of mitigating its risk by accepting wagers from illegal bookmakers in other jurisdictions.[48] If proven, this would have violated federal gambling laws. Cantor Gaming ultimately settled the matter by signing a non-prosecution agreement and agreeing to pay $16.5 million to the United States Attorney's offices in New York and Nevada, $6 million to the Treasury Department's Financial Crimes Enforcement Network,[49] and an additional penalty of $5.5 million to the Nevada Gaming Commission.[50]

Asian Handicapping

In 1998, Joseph Phan, a bookmaker from Indonesia, decided to launch a new internet sports wagering platform based on a new

46 Brett Lillian Levine Abarbanel, Estimating the Indirect Contribution of Sportsbook: Sports Wagering as a Driver of Other In-House Revenues. (2009) (unpublished Ph.D. dissertation, University of Nevada, Las Vegas).

47 *See* Liz Benston, *Will Las Vegas Sportsbook Adopt More Bettor-Friendly British Wagering Style?* Las Vegas Sun, Apr. 27, 2011, http://www.lasvegassun.com/news/2011/apr/27/will-sports-books-take-british-betting-style ("Cantor [Gaming] welcomes large wagers and professional gamblers . . . [and] could significantly increase the market for big-time sports betting.").

48 Keith Romer, *When A Wall Street Firm Took A Stab at Casino Capitalism*, NPR, Jan. 5, 2017, http://www.npr.org/2017/01/05/508408521/when-a-wall-street-firm-took-a-stab-at-casino-capitalism.

49 Michael J. de la Merced, *Cantor Fitzgerald Gambling Affiliate Settles Investigation,* NY Times, Oct. 3, 2016, https://www.nytimes.com/2016/10/04/business/dealbook/cantor-fitzgerald-gambling-affiliate-settles-investigation.html.

50 A copy of the settlement with the Nevada Gaming Commission is available at http://gaming.nv.gov/modules/showdocument.aspx?documentid=8600.

Favorite Handicap	Game result	Bet result	Underdog Handicap	Game result	Bet result
0	Win	Win	0	Win	Win
	Draw	Push (Wager Returned)		Draw	Push
	Loss	Loss		Loss	Loss
- 0.25	Win	Win	+ 0.25	Win	Win
	Draw	Half loss		Draw	Half win
	Loss	Loss		Loss	Loss
- 0.50	Win	Win	+ 0.50	Win	Win
	Draw	Loss		Draw	Win
	Loss	Loss		Loss	Loss
- 0.75	Win by 2+	Win	+ 0.75	Win	Win
	Win by 1	Half win		Draw	Win
	Draw	Loss		Loss by 1	Half Loss
	Loss	Loss		Loss by 2+	Loss
- 1.00	Win by 2+	Win	+ 1.00	Win	Win
	Win by 1	Push		Draw	Win
	Draw	Loss		Loss by 1	Push
	Loss	Loss		Loss by 2+	Loss
- 1.25	Win by 2+	Win	+ 1.25	Win	Win
	Win by 1	Half loss		Draw	Win
	Draw	Loss		Loss by 1	Half win
	Loss	Loss		Loss by 2+	Loss
- 1.50	Win by 2+	Win	+ 1.50	Win	Win
	Win by 1	Loss		Draw	Win
	Draw	Loss		Loss by 1	Win
	Loss	Loss		Loss by 2+	Loss
- 1.75	Win by 3+	Win	+ 1.75	Win	Win
	Win by 2	Half win		Draw	Win
	Win by 1	Loss		Loss by 1	Win
	Draw	Loss		Loss by 2	Half loss
	Loss	Loss		Loss by 3+	Loss
- 2.00	Win by 3+	Win	+ 2.00	Win	Win
	Win by 2	Push		Draw	Win
	Win by 1	Loss		Loss by 1	Win
	Draw	Loss		Loss by 2	Push
	Loss	Loss		Loss by 3+	Loss

method of wagering. Joe Saumarez Smith, a gaming magazine reporter, learned of this new system and coined it "Asian Handicapping" because it was based on an Asian style of wagering with the name "hang cheng."[51] Asian handicapping is a type of point spread wagering

51 BETASIA, *Origin of Asian Handicap*, https://web.archive.org/web/20091031041314/http://www.betasia.com/features/how-to-win/general/5874/origin-of-asian-handicap.html.

used primarily for soccer. Like American point spread wagering, the underdog is given a given a point or goal advantage. If the actual score plus their goal advantage exceeds their opponent's score, the bettors that wagered on the underdog win the wager. Likewise, if their actual score plus their goal advantage is less than their opponent, the bettors that wagered on their opponent win. If their score plus the goal advantage equal their opponent's score, then it is a draw and the bets are refunded. Obviously, on .5 handicaps, no draws are possible.

With both whole and half-point handicaps, Asian handicapping is identical to point spread wagering. What distinguishes Asian handicapping, however, is that the sportsbooks also offer .25 and .75 handicaps. These are actual combination bets. If a bettor wagered $100 on a +.25 handicap, he effectively is placing half his bet at 0 and the other half at .5. Stated a different way, the bettor who wagered $100 on a +.25 handicap bet the equivalent of $50 on a 0 handicap and $50 on a .5 handicap. Likewise, a +.75 wager is a combination of a +.5 handicap wager and a +1.0 handicap wager. A sportsbook can write a quarter-goal handicap as 0,25, 0.25, or 1/4. A half-goal handicap can be written as 0.5, 0.5, 1/5.

At the book, betting on a soccer game may be posted as follows:

Southampton -.5 (1.90) | *Brighton* +.5 (2.10)

If Southampton wins the game by a score of 1-0 over Brighton, a $100 wager placed on Southampton will result in a win and return $190 (the original wager plus a profit of $90). If the final score is 1-0, the bet on Southampton is lost.

Suppose the book posted the same soccer game as follows:

Southampton -.75 (1.80) | *Brighton* +.5 (2.20)

If Southampton wins the game by a score of 1-0 over Brighton, a $100 wager placed on Southampton will result in a win and return $140 (the original wager plus a profit of $40). The calculation of that payout is set forth below:

	Half Bets		Overall Bet
Handicap	-0.5	-1	-0.75
Wager	$50.00	$50.00	$100.00
Result	Win	Push	Half Win
Payout	$90.00	$50.00	$140.00
Profit	$40.00	$0.00	$40.00

Parlay Wagering

Parlay wagers are where the bettor must choose the winners of multiple games, often single game outcomes against the point spread, and correctly pick all winning teams to win the bet. If a person loses any of the individual games, he loses the parlay wager. For example, if he correctly picks seven of the eight games in an eight-team parlay, he would lose his bet. Parlay cards are attractive to some bettors because high payoffs can be won without risking significant sums of money.

Examples of the typical payouts for parlays are:

- Two Team Parlay: 13 to 5 (bet $100 to win $260)
- Three Team: 6 to 1 (bet $100 to win $600)
- Four Team: 10 to 1 (bet $100 to win $1,000)
- Five Team: 20 to 1 (bet $100 to win $2,000)
- Six Team: 40 to 1 (bet $100 to win $4,000)
- Seven Team: 75 to 1 (bet $100 to win $7,500)
- Eight Team: 100 to 1 (bet $100 to win $10,000)

On a parlay card where ties go to the player, and the payouts are as described above, the house advantage on a randomly selected card is between 20% and 31% depending on the number of games selected.[52] As the Nevada statistics reveal, the actual win percentage on parlay cards is considerably higher (29% in 2015 and 17% in 2016) than for straight wagers.[53]

Books do not manage risk with parlay card the same as with straight wagers. The books have no practical way to move the lines on the parlay cards so they must manage risk by having bet limits and maximum aggregate payout limits, i.e., the total amount paid out to all bettors in each week.[54] The total amount wagered on parlay cards, however, is small in comparison to straight wagers.[55]

Some books offer "Off The Board Parlays." "Off the Board" parlays use the point spreads on the betting board instead of those printed on a parlay card. The better does not complete a parlay card but tells the writer he wants to bet a parlay, provides the bet numbers for the parlay, and indicates the amount of the bet. If all the games parlayed are standard -110 (pay $11 to win $10), then the payouts are typically

---

52 THE WIZARD OF ODDS, *Parlay Bets in the NFL*, Dec. 19, 2014, https://wizardofodds.com/games/sports-betting/nfl-parlay/.

53 *See infra* note 72 and accompanying chart.

54 NEVADA SPORTSBOOK, *Sportsbook House Rules*, https://nvsportsbooks.com/houserules/.

55 *See supra* note 5, and accompanying chart.

listed by the sportsbook. An example would be:

2 TEAMS	13/5
3 TEAMS	6/1
4 TEAMS	11/1
5 TEAMS	22/1
6 TEAMS	45/1
7 TEAMS	90/1
8 TEAMS	180/1
9 TEAMS	360/1
10 TEAMS	720/1

If any of the games are not the standard -110 line, the computer will generate the payouts based on the different odds.

Some sportsbooks offer "teasers" or "pleasers" parlays. Teaser cards are point spread based, and the bettor gets extra points on the teams that he chooses. For example, if the Oakland Raiders are 8-point favorites to win the game, a bettor can choose the Raiders to be only a 2-point favorite as one selection on a teaser parlay card. To compensate for the changes in the point spread, the payout on teasers is significantly less than regular parlay cards. Pleasers are the opposite, where the bettor must give up typically between 7 and 14 points on each game, but the payouts are significantly higher than regular parlay cards. The house advantage on teaser cards varies based on the number of extra points given and the number of games chosen, but are favorable to the sportsbook and range from about 11% to over 80%.[56]

56 THE WIZARD OF ODDS, *Teaser Bets in the NFL*, Sept. 26, 2014, https://wizardofodds.com/games/sports-betting/nfl-teaser/.

Proposition Wagers

Proposition or "prop" bets, also called "derivatives," are "exotic" wagers on the outcome of events that occur within a game or season that are unrelated to game outcome.[57] For example, in a football game a person can bet on whether a quarterback will throw for more or less than 200 yards, or which team will kick the first field goal. Here are examples of proposition bets offered in Las Vegas on the 2017 NFL Super Bowl.[58]

MOST PENALTY YARDS
**(Declined penalties do not count)
PATRIOTS +105
FALCONS -125
WILL THERE BE A MISSED EXTRA POINT KICK?
**(If no TD is scored—all bets are refunded)
YES +330
NO -400
WILL BOTH TEAMS MAKE 33 YARD OR LONGER FIELD GOALS?
**(If no Field Goal is made, no is the winner)
YES -150
NO +130
TEAM TO USE COACHES CHALLENGE FIRST
**(Official Challenges from the league are excluded)
PATRIOTS -110
FALCONS -110

In-game wagering

In-game wagering is the ability to place wagers, typically through electronic means, during the progress of a game and often on each play. For example, in American football, a person may wager on whether the next play will be a run or a pass. In-game wagering makes up about one-third of online sports betting revenue in the United Kingdom. While it is not prevalent in Nevada, it is gaining in popularity.[59]

Futures

A futures wager is typically a fixed odds wager on a future event. Nevada

57 David Forrest, MATCH-FIXING IN INTERNATIONAL SPORTS (Springer International Publishing, 2013).

58 WESTGATE LAS VEGAS SUPERBOOK, *Super Bowl LI Propositions*, http://www.vegasinsider.com/visports/nfl/westgate-super-book-2017.pdf.

59 GAMBLING COMMISSION, *In-play (in-running) Betting: Position Paper*, (Sept. 2016), http://www.gamblingcommission.gov.uk/pdf/In-running-betting-position-paper.pdf.

sportsbooks post futures as fractional wagers. The most popular are futures wagers as to which team will win the next season's championship. For example, the chart below shows the odds for who would win the 2018 NBA Championship about six months before the season was even set to begin.

Team	Odds	Team	Odds
Golden State Warriors	10/17	**Philadelphia 76ers**	80/1
Cleveland Cavaliers	5/1	**Denver Nuggets**	100/1
Boston Celtics	15/2	**LA Clippers**	100/1
Houston Rockets	10/1	**Los Angeles Lakers**	100/1
San Antonio Spurs	10/1	**Memphis Grizzlies**	100/1
Minn. Timberwolves	33/1	**Miami Heat**	100/1
OKC Thunder	40/1	**Orlando Magic**	100/1
Washington Wizards	40/1	**Charlotte Hornets**	125/1
Milwaukee Bucks	50/1	**Port. Trail Blazers**	125/1
Toronto Raptors	50/1	**Dallas Mavericks**	150/1
Utah Jazz	66/1	**Detroit Pistons**	150/1
NO Pelicans	66/1	**New York Knicks**	150/1

Futures wagers typically have strong house advantages. For example, the typical house advantage on future Super Bowl Champions in Nevada books can range from 20 to 60%.[60]

Betting Exchanges

Flutter, a British company, introduced the concept of a betting exchange to the public in May 2000, followed closely by UK-based Betfair in June 2000.[61] Below is a snippet of an exchange on an NBA basketball game between the Cleveland Cavaliers and the Houston Rockets, November 9, 2017.

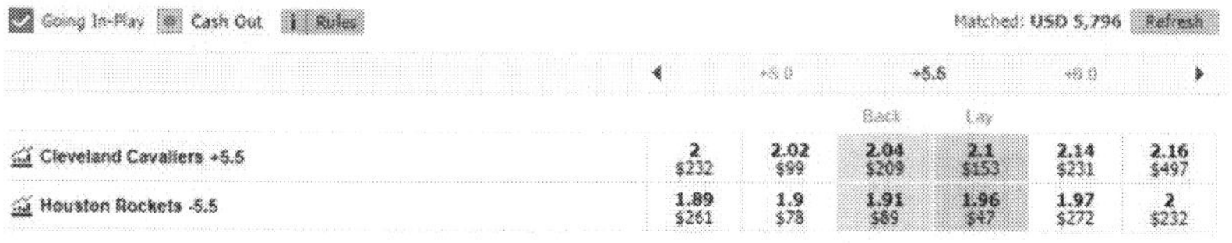

Going In-Play Cash Out Rules — Matched: USD 5,796 Refresh

+5.5

			Back	Lay		
Cleveland Cavaliers +5.5	2 $232	2.02 $99	2.04 $209	2.1 $153	2.14 $231	2.16 $497
Houston Rockets -5.5	1.89 $261	1.9 $78	1.91 $89	1.96 $47	1.97 $272	2 $232

This shows the back and lay offers on a wager for Cleveland +5.5. Betting exchanges offer the opportunity for players to lay outcomes, such as to bet that a participant in an event will lose. In other words,

60 The Wizard of Odds, *Sports Futures*, Sept. 12, 2014, https://wizardofodds.com/games/sports-betting/appendix/5/.

61 Greg Wood, *Flutter's Departure Leaves Bitter Taste*, The Guardian, Jan. 16, 2002, https://www.theguardian.com/sport/2002/jan/16/horseracing.gregwood.

a player can post a wager and stake on a sporting event, and other players can choose to match it. The opposite is to be willing to accept the proposition that participant will win that particular bet.[62] This is the way that a stock exchange operates as a forum for buyers and sellers of stocks. Players have a choice of what odds to accept.[63] Betting exchanges use decimal odds, so 2.04 in the above example means that a bettor backing that wager would receive $2.04 for every dollar invested including his stake.[64] The dollar figure below each decimal odds is the amount available for each wager, that is, the total amount other bettors have made offers at with that point spread and odds.

Once another user accepts that offer, a binding wagering contract is entered. If a player wants better odds than are available, he or she can place an order for a better price. The bet exchange sites track the lays, backs, and orders in the order they are matched. A betting exchange effectively allows the public to become the bookmaker by offering a wager of their making.[65] Betting exchanges also allow bettors to sell their wagers "in-running."[66] In other words, a player can sell a bet, provided there is a willing buyer, at any time from the acceptance of the wager until the conclusion of the contest that was the subject of the wager. The exchange is never at risk and makes its revenues by charging a commission on every wagering contract. The customers in the exchange, and not the exchange itself, are responsible for creating the liquidity in the pools. These fees are often lower than in traditional bookmaking because (a) the commission rate does not need to reflect the risk of loss, and (b) the ability to trade bets in-running creates a much greater turnover on which to base commissions. For example, Betfair starts at a 5% commission rate but discounts it up to 60%, lowering it to an effective 2% rate for members that have high bet volumes.[67]

---

62 ALL ABOUT GAMBLING, *Betting Exchanges*, http://www.allgam.com/betting-exchanges.php (accessed March 31, 2017).

63 BETFAIR, *Help*, http://www.betfair.com/IRL/help/Help.Introduction/ (accessed March 31, 2017).

64 BETFAIR, *How to Read the Betfair Screen Part One*, https://betting.betfair.com/how-to-read-the-betfair-screen-part-one.html (accessed Nov. 14, 2017).

65 Helmut Dietl and Christian Weingärtner, *Betting Scandals and Attenuated Property Rights–How Betting Related Match-Fixing Can Be Prevented in Future*, 14 THE INTERNATIONAL SPORTS LAW JOURNAL 128 (June 2014).

66 Gambling, *supra* note 62.

67 Betfair, *Exchange: What is the Discount Rate?*, https://en-betfair.custhelp.com/app/answers/detail/a_id/414/related/1/session/L2F2LzEvdGltZS8xNTAwNzQ4MzI0L3NpZC96emZhcmZvbg%3D%3D.

Pari-mutuel Wagering

The name, "pari-mutuel," roughly translates from the French as "to wager among ourselves." All bets of the same type go in a common pool, and then a specified percentage is deducted for taxes and the house take. The winners then share the remaining pools on a basis proportionate to the amount of their wager. This system of betting is sometimes called "pool sharing." The pool remains open even after one places a bet until a specified time, for example, when a horse race begins, and the pool is closed. Between the time the pools open (betting commences) and when the pools close (betting ends), the pool operator typically shows the estimated payouts for most bets based on the bets already placed. The operator does not determine the payouts until after the event ends. This differs from the "fixed odds" bets, like point spread or money line wagers where the potential payout is known at the time the bet is made.

Here is an example of pari-mutuel betting on a tennis tournament with four competitors where the pools of wagers is as follows:

Player A $300   Player B $400   Player C $100   Player D $200

Here the total pool is $1000. If the operator has a commission of 20%, this is subtracted from the pool before distribution of the prizes. This leaves $800 to be shared among the winning bettors. If Player B won the tournament, those who wagered on that player would receive two dollars for every dollar wagered ($800/400). If Player C won, the bettors would receive eight dollars for every dollar wagered ($800/100).

The example above is based on the player winning the tournament. In horse racing, a bettor also can bet on the horse placing or showing. A person betting a horse to "place" will be in the winning pool if the horse finishes first or second. A person betting a horse to "show" will be in the winning pool if the horse finishes first, second, or third. There are a myriad of other wagers, often called exotic bets, such as the daily double (picking winners in two specified races, often the first two), exacta or perfecta (picking the winner and the second place finisher in a race in exact order), quinella (picking the winner and the second place finisher in a race regardless of order), trifecta (picking the winner, the second place and third place finishers in a race in exact order), and pick six (picking the winners in six consecutive races).

FIRST RACE
Finger Lakes
JULY 19, 2017

1 MILE 40 YARDS. (1.40[illegible]) CLAIMING . Purse $9,000 FOR FILLIES AND MARES THREE YEARS OLD AND UPWARD WHICH HAVE NEVER WON TWO RACES. Three Year Olds, 118 lbs.; Older, 124 lbs. Non-winners Of A Race At A Mile Or Over Since June 18 Allowed 2 lbs. Such A Race Since May 18 Allowed 4 lbs. Claiming Price $5,000 (Clear. [illegible])

Value of Race: $9,000 Winner $5,400; second $1,800; third $900; fourth $450; fifth $180; sixth $135; seventh $135. Mutuel Pool $39,894.00 Exacta Pool $31,300.00 Superfecta Pool $13,168.00 Trifecta Pool $24,100.00

Last Raced	Horse	M/Eqt. A. Wt.	PP	St	¼	½	¾	Str	Fin	Jockey	Cl'g Pr	Odds $1
5Jly17 3FL4	Uwandadance	L b 5 120	3	1	1^{1}	1^{1}	1^{1}	1^{2}	1^{5}	Flores Jeremias	5000	6.90
15Jly17 5FL5	Chica Zoom	L b 4 115	7	7	7	7	$6^{1/2}$	[illegible]	2^{3}	Valdes A5	5000	a-0.35
21Jun17 4FL2	Twofreeknights	L b 3 118	4	5	[illegible]	3^{hd}	2^{hd}	2^{1}	[illegible]	Perez L E	5000	a-0.35
5Jly17 3FL2	Midswellswing	L bf 4 120	2	3	[illegible]	5^{1}	4^{1}	[illegible]	4^{6}	Cruz J	5000	7.40
25Jun17 5FL6	Campobasso	L 4 120	6	6	2^{2}	2^{1}	[illegible]	[illegible]	[illegible]	Ignacio R	5000	16.90
5Jly17 3FL3	Sam Little Lady	L b 3 118	5	2	[illegible]	[illegible]	5^{1}	6^{25}	[illegible]	De Diego E	5000	13.60
5Feb17 9Aqu11	Go Go Beans	L bf 6 120	1	4	[illegible]	6^{2}	7	7	7	Sone Y	5000	6.90

a-Coupled: Chica Zoom and Twofreeknights.

OFF AT 1:11 Start Good. Won driving. Track fast.

TIME :23[illegible], :48[illegible], 1:14[illegible], 1:42[illegible], 1:45[illegible] (:23.63, :48.48, 1:14.56, 1:42.58, 1:45.24)

$2 Mutuel Prices:				
	4 -UWANDADANCE	15.80	5.30	3.80
	1A-CHICA ZOOM(a-entry)		2.10	2.10
	1 -TWOFREEKNIGHTS(a-entry)		2.10	2.10

$1 EXACTA 4-1 PAID $13.30 $1 SUPERFECTA 4-1-3-6 PAID $118.70 $1 TRIFECTA 4-1-3 PAID $29.00

The invention that made pari-mutuel betting more popular was the totalisator.[68] Initially conceived in the 19th century in Europe, a totalisator is a specialized, mechanical calculating machine that can calculate the odds and approximate payouts for the different types of bets as the betting pool grows and before the event begins.

Spread-betting

Even though they share a similar name, UK-style spread betting is different from the US-style point-spread wager system. The United Kingdom allows companies licensed by the Financial Services Authority to offer spread betting on sporting events. Bettors in this type of wager are risking funds on the accuracy of their predictions on any of a number of aspects of a sporting event. For example, the book may set a spread of 25-28 minutes for either team to score the first goal in a soccer game. This would be expressed as Sell 25, Buy 28. If a person takes the Sell 25 side, he is betting that the first goal will occur before the 25th minute. If the first goal occurs at the ten-minute mark, he would make the amount of his bet times 15 for every minute the first score occurred before the 25th minute. If he bet $10, he would win $150. If, however, the first goal did not happen until the 38th minute, he would lose 13 times his bet or $130 on a $10 wager. The operator offering the spread has a built-in advantage in the pricing differences between the Sell and Buy prices. UK-style spread betting has a small audience in the UK and elsewhere and has not expanded to the United States. In the U.K., the approximately 100 licensed spread betting firms have about 125,000 domestic customers and 400,000 foreign customers, of which about 82% have lost money

68 *Quiniela Wager*, BRITANNICA.COM, https://www.britannica.com/topic/quiniela-wager (last accessed Nov. 12, 2017).

Nevada Sports Wagering Summary[70]				
Year	# of locations	Handle in thousands	Win in thousands	Win %
1995	119	2,428,596	79,415	3.27
1996	133	2,483,312	76,486	3.08
1997	136	2,431,382	89,718	3.69
1998	146	2,269,032	77,375	3.41
1999	156	2,470,407	109,192	4.42
2000	165	2,323,377	123,836	5.33
2001	162	2,042,855	118,077	5.78
2002	149	1,936,544	110,383	5.70
2003	150	1,863,678	122,630	6.58
2004	159	2,087,273	112,504	5.39
2005	164	2,257,174	126,176	5.59
2006	168	2,427,605	191,538	7.89
2007	169	2,594,191	168,363	6.49
2008	177	2,578,225	136,441	5.29
2009	185	2,568,362	136,380	5.31
2010	183	2,762,267	151,096	5.47
2011	183	2,877,935	140,731	4.89
2012	182	3,449,533	170,062	4.93
2013	180	3,622,107	202,838	5.60
2014	182	3,901,117	227,045	5.82
2015	197	4,237,422	231,787	5.47
2016	193	4,509,753	219,174	4.86
2017	192	4,868,434	248,777	5.11

in 2016, with the average customer suffering annual losses of about $2900.[69]

UNDERSTANDING THE ECONOMICS OF LEGAL SPORTSBOOKS

Sportsbooks Have Low Margins

The size and profitability of legal sportsbooks in Nevada are often misunderstood. While the amount wagered is substantial and attracts headlines, the actual profitability is modest because of low margins and taxes on handle.

69 Julia Bradshaw, *What is Spread Betting and Why Does the FCA Want to Tighten Up the* Rules, The Telegraph, Dec. 6, 2016, http://www.telegraph.co.uk/business/2016/12/06/spread-betting-does-fca-want-tighten-rules/.

The next chart shows both the amount wagered and the win from sports wagering in Nevada.

Three important observations come from this chart. First, despite the large volume of wagers—over $4.5 billion in 2016—the sports wagering business does not generate a large win, or gross revenue, before expenses and taxes. Gross revenue in the gambling industry means all moneys received as bets (the handle) less all money paid out as losses. Gross revenue does not take into account the myriad of expenses and taxes that sportsbooks must pay.

In 2016, the gross revenue for all of Nevada books was $219 million. While in isolation this may seem like a large number, the gross revenue for all gaming in Nevada was $11.26 billion. In other words, only about 2% of the casino industry's revenue comes from sports wagering. Moreover, on average, a licensed sportsbook in Nevada has gross revenues of just over $1.13 million before paying all overhead including salaries, utilities, space costs, state gaming taxes, federal excise taxes, and communication costs.

Second, Nevada sportsbooks have improved their margins since the 1990s. In the 1990s, the win percentage was between 3.08 and 4.42. This improved by the 2010s where the win percentage has risen to between 4.86 and 5.82. This improvement in win percentage reflects some fundamental changes to the sportsbook industry in Nevada.

Third, low margins contribute to the low gross revenues. The blended win rate of about 5% is a low margin for most businesses.

Low Margins Are Important in Setting Tax Rates

This low margin should be an important consideration when policymakers set taxes or other assessments. A tax on gross revenues, which is a common basis for states to use in imposing taxes on the casino industry, cuts into these already low margins for sports wagering. In the casino industry, state gross revenue taxes range from a low of 6.75% in Nevada to as much as 69% in New York.[70]

A tax on the handle (the amount wagered) has even more impact. This next chart shows how much the Nevada sportsbooks retain from every dollar bet on every sport. In 2016, the total retained from every sport on average, was 4.86%. In this case, a .25% tax on the handle would equate to about a 5% tax on win or net revenues before

70 National Conference of State Legislatures, *2015 Casino Tax and Expenditures*, (Sept. 28, 2015), http://www.ncsl.org/research/financial-services-and-commerce/casino-tax-and-expenditures-2013.aspx.

Win Percentage By Sport[74]						
	Football	Basketball	Baseball	Parlay	Other	Total
1995	3.13	2.70	0.86	27.93	3.93	3.27
1996	2.76	2.84	1.66	27.57	-1.87	3.08
1997	3.39	2.22	2.56	29.79	5.17	3.69
1998	3.15	3.82	0.78	23.20	4.76	3.41
1999	5.07	4.51	0.63	31.08	5.64	4.42
2000	5.39	4.27	3.41	32.07	4.82	5.33
2001	5.76	5.21	3.50	32.22	5.36	5.78
2002	4.69	5.91	2.86	32.81	6.29	5.70
2003	5.91	6.96	3.20	32.93	6.15	6.58
2004	4.82	5.60	2.13	33.27	7.28	5.39
2005	3.84	6.62	5.63	24.86	5.69	5.59
2006	8.02	7.27	4.84	30.89	8.37	7.89
2007	6.25	5.45	4.80	29.56	8.80	6.49
2008	3.50	5.89	4.52	31.36	7.47	5.29
2009	4.45	4.76	4.38	32.57	6.98	5.31
2010	4.76	4.74	4.28	33.50	8.63	5.47
2011	3.30	6.62	3.52	28.10	5.79	4.89
2012	4.37	4.91	4.34	23.33	6.37	4.93
2013	4.98	5.62	4.27	34.63	6.73	5.60
2014	6.50	4.89	2.95	36.83	6.18	5.82
2015	4.86	5.83	4.39	29.56	6.27	5.47
2016	5.39	4.75	3.08	17.28	6.07	4.86
2017	4.38	5.90	3.23	24.12	7.56	5.11

the books pay all expenses. Likewise, a 4.86% handle tax would be equivalent to a 100% tax on gross revenues.

Handle taxes need to be carefully considered because they can have unintended consequences if they are too high. Congress passed the Wagering Excise Tax[71] in 1951, which imposed a 10 percent tax on sports betting revenues, and required a $50 occupational stamp for each person employed in book operations. This tax negatively affected the legal Nevada sportsbook market until the government reduced the tax to 2% in 1974, and then to its current .25% in 1982.[72] It is likely that the only reason most Nevada sportsbooks survived before 1974 was that they evaded paying the Wagering Excise Tax on large wagers. Back then, at least a few of the operating Nevada books had two sets of

71 26 U.S.C. § 4401 (2012).

72 Charles T. Clotfelter, Theory and Practice of Excise Taxation: Smoking, Drinking, Gambling, Polluting, and Driving (Oxford University Press 1st ed. 2005).

73 David G. Schwartz. *Nevada Sports Betting Totals: 1984-2017*. Las Vegas: Center for Gaming Research, University Libraries, University of Nevada Las Vegas, 2018.

accounting records: one set of books reflected actual figures, the other set of books was what the book recorded for tax purposes. For example, a large $1200 bet on a football game was registered for tax purposes as a $12 bet and the book paid $1.20 in Federal Excise Taxes instead of $120.[74] The actual set of books recorded it as a $1200 bet and a $2200 payout if the player won.[75] Because of the tax, the books required the average bettor to risk $12 to win $10 on point spread bets instead of the current 11 to 10.[76] Even at 12 to 10, however, sportsbooks could not make a profit if they paid all their federal and state taxes.

When the federal government first imposed the 10% wagering excise in 1951, it devastated the sportsbook industry in Nevada.[77] Of the 24 books that existed before the excise tax, only four continued operations after the tax was adopted.[78] All 13 books in Las Vegas closed.[79] Gaming regulators did not have the regulatory power to close sportsbooks in the state, although this was considered. Instead, Nevada regulators made the economic survival of sportsbooks even more precarious in 1952 when they required that sportsbooks only be operated in a building separate from the casinos, as well as prohibiting them from offering food and beverages.[80] Proposals to prohibit sports wagering in Nevada, however, were blocked by legislators who feared it would be the first step toward ending the casino industry.[81]

Sportsbooks Thrive on Increased Volumes

The Nevada sportsbook industry's fortunes began to change in the early 1970s after the excise tax was reduced to 2%. While this was a very heavy tax on the industry, it was not prohibitive.[82]Some major casino interests, including those that were part of Howard Hughes's large casino empire, opposed allowing sportsbooks back into Nevada's casinos.[83] The Nevada Gaming Commission, however, allowed sportsbooks back into the casinos in 1975.[84] Almost

74 Manteris & Talley, *supra* note 26.

75 Davies & Abram, *supra* note 14.

76 *Id.*

77 Arne Lang, SPORTS BETTING AND BOOKMAKING, AN AMERICAN HISTORY 182 (Rowman & Littlefield, 2016).

78 *Id.*

79 *Id.*

80 *Id.* at 183.

81 *Id.*

82 *Id.* at 185.

83 *Id.*

84 *Id.*

immediately sportsbooks reappeared in Harrah's Club in Reno and the Union Plaza in Las Vegas.[85] Perhaps most dramatic, however, was the opening in 1976 of the sportsbook at the Stardust, which, at 9000 square feet, was the genesis of the the "superbook" designed to cater to both tourists and local bettors.[86]

After Congress lowered the Wagering Excise Tax to .25% in 1982, Nevada experienced a significant expansion of the sportsbook industry. By 1984, 50 sportsbooks existed in Nevada. Casinos competed for who would open the largest and most elaborate books with the Las Vegas Hilton Superbook and the Olympiad Sportsbook at Caesars Palace being prime examples.[87] Statewide handle increased from $8 million in 1974 to over $929 million in 1984.[88] The competition among the casino sportsbooks had one significant effect: in the early 2000s, Leroys, the last remaining stand-alone sportsbook, closed its doors. By 2010, the number of sportsbooks had quadrupled, with all of these books serving as an ancillary amenity to a casino. Unlike the professional gamblers that made up a significant percentage of the Nevada sportsbooks' business in the 1990s, the casino sportsbooks brought in higher numbers of casual bettors or "square" bettors, many of whom were staying at the tourist-centric casino resorts.[89] A respected odds maker and bookmaker, Pete Korner, noted:

> The sportsbook industry thrives on volume and churn on the betting dollar. Back in 1990, fewer outlets existed. The people who were betting were people who knew how to bet. "Wise-guy" money ruled a larger percentage of the total betting volume. Today, the sheer amount of "square" play, particularly on a football Sunday can easily temper the larger single wagers that sportsbooks lived and died on in years past.[90]

Moreover, by increasing the number of bet offerings, sportsbooks could reduce overall volatility by spreading risk over more events.[91] Up until the mid-1990s, the limited number of televised national and regional games resulted in the sportsbooks offering more limited wagers,[92] as sportsbooks could not spread their risk over large numbers of betting pools. But with advances in broadcasting many

85 *Id.*
86 *Id.* at 186.
87 *Id.* at 188.
88 *Id.* at 189-190
89 Korner, *supra* note 7.
90 *Id.*
91 *Id.*
92 *Id.*

more games were televised, increasing betting interest. This permitted sportsbooks to increase the number of wagering opportunities, while reducing profit volatility.[93]

As Pete Korner stated:

> The number of offerings that a sportsbook exposed themselves to in the 1990s and before was minimal comparatively speaking to today's sports wagering menu. National and regionally televised games were fewer and these games (like today) were the games being bet on. With limited decisions, the day's outcome became quite a hit-or-miss proposition for most sportsbook bookmakers on fewer key games of the day.[94]

More casual bettors wagering on a larger number of games provided more "churn" and a higher win percentage.[95] Churn, meaning the volume of wagering, is the bookmaker's expression for the effect of the law of large numbers. Expectation that the book will meet the desired win percentage is based on long-run averages. That is, for a large number of trials (wagers) these values represent what can be expected to occur. Actual play will deviate from these values, but when the number of trials is large enough, the percentage of the total amount wagered that is retained by the sportsbook should be close to the house advantage. In other words, making enough trials essentially ensures that the ratio of successes to total trials will be about equal to the house advantage (theoretical probability). Thus, as the number of bet types and numbers increase, the total book win divided by the total action will tend to get closer and closer to the expected book win divided by the total action. If the book has only a few bet types and offerings, the chances that a single game can cause the book to deviate from expected win increases.

As the market share of the largest competitors has increased, there has been an increase in handle that allows the book makers to better manage risk. The increased number of sportsbook locations, however, does not mean additional competitors. The casino industry consolidated considerably in the 2000s. As one researcher noted,"a fundamental shift had changed the structure of casino ownership in Nevada, and particularly along the Las Vegas Strip, as casino ownership became concentrated in the hands of fewer, larger operators."[96]

Along with this casino consolidation came a consolidation

93 *Id.*

94 *Id.*

95 Korner, *supra* note 7.

96 David G. Schwartz, *Concentration on the Las Vegas Strip: An Exploration of the Impacts*, 17 GAMING L. REV. & ECON. 619 (2013).

of the sportsbooks within the casinos. Moreover, the market for companies that operated sportsbooks in other companys' casinos also consolidated. As Pete Korner noted, "Today, however, networks dominate the Nevada landscape. William Hill, Stations, MGM-Mirage are the big networks. They encompass a majority of the sportsbooks in the state."[97] No statistics are available on the exact market concentration in Nevada, but it is evident that a small number of companies dominate the market. William Hill does not own a casino but operates 55% of all sportsbooks in Nevada, including 74 full service books.[98] While most of their clients are middle size to smaller casinos, they combine to possess significant market share. CG technologies, a smaller network competitor, operates books at nine locations including the Venetian. MGM and Caesars have the most casinos on the Las Vegas Strip. MGM has ten casinos including the Aria and Bellagio. Caesars Entertainment has 13 Nevada casinos including Caesars Palace. Stations Casinos is a leader in casinos that cater to locals and has ten casinos, including the upscale Red Rock Casino and Resort. Boyd Corporation, also predominately a locals' casino company, has twelve casinos. These six larger networks have greater liquidity that promote better risk management and lower volatility.

Risk Management Has Evolved Significantly

The tools and information available to manage risk improved significantly.[99] In 1990, the line makers had limited data and inadequate tools to do the analytics necessary to create the opening line. For example, on a Sunday during college basketball season, a line marker would have to spend almost the full day working through about 100 feet of dot matrix printouts from the previous day's games to log every single player's contribution, and determine who may have been injured or didn't play.[100] The key games that determined the day's outcome were only then discovered to have an injury to a key player.[101] The databases available then consisted of archaic (by today's standards) logs maintained by Computer Sports World, then the leading provider of sports information.[102]The wise guys who had access to better information

97 Korner, *supra* note 7.

98 William Hill Race & Sportsbook, https://www.williamhill.us/.

99 Korner, *supra* note 7.

100 *Id.*

101 *Id.*

102 *Id.*

than the odds maker could take advantage of inaccurate opening lines. The internet took this advantage away from the professional bettor. The line makers and book managers now have almost real-time access to injury reports and other key information.[103] Bookmakers can limit their exposure with advanced computer programs that can suspend wagering on a game pending the book manager's review.[104] The increased access to information sharpens the odds and offers less opportunity for professional bettors to capitalize.[105]

Understanding Sportsbook Operations

Nevada's legal full-service sportsbooks may serve as business models if other states or the federal government permit sports wagering. The expansion of sports wagering would be an opportunity for Nevada sportsbook operators to extend their brands and expertise to sportsbook in other states. Despite Nevada's prominence in the sportsbook industry, other states may not adopt the Nevada requirement that sportsbooks be physically on the premises of licensed casinos. Instead, they may look to other countries where sportsbooks can be independent operations, or be offered at locations like clubs and taverns.

Race and sportsbooks in Nevada casinos are often adjacent but with separate areas. The race book overwhelmingly accepts a bet or wager using a pari-mutuel system of wagering, but can offer fixed odds (or track odds) based on the outcome of racing. In most cases, Nevada race books accept pari-mutuel wagers from their patrons that are then merged with a common pool at the race track where the race is being conducted. The races are simultaneously televised from tracks on closed loop systems. Fixed odds wagers, where the bettor can bet against the race book (or the house), which sets the odds on each racing event, are usually only offered on wagers not available at the track. An example might be a quinella where the bettor attempts to select the top two finishers in either order.

How Customers Place Wagers with a Sportsbook

In-Person Wagering

A typical sportsbook at a major Nevada casino will have large projection screens and big-screen televisions that display available sporting events. These books pay the providers for the rights to broadcast the events at their book. The cost for the broadcast rights

---

103 *Id.*
104 *Id.*
105 *Id.*

vary based on the occupancy of the sportsbook, but fees in excess of $150,000 for the broadcast rights for a single book are not uncommon. The book will have seats often arranged stadium style where customers sit and watch the games. Some books have special seating with desks and individual monitors for regular or high-betting customers. Besides the television monitors, the books have large monitors that display the games and the odds of those games along with the results of other ongoing games. Immediately below the screens in the front of the sportsbook is a counter with multiple counters, much like in a bank. Behind the counters are ticket writers.

If a bettor wants to place a wager, he will go to the ticket window and inform the ticket writer of the wager or wagers that he would like to place. Suppose the odds board showed the following game:

405	Redskins	37.5 +165
406	Panthers	-3.5 -185

This is displaying three different bets. The 37.5 is the over/under number on the total number of points scored in the game. The point spread wager has the Panthers has a 3.5-point favorite, and the +165 and -185 are the money line bets. To bet the Panthers and lay the points, a bettor would inform the teller that he would like to place a bet and would provide: (1) the number of the team, in this case, 406, (2) the type of bet, in this case a straight bet on the Panthers -3.5, and (3) the amount of the bet, in this case as an example, for $220 straight. The bettor would then tender the amount of the wager to the ticket writer. In turn, the ticket writer will enter the information into the book operations computer system through a terminal. The terminal will issue a ticket that the teller gives to the patron.

Interactive Wagering on Sports

Interactive wagering is a type of wagering where the bettor does not have to be physically at the sportsbook to make a wager. This has become extremely popular in Nevada and is the preferred method of wagering outside Nevada. From its introduction in 2010 by Vic Salerno's company, American Wagering, interactive sports wagering has captured about 30% of the betting market in Nevada.[106] Bettors do most interactive wagering on sports using mobile telephones or tablets that run either Apple or Android operating systems.

106 The Oral History Of Vic Salerno, *Special Issue: A Collection of Oral Histories from Prominent Gaming Industry Figures*, 7 UNLV Gaming L.J. 15, (Spring 2017)[hereinafter *Oral History*].

To use an interactive wagering account in Nevada, the bettor must first open an account. Because of Nevada regulations requiring the in-person verification of the bettor's government identification, a person cannot open an account online.[107] Instead, the bettor must either physically go to a sports location or have a representative of the sportsbook come to them to verify the government identification. Some sportsbooks will come to the bettor's home, place of business, or other location to verify identification if the bettor agrees to deposit a minimum amount of money, usually $500. Once the account is opened, the bettor must download the mobile betting application on their mobile device including an Apple iPhone, Apple iPad, Android phone, or Android tablet.

All wagering on mobile devices is by advance-deposit wagering (ADW), where the bettor must fund the account before the sportsbook will accept his bets. Cash deposits can be made at the sportsbook, or at designated locations such as taverns and convenience stores. Some books accommodate funding through pre-paid cards that can then be transferred to the bettor's ADW account.

After opening and funding the account, the bettor can use the application on the mobile gaming device to place bets from anywhere in the state of Nevada. The application uses geolocation technology built into the mobile device to determine the physical location of the device. These technologies incorporate GSM-based methods that measure the relative signal strength of the mobile device to nearby cell tower antenna masts. To determine the location of the mobile device, GPS-based mobile devices use the US government-owned space-based global navigation satellite system to determine location.

If the bettor is physically in Nevada, he can use the application to place bets. Before being able to do so, the bettor must enter his username and password. After that, the bettor can make any wager that the sportsbook offers at its physical location, including in-game wagering. The application will provide account information such as current balance and a summary of current and historical bets. If the bettor wants to withdraw money, he can do so at the physical book or, in some cases, request that the money be sent by check, or be moved to a prepaid debit card.

107 Nev. Gaming Comm. Reg. 22.140(6).

Who Is Involved In The Sportsbook Operations?

Race and sportsbook personnel are responsible for ensuring the operational integrity of race and sportsbooks.[108] Because sportsbooks must be in licensed casinos, it often operates as a department under casino operations. In this respect, it may have specific shared services with the other casino departments. For example, the same accounting and internal audit departments have authority over both the sportsbook and the slot department. Book operations have different organizational structures and titles depending on several factors, including the size of the operation and its integration into the casino. The Nevada government does not require the casino licensee to own or operate the sportsbook. Therefore, a casino may lease the sportsbook to a third-party. These companies may pay a flat fee rent or have a revenue-sharing agreement with the casino. In these cases, the employees at each leased location are similar to a casino-operated sportsbook, but the independent company maintains a central staff that will perform accounting, internal audit, technology, and compliance functions.

In all cases, however, individual race and sportsbook employees include the following:

- **Director or Manager of Race Book and Sports Operations** - has supervisory authority over an operation of a race and sportsbook department, including staffing, patron relations, the integrity of betting and payouts, compliance with related internal control procedures (*see* Accounting discussion *infra*), and gaming regulations. The manager has bookmaking authority to manage company or property liability exposure, maintain and move games lines, update futures odds for specified events, and balance wagering on games and events. The manager develops and implements the operating plan to ensure operating expenses meet established forecast goals. The manager monitors competitors' practices and technological innovations affecting the Race & Sports book betting industry and remains aware of legislative action affecting business opportunities.
- **Race Book and Sports Pool Shift Manager/Supervisor** - has supervisory authority over the daily operations of race and sportsbook and supervises the ticket writers. The supervisor may open the sportsbook and assures facilities and equipment, including the video screens, are available and functioning. Additionally, the supervisor sets up, posts, and

108 In all states that have casinos, except Nevada, this would include race book personnel only.

updates event information in a book's computer system for display to the public. The supervisor verifies large payouts on winning wagers. The supervisor oversees personnel development including hiring, training, discipline, and administration of a merit system, and maintains work schedules for assigned personnel. The supervisor counsels, guides, and instructs personnel in the proper performance of duties, and administers evaluations, performance reviews, and merit compensation. The supervisor has a responsibility to maintain customer relations including customer recognition and development. The supervisor ensures that departmental procedures conform to all regulatory requirements, with an emphasis on requirements to prevent money laundering, and to provide maximum security for the company's assets.

- **Race Book and Sports Pool Writer and Cashier** - provides services to patrons by accepting race and sportsbook wagers and handling of payouts on winning tickets. The ticket writer greets the bettors when arriving at his/her window, provides information and assistance mainly on how to place wagers, and handles and solves any patron concerns or questions. If the patron wants to place a bet, the ticket writer enters the betting requests into the race and sports computer system on the terminal behind the counter. The ticket writer verifies and presents the ticket to the bettor after receiving payment.[109] The ticket writer maintains the cash bank for his/her shift with responsibility for accepting payment and making correct change, verifying tickets and payoffs, and making payments on winning tickets. At the end of every shift, the ticket writer must reconcile his cash drawers to account for each bet accepted and recorded by the system, every payout made on winning tickets, and every fill from the cashier.[110]

The ticket writer handles writing/cashiering according to department policy and procedures and ensures compliance with Nevada gaming statutes and regulations including cash transaction reporting, suspicious activity reporting, and prohibitions against messenger/runner betting.

Others

Auditing and Accounting

At the end of each shift, the ticket writers count their banks and submit the results to the main cashier, who adjusts for fills and

---

109 Nevada Gaming Control Board, *Race and Sports*, STATE OF NEVADA (Sep. 2017), http://www.gaming.nv.gov/modules/showdocument.aspx?documentid=4549.

110 Malcolm E. Greenlees, CASINO ACCOUNTING AND FINANCIAL MANAGEMENT (University of Nevada Press, 1998).

makes sure that all the banks reconcile. If they do not, then a review is undertaken as to where the errors may have occurred. At the end of each day, the main cashier submits the amount of the handle broken down by current and futures wagers to the accounting department.

The accounting department maintains the book operation's financial records, prepares license and tax forms, balances the operation's books, and creates the internal controls. Internal controls are systematic measures including reviews, checks and balances, methods and procedures that the book operations put into place to safeguard assets, maintain accurate accounting data and financial statements, and assure compliance with all applicable laws and regulations. Internal controls should be designed to protect the assets while promoting efficient operations. The costs related to implementation and internal controls should not exceed the benefit to be derived from the internal controls. The accounting department should work with the operations department to properly balance both objectives.

Internal controls can often prescribe a simple process to maintain integrity in the system. For example, a ticket writer may have paid several winning tickets causing him to run low on cash in his drawer. He will need additional cash (called a "fill") to pay other winning tickets. Internal controls will dictate how the money is transferred from main book bank to the cashier.[111] A transfer slip for this transaction may require three signatures, the main bank cashier who counts the additional funds, a book supervisor who transfers the cash to the ticket writer, and the ticket writer who recounts the cash before putting it into his cash drawer.[112] Surveillance cameras observe the physical book facility and observe or record this entire transaction. Lower level accounting employees may direct, supervise, and maintain all general financial records.

A chief accountant leads the finance department of a book operation. The book operations may have a controller who manages and directs all financial activities. The controller may set policies and practices to protect property assets, comply with federal, state, and local regulations, and to meet cost-control objectives. He is responsible for the control of all revenues and disbursements, and internal controls. The controller also prepares management reports and reports to regulatory and tax agencies. He may develop the operating budget for the property and produce financial reports to

111 *Id.*
112 *Id.*

inform management of the performance of the departments. He reconciles all the accounting transactions in the book and enforces all internal controls and administrative controls. The controller and staff may prepare federal, state, county, and city licenses and tax forms. They also may install and maintain accounting procedures, and design or modify accounting systems to provide exacting records of assets, liabilities, and financial transactions. In addition, they prepare accounting procedure manuals and procedure training for accounting personnel. They also monitor and survey department operations to determine if accounting methods are adequate and up-to-date.

A director supervises the activities of the internal audit department. He decides the adequacy of internal controls including the adequacy and proper application of all accounting, financial, and operating controls. The director also coordinates the internal audit with the external audit that is conducted by independent public accountants. Internal auditors, led by the director, determine if the gaming departments are following accounting rules, custodial policies, and control procedures. While internal auditors are focused on the workings of gaming departments, audit clerks audit revenue generating areas. They determine if departments are correctly following accounting, custodial or control rules, policies, and procedures. Audit clerks verify the accuracy of revenue and expenditure figures, correct discrepancies, audit account balances, and prepare reports about daily operations. Internal auditors seek to verify information post-event, so they are not directly involved in actual gaming operations. They evaluate the adequacy and effectiveness of management controls. They also prepare reports of the results of the audit examinations, report audit findings, and suggest corrections of poor performances and cost reductions. Internal auditors may conduct special reviews for management.

The audit director reviews the accounting systems and records of vendors and subcontractors to decide if they are correct and comply with negotiated agreements. He sets rules, policies, and procedures affecting financial reporting to assure they comply with all federal, state, and local law. He also monitors the consistency of organizational objectives, industry trends, business conditions, and government legislation. Internal auditors analyze and verify the gaming operation's transactions to ensure they meet established regulatory and internal guidelines.

Surveillance

Surveillance personnel use a system of video cameras that can be virtually everywhere on the book's premises to transmit a video signal to a specific surveillance room. There, surveillance employees can review either real-time or recorded video to detect crimes or improper activities, with a concentration on high stakes gambling and sensitive areas such as cage and count. Surveillance plays a role in internal control procedures by observing controlled transactions including large wagers and payouts. Surveillance personnel have access to player data to help profile undesirable players and third-party databases of known or suspected criminals, and known messenger bettors.

Technology

The chief technical officer is the executive who focuses on technology issues within the book environment. The chief technical officer can have many different roles depending on the size of the operation. Small books with third-party supplied management systems may not have any technology personnel; they instead rely on the third-party contractor to supply and maintain segregated systems. In sportsbooks in larger casinos, the chief technical officer can be the infrastructure manager and external facing technologist who identifies, adapts, and integrates new technologies, leverages technologies across the profit centers of an integrated resort, helps drive business strategies, enhances client relations, drives revenues, and reduces costs through technology.[113] The chief technical officer can also have prominence in larger organizations as the visionary on the future of the sportsbook services, delivery services, and design.

Compliance

The compliance officer coordinates, monitors, tests, and reports on company compliance efforts. Some companies have both a compliance officer and a compliance committee. Others simply have a compliance officer that reports to senior management or the board of directors. A compliance committee is usually a group of senior executives along with knowledgeable outside members that review major hiring decisions and transactions, regulatory issues as they arise, compliance history, and other regulatory issues. They also make recommendations to senior management or the board of directors on appropriate courses of action. The compliance officer has the

113 Tom Berray & Raj Sampath, *The Role of the CTO: Models for Success*, Cabot Consultants (Apr. 2002), http://www.brixtonspa.com/Career/The_Role_of_the_CTO_4Models.pdf.

responsibility for collecting information needed by the compliance committee to make informed decisions. The compliance officer should have the ability to conduct employee training, document all compliance activities and functions, and coordinate internal investigations. Documenting all activities and preparing all reports for the compliance committee, as required by the compliance plan or by law, is essential.

The compliance officer may have multiple responsibilities, including:

- Conducting and coordinating background investigations, including prospective management and key employee hiring, review of suppliers and vendors, and material litigation.
- In-taking and coordinating review and investigations of business practices that may be an unsuitable method of operation, employee-reported violations, regulatory, civil or criminal investigations of or involving the company or management.
- Assuring that the book is complying with all regulatory requirements particularly those involving operations such as anti-money laundering reporting, underage gambling, and messenger betting.
- Interacting with the corporate divisions to determine situations requiring reporting under the internal reporting system and review by either senior management, the board of directors, or the compliance committee.
- Providing the necessary reports to senior management, the board of directors, or the compliance committee that establishes the information upon which the Committee makes recommendations.
- Interfacing with regulatory authorities to report all events that are required by law to be reported.
- Maintaining systems for employee or patron reporting of illegal or unethical practices.

Third Parties

Odds Makers

Sportsbooks may hire odds makers to provide the opening line. The value of the odds maker is to consistently deliver opening lines that ensure balanced action on the game, and that close not too far from the opening line. Nevada law requires line markers to obtain a privileged license before doing business with licensed books.[114] Nevada law includes odds makers within a slightly broader definition of "information services," which includes companies that sell and provide information to a licensed book "that is used primarily to aid the placing of wagers on events of any kind."[115] The term includes: (1) line, point spread or odds; (2) information, advice or consultation that a licensee considers in establishing or setting lines, point spreads, or odds; or (3) "advice, estimate or prediction regarding the outcome of an event."[116]

Nevada still has some licensed odds makers, but many Nevada books set their opening lines off the point spreads posted by offshore books. These offshore books often have considerably larger pools, maintain sophisticated odds makers, and employ advanced analytics. Also, they typically set their opening lines about 3 hours earlier than the Nevada books. Using the offshore lines that are maintained three hours after their opening and that have already been adjusted to market forces saves the cost of paying an independent odds maker and may offer a better prediction of balanced action on the game.

Sportsbook Systems Providers

In the 1970s, Las Vegas sportsbooks did everything by hand. The boards that displayed the games and odds were chalkboards or manual wall boards. All the betting information needed to place a wager was entered by "board men" using chalk to write the games, betting number, game times, and other information.[117] When a line changed, the book employees simply erased the old number and wrote the new number in chalk.[118] Ticket writers wrote the tickets on a device that made triplicate copies that were stored separately and later verified by audit staff. When the sportsbook used a three-part form, one copy was given to the bettor as proof of his wager, the second copy was retained by the sportsbook, and the third copy remained in the ticket

---

114 Nev. Rev. Stat. Ann. § 463.160.

115 Nev. Rev. Stat. Ann. § 463.01642.

116 *Id.*; Nevada Gaming Control Board, *Instructions to Applicants*, http://gaming.nv.gov/modules/showdocument.aspx?documentid=2371 (accessed September 09, 2017). Nevada does not require licensing of general circulation newspapers or magazines, or television or radio broadcasts whose primary purpose is not to aid the placing of wagers.

117 Scott Schettler, We Were Wiseguys And Didn't Know It 16 (BookSurge Publishing 2010).

118 *Id.*

machine under lock until removal by the accounting department.[119] The ticket writers also would verify the time of issuance using a separate timestamp machine.[120]

Book managers managed their risk by tracking only larger bets with pencil and paper.[121] A supervisor in the sportsbook would have to sort and tabulate the copies retained by the book by event to obtain the data needed to make line movements strategically.[122]

Game results came over a Western Union Ticker or a UPI ticker tape machine.[123] Before paying winning tickets, the supervisor would have to separate the winning and losing tickets based on the game results.[124] A single cashier in the sportsbook would pay winning tickets.[125] That cashier would have to match the customer's winning ticket with the book's copy of the winning ticket before making the payout.

The first computerized book making system in Nevada debuted in 1981. It automated the ticket writing process and provided basic accounting and auditing functions, but was very slow.[126] By 1986, a system called Computerized Bookmaking System was the prevailing standard throughout Nevada.[127] The computerized systems provided much greater accountability. Ticket writers, for example, could no longer write tickets after the game had started (past posting), [128] or write tickets where the line was more favorable than that set by book management.[129] Moreover, the data collected allowed managers to control risk better. As Vic Salerno, who owned the company and was a bookmaker himself, noted, "The system had the ability to put in a predicted score, and the system would go through all the bets and would calculate how much you were going to win or lose if that was the final score. That ability aided us with adjusting the odds."[130]

Licensed sportsbooks now have a variety of sophisticated computerized systems that both operate and provide their books

---

119 Greenlees, *supra* note 111.
120 Oral History, *supra* note 107.
121 *Id.*
122 Greenlees, *supra* note 111.
123 Schettler, *supra* note 118.
124 Greenlees, *supra* note 111.
125 *Id.*
126 Schettler, *supra* note 118.
127 *Id.*
128 Oral History, *supra* note 107.
129 Schettler, *supra* note 118.
130 Oral History, *supra* note 107.

with an integrated solution to all their needs.[131] These systems offer accounting, auditing, analytics, risk and line management, customer service, customer relationship management, and other assorted features. The systems can automate much of the risk management by inputting data from the live feed of the games and using advanced mathematical algorithms to recalculate the odds automatically.[132]

These systems interface with all the systems that a sportsbook may use including electronic displays, betting terminals and kiosks, video streaming, and betting odds and results. The systems have data security, conform to internal control standards, data warehousing, and support communication technologies. Most have pricing algorithms that allow the sportsbook to create and post customizable betting propositions and are scalable to handle almost any level of betting activity.

Third-Party Line Aggregators

On a subscription basis, sports information services electronically disseminate consolidated information related to publicly-available sports wagering lines or odds from the United States and international sportsbooks.[133]

These services offer customers the option of either a regular or premium subscription service with the latter offering real-time odds. Bookmakers can see the current odds from all major US and some non-US sportsbooks. These services also provide real-time XML data feeds so that the odds information directly feed into the sportsbook management system. The chart on the following page is an example of the sportsbooks whose information is available through an aggregator.

Touts

Touts typically sell their opinions, betting lines, and picks on games, races or contests for their clients to use when placing bets. Touts typically claim that they have advanced skills that will allow their customers to win money consistently through wagering.[134] Touts have a long history. The famous Jimmy "the Greek" Snyder had both a sports betting column with his preferred picks and a company

131 *Id.*

132 *Id.*

133 One of the leaders in this area is Don Best Sports. A description of their real-time-odds subscription service is found on their website. http://www.donbestcorp.com/real-time-odds/.

134 Ryan Goldberg, *How America's Favorite Sports Betting Expert Turned A Sucker's Game into An Industry*, Deadspin, June 23, 2016, http://deadspin.com/how-america-s-favorite-sports-betting-expert-turned-a-s-1782438574.

5Dimes	Ace Sportsbook	Aliante (Nevada)	Atlantis	Atlantis Bahamas
Bet365	Bet Online	Bet Phoenix	Bet QuickSilver	Bet US
BookMaker	Bet Mania	Bovada	Buckeye	Caesars (Nevada)
Carib	CAT Sport	Coast (Nevada)	BetCris	Bet33
BetFair	BetHongKong	BetISN	CG Tech	BetEagle
DSI	Dollar Per Head	Easy Street	EVO	Golden Nugget (Nevada)
Grande	Greek	HotelNV	IASport	Intertops
Jazz	Jerrys Nugget (Nevada)	Just Bet	Loose Lines	Low Vig
LVH (Nevada)	Matchbook	Mirage (Nevada)	Option	OSC
Pinnacle	PPH	QBT	Resorts	Sports Betting AU
SB Global	SIA	Skybook	SouthPoint (Nevada)	Sports Betting
Sport Bet	Stations (Nevada)	Stratosphere (Nevada)	Treasure Island (Nevada)	UCA Bet
Vietbet	Wager ABC	William Hill (Nevada)	World	WWWager
Wynn (Nevada)	YouWage			

that offered betting advice in the early 1960s.[135] These services are rarely free but require the clients to pay fees such as a flat rate plus a percentage of the client's winnings from the proffered advice.

Honest tout services are generally legal.[136] Many touts, however, are simply frauds.[137] In 1981, *Sport Magazine* reported that "for every good

135 Davies & Abram, *supra* note 14, at 133.

136 Tout services alone do not violate the Federal Wire Act. United States v. Alpirn, 307 F. Supp. 452 (S.D.N.Y. 1969). In that case, the court held that a person engaged in "touting" - providing paying clients with picks as to which horse would win a given race - was not "engaged in the business of betting or wagering" under § 1084(a) because, among other things, his clients were not "contractually bound to wager at all." *Id.* at 455. "Betting or wagering," the court reasoned, involves "situations where the defendant was himself making or accepting bets directly." *Id.* at 454 (emphasis added). The court concluded that the arrangement between Alpirn and his clients was not a betting or wagering contract as that arrangement is normally understood and was not the type of activity Congress had in mind when Section 1084(a) was enacted. Had Congress intended to prohibit "touting" activities of this sort, it could have chosen to broaden the opening language of Section 1084(a) rather than to limit coverage to persons engaged in betting and wagering activities. Moreover, the court found that Alpirn and each client did not become joint venturers even though some of Alpirn's clients may have acted upon his advice and placed wagers on the recommended horse. Rather, all that the stipulated facts established was that Alpirn's clients agreed to share their winnings with him - if in fact they wagered and were fortunate to win. These facts did not show that his clients were contractually bound to wager at all. Unlike a true joint venture, Alpirn did not share in the losses from the alleged venture.

137 Jacob Lewis, *Slim Pickings*, SLATE, Oct. 7, 2005, http://www.slate.com/articles/

service there are 10 imposters, cheats and pirates."[138] An advertisement for a tout often may claim incredible success, such as correctly picking 80% of their top picks.[139] The best legitimate handicappers and professional bettors rarely exceed 57% in a season and are pleased with a 55%-win rate. Tout scams are almost always sales related, not result oriented. Some touts simply seek high volumes of clients because if they only have 50% success rates, half of their clients in each week are led to believe that they have special skills.[140] As one reporter noted:

> As touts bounce from site to site, sometimes under different names, there really is no way to determine their true track records. And in addition to aliases and high turnover, there's a simpler, more effective smoke screen: obscured or altered pick histories. Touts plug away despite columns of red, all the while advertising useless cherry-picked short-term streaks or outright falsified ones.[141]

Some touts also make money through referral fees from foreign internet sports sites that illegally accept players from the United States. The touts direct players to internet sites where they can place wagers. In turn, the internet sites compensate the touts either based on a percentage of the player's initial deposit or his losses, estimated to reach as high as 40%.[142] This creates a conflict between the "winning" advice sold and the prospects for compensation based on the player's loss.

Conceivably, touts and others could be involved in the sports wagering market equivalent of "pump and dump," which is a form of microcap stock fraud that involves artificially inflating the price of an owned stock through false and misleading positive statements, and then selling the cheaply purchased stock at a higher price.[143] Sports touts could use their services to promote a wager that has low liquidity so that the books move the line off of a sound number based on all available metrics, including the relative performance value of the competitors. Once the line moves sufficiently to provide the touts with a positive expectation (that is, they are more likely to make money than lose money), the touts can bet the opposite of the selection that they promoted and sold to clients.

---

news_and_politics/life_and_art/2005/10/slim_pickings.html.

138 Davies & Abram, *supra* note 14, at 141.

139 Manteris & Talley, *supra* note 26.

140 *Id.*

141 Goldberg, *supra* note 135.

142 *Id.*

143 Ryan Rodenberg & Jack Kerr, *Fake News, Manipulated Data and the Future of Betting Fraud*, ESPN, June 28, 2017, http://www.espn.com/chalk/story/_/id/19752031/future-sports-betting-fake-news-manipulated-data-future-betting-fraud.

A few states have laws governing tout services, but the restrictions apply only to those selling predictions for horse racing. Arizona has a statute prohibiting anyone from advertising, selling, or offering for sale predictions on horse races, unless there is compliance with regulatory and statutory requirements.[144] The statutory requirement is that the regulatory department must be notified of the picks in writing on forms created by the department no later than three hours before the race.[145] Therefore, a tout charging for picks without the appropriate notice to Arizona regulatory authorities would violate the Arizona statute. Like Arizona, California has a statute prohibiting anyone from advertising, selling, or offering for sale predictions on horse races unless there is compliance with regulatory and statutory requirements.[146] The statutory requirement is that the regulatory department must be notified of the picks in writing on forms created by the department no later than three hours before the race.[147]

The Bettors

Without bettors there would not be any wagering contracts and, as a result, no sportsbooks. If the government decides to regulate the wagering contract, the bettors are an integral part of that contract. The notion of regulating bettors may seem strange but is similar to the regulatory functions of a commission over a financial stock exchange. For example, the U.S. Securities and Exchange Commission has jurisdiction over investors that engage in market manipulation or insider trading. Similarly, gaming regulators should be concerned about bettors who are manipulating the markets by fixing games, manipulating lines, or using insider information, which is information possessed by a person because of their relationship to a sport or competition that is not public, a matter of common knowledge, or disclosed by the sports governing body.[148]

The government also needs to understand the differences between professional and casual bettors. The latter are often sports fans or sports betting fans who view betting as recreational because they are either loyal to a particular team or merely enjoy wagering. While casual bettors want to win, having action on the game is often more

144 ARIZ. REV. STAT. ANN. § 5-115 (2003).

145 *See id.*

146 CAL. BUS. & PROF. CODE § 19664 (2003).

147 *See id.*

148 Nevada does not prohibit wagering using insider information, so a trainer or other athletic support personnel who knows the true extent of a star athlete's injury would not be violating the law by wagering on that event in Nevada.

important than the result. On the other hand, professional bettors have no personal stake in their selection; they are looking for a return on their bets, which they consider investments.[149] To do this, they need to deploy strategies sufficient to not only beat the other bettors but also to overcome the bookmaker's commission.

Professional bettors can use various methods to achieve their desired economic results. Some professional bettors will use computer modeling and analytical techniques to determine when the betting odds or lines are inconsistent with expected results.[150] Professional bettors may focus on point-spread betting because the sportsbook sets the line attempting to induce equal wagering on both teams rather than the expected result.[151] These professional sports betting entities will use computer modeling and analytical techniques to determine when the betting odds or lines are inconsistent with expected results. When the line is sufficiently inconsistent with their data analytics, they will place wagers. These models may use massive amounts of publicly available data to assist in predicting results. A casual bettor may not care about the wind speed and direction on any given Sunday baseball game, but it is a data point for the professional bettor. Some professional sports betting entities also seek and use non-public insider information regarding a sporting event to gain an advantage,[152] including the extent of a player's injury or the coach's decision on starting lineups, which can be valuable information in predicting the outcome.

Still other professional bettors are involved in arbitrage and exploit differences in odds or lines between bookmakers or between betting

---

149 Steve Donoughue & Fabian Adams-Sandiford, *Improving the Integrity of Sports Betting*, GAMBLING CONSULTANTS, Nov. 2010, http://www.gamblingconsultant.co.uk/articles/improving-the-integrity-of-sports-betting.

150 *Id.*

151 *Id.*; Anthony Cabot, *Betting on the Edge*, GLOBAL GAMING BUSINESS MAGAZINE, June 19, 2015, https://ggbmagazine.com/article/betting-on-the-edge/.

152 This last category of professional bettors, i.e., the ones who seek to obtain inside information and profit from it, are the ones most commonly cited as presenting a danger to a game's integrity. In its simplest terms, a "bad guy" can pay money (bribes) to a trainer, coach, or player, in exchange for material inside information, or even pay money to affect the outcome of a game or its components. The first two categories, i.e., professional gamblers who use statistical analyses to inform a betting decision, and those who use arbitrage, are analogous to stock traders, who also use statistical analyses to inform a buy-sell decision and arbitrage to take advantage of spreads in the markets. These types of professional gamblers are much less reliant on "inside information" and therefore may be of less concern to sports leagues and franchises.

platforms.[153] The following chart is an example of how an arbitrage sports bet might work.

Money Line Baseball Game: Cleveland vs. Detroit		
Outcome 1	Outcome 2	Profit
Cleveland Wins **Bookmaker:** Wynn **Money Line:** -285 **Stake:** $80 **Return:** $108.	Detroit Wins **Bookmaker:** Caesars **Money Line:** **+450** **Stake:** $20 **Return:** $110	**8-10%**

Many professional sports betting entities raise capital through equity investment based on the perceived value of their prediction methodology. In marketing their company to potential investors, they can make claims, like some tout services, of unbelievable profitability. Some of these firms will be legitimate, others not. Some may be Ponzi schemes and others simply thieves, while others are genuine sophisticated sports analytics investors.[154]

Besides regulating conduct, the design of sports wagering markets can either encourage or discourage professional bettors. Nevada decided to encourage professional bettors by allowing business entities to place race and sports pool wagers with Nevada licensed race and sportsbooks.[155]

A primary question is whether the legitimate professional wagering companies will even bother with Nevada.[156] The sports handle in Nevada is only about $5 billion, while the legal handle outside the United States is about $1.2 trillion. The illegal handle is about the same as the legal handle. Both the legal and illicit markets are available through the internet, with over 8000 wagering sites. The legitimate professional wagering companies may prefer the non-Nevada markets because they can realize higher profits for several reasons.

The massive liquidity of these markets will allow them to place much larger wagers before the book mitigates the expected statistical advantage by moving the line. Second, many illegal books operate in low (or no) tax, or tax reporting, environments. Third, the illegal books may offer lower commissions or rebates. Regardless of the method, professional sports betting entities may prefer to use bookmakers that offer the lowest commissions. Thus, bookmakers in unregulated

153 Cabot, *supra* note 152.
154 *Id.*
155 Buck Wargo, *Entity Bettiing Off to Slow Start with Nevada Sportsbook*, LAS VEGAS REVIEW JOURNAL, Sept. 17, 2016, https://www.reviewjournal.com/business/casinos-gaming/entity-betting-off-to-slow-start-with-nevada-sports-books/.
156 *Id.*

or under-regulated jurisdictions may have advantages because they may have lower taxes, less regulatory expense, and no requirements to maintain a physical sportsbook.

Casual bettors are at a disadvantage when they place bets in markets where legitimate professional wagering companies are allowed to wager. Legitimate and competent professional wagering companies are the sharks in the market and want to promote a Wall Street-like approach in the betting market. In contrast, sports fans or casual sports betting fans view betting as recreational, often consistent with fan loyalty for a team or for the enjoyment associated with betting. That the fans may end up the big losers in the equation is simple economics. The sportsbooks anticipate a positive return based on the house advantage. Likewise, the professional sports betting entity is seeking a positive return. To overcome the house advantage, the sports betting entity in point spread wagering world need to win more than 11 times for every 10 losses for bets of equal size. This would be 11 out of every 21 times or over 52.4% of the time. So, assuming the sharks win over 52.4% of the time and the house has an edge of 4.55% (on straight bets at 11 to 10), who are the losers? It would be the casual bettors, who will necessarily lose more than if the entire pool was made up of other casual bettors. Sports governing bodies, therefore, may be concerned about how the commoditization of sports wagering can negatively impact its value for fan engagement.

ILLEGAL BOOKMAKING IN THE UNITED STATES

Old School Illegal Bookmakers

Illegal bookmaking before the internet was much different from today. Illegal bookmakers then conducted all transactions in person or using the telephone.

Two types of illegal bookmaking were common, straight wagers and parlay cards. The former required the personal attention of a street bookmaker who recruited and serviced the customers.[157]

Parlay cards were distributed early in the week for the upcoming weekend football games.[158] If the person won, he would be paid the following week often on the same day as the parlay cards for the next

157 Sean Chaffin, *Old School Action: A Life of Booking Illegal Sports Bets*, Poker News, Feb. 2, 2017, https://www.pokernews.com/news/2017/02/old-school-action-a-life-of-booking-illegal-sports-bets-27020.htm.

158 This was based on Author Cabot's personal experience when he worked in an awning factory in Cleveland in 1974-75 while attending college.

week were distributed. Parlay cards came with a stub, so that if the bettor won, he could redeem it the next week. A distribution network existed for the cards. At some factories, the food truck drivers would be responsible for distributing the cards, collecting the completed cards, and paying the winning cards. Minimum bets were low, making the betting opportunity affordable to the workers. The process was recurrent across the country in different forms.

Straight wagers, however, required more personal attention. An old-school bookie was responsible for cultivating and servicing bettors. New customers could be recruited at sport or country clubs, bars, and through veterans or other service groups.[159] Once the bookie had a client base, he would have to communicate with the bettors on a regular basis to accept bets and make payouts.[160] While this could be by telephone, bookies often worked taverns, restaurants, and delicatessens. A popular bookie with 100 or more clients had considerable work merely keeping up with these telephone communications, personal visits, recording every wager that he accepted, collecting money, and paying winning wagers.

Bookies could either work alone or be part of a larger syndicate. In the former case, they had to set the point spread and manage risk. If they were part of a larger syndicate, they would only be an agent to accept the wagers and transmit them to a central location. The agent would have to be aware of the current point spreads and had bet limits on what he could accept without authorization. The bookmaker at the central location would set the lines and manage risk. In either case, the street level bookmaker would have to record each wager for tracking and accounting purposes. The street level bookmaker would have to make decisions on whether the bettor had to pay upfront or could settle later. If a street book worked alone, he would set his line. He would have to set limits on the size of the wagers that he accepted to avoid too much exposure. With substantial bets, the bookie would either attempt to lay it off with another bookie or accept the risk on the wager.[161]

Bookies would grant credit to some customers but rarely had difficulties in collecting because they worked specific neighborhoods and the customers would not have alternatives if they wanted to make future bets.[162]

---

159 James Jeffries & Charles Oliver, THE BOOK ON BOOKIES: AN INSIDE LOOK AT A SUCCESSFUL SPORTS GAMBLING OPERATION, (Paladin Press, 1st ed., 2000).

160 Chaffin, *supra* note 158.

161 *Id.*

162 *Id.*

Post-Internet Illegal Bookmaking

While some old school bookmakers exist in the United States,[163] the ubiquity of the internet has transformed almost all illegal wagering. In 2016, Florida authorities arrested about two dozen people who were running a traditional parlay card operation out of stores offering check cashing and selling cell phones.[164]

When internet sports wagering first emerged, the contact between the bettors and the off-shore sportsbook was direct. To bet illegally, a person simply did an internet search for sportsbooks, picked a sportsbook, established an account, funded that account using a credit card, and then placed wagers on the site using their sports wagering interface. For example, a player could fund his account using a MasterCard or Visa. If the player transferred $100, that amount would show up in their online account. If the player made a wager, the amount of the wager would be deducted from the account. If they tied or won a wager, the corresponding amount would be credited to their account. If they wanted to withdraw money from their account, they would make an online request and typically a check for that amount would be mailed to the player.

This relatively straightforward method of doing business, however, was disrupted when banks and credit card companies began to exercise greater due diligence to determine the business of their customers before providing them with merchant credit card accounts. At first, some books evaded these bank inquiries by merely lying to the bank as to the nature of their business. This method, however, became more difficult after the banks improved their due diligence and prosecutors targeted those who misled the banks and credit card companies. An example of this involved a Florida man who received a 41-month prison sentence for wire fraud and bank fraud after he convinced the banks to open merchant credit card accounts by

---

163 A prosecution in Colorado in 2015 was a variation of old school bookmaking. The defendant recruited bettors at exclusive golf courses. He would accept cash or checks from his customers. After establishing an account, the bettors could place bets using either the telephone or internet. In this case, the dependent operated his own sportsbook located in Costa Rica. If the bettors won and requested their money, he would pay them either in cash or by check. This was a rare modern case where the person servicing the customers was also the person operating the sportsbook. The operation ran from 2006 to 2015.

164 Will Green, *Big US Sports Betting Busts In 2016 Serve as Backdrop for Legalization Effort*, Legal Sports Report, July 5, 2016, https://www.legalsportsreport.com/10643/2016-illegal-us-sports-betting/.

claiming that his company was selling internet television and movie subscriptions when in fact they were to fund gambling accounts.[165]

With restricted access to credit cards, the illegal bookmakers needed alternative methods to receive and send money to bettors. The predominant method, especially for those who placed larger bets, uses a network of agents and subagents. The sportsbooks would still maintain internet sports wagering sites, but they would also employ agents throughout the United States to service customers.

An example of this occurred in Pennsylvania, which has legal casinos but not sports wagering. A man was arrested for recruiting and servicing sports bettors out of the Sands Casino Resort Bethlehem in locations such as the casino high roller lounges and the poker room. The defendant would establish accounts and accept cash from bettors at the casino, then provide log-in information and passwords to access an offshore sportsbook where the bettors could then make wagers. He would pay the bettors in cash at the casino.[166]

In some cases, these agents would employ subagents that dealt directly with the bettors.[167] This multilevel marketing scheme has the benefit of putting two layers between law enforcement and the sportsbook. In this case, agents are like distributors and can hire subagents, also called runners, who service the bettors. The runners may have limited knowledge of the identity of distributors, who may operate in different states or countries. The runner may also be unaware of the operator of the internet sportsbook that operates in a friendly foreign country and would have limited responsibilities. Thus, the arrest of the runner would have no impact on the sportsbook's operations.[168] In some cases, the sportsbook operation, the distributors, and the runners have had direct ties to organized crime syndicates such as the Genovese family and the Lucchese crime families.[169]

---

165 INTERNAL REVENUE SERVICE: EXAMPLES OF GAMING INVESTIGATIONS-FISCAL YEAR 2015, https://www.irs.gov/uac/examples-of-gaming-investigations-fiscal-year-2015.

166 Sara K. Satullo, *Lower Macungie Man Operated Illegal Sports Betting at Sands Casino, Police Say*, LEGHIGH VALLEY LIVE, Sept. 30, 2014, http://www.lehighvalleylive.com/bethlehem/index.ssf/2014/09/lower_macungie_man_operated_il.html.

167 U.S. ATTORNEY'S OFFICE DISTRICT OF NEW Jersey, *Two New Jersey Men Sentenced to Prison for Their Roles in Illegal Online Gambling* Enterprise, FBI (June 16, 2015), https://www.fbi.gov/contact-us/field-offices/newark/news/press-releases/two-new-jersey-men-sentenced-to-prison-for-their-roles-in-illegal-online-gambling-enterprise.

168 Puneet Pal Singh, *How Does Illegal Sports Betting Work and What Are the Fears?*, BBC NEWS, Feb. 19, 2013, http://www.bbc.com/news/business-21501858.

169 U.S. Attorney, *supra* note 168.

2

Legal Status of Sports Wagering

GENERALLY

The legal environment for regulated sports betting in the US is a product of history, politics, and debates about the role of government. It also reflects the cultural and moral ambivalence our society has about gambling generally. Sports betting enjoys wide popularity in the US and the public often views it as the least objectionable form of gambling. This popularity has not translated into a coherent legal treatment of sports betting, however, by either legislative bodies or courts. However, on May 14, 2018, the United States Supreme Court clarified and transformed the law of sports wagering with its ruling that the federal law that had restricted sports betting in the US was unconstitutional.[1] This chapter sets out the legal treatment of sports betting leading up to and including this momentous Supreme Court decision.

SPORTS BETTING BEFORE 1992

To understand the current legal environment for sports betting, a bit of history is necessary. For all its current popularity, sports betting as a regulated form of gambling didn't begin to develop until after World War II. In the early 1950s, legal sports betting in Nevada enjoyed a spike in interest, but a high federal excise tax inhibited growth in the industry.[2] At venues called "turf clubs," the betting on horse races was much greater than on sports betting.[3]

1 Murphy v. NCAA, 138 S. Ct. 1461 (2018). Lower court decision Christie v. NCAA, 832 F.3d 389 (3d Cir. 2016), cert granted, 137 S. Ct. 2327 (2017)

2 Revenue Act of 1951, 82 Pub. L. No. 82-183, 65 Stat. 452, 82 Cong. Ch. 521; *See also The Federal Gambling Tax and the Constitution*, 43 J. Crim. L. Criminology 637 (1952-1953).

3 David Schwartz, Cutting the Wire 169 (Univ. of Nevada Press, 2005).

It was in the mid-1970s when sports betting as a distinct form of wagering was born. By this time, Congress had lowered the tax on sports bets and interest in sportsbooks expanded beyond the "stand-alone" sportsbook. When the Stardust Casino opened its Race and Sports Book in that year, it marked the entry of Nevada casinos into the sports betting market.[4] Soon, other casinos in Nevada made sportsbooks a part of their operations, and the new era of sports betting began.

In the late 1970s and 1980s, sports betting's popularity grew steadily as the handle in Nevada evidenced.[5] Part of the growth was attributable to the proliferation of sports programming on American television. When ESPN began operations in the fall of 1979, few could have anticipated the appetite for sports betting in the US.

One needs to keep in mind that until 1976, Nevada was the only state where legal casino gambling existed. State lotteries had begun to re-emerge in the 1960s, and pari-mutuel wagering on horse racing still had a substantial following. But until New Jersey legalized casino gambling in 1976, with its first casino opening in 1978, Nevada was the only state where casino gambling, and sports betting, could take place.

Looking back, many states likely consider this as a time of lost opportunity for establishing legal, regulated sports betting. In the 1970s and 1980s, no federal law barred states from offering sports betting. Why didn't states jump on this opportunity?

New York is a good case in point. As a populous state with numerous horse tracks and, beginning in 1967, a state lottery, New York would seem to be an attractive market for sports betting. But, as noted above, politics often plays a role in the legalization of gambling, including sports betting. Infighting among affected parties, the opposition of state lottery officials, and concerns about the effects on the pari-mutuel industry combined to thwart efforts to legalize sports betting in New York.[6]

By the late 1980s and early 1990s, however, many states had begun to consider legalizing sports betting to alleviate budget pressures and to meet the growing demand. Nevada had established that sports betting was popular and could generate considerable tax revenues for states. Around this same time, those opposing sports betting,

---

4 *Id.*

5 *See* discussion in Chapter 1.

6 *See generally* Arne K. Lang, SPORTS BETTING AND BOOKMAKING: AN AMERICAN HISTORY 170-77 (2016).

especially the leadership of the major sports leagues and the NCAA, began a drumbeat of opposition to the spread of gambling on sports.

This coalescence of parties claimed sports betting was a corrupting influence that affected the character and integrity of the games. Additionally, if states added their imprimatur to sports betting, they were sending a mixed message to young people: rather than sports contests being about healthy competition, the focus would be on a "something for nothing" mentality that was inherently corrupt.[7]

These moralist arguments led to efforts to entirely outlaw sports betting, or to pass a law that would limit sports betting to professional sports only. By the early 1990s, the proponents of regulated sports betting were losing out to those seeking its abolition. All the abolitionist cause needed was a champion. And it found one.

THE PROFESSIONAL AND AMATEUR SPORTS PROTECTION ACT OF 1992

Bill Bradley was a Princeton graduate, All-American basketball player, Rhodes Scholar, a member of an NBA championship team, and a United States Senator from New Jersey. He also was a fierce opponent of sports betting. Bradley was frustrated that he could not garner sufficient support for a law that would eliminate sports betting in the country. Instead, he had to settle for a law that would ban the *spread* of sports betting beyond its current status in 1992.

The bill that was signed into law, the "Professional and Amateur Sports Protection Act of 1992,"[8] known as PASPA, is one of the most controversial federal gambling statutes on the books. PASPA has several parts. The first portion establishes the law's basic prohibitions:

- States or other governmental entities are not permitted to "sponsor, operate, advertise, promote, license, or authorize by law or compact," sports gambling schemes;[9]
- A separate provision extends the prohibition to private persons. That is, a person may not "sponsor, operate, advertise, or promote" a sports betting scheme "pursuant to the law or compact of a governmental entity."[10]

---

7 A detailed discussion of the arguments favoring and opposing regulated sports betting is in Chapter 5.

8 Professional and Amateur Sports Protection Act of 1992, 28 U.S.C. §§ 3701-3704 (2017).

9 28 U.S.C. § 3702(1) (2017).

10 *Id.* at (2).

• Both provisions extend their coverage to a "lottery, sweepstakes, or other betting, gambling, or wagering scheme based . . . on games in which amateur or professional athletes participate. . . ." [11]

Who was to enforce the prohibitions set out in section 3702? In section 3703, PASPA declared that "the Attorney General of the United States, or . . . a professional sports organization or amateur sports organization whose competitive game is alleged to be the basis of such violation" could seek injunctive relief in federal court."[12]

While Section 3702 contained PASPA's core prohibitions, Section 3704 sets out exceptions that have created significant controversy:

- "[P]ari-mutuel animal racing," that is, betting on horse and dog races was exempted, as was jai alai, another sport where pari-mutuel wagering was used.[13]
- Without expressly identifying Senator Bradley's state, New Jersey was given one year from the effective date of the Act to authorize sports betting.[14]
- In the most controversial exceptions, certain states were "grandfathered" so that PASPA would not apply to their sports betting operations. Section 3704(a)(1) exempted sports lotteries "to the extent that the scheme was conducted

---

11 *Id.*

12 *Id.* at (3).

13 28 U.S.C. § 3704(a)(2)(B) (2017); George Richards, *ESPN Asks 'What the Hell Happened To Jai-alai?'*, MIAMI HERALD, Aug. 2, 2016, http://www.miamiherald.com/sports/article93237822.html (reporting on an ESPN documentary examining the disappearance of jai-alai); Peter Wedderburn, *Greyhound Racing: An Industry in Terminal Decline?*, THE TELEGRAPH, Aug. 31, 2016, http://www.telegraph.co.uk/pets/news-features/greyhound-racing-an-industry-interminal-decline/ (describing the worldwide decline in greyhound racing); Horseracing has enjoyed a favored status under federal law for decades; *See* Interstate Horseracing Act of 1978, 15 U.S.C. § 3001 (2017) (exempting horseracing from many of the provisions of the Wire Act, allowing for "off-track" and online wagering).

14 The language in PASPA granting New Jersey this exemption is somewhat obscure. Subsection 3 stated that the prohibition did not apply to:

> (3) a betting, gambling, or wagering scheme, other than a lottery described in paragraph (1), conducted exclusively in casinos located in a municipality, but only to the extent that--
>
> (A) such scheme or a similar scheme was authorized, not later than one year after the effective date of this chapter, to be operated in that municipality; and
>
> (B) any commercial casino gaming scheme was in operation in such municipality throughout the 10-year period ending on such effective date pursuant to a comprehensive system of State regulation authorized by that State›s constitution and applicable solely to such municipality.

Only Atlantic City, New Jersey satisfied the terms of this provision.

> . . . at any time during the period beginning January 1, 1976, and ending August 30, 1990." Section 3704(a)(2) exempted sports gambling that was "authorized by statute as in effect on October 2, 1991 [and] actually was conducted . . . at any time during the period beginning September 1, 1989, and ending October 2, 1991." The legislative history of PASPA, in one way or another, refers to at least nine states fitting within one or the other of these exceptions.[15] But it was clear that this exception was meant primarily to preserve the sports betting industry in Nevada, a state whose economy was heavily dependent on gambling.[16]

As noted above, PASPA has been the object of severe criticism over the years. These attacks have found their way into judicial proceedings and appeals for Congress to overturn or modify the law. These arguments will be analyzed in detail below as the litigation over PASPA is presented. For now, however, two important points should be made.

First, PASPA does not make sports betting illegal as a matter of federal law. It simply prohibits the *states* from authorizing or licensing sports betting schemes. This may seem to be a subtle distinction, but it plays an important role in the judicial challenges to the validity of PASPA under the United States Constitution.

Second, PASPA is anomalous because it fits neither category of instances when the federal government typically has passed gambling laws: to fortify state laws against gambling,[17] and as a way of thwarting organized crime efforts to operate in interstate commerce.[18] In this second category is the infamous federal Wire Act.[19]

The Wire Act was a product of Attorney General Robert Kennedy's efforts to combat organized crime in the US. The law makes it a crime for one to:

---

15 Sen. Rep. No. 102-248 at 8 (1992), *reprinted in* 1992 U.S.C.C.A.N. 3553, 3559.

16 *Id.*

17 *E.g.*, Travel Act, 18 U.S.C. § 1952(b) (2017) ("any business enterprise involving gambling. . . in violation of the laws of the State in which committed"); Illegal Gambling Business Act, 18 U.S.C. § 1955(b)(1)(i) (2017) ("illegal gambling business means a gambling business which is a violation of the law of a State or political subdivision in which it is conducted").

18 In the mid-twentieth century the federal government enacted several laws aimed at eliminating organized crime's influence on gambling. Among these laws were the Travel Act, 18 U.S.C. § 1952; Interstate Wagering Paraphernalia Act, 18 U.S.C. § 1953; and the Illegal Gambling Business Act, 18 U.S.C. § 1955.

19 The Interstate Wire Act of 1961, 18 U.S.C. §§ 1081-1084 (2017).

> be[] engaged in the business of betting or wagering [to] knowingly use . . . a wire communication facility for the transmission in interstate or foreign commerce of bets or wagers or information assisting in the placing of bets or wagers on any sporting event or contest.[20]

Note that the law offers safe harbor for the transmission of information to assist in the placing of sports bets between two states that allow sports betting.[21] Also, the Wire Act requires a transmission "in interstate or foreign commerce."[22]

The effect of the Wire Act was to place limitations on the use of wire facilities to transmit sports betting information between states. PASPA is notable because, with limited exceptions, it interferes with a state's ability to offer purely *intra-state* sports betting. Few federal laws on gambling limit a state's authority over gambling. Thus, it is not surprising that challenges have been made to PASPA. Not all the challenges have been full-on attacks, but most have been just that.

EFFORTS TO WORK WITHIN PASPA

As noted above, the "grandfathering" provision in PASPA has been the source of constitutional challenges. But one state didn't challenge PASPA; it tried to operate within its terms, albeit in a slightly different manner.

During the football season of 1976, Delaware offered several contests that allowed betting on NFL games. All the betting schemes required that the bettor wager on more than one game at a time. The NFL challenged Delaware's games, claiming they amounted to the league's "forced association with gambling," and that they were a misappropriation of the product of the league's efforts to build its business into the commercial success that it was (and is today).[23] Except for holding that the state had to make a conspicuous statement that the NFL was not associated with the state-sponsored contests, the court rejected all claims of the league.[24] Despite its victory, the state discontinued the games the very next year due to their unprofitability.

---

20 18 U.S.C. § 1084(a) (2006).

21 18 U.S.C. § 1084(b) (2017). *See also United States v. Cohen,* 260 F.3d 68 (2d Cir. 2001) (ruling that it was irrelevant that the jurisdiction accepting the bet had legal wagering, as both jurisdictions must allow wagering to be legal under Wire Act).

22 18 U.S.C. § 1084(a) (2017).

23 In addition to the league's "forced association" claim they raised arguments of misappropriation, violation of trademark, and unfair competition claims. NFL v. Governor of Del., 435 F. Supp. 1372, 1377-82 (D. Del. 1977).

24 *Id.* at 1391.

But that was 1977. In 2009, Delaware's governor proposed legislation that authorized sports betting at facilities in the state. In May, he signed such a proposal into law. The legal basis for doing this was that PASPA grandfathered Delaware's ability to offer sports betting because it had a sports betting scheme in 1976. Delaware was simply taking advantage of the clear legislative opportunity PASPA offered. All the major US sports leagues and the NCAA sued Delaware claiming its new law violated PASPA.[25]

Although Delaware maintained that it was simply reinstituting the system of sports betting that it authorized in 1976, there was one fundamental difference: while the games in 1976 allowed bettors only to wager on parlay bets that required picking a minimum of three games, the new law allowed bets on individual games. This difference, which was at the core of the parties' dispute, was substantial because bettors prefer to wager on single games.

Delaware argued that the plain language of PASPA allowed it to reintroduce sports betting; the language of PASPA put no restriction on the types of betting opportunities that could be offered. The state had previously authorized many types of betting games and now it was offering them.[26]

The argument of the leagues required a closer look at the grandfathering provision in PASPA. PASPA's general prohibition did not apply to a:

> lottery, sweepstakes, or other betting, gambling, or wagering scheme in operation in a State or other governmental entity, *to the extent that the scheme was conducted by that State* or other governmental entity at any time during the period beginning January 1, 1976, and ending August 31, 1990. 28 U.S.C. § 3704(a) (emphasis added).

It wasn't enough that a state had contemplated or authorized a particular "scheme" of betting, the leagues argued; only those schemes that had been implemented—conducted—were within the PASPA exception. Because Delaware did not conduct single-game wagering as a betting scheme in 1976, PASPA prevents Delaware from implementing it now.

The court agreed with the leagues. Congress used unambiguous language that intended that the type of betting being proposed now was a "scheme" that had been *conducted*, not simply authorized,

25 Office of the Comm'r of Baseball v. Markell, 579 F.3d 293 (3d Cir. 2009).

26 Brief for Appellee at 49-50, Office of the Comm'r of Baseball v. Markell, 579 F.3d 293 (3d Cir. 2009) (No. 09-3297).

earlier.[27] This meant that only parlay-type betting was permitted now, as that was the only type of betting that Delaware offered in 1976. *De minimis* alterations such as allowing betting on teams that weren't in existence in 1976 were allowed because they wouldn't "effectuate a substantive change from the scheme that was conducted during the exception period."[28] But the move from parlay contests to single-game betting was a fundamental change and was not within the purview of PASPA's grandfathering provision.

Delaware still has a parlay style system of sports betting. So does Montana, another grandfathered state, which has expanded its contests to NASCAR.[29] Oregon formerly had NFL parlay betting but caved in to pressure from the NCAA and eliminated it as of 2007.[30] Because of the restrictions to parlay betting, states have not garnered significant revenue from sports betting. The only grandfathered state that has realized notable revenues under PASPA's regime is Nevada,[31] as it was the only state that had single-game wagering at the time Congress enacted PASPA. Given the revenues that Nevada has generated from its regulated sports betting licensees, with time other states would want in on the opportunity. To do this, PASPA would have to go.

NEW JERSEY'S BATTLE TO GET SPORTS BETTING: WHAT A LONG, STRANGE TRIP IT'S BEEN

New Jersey and PASPA

There is little doubt that New Jersey missed a golden opportunity to have sports betting. Much to the chagrin of PASPA's sponsor Senator Bill Bradley, a provision in PASPA gave the state until January 1, 1994, to pass a sports betting law. The plan was to put a constitutional amendment on the ballot for a vote in November 1993 so that a sports betting law could then be passed. But other political considerations,

---

27 Markell, 579 F.3d at 301.

28 *Id.* at 303.

29 MONTANA DEPT. OF JUSTICE GAMBLING CONTROL DIVISION, GAMBLING LAWS, https://dojmt.gov/gaming/gambling-laws-administrative-rules/ (last visited Aug, 29, 2017).

30 SPORTS BUSINESS DAILY, *Oregon Lottery Canning Sports Betting Games After Super Bowl*, Jan. 30, 2007, http://www.sportsbusinessdaily.com/Daily/Issues/2007/01/Issue-90/Collegiate-Sports/Oregon-Lottery-Canning-Sports-Betting-Games-After-Super-Bowl.aspx (last visited Sept. 1, 2017).

31 *See* "Nevada Sports Wagering Summary", *supra*, Chapter 1.

primarily relating to the state's gubernatorial race, interfered with this and it became clear that the constitutional amendment proposal for sports betting was not going to be on the November ballot.

Panic ensued, and the operators of all the Atlantic City casinos petitioned the state Casino Control Commission. They asserted that a constitutional amendment was not required for the Commission to authorize sports betting. The 1976 constitutional amendment that authorized casino gambling, and the implementing legislation, allowed "gambling games" to be offered. The casinos argued that sports betting fell under the definition of a gambling game. The Commission rejected the plea and the casinos swiftly challenged that rejection.

The federal district court gave the state no relief. It ruled that the phrase "gambling games" was limited to games which take place within the casino and could not be read broadly. As the court put it:

> The evolution of legalized gambling in New Jersey has been grudging. Because of widespread abuses in various gambling activities and the attendant social and economic ills engendered, gambling has historically been viewed as an undesirable activity.[32]

A specific constitutional amendment was required to allow for casino games, just as had been the case for simulcasting of horse racing. Legalizing forms of gambling in the state had been an incremental process, and this meant New Jersey's path to legal sports betting, within PASPA, had come up empty. All that was left was to challenge the law itself.

Interactive Media Entertainment and Gaming Association, Inc. v. Holder

The first constitutional broadside against PASPA came in 2011,[33] when several New Jersey thoroughbred associations, New Jersey State Senator Raymond Lesniak, and the named plaintiff, asserted that PASPA:

- exceeded Congress's powers under the Commerce Clause,
- violated the Equal Protection Clause of the Fourteenth Amendment because it granted differential privileges to engage in sports betting depending upon one's residence, and
- offended the Tenth Amendment which reserved to the states the power to raise revenue from sports betting.[34]

The court reached none of these arguments, however, holding that

32 Atl. City Racing Ass'n v. Atty. Gen. of N.J., 489 A.2d 165, 167 (1985).

33 Interactive Media Entertainment and Gaming Association, Inc. v. Holder, 2011 WL 802106 (D.N.J. March 7, 2011).

34 *Id.*

none of the plaintiffs had standing to bring the Commerce Clause and Equal Protection Clause claims, and that only a state could assert a violation of the Tenth Amendment and the state of New Jersey was not a party.[35]

But while the case was pending, supporters of sports betting in New Jersey were busy. They prepared a constitutional amendment as a referendum item for the November 2011 general election which permitted sports betting in the state. The amendment received the support of 64 percent of New Jersey voters.[36] Soon after that, the state legislature passed laws authorizing the state to permit and regulate sports wagering at Atlantic City casinos and horse racetracks. The legislation gave the Division of Gaming Enforcement authority to approve applications for sports wagering operations. Interestingly, the law came with a proviso that no sports betting operation could accept wagers on any college sporting events taking place within New Jersey, or on any New Jersey college team's game, regardless of where it was played.[37]

Christie I

New Jersey's plan seemed to be one of "stop us if you can," as the state prepared to offer sports betting in time for the NFL season beginning in the fall of 2012. The major sports leagues and the NCAA took the state up on the challenge and sought and received injunctive relief from the federal district court in New Jersey. The court issued its opinion on February 28, 2013, holding "that Congress acted within its powers and the statute in question does not violate the United States Constitution."[38] The state then appealed the decision to the Third Circuit Court of Appeals. The analysis of the Third Circuit was quite similar to the district court's decision, so the discussion below refers to the court of appeals decision.

Issue # 1 —Do the Leagues Have Standing to Challenge the New Jersey Plan?

New Jersey claimed that the leagues were unable to show a concrete injury from a potential increase in legal gambling. Without

35 *Id.* at 8.

36 Sarah Coffey, *N.J. Moves Towards Legal Sports Betting This Fall, in Time for NFL Season*, THE NAT'L LAW REV., May 25, 2012, https://www.natlawreview.com/article/nj-moves-towards-legal-sports-betting-fall-time-nfl-season (last visited Aug. 25, 2017).

37 Nevada had a similar provision in their gambling regulations until 2001. The previous regulation was repealed by Gaming Regulation 22.120(b).

38 NCAA v. Christie, 926 F. Supp. 2d 551 (D.N.J. 2013), aff'd 730 F.3d 208 (3rd Cir. 2013), cert denied, 134 S. Ct. 2886 (2014)(*Christie I*).

this, they lacked standing to bring the challenge to New Jersey's law.

But the court thought this it was a "straightforward conclusion" that the leagues did have standing.[39] Their games were the subject of PASPA and the leagues offered plausible evidence that the New Jersey plan threatened harm to their reputation.

Issue # 2 —Is PASPA within Congress's Commerce Clause Power?

The court ruled that wagering on sports is an economic activity that transcended state borders. To the extent the wagering activity had an intrastate quality, it can be regulated if the intrastate activity, in the aggregate, substantially affects interstate commerce. Both the sporting events that are the object of wagers and the actual wagering did have a substantial effect on interstate commerce, the court held. Congress should be given considerable deference in making judgments of how to regulate economic activity that substantially affects interstate commerce. Here, the court ruled that PASPA was a "rational means of regulating commerce."[40] Consequently, Congress was acting within its authority under the Commerce Claus in enacting the law.

Issue # 3—Does PASPA Commandeer State Legislatures in Violation of the 10th Amendment[41]?

This issue begins to develop the core attack on PASPA, which did not make sports wagering illegal in the US. If one accepts the court's analysis of Congress's Commerce Clause powers in the case, Congress would be constitutionally justified in passing a law that completely prohibited sports betting. Instead, with PASPA, Congress prevented *states* from passing laws that authorized or licensed sports betting, subject to the grandfathering provisions.

The idea of "commandeering" is that the 10th Amendment and conceptions of state sovereignty and federalism do not allow Congress to pass a law that has the effect of compelling a state to enact and enforce a federal regulatory program. New Jersey argued that PASPA conscripted the state to do the work of federal officials thereby violating the dual sovereignty concept that is at the heart of limited federal authority. What was it that PASPA compelled New Jersey to do? The state argued that the federal law prohibited the state from repealing its laws that prohibited sports wagering. This prohibition

39 Christie I, 730 F.3d at 224.

40 *Id.* at 225.

41 The Tenth Amendment to the United States Constitution provides: "The powers not delegated to the United States by the Constitution, nor prohibited by it to the States, are reserved to the States respectively, or to the people."; U.S. Const. amend. X.

acted as an affirmative requirement on the state that exceeds the inherent limitations on the reach of federal power.

In analyzing this argument, the court noted that there were only two cases where the Supreme Court had applied the commandeering idea to strike down a federal law. In one case, *New York v. United States,*[42] the federal law provided that a state had to make arrangements for the disposal of radioactive waste by a certain date. If it did not, the state itself "took title" to the waste, with accompanying obligations under federal law. The Supreme Court held that the law exceeded Congress's power because it compelled states to enact a regulatory program or expend resources for disposal of the radioactive waste. This crossed the line between encouragement and coercion.[43]

In the other case, *Printz v. United States,*[44] the federal law known as the Brady Act required states at their own expense to do background checks on gun purchasers. The Court ruled that Congress could not command state officials to enforce a federal regulatory program and to absorb the financial burden of implementing a federal program relating to gun control.[45]

The court of appeals did not agree that PASPA was a case of improper commandeering. In fact, the court ruled, PASPA didn't require a state to do anything; rather than telling a state what to do, it simply barred them from doing something they might want to do.[46] Commandeering required an affirmative command from Congress that was lacking here. PASPA simply operated to invalidate state laws that would authorize or license sports betting, and the Supremacy Clause of the Constitution gave precedence to federal law.

The court also was unpersuaded by New Jersey's argument that PASPA required it to keep its anti-gambling laws in force and this was a form of commandeering. PASPA prohibited the issuance of sports gambling licenses, and the affirmative authorization by law of sports gambling schemes, the court held. States don't have to keep a sports betting ban on books; that would, the court held, create a "false equivalence between repeal and authorization."[47]

PASPA, rather than forcing states to take a certain action, gave

42 New York v. United States, 505 U.S. 144 (1992).

43 *Id.* at 175.

44 Printz v. United States, 521 U.S. 898 (1997).

45 *Id.* at 926.

46 NCAA v. Christie, 926 F. Supp. 2d 551 (D.N.J. 2013), aff'd 730 F.3d 208 (3rd Cir. 2013), cert denied, 134 S. Ct. 2886 (2014)(*Christie I*).

47 *Id.* at 233.

states options. One option was to repeal its laws prohibiting sports wagering. A repeal was permissible under PASPA because the law forbade the licensing and authorization of sports betting, and there was no "equivalence between repeal and authorization."[48] In other words, the court suggested that one option New Jersey had was to take its anti-sports wagering laws off the books and allow for unregulated sports betting.

If this suggestion seemed a bit outlandish, the court's description of New Jersey's other option offered what New Jersey saw as a path forward:

> On the other hand, a state may choose to keep a *complete* ban on sports gambling, but [each] state [can] decide how much of a law enforcement priority it wants to make of sports gambling, or *what the contours of the prohibition will be.*[49](all emphasis added)

Because New Jersey had these options, the court ruled, PASPA did not commandeer the state legislature in a way that offended the 10th Amendment.

Issue #4—Equal Sovereignty of the States

New Jersey's final substantive argument was fairly direct: PASPA is invalid because the grandfathering provision that allowed Nevada to have a monopoly on single-game sports betting was at the expense of all other states. The Constitution does not allow Congress to favor one state over others.

As the court put it, the "centerpiece" of the state's argument here was the analysis the Supreme Court gave to two cases involving the Voting Rights Act of 1965.[50] In these cases, the Court ruled the Act's requirements that certain jurisdictions obtain Department of Justice preclearance before changing election details raised federalism issues because they treated states differently. New Jersey wanted to "leverage" the Court's statements of concern in those cases to strike down PASPA's allowance of sports betting for Nevada and no other state.

The court declined to draw the parallel advanced by the state. Statutes enacted under the Commerce Clause often treat states differently when addressing matters of national concern.[51] The Voting Rights Act cases themselves acknowledged that distinctions between states were often permissible.[52] PASPA was designed to keep sports

48 *Id.*

49 *Id.*

50 *Id.* at 237.

51 *Id.* at 238.

52 *Id.* at 238-39.

betting from spreading; targeting states where it didn't yet exist made complete sense. As the court saw it, PASPA didn't disfavor states, it favored Nevada, and New Jersey wasn't seeking to have Nevada's special status removed. Finally, regulating voting rights—an area of law with a fraught history of sensitive interaction between the federal and state governments--was a very different type of policymaking compared to gambling.[53]

No one could miss the tone of humility to the court's decision, as the court noted the absence of any "Eureka moment" where an "easy solution" presented itself.[54] The two doctrines emphasized by the state—commandeering and equal sovereignty—were important principles but had "only been used to strike down notably intrusive and, . . .extraordinary laws."[55] Extending those principles to the situation here would do damage to the Supremacy Clause. In echoing the refrain raised by many people, PASPA may be an unwise and unpopular law, but it is not unconstitutional, the court ruled. The remedy for curing its errors is an appeal to Congress.

The panel decision was not unanimous. The dissenting judge found little practical significance to the "commanding to regulate" vs. "commanding non-regulation."[56] PASPA controls the way states regulated private parties rather than directly regulating commerce, and this went beyond Congress's authority. The Supreme Court denied certiorari,[57] an unremarkable action at the time, but one that resonated later.

The Reaction to Christie I and New Jersey's Next Step

Some commentators attacked the approach taken by New Jersey, and the court's decision, as having gotten "lost in a thicket of obscure constitutional doctrines."[58] Rather than complicated constitutional doctrines like commandeering, the real key to the case was that Congress cannot pick winners and losers as it did in PASPA. But New Jersey did not accept defeat. The state looked at the court's decision and set out on a new tack.

The state passed legislation that removed state law prohibitions on sports betting. Governor Christie initially balked at this and vetoed the law. But less than two months later he signed a slightly revised

53 *Id.* at 239.

54 *Id.* at 240.

55 *Id.*

56 *Id.* at 245.

57 Christie v. NCAA, *cert denied*, 134 S. Ct. 2866 (2014).

58 I. Nelson Rose, *New Jersey Sports Betting—Court Gets It Wrong. Again.* 19 GAMING L. REV & ECON. 566 (2015).

provision. So what had the state done? Had they repealed *all* their laws that prohibited sports betting? And why would a repeal of these laws help them in light of PASPA?

As for the scope of the repeal of the laws prohibiting sports betting, it was limited:

> to the extent [the restrictions] apply . . . at a casino or gambling house operating in this State in Atlantic City or a . . . racetrack in this State, . . . by persons 21 years of age or older.[59]

In other words, casinos and racetracks in the state were the subjects of the *repeal* of the state's anti-wagering laws and were thereby not breaking the law if they offered sports betting. In all other respects, the laws prohibiting sports betting were still in place. What was New Jersey's strategy with this approach?

Christie I said "[a]ll that is prohibited" by PASPA "is the issuance of gambling 'licenses' or the affirmative 'authorization by law' of gambling schemes."[60] The 2012 Law violated PASPA solely because it was an *affirmative authorization* and licensing of sports wagering. PASPA does not prohibit a State from repealing a ban; a mere repeal does not "license" or "authorize" wagering. That is, there is no "equivalence between repeal and authorization," and the repeal here doesn't authorize or license sports betting.[61]

As the state put it, the key was ***not*** whether sports betting would be taking place; instead, whatever sports wagering that was taking place was *not* affirmatively authorized or licensed by the state. Therefore, PASPA was not violated by such a system.

The leagues declared the state's argument to be a cherry-picking of the court's language from *Christie I*. That decision didn't allow for a partial repeal. The state's choice was binary: *EITHER* maintain its laws prohibiting sports betting OR deregulate the area *completely* and allow sports betting without limits. The crafty halfway measure reflected in the 2014 law could not be squared with PASPA.

Christie II—The Case with Nine Lives

The path of the second challenge to PASPA by New Jersey, leading up to the Supreme Court's grant of certiorari in June 2017, has been one marked by twists and surprises. It started simply enough when federal district court Shipp, the same judge who decided *Christie I*, ruled that New Jersey's partial repeal of its sports betting prohibitions

59 New Jersey P.L. 2014, c. 62 (2014).

60 Christie I, 730 F.3d at 232.

61 *Id.* at 233.

violated PASPA.[62]

In his opinion, Judge Shipp began by making it clear that the constitutionality of PASPA had been resolved; the issue now before the court was whether PASPA pre-empted the 2014 law.[63] In making that judgment, Judge Shipp stated that Congress did not want the "label of legitimacy" that would come from a state "scheme" of sports gambling.[64] The legislative history of PASPA also made it clear that Congress's concerns about sports betting extended beyond the form of regulation.[65] Ultimately, he said, the choice the state has is a binary one: maintain a complete prohibition on sports wagering or completely repeal all laws that forbade sports betting.[66] A partial repeal just doesn't cut it.

A panel of three judges of the 3rd Circuit affirmed this ruling. In a rather terse opinion, the court declared that the 2014 Law authorized conduct that was otherwise completely prohibited by PASPA.[67] This authorization came from the law selectively dictating where sports gambling could occur, who could place bets, and which athletic contests the casinos and racetracks accept wagers on. The state might call what it did a repeal, but the law essentially provides that, regardless any other prohibition by law, casinos and racetracks shall hereafter be permitted to have sports gambling. This is not a repeal; it is an authorization.[68]

But there were signs that the case was on a different trajectory this time around. First, Judge Fuentes, who wrote the majority opinion in *Christie I,* dissented in *Christie II.* He maintained that New Jersey's partial repeal did not authorize sports betting and that it did not offend PASPA.[69]

Second, the court filed the opinion on August 25, 2015. But on October 14, the full 3rd Circuit vacated the opinion and granted a motion for rehearing *en banc.*[70] Such a step occurs in less than 1% of the cases ruled on by panels in the circuit.[71] Vacating the panel

62 NCAA v. Christie, 61 F. Supp. 3d 488 (D.N.J. 2014).

63 *Id.* at 498.

64 *Id.* at 499.

65 *Id.*

66 *Id.* at 501.

67 NCAA v. Governor of N.J., 799 F.3d 259 (3d Cir. 2015)(*Christie II*).

68 *Id.* at 266.

69 *See id.* at 268-32 (Fuentes, J., dissenting).

70 NCAA v. Rebuck, Nos. 14-4546, 14-4568, 14-4569, 2015 U.S. App. LEXIS 17839 (3d Cir. Oct. 14, 2015).

71 Matthew Stiegler, *A Closer Look at the Third Circuit's Recent En Banc Cases*, CA3BLOG,

decision effectively nullified the panel decision.

Speculation immediately began to swirl regarding why the court would take such an unusual approach in this case. It seemed unlikely the court wanted to rule on the case *en banc* simply to reaffirm the validity of PASPA. Were PASPA's days numbered?

During oral argument to the full 3rd Circuit on February 17, 2016, some questions from the bench suggested the court might reconsider the constitutionality of PASPA. Other exchanges between the lawyers and the court indicated that PASPA might be constitutional, but New Jersey's 2014 partial repeal law had found the "sweet spot." That is, sports betting was permitted in the manner prescribed by the law.

The anticipation that the 3rd Circuit was going to rule in such a way that allowed for sports betting in one way or another gained steam as the months went on. Perhaps the court was about to declare PASPA unconstitutional and knew it would be a controversial decision. The delay might allow the court to forge a strong consensus opinion.

The decision, released on August 9, was a bit of an anti-climax.[72] Part of the opinion was a reinforcement of the district court's ruling that the legislative characterization of the 2014 statute as a repeal was not binding on the court. In fact, the court held, the law selectively authorized casinos and racetracks to offers sports betting while maintaining the general prohibitions against that activity.[73] This was an authorization forbidden by PASPA. But a significant part of the court's opinion was a walking back of language used in the *Christie I* decision, and a clarification of the law as expressed by the federal district court in *Christie II*.

First, the court announced that its analysis of the relationship between an "authorization" of sports betting by a state and a "repeal" of prohibitions on sports betting had been, to use the court's term, "too facile."[74] In other words, the gap between the two might not always be so great. In any event, "[t]o the extent . . . we took the position that a repeal cannot constitute an authorization, we now reject that reasoning,"[75] and the court pronounced the discussion from *Christie I*

Mar. 17, 2015, http://ca3blog.com/judges/a-closer-look-at-the-third-circuits-recent-en-banc-cases/ (last visited Aug. 29, 2017); The Third Circuit's own rules indicate that en banc hearing is "disfavored." L.A.R. 35.0 Determination of Causes By The Court En Banc 35.4 at 38. (available at http://www2.ca3.uscourts.gov/legacyfiles/2011_LAR_Final.pdf.).

72 NCAA v. Governor of N.J., 832 F.3d 389 (3d Cir. 2016).

73 *Id.* at 401.

74 *Id.*

75 *Id.* at 396-97.

to be "unnecessary dicta."[76]

Stripped to its essentials, the court ruled that the partial repeal still acted as an authorization. "States may not use clever drafting or mandatory construction provisions to escape the supremacy of federal law."[77] The anti-commandeering analysis did not need reconsideration and PASPA did not exceed the constitutional powers of Congress.

Second, the court rejected the analysis of Judge Shipp in *Christie II* that the state had only two options. The "binary choice" approach—either completely ban sports betting or completely repeal their anti-sports betting laws—was also dicta, and misleading dicta at that. While the partial repeal New Jersey wanted to implement violated PASPA, that "does not preclude the possibility that other options may pass muster."[78] Even the leagues had conceded, the court ruled, that "not all partial repeals are created equal."[79]

> For instance, a state's partial repeal of a sports wagering ban to allow *de minimis* wagers between friends and family would not have nearly the type of authorizing effect that we find in the 2014 Law.[80]

This tantalizing reference to the types of partial repeals that might not offend PASPA was all the court was willing to offer, however. It did not wish to "articulate a line whereby a partial repeal of a sports wagering ban amounts to an authorization under PASPA, if indeed such a line could be drawn"[81] Simply, the 2014 law "overstepped" the boundary.[82]

The *en banc* decision did seem a bit underwhelming. PASPA was again upheld. So why did the court go to the trouble of an *en banc* hearing? Was it because the "authorization" and "repeal" analysis had become muddled? Did the "binary choice" analysis simply go too far? Or was it that the court wanted to make it clear that PASPA was constitutional and states shouldn't continue to try end runs around it? This last rationale is difficult to square with the court's "not all partial repeals are the same" language. Rather than dampen a state's enthusiasm for probing the soft spots of PASPA, the decision added fuel to the fires of creativity. What kind of partial repeal can we enact that slips past PASPA?

---

76 *Id.* at 401.
77 *Id.* at 398.
78 *Id.* at 401.
79 *Id.* at 402.
80 *Id.*
81 *Id.*
82 *Id.*

Christie II—The Case That Refuses to Die!

In one sense, after the 3rd Circuit ruling in August 2016, there was little reason to think that New Jersey's pursuit of a writ of certiorari from the Supreme Court would have any better chance of success the second time around. On the other hand, arguments continued to be made that PASPA was not only anachronistic, but its selective treatment of Nevada undermined basic tenets of fairness.[83] But when the state sought the writ in *Christie II*, the prevailing sentiment was that New Jersey was running out of chances.

As with the 3rd Circuit's granting the motion to hear the case *en banc*, however, the Supreme Court upset expectations when in February 2017, it issued a "call for the views of the Solicitor General."[84] Known as a CVSG, this action is the Supreme Court's way of seeking the counsel of the United States Solicitor General about the cert-worthiness of a case that the United States does not have a direct interest. Historically, if the Solicitor General recommended the Court grant certiorari, the Court usually did.[85] But even when no such recommendation was made, the Court's action of issuing the CVSG indicated its interest in the case and increased the likelihood that the Court would grant the petition.

The Solicitor General found little merit to the petition. States were not compelled to do anything by PASPA; the law simply prohibited the licensing or authorization of sports betting by states. Moreover, the 3rd Circuit was the only federal circuit that had ruled on PASPA. Typically, the more a case "percolates" with differing holdings in the various federal circuits, the more likely it is for the Supreme Court to determine it needs to step in and resolve the conflict. That dynamic was completely absent here. The case did not warrant the scrutiny of the Court, the Solicitor General opined.[86]

Slightly more than one month later, however, the Court issued its order granting the petition for the writ of certiorari.[87] The case was

---

83 In its application for cert, New Jersey also cited similar arguments they previously have including: Congress may not require states to regulate their citizens, their anti-commandeering argument, and federalism arguments; Brief for Petitioners, Christie v. NCAA, 137 S. Ct. 2327 (U.S. June 27, 2017) (No. 16-476).

84 Lisa McElroy, *"CVSG"s in Plain English*, SCOTUSBlog, Feb. 10, 2010, http://www.scotusblog.com/2010/02/last-week-in-plain-english-2/ (last visited Aug. 30, 2017).

85 *Id.*

86 Amicus Curiae Brief for United States at 21, Christie v. NCAA, 832 F.3d 389 (3d Cir. 2016), *cert granted*, 137 S. Ct. 2327, 85 U.S.L.W. 3602 (U.S. June 27, 2017) (No. 16-472).

87 Christie v. NCAA, 832 F.3d 389 (3d Cir. 2016), *cert granted*, 137 S. Ct. 2327, 85 U.S.L.W. 3602 (U.S. June 27, 2017) (No. 16-472).

argued on December 4, 2017 and it was clear that several justices had deep reservations about the constitutionality of PASPA.[88] This was confirmed when the Court announced its decision on May 14, 2018.[89]

Writing for the Court, Justice Alito declared emphatically that PASPA violated the U.S. Constitution. Congress did not have the constitutional authority to tell a state how to legislate. PASPA's provision that states could not authorize sports betting unequivocally dictated to state legislatures what they were permitted to do and not do. The opinion made short work of the leagues' argument that PASPA didn't require action by states, it only prohibited certain action. That distinction was "empty," the Court ruled; whether PASPA commanded the states to act or prohibited them, "The basic principle—that Congress cannot issue direct orders to state legislatures—applies in either event."[90] With PASPA:

> state legislatures are put under the direct control of Congress. It is as if federal officers were installed in state legislative chambers and were armed with the authority to stop legislators from voting on any offending proposals. A more direct affront to state sovereignty is not easy to imagine.[91]

The Court also ruled that PASPA's provisions prohibiting private parties from operating sports books pursuant to state law were not severable. Those provisions "were obviously meant to work together with the provisions" that barred states from authorizing or licensing sports books.[92] Once the state prohibition failed, all of PASPA collapsed.

Seven justices ruled PASPA was invalid because it commandeered state legislatures. Justices Ginsburg and Sotomayor dissented, disagreeing both with the commandeering conclusion and the ruling of non-severability.[93] Justice Breyer agreed with the dissenting justices on the severability issue, while joining with the Court on the commandeering point.

So, after six years of court battles, New Jersey had finally won the day. The controversy could now finally pivot from whether states could offer sports betting, to how they should regulate it.

---

88 Transcript of Oral Argument at 31, Christie v. NCAA, 137 S. Ct. 2327 (2017) (No. 16-476).

89 Murphy v. NCAA, 138 S. Ct. 1461 (2018)

90 *Id.* at 1478

91 *Id.*

92 *Id.* at 1483

93 "The Court wields an ax . . .instead of a scalpel to trim the statute." (*Id.* at 1489) (Justice Ginsburg dissenting)

3

Regulatory Models for Wagering

Whether through legislation or judicial decision, the "legalization" of sports betting in the US is only the beginning point for offering sports betting. A fundamental question for the regulation of sports wagering is what the methods and structure of regulation should be. In other words, should the locus of regulation reside with the federal government, with the states, or with a combination of both? Even after answering this question, numerous details of regulation must be addressed. Because the regulatory model established will likely be a product of political compromise, many variations are possible. But the models described below offer a template for discussion. This Chapter sets out different potential models of regulation, with a description of their features and advantages and disadvantages.

Before discussing the models, however, two foundational issues will supply necessary context. The first is a description of the historical relationship between the federal and the state governments as it relates to the regulation of gambling. Regulatory models that deviate from this association may create problems of implementation as the federal-state relationship is restructured. The second is an explanation of the factors that will be the basis for consideration of the advantages and disadvantages of the potential models of regulation.

HISTORICAL RELATIONSHIP BETWEEN THE FEDERAL AND STATE GOVERNMENTS

Before the passage of the Professional and Amateur Sports Protection Act (PASPA),[1] federal policy towards gambling was relatively simple. Rather than preempting state laws, federal gambling laws were to aid states in enforcing their laws that prohibit gambling. There are several examples.

---

1 28 U.S.C. 3701 et seq.

In adopting the Federal Wire Act,[2] Congress in 1961 made clear its respect for the rights of individual states to regulate gambling within their borders. [3] The Travel Act,[4] the Wagering Paraphernalia Act,[5] and the Illegal Gambling Business Act[6] are laws enacted during the 1960s and 1970s that also illustrated the supplementary role of federal gambling laws. Congress passed these laws in response to the proliferation of illegal multistate gambling operations conducted by organized crime.[7] The federal government intervened because states could not adequately investigate and prosecute criminal organizations that operated in multiple states. The creation of separate federal offenses based on a predicate state law violation gave the Federal Bureau of Investigation the authority to investigate and the Department of Justice the ability to prosecute national crime organizations.

These considerations also have application to the regulation of sports betting. Once again, a lack of resources or jurisdictional authority limits the ability of state governments to regulate interstate or foreign businesses. Federal intervention is necessary to achieve goals that are beyond the jurisdictional reach of the states. In the context of sports wagering, these goals can include: (a) international criminal cooperation for the exchange of intelligence and information related to the investigation and prosecution of manipulation of sports results at national and international levels; (b) establishing common standards for extraterritorial jurisdiction and international extradition; (c) agreeing to collect, preserve, and share evidence (including electronic data) with foreign governments relating to competition manipulation; and (d) agreeing to require licensed sportsbooks to provide betting data to national and international data bases to detect criminal behavior.

Since the passage of the Interstate Horseracing Act, however, federal intervention into gambling regulation has become more

---

2 18 U.S.C. 1804.

3 See United States v. Yaquinta, 204 F. Supp. 276 (N.D. W. Va 1962). The purpose" of the Wire Act " is succinctly stated in Report No. 588 of the Senate Judiciary Committee of the 87th Congress, on July 24, 1961, as "* * * to assist the several States in the enforcement of their laws pertaining to gambling and to aid in the suppression of organized gambling activities by restricting the use of wire communication facilities." *Id.*

4 18 U.S.C. 1952.

5 18 U.S.C 1953.

6 18 U.S.C. 1955.

7 United States v. Roselli, 432 F.2d 879, 891 (9th Cir. 1970): *See also* United States v. Aquino, 336 F. Supp. 737, 739 (E.D. Mich. 1972).

prevalent. With this law, first passed in 1978,[8] Congress exercised control over the economics of the sport of horseracing. The law requires that race books share a portion of each wager with the race tracks and the horse owners on whose racing events the race books were accepting wagers.[9] The legislative history of the law indicates that Congress saw this revenue sharing as promoting the stability of horseracing and off-track betting in the United States.[10] As a practical matter, the off-track race books have to negotiate a contract with the track to conduct wagering on the track's races.[11] Because both parties need the other to maximize profits they have relatively equal bargaining power. The Act also seeks to assure that horsemen receive fair shares of interstate wagers by including their consent as a "condition precedent" to the agreements.[12]

Congress's intervention in horseracing may have relevance to sports wagering. PASPA prevented states from determining their policy towards gambling on sporting events involving humans, as the IHA did with sporting events involving horses. If in a system of widespread regulated sports betting sportsbooks had to pay to the leagues a portion of every bet, the Interstate Horseracing Act would be a valuable precedent.

PASPA and IHA are consistent in one other important aspect.[13]

---

8 15 U.S.C. §§ 3001-3007 (2012).

9 To this end, the original version of the Interstate Horseracing Act ("IHA") prescribed rules for "interstate off-track wagering," which Congress defined as a "legal wager placed or accepted in one State with respect to the outcome of a horserace taking place in another state." 15 U.S.C. § 3002 (2012).

10 Congress envisioned an interstate pari-mutuel scheme to ensure that states would "cooperate with one another in the acceptance of legal interstate wagering."

11 The IHA governs the relationship between the OTB operators, licensed internet and interactive television horse race betting services, the tracks, the horse owners and trainers, and the state racing commissions. All other aspects of horseracing, such as licensing and policing, are left to the discretion of the various state racing or gaming commissions. Before an OTB operator can accept an interstate off-track wager, "consent" must be obtained from three parties: (1) the track, (2) the racing commission in the state where the track is located, and (3) the racing commission in the state where the OTB operator is located. The use of the word "consent" should not mask the true intent of the Act, however. Consent comes with a price, either in the form of an agreement to provide wire information or a simulcast, or to conduct pari-mutuel wagering.

12 The IHA has met its original objective of assuring that the tracks receive a fair share of interstate wagers on races conducted at its track. The respective rights of the OTB operator and the track are well defined under the IHA. This usually includes provisions for the merging of pari-mutuel pools and the receipt by the OTB operator of the race simulcast and instantaneous transmission of all tote (i.e., wagering) and other track information. 15 U.S.C. § 3002(a)(1).

13 What is striking about the PASPA and IHA is that while both laws address sporting

Neither Act attempts to create a federal regulatory scheme over the gambling activity itself. In the case of PASPA, the intention was to create a national prohibition against state-authorized sports wagering. With the IHA, the intention was to assure that the race books compensated the parties that created the event upon which race books offered wagering. While the decision in the *Christie* case may negate PASPA's exercise of control over state sports betting policies, Congress may seek other ways to intrude on these state prerogatives.

The federal government has historically played no role in the discharge of the traditional regulatory functions of licensing, enforcement, and audit. It has, however, asserted regulatory authority over some aspects of casino operations, the most prominent being anti-money laundering laws.[14] For example, casinos and sportsbooks

---

events with highly skilled athletes their treatment of the activities is quite different. In the case of horseracing, Congress shows no concern for the impact of wagering on the integrity of the sport. Instead, Congress's concern is to assure that the various stakeholders in the sport are fairly compensated when persons accept wagers on their events. No proof exists that horseracing is any more tainted with scandal than other sports. The only difference is that the powerful horseracing industry wants wagering on their sport and the powerful professional sports leagues want a ban on sports wagering that does not involve horses.

14 Money laundering is the process by which criminals transform the money that they receive from criminal activities into funds that appear to have been generated by lawful means and cannot be traced by law enforcement to their illicit sources. Money laundering involves three steps. The first is placement, which involves changing the form of the funds into a less suspicious, more easily manipulated form. Placement is the most well-known phase of money laundering. Criminals, particularly drug dealers, tend to accumulate their money from the sale of drugs to customers in smaller denominations. These funds tend to be bulky and difficult to transport. Therefore, methods need to be devised to convert the smaller bills into larger bills, bank checks, money orders, traveler's checks, or some other form of cash equivalent.

The next step is to layer the funds. Layering is the method by which criminals distance themselves from the converted funds. The idea is to provide a series of financial transactions that inhibit the ability of law enforcement to track the money back to their owner or source. This frequently involves wire transfers between bank accounts, often in foreign countries.

The final step is integration, which involves transferring the layered funds from the foreign country into a mainstream financial world in the US through a transaction that has legitimate commercial purpose. Anthony N. Cabot & Keith C. Miller, THE LAW OF GAMBLING AND REGULATED GAMING 58-59 (Carolina Academic Press, 2nd ed. 2016).

Using wagering operations for "placement" is different for land-based and internet operators. The latter generally are not set up to accept cash. Instead, they typically use a third-party intermediary to obtain money from the customer. In some cases, however, illegal internet operators have used runners to accept large cash deposits from patrons in person and establish on-line account wagering. The patrons will simply wager against the moneys held on account and at his request have amounts debited from the account and returned in cash to the patron in person.

must report certain currency payments and suspicious activity to comply with BSA regulations of a federal agency called the Financial Crimes Enforcement Network (FinCEN).[15] Sportsbooks must file Currency Transaction Reports (CTR) for all cash transactions over $10,000, either individually or in the aggregate, in one gaming day.[16] While all suspicious activity may not warrant a CTR because of the currency transaction value,[17] the sportsbook must file a Suspicious Activity Report (SAR) if it observes a suspicious activity whether attempted or completed and involving $5,000 or more in funds or other assets.[18]

Wagering operations can assist in in the layering process of laundering money. A value of involving wagering operations is that the funds can be disguised as winnings when, in fact, no "gambling" transaction has ever taken place. Take, for example, an unscrupulous operator in an unregulated environment. A drug dealer could set up multiple accounts with the operator. Some accounts result in the drug dealer "losing" all the deposited funds, while other accounts result in the drug dealer "winning." The funds from the winning accounts are then transferred to an internet bank in the "layering" process. To anyone investigating the trail, the funds appear to be legitimate internet casino winnings. For example, if a patron bets $100,000 on one side of a football game in one account and $100,000 on the other side in a different account, then one account will show a large gain and the patron is only out the vigorish. In both scenarios, the account with the large gain will look like a legitimate gambling win. More pertinent to sports integrity, however, is when the criminals rather than simply using the wagering operations to launder money at the standard vigorish, attempt to use the markets to both launder money and make a profit by fixing the games on which they place wagers.

SportAccord estimates that sports betting could now be used to launder more than €11,000m worldwide and that the winnings of fixed matches could represent up to €6.8bn. Criminals, however, make wagering money laundering operations profitable by corrupting the games on which they bet. Emine Bozkurt, *Match Fixing and Fraud in Sport: Putting the Pieces Together*, Sept. 17, 2012, http://www.europarl.europa.eu/document/activities/cont/201209/20120925ATT52303/20120925ATT52303EN.pdf.

The wagering industry is particularly susceptible to layering because: there is high liquidity; is a cash business and has fluid cash flow; has easily accessible global markets; has significant unregulated markets; has a lack of harmony in regulations and a lack of cooperation between regulated markets; winnings are tax free in some jurisdictions and/or winnings can be easily transferred to other jurisdictions.

15 The forms used to report such activities are FinCEN Form 112: Currency Transaction Reports (CTR) and FinCEN Form 111: Suspicious Activity Report (SAR).

16 Besides the standard CTRs filed for a single currency transaction, casinos must file CTRs for reportable multiple transactions identified through the aggregation of daily records. As such, the sportsbook will periodically update records used to assist with customer verification to ensure their accuracy.

17 A sport book must have internal controls to detect suspicious activity, using a risk-based approach to the areas of products and services, customers, geographic areas, and transaction types.

18 Press Release, Financial Crimes Enforcement Network, Final Rule Amending Casino Currency Reporting Requirements Announced (June 21, 2007) Retrieved from http://www.fincen.gov/news_room/nr/pdf/20070621b.pdf. The FinCEN casino-specific Web

FACTORS TO CONSIDER

This section sets out seven primary factors that policymakers can consider in evaluating different models that assign control over the regulation of sports wagering to the federal government, the states, or a combination of both. Then, the relevant factors will be used to examine the advantages and disadvantages of each model and, in some cases, the political dynamics of gaming regulation that may favor or disfavor a model.

Regulation can promote inefficiencies in a market in several ways: by setting prices above competitive rates, restricting information that consumers use to price shop, and by creating "barriers to entry." Governments, the public, and the casino industry should understand the consequences of regulation and the factors that produce those consequences. An awareness of the costs of regulation on price and innovation can help to make regulation more efficient and the price of the gaming product lower.

Barriers to entry/Pricing

Most common among the indirect economic consequences of regulation is the creation of barriers to entry. The absence of barriers to entry helps to promote competitive market models. Markets are fluid; demand can rise and fall. If demand increases and prices do not change, excess demand would occur, and prices would inevitably rise. With higher prices, firms supply more, and prices may rise until supply increases. A common means of increasing supply is when new participants enter the market because they are attracted by the potential return on investment. If barriers to entry inhibit potential

---

site also provides the casino industry with BSA compliance information and is available at http://www.fincen.gov/financial_institutions/casinos/. FinCEN expects the following types of information in SARC:

- Complete customer information, such as name, permanent address, government-issued identification number, date of birth and patron account number
- A narrative that describes the suspicious activity including:
  - o describing the suspicious activity in a complete and chronological way;
  - o identifying "who," "what," "when," "why," "where," and "how";
  - o identifying whether the transaction was attempted or completed;
  - o noting any actions (taken or planned) by the sports book, including any internal investigative measures to maintain records of the suspicious activity; and
  - o including contact information for persons at the sports book with additional information about the suspicious activity.

entrants, existing market participants can enjoy the benefits of higher prices and, most likely, positive economic profits.

The costs and burdens of regulatory compliance on the sportsbooks can create barriers to entry that have a significant impact on pricing and competition. An unintended economic consequence of gaming regulation is higher prices for gaming products. Regulatory compliance costs include the direct costs of government regulation, as well as the indirect costs that come from any economic inefficiencies created by regulation. In contrast, illegal sportsbooks have minimal regulatory costs, low or no taxes, and high liquidity. This permits them to offer lower "pricing" in the form of better odds than the regulated sportsbooks.

That regulation has an economic impact by restricting entry does not mean the regulation is necessarily good or bad. Achieving policy goals may be worth the costs of regulation. For example, the legal requirement for medical doctors to obtain a license to practice is intended to protect the public from possible harm to their health. The consequences that unqualified persons may poorly administer medical treatment may justify limiting the number of medical providers. It will, however, raise the costs of medical services.

Gaming licensing is *supposed to* create a barrier to entry. Few would dispute that keeping persons who are likely to cheat customers or who are members of organized crime from entering the industry is a desirable goal. The imposition of reasonable costs is necessary to achieve such goals. If a jurisdiction's licensing system were perfect, only those who met the government's standards would obtain a license. Licensing, however, cannot be done with total efficiency because the process erects barriers relating to costs, risks, delays, or potential adverse publicity that may keep out *suitable* potential entrants.

State licensing requirements also can create absolute barriers to entry. If sportsbooks can only operate in casinos or racetracks, that prevents other qualified companies from providing services in that state. This restricts a bettor's choice of potential sportsbooks and will almost certainly produce higher prices to the detriment of the bettors and the advantage of the illegal offshore bookmakers.

Moreover, a lack of regulatory uniformity between governmental entities also raises costs and barriers to entry. For example, if states individually regulate sports wagering and each requires a separate license, the costs of getting licensed in each state favors companies with large capital resources and creates a significant barrier to entry for other companies. The same is true when sportsbooks must operate within numerous regulatory systems having dissimilar regulations, standards, processes, and enforcement. Uniformity in regulation, on the other hand, lowers entry barriers for new companies and reduces costs.

Liquidity

Liquidity in this context refers to the amount of money wagered (handle), which is functionally related to the amount of money that players can wager and win. Greater liquidity lowers pricing because fixed costs are spread over a larger base. It also increases the choice of wagers because sportsbooks can offer less popular wagers if a sufficient market exists to justify the cost of implementation. Lower liquidity on the other hand may result in the sportsbooks setting lower bet limits to manage risk better.[19]

High liquidity in illegal markets makes competition manipulation more difficult to detect. This is because the amounts wagered from corrupt sources may still not be enough to trigger suspicions of unusual activity. On the other hand, high liquidity is good for regulated markets because the more data that is subject to analysis and early warning systems, the more likely that corruptors will be deterred or discovered. As one commentator noted:

> Attempts to reduce liquidity by imposing restrictions in domestic betting markets may, if anything, prove counter-productive. For example, if certain bet types are prohibited, or if domestic operators are constrained to offer 'unattractive' odds, serious bettors, who are responsible for a disproportionate share of volume, may shift their activities to the international market, further enhancing liquidity in the part of the market where regulatory supervision is weak or non-existent. This appears to be the opposite of what is needed. There is a prima facie argument for improving choice and value for bettors willing to trade in a supervised environment because, where they do so, this will reduce liquidity in the unsupervised sector.[20]

Revenue Potential

This factor looks at which model is most likely to result in the highest gross revenue, which, after expenses, leads to net income and taxable revenue. Revenue potential is important because it impacts the number of potential competitors and their willingness to commit

19 *See* "State Regulatory Approaches" discussion *infra*.

20 David Forrest, "Match Fixing: An Economics Perspective." MATCH-FIXING IN INTERNATIONAL SPORTS, 177-197. (Springer International Publishing, 2013).

capital. It also affects the ability of the government to maximize tax revenues based on the net income of sportsbooks.

Fan Engagement

Fan engagement is a phrase used to describe the behaviors that followers of a sport, team, or athlete engage in. This includes such things as watching games in-person, on mobile devices or television, buying team or athlete-related products, reading sports print or digital media, and communicating with others regarding their interests or experiences.[21] Sports leagues have a keen interest in sports wagering as a method to increase fan engagement.[22] Television ratings for most sports have declined,[23] for reasons that are not clear. One possibility is the "cord-cutting" that has been a result of the growth of mobile technology and viewing options for viewers.[24] In any event, one of the reasons the leagues have been supporters of fantasy sports, and more recently, daily fantasy sports, is a belief that having a financial stake in a sporting contest promotes "fan engagement."[25] This may

---

21 Masayuki Yoshida, Brian Gordon, Makoto Nakazawa, & Rui Biscaia. *Conceptualization and Measurement of Fan Engagement: Empirical Evidence from A Professional Sport Context*, J. of Sport Mgmt. 28, no. 4 (2014): 399-417.

22 See footnote 26, *infra*, and accompanying text.

23 The ratings decline for the NFL has been a well-documented trend over the past several years and has continued into the first half of the 2017 season. Through the first six weeks of the 2017 NFL season, networks witnessed a decline of 7.5 percent compared to the same time period in 2016. Compounded with the 8 percent decline in ratings in 2016 compared with 2015, the National Football League has lost a substantial amount of television viewers over the last few years. Scooby Axson, *NFL TV Ratings Down 7.5 Percent*, Sports Illustrated, Oct. 18, 2017, https://www.si.com/nfl/2017/10/18/nfl-television-ratings-decline; the ratings decline has not been limited solely to professional football as the NBA has experienced a decline in viewership on their regional sports networks. John Ourand and John Lombardo, *NBA's RSN Ratings Down 15 Percent This Season*, Sports Business Daily, Feb. 20, 2017, http://www.sportsbusinessdaily.com/Journal/Issues/2017/02/20/Media/NBA-RSNs.aspx.

24 Cord cutting has accelerated in recent years with cord cutters in 2017 far outpacing previous projections. It is estimated that by 2021, there will a be 10% decline in cable subscriptions from 2016 numbers. Todd Spangler, *Cord-Cutting Explodes: 22 Million U.S. Adults Will Have Canceled Cable, Satellite TV by End of 2017*, Variety, Sept. 13, 2017, http://variety.com/2017/biz/news/cord-cutting-2017-estimates-cancel-cable-satellite-tv-1202556594/ (noting cord cutters have increased 33% from 2016, up to over 22 million former cable and satellite TV subscribers).

25 In recent years, several of the leagues and player associations have engaged with some form of relationship with the two major players in the industry, DraftKings and FanDuel. *See* Kristi Dosh, *NFL Players Association Inks Licensing Deal with DraftKings*, Forbes, Sept. 29, 2015, https://www.forbes.com/sites/kristidosh/2015/09/29/nfl-players-association-inks-licensing-deal-with-draftkings/#9ca4338374cc; Darren Heitner, *DraftKings and Major League Baseball Extend Exclusive Partnership*, Apr. 2,

be another way of saying that people may watch a game they are not otherwise interested in, or that they may continue to watch a game after the overall result is clear, when they stand to win or lose money on the contest.

Until recently, the leagues have substantially opposed the idea of fan engagement produced by single-game wagering. While this view is evolving, single-game betting is not the only way to promote engagement, as fantasy sports has illustrated. The leagues are seeking new and innovative ways for fans to interact with the games and the athletes to promote increased viewership and interest in the sports. States might be incentivized to develop novel forms of wagering that will promote liquidity for the sports betting markets and perhaps boost viewership. This will inure to the benefit of the sports leagues as well as those involved in operating these new sports betting products. While single game wagering alone is a vehicle for increased fan engagement, other wagering products designed to be more interactive with the player might also have appeal. These wagering products would serve the same function as fantasy sports did for skill based contests.

Fantasy sports was a disruptive product that changed the way that sports leagues and media outlets delivered sports to the consumer. For example, the "RedZone" is a television channel that switches from stadium to stadium to capture highlights of significant plays in the games, and offers live coverage when one team is threatening to score based on its field position. The NFL and media partners designed this channel for the fantasy player.[26] Other innovative sports betting products will be an essential part of enhancing fan engagement by embracing the way fans consume sports. It is likely that these products will surpass traditional sports wagering in encouraging engagement.

2015, FORBES, https://www.forbes.com/sites/darrenheitner/2015/04/02/draftkings-and-major-league-baseball-extend-exclusive-partnership/#3eeefa006ba7; Darren Heitner, *NHL Does Multi-Year Exclusive Deal With DraftKings*, Nov. 10, 2014, FORBES, https://www.forbes.com/sites/darrenheitner/2014/11/10/nhl-does-multi-year-exclusive-deal-with-draftkings/#26a1e99f7a34. For a comprehensive tracker of the partnerships between sports leagues and franchises and DraftKings and FanDuel *see* DFS Partnership / Sponsorship Tracker, LEGAL SPORTS REPORT, https://www.legalsportsreport.com/dfs-sponsorship-tracker/ (last visited Nov. 1, 2017).

26 Nick Greene, *RedZone is the Cause of and Solution to All of the NFL's Problems*, SLATE, Sept. 17, 2017, http://www.slate.com/blogs/the_slatest/2017/09/17/redzone_is_the_cause_of_and_solution_to_all_of_the_nfl_s_problems.html.

Speed to Market

Speed to market has two aspects. The first is how quickly operators can offer a sports wagering product to the public in places where legal. The second is how quickly individual competitors can bring new products or product innovations to market considering regulatory hurdles such as product approvals.

Effectiveness

Effectiveness looks at whether the regulatory processes accomplish the public policy goals. Four common ways that regulatory processes fail to meet their goals are knowledge failure, instrument failure, implementation failure, and motivation failure.[27] Knowledge failure occurs where the government has insufficient knowledge: (a) to identify what the regulation is attempting to accomplish, and (b) to design appropriate laws or regulations or identify non-compliance.[28] Instrument failure is where the laws or regulations (the instruments) are inappropriate or unsophisticated.[29] Implementation failure occurs when enforcement mechanisms fail to accomplish policy goals.[30] This can occur because the government does not have the knowledge, competence, resources, or money to regulate effectively. Motivation failure takes place when those regulating are insufficiently motivated to enforce the law because of inaction or corruption.[31]

Political Viability

States are hesitant to give up control over gambling to the federal government. Part of this is a fundamental states' rights argument. Another factor, however, may be to protect their home state industries. For example, exclusive licenses to conduct sports wagering are likely to go to the state lottery in a state with a dominant state lottery and a weak or non-existent casino industry. Similarly, in states with a politically powerful casino (or horseracing) industry, licenses may be issued only to those companies that already have licenses. The political strength of casinos, horse race interests, and lotteries within a state can complicate a uniform federal approach to regulation.

---

27 Julia Black, *Critical Reflections on Regulation*, 27 AUSTRALIAN J. LEGAL PHIL. 1, 11 (2002).

28 *Id.*

29 *Id.*

30 *Id.*

31 *Id.*

POSSIBLE REGULATORY MODELS

Category One— State Regulatory Approaches

Within a framework of state-by-state regulation, there are several possibilities. Each would draw from models of regulation for other forms of gambling.

State Model #1: The Status Quo. A basic state regulatory approach would be a purely intrastate system where an operator would need to have a physical presence and obtain a gaming license in the specific state to offer sports wagering there. The federal government's role would be limited to providing enforcement for interstate or foreign crimes, which does not extend to regulation. As noted earlier, for the most part, this is the existing approach that is used for casino wagering.[32] The trade association for the casino industry contends that maintaining the current division of responsibilities between the state and federal governments is the best structure.[33] This model preserves both the status quo and where applicable, the exclusivity of the casinos' existing licenses.

Benefits might include:

- Speed to Market. States already have regulatory apparatuses in place that could create the foundation for sports regulation. For example, former New Jersey Governor Chris Christie stated that if New Jersey won the Supreme Court case its casinos and racetracks could begin offering sports wagering within two weeks because the state has prepared for the contingency.[34] Other states could quickly emulate Nevada or New Jersey by piggybacking off their existing regulatory processes. Nevada uses the same licensing, accounting, audit, and enforcement agents

32 Nevada would be an obvious example of the intrastate regulatory approach. The Nevada Gaming Control Board's New Applicant Pre-Opening Checklist for a Non-restricted Licensee can be found here: http://gaming.nv.gov/modules/showdocument.aspx?documentid=2214.

33 The American Gaming Association, which is the lobbying arm of the casino industry, supports a new organization called the American Sports Betting Coalition. The official position on how the government should regulate sports wagering is on its website. http://www.sportsbettinginamerica.com/industry-positioning/ In short, a key goal is to "ensure the integrity of sports betting and sports themselves through appropriate licensing and regulation by state and tribal gaming commissions."

34 *Christie: Sports Betting Could Begin Quickly*, USA TODAY, Dec. 4, 2017, https://www.usatoday.com/videos/news/nation/2017/12/04/christie-nj-sports-betting-could-begin-quickly/108305738/.

to regulate both the casinos and sportsbooks. Due to the limitations set by PASPA, Nevada has enjoyed a substantial head start over other states and has a well-developed sports wagering system.[35] Consequently, states may initially look to Nevada for how a model of the regulation of sports wagering should operate within existing regulatory structures. But this would likely evolve as states began to improve on and adapt the Nevada model. Moreover, states could develop their regulatory structures as "laboratories" for other states to learn from. This process of learning from the examples of other states is one of the most widely-valued characteristics of our federal structure.[36]

- Effectiveness of Wagering Integrity. States would have autonomy to tailor a sports wagering system that fit their own peculiar set of values and regulatory goals; the tradition of local control of gambling would be promoted. Finally, states might be more responsive to technological change and would be able to adapt more quickly to proposals for innovation.
- Political Viability. A state model may be the only viable option given the difficulties of enacting legislation in an intensely partisan Congress.

Drawbacks might include:

- Potentially High Barriers to Entry Due to High Compliance Costs. Companies with a presence in multiple states have extremely high compliance costs. For example, if states did not limit sportsbook licenses to their existing casinos, racetracks, or tribal gaming operations, a company wanting to obtain licenses nationwide would be in the same position as manufacturers of gaming equipment. A licensed manufacturer of slot machines may need over 100 gaming licenses between state and tribal governments to sell their wares in the United States. Moreover, the technical standards for sportsbook systems and methods for communicating remotely with bettors may differ

35 Professional and Amateur Sports Protection Act, 1992 Enacted S. 474, 102 Enacted S. 474, 106 Stat. 4227 Sec. 3704(a)(1); For an extended discussion of this topic, *See* Chapter 2 on legality of sports wagering.

36 New State Ice Co. v. Liebmann, 285 U.S. 262 (1932) (Brandeis J., dissenting)("a single courageous State may, if its citizens choose, serve as a laboratory; and try…experiments without risk to the rest of the country.").

among jurisdictions. If, for example, states required functionality such as computer servers and key personnel to be physically located in the state, massive inefficiencies that raise costs and create significant barriers to entry would exist. These costs increase prices to the betting public and affect the legal industry's ability to compete against illegal off-shore sportsbooks which can offer better odds because they have lower costs.

- Absolute Barriers to Entry Based on Licensing Criteria. Politics can play a significant role in shaping a state's regulatory policy. Those influencing policy may promote a protectionist ("ring fence") approach where states have the incentive to implement laws that would benefit existing operators. An existing system can serve as an anticompetitive tool that allows existing casinos, racetracks, and tribes to maintain their exclusive licenses to the determent of other competitors that may be better financed, have superior technology and experience, and have more innovative products. For example, New Jersey's sportsbook law limits the granting of licenses to existing casinos and racetracks, neither of which have experience in sports betting. This absolute barrier to entry may stifle innovation and create uncompetitive odds that could disadvantage the sports betting public.[37]
- Placing Small States at a Disadvantage. A small state would have the same fixed costs as larger states in establishing the regulatory infrastructure that is essential to the proper regulation of sports wagering. These costs include adequately trained personnel such as licensing agents, audit and accounting staff, and enforcement agents, as well as equipment. Small states would face liquidity problems as small betting pools produced low revenues, fewer bet options, and higher pricing. All this would damage the ability of a small population state to offer a competitive range of sports wagering products
- Difficulties of Ensuring Sports Integrity. A state-centric approach may complicate if not frustrate the pursuit of

37 Protectionism's harm on consumers has long been identified and analyzed by economists. *See* Robert Z. Lawrence and Robert E. Litan, *Why Protectionism Doesn't Pay*, HARV. BUS. REV., (May 1987), accessed at https://hbr.org/1987/05/why-protectionism-doesnt-pay.

sports integrity. Regulatory structures in place to protect the integrity of casino gambling have limited application to sports wagering. States and tribes have vast experience in regulating land-based gaming, including casinos and gaming devices outside of casinos. The regulation of wagering integrity and sports integrity, however, is very different. Regardless of whether the government is regulating casinos to protect the bettor, maximize taxes, or create jobs, a standard policy goal of every regulatory system is to assure the honesty of the games offered to the public. Casino patrons are susceptible to fraud if an unscrupulous casino operator uses cheating methods to assure that a random event does not determine the gambling contracts. A dishonest casino can cheat the players by predetermining or influencing the result to its advantage. Gamblers who are cheated are unlikely to play at the casinos; this impacts taxes, jobs, and the general economy of the jurisdiction. A casino operator is honest if it offers games whose determinative outcomes are random. Given the importance of honesty to the gaming industry, governments that regulate casino gaming implement multi-faceted regulatory schemes such as licensing, technical standards, extensive testing, field observation and review, periodic audit, and internal control requirements.

- Sports casino wagering share similar aspects. Legally, all wagers are contracts; the price (amount won or lost) is honored according to the terms of the contract when the bettor and a bookmaker enter it. The distinctive part of a wagering contract is that the promise of performance is based on a future contingent event (the outcome of the casino game or the sports competition) not under the control of the casino or sportsbook, on the one hand, or the bettor, on the other. After that, whether the sportsbook or the casino must fulfill its promise to pay the bettor is dependent on the terms of the bet and the outcome of the future contingent event, either the casino game or sporting event. The difference between casino wagering contracts and sports wagering contracts is that state regulators tightly control the regulation of the future contingent event in casino contracts. Assuring the honesty of the underlying event that determines the outcome of a sports wager, in contrast, is much different. These uncertain contingent events do not occur in the casino nor typically in the jurisdiction where the casino is located. As a result, the integrity of the sporting event is largely outside the control of the state regulators. Therefore, state government must accept the risk that those who place sports wagers with the sportsbook could be the victim of fraud by competition manipulation.

- Limited Fan Engagement. State-ringed sports wagering will likely produce smaller, disaggregated wagering pools. This will affect traditional types of wagers, such as single-game wagering, because it limits the number of wagering opportunities, creates greater odds fluctuations, and limits liquidity. However, the bigger impact will be on new products designed to increase fan engagement. As online poker experienced, state-based ring fencing produced smaller betting pools and poker game options that were not attractive. A similar result may occur with sports wagering where more immersive game products may only have viability with high liquidity.

State Model #2: State Regulation with Open Markets. Under this model, the regulation of sports betting would be the responsibility of the respective states. Unlike state model one, however, any operator who submitted to the licensing authority of a state could offer sports wagering in the state. In other words, the operator would not be required to have a physical presence in the state. This approach would resemble that used in the daily fantasy sports industry.[38] In the United States, a firm can offer fantasy sports in multiple states, thus creating the liquidity necessary to operate a viable business. However, the company must comply with licensing and other standards imposed by the individual states. About a dozen states allow daily fantasy sports

38 Approval for licensure in DFS varies by state. In Tennessee, approval is from the Secretary of State's office. *Fantasy Sports*, TENNESSEE SECRETARY OF STATE, https://sos.tn.gov/fantasysports; The Indiana Gaming Commission grants licenses in Indiana. Scott L. Miley, *Fantasy Sports Operators Get First State Licenses*, GREENSBURG DAILY NEWS, June 29, 2017, http://www.greensburgdailynews.com/news/fantasy-sports-operators-get-first-state-licenses/article_24557c23-4372-5688-b9ef-2f490519514d.html.; Regulation of DFS in Maryland is overseen by the Comptroller of the state. Dustin Gouker, *Maryland Comptroller Officially Implements Fantasy Sports Regulations*, LEGAL SPORTS REPORT, Jan. 3, 2017, https://www.legalsportsreport.com/12544/maryland-comptroller-dfs-reguation/.

companies to offer their national contests within their state provided they comply with state laws for licensing, operational requirements, and consumer protections.[39]

Benefits might include:

- Barriers to Entry. Barriers to entry would be reduced compared to the first state model because operators can determine which states they want to operate in based on factors like regulatory burden, costs, and business potential. Non-traditional gaming companies would have the opportunity to develop innovative forms of sports wagering in states they choose to operate in. Because companies would be subject to licensing and regulations in each state where they do business, however, the model does not guarantee uniformity. This will raise costs and potentially result in new products being either slow to market or only being offered in certain states.
- Increased Liquidity. While sports wagering is not as dependent on liquidity as daily fantasy sports, a non-national approach makes it difficult for small states to offer competitive pricing and hurts the ability of innovators to offer new products that have the prospect for higher fan engagement. This model reduces but does not eliminate the problems created by ring-fencing states that permit intrastate wagering only.
- Speed to Market. States can determine how quickly to license and permit operators to access their markets. A new company may choose states with the fastest and least expensive regulatory path to licensing and operations and then expand to other states as it has resources to do so.
- Fan Engagement. Unlike model one that ring-fences activity into a particular state, this model allows companies to increase liquidity by leveraging multiple markets. This may promote innovative products that work better with higher liquidity or a more diverse fan base.
- Effectiveness of Ensuring Wagering Integrity. Like State Model #1, this model relies on states to ensure wagering integrity. As most states already have some form of gaming

39 Ryan Rodenberg, *Daily Fantasy Sports State-by-State Tracker*, ESPN, July 26, 2017, http://www.espn.com/chalk/story/_/id/14799449/daily-fantasy-dfs-legal-your-state-state-state-look. Nevada is the only exception that requires ring-fencing – which effectively eliminates any prospect for a viable industry.

regulation, this model should be efficient and effective to ensure wagering integrity.

Drawbacks might include:

- Barriers to Entry. Like State Model #1, entities wanting to offer sports betting in multiple states will have to obtain licenses in each of them, making licensing more expensive. Likewise, varying audit, accounting, operational and technical rules in states are burdensome and deter all but the most heavily capitalized companies from entering state markets.
- Ineffectiveness of Ensuring Sports Integrity. This model does not alter the concerns raised for State Model #1 regarding ensuring sports integrity.
- Political Viability. This model is based on an open market. Companies without ties to a particular state, such as owning or operating a racetrack or casino, would have access to the sports wagering market. Casinos, tribes, and racetracks with powerful lobbies, or states with an influential state lottery, are likely to fight this approach.

State Model #3: State Regulation with Reciprocity. This model subjects operators to the regulatory authority only in the states in which they conduct operations and maintain servers, but allows them to accept wagers from bettors in any state that has authorized sports wagering. This is similar to how the Interstate Horseracing Act (IHA) works in practice.[40] According to the popular interpretation of that law, a company wishing to engage in account-based wagering on horse races must obtain a license from a state that regulates that form of race wagering. The company has the choice of about 20 states that license race book operators.[41] Once licensed, the race book can accept wagers from any state where betting on pari-mutuel horseracing is legal, which includes about 36 states.

Benefits might include:

---

40 Interstate Horseracing Act 15 U.S.C. §§ 3001-3007 (2012). The Interstate Horseracing Act (IHA) was passed to "regulate interstate commerce with respect to wagering on horseracing, in order to further the horseracing and legal off-track betting industries in the United States." There is a general prohibition on "interstate off-track wager[ing]," but there are exceptions for simulcast wagering with consent from the local jurisdiction.

41 These states include: Arizona, California, Colorado, Connecticut, Idaho, Illinois, Indiana, Iowa, Kentucky, Louisiana, Maine, Maryland, Montana, Nevada, New Jersey, New Mexico, New York, Ohio, Oklahoma, Oregon, Pennsylvania, Virginia, Washington, Wisconsin, and Wyoming. *Off Track Betting Locations*, OTB.US, http://www.otb.us/off-track-betting-locations.html.

- Lower Barriers to Entry. The lowered regulatory burden of having to obtain a single license and comply only with the laws and regulations where a company is licensed would make it easier for operators to get to market.
- Liquidity and Revenue Potential. This state model provides the greatest liquidity because an operator can decide which jurisdiction to obtain a license and, after obtaining a license and other necessary approvals, have access to the liquidity in all other states that permit sports wagering.
- Speed to Market. This state model provides the quickest speed to market because an operator can decide which jurisdictions to obtain a license. After obtaining a license and other necessary approval the operator would have access to all other markets. This would stoke competition between states to create regulatory systems that can issue licenses expeditiously and provide for the least costly regulatory burdens.
- Fan Engagement. Like model #2, this model allows companies to increase liquidity by offering wagering in multiple markets. This liquidity will contribute to new products that may incease fan engagement.

Drawbacks might include:

- Political Viability. States might be wary of permitting wagering in other jurisdictions where sports integrity and patron protection provisions are inadequate.
- Lack of Uniformity. Conflicts between state laws would complicate operations and revenue sharing between states.
- Ineffectiveness of Ensuring Wagering Integrity. Operators would migrate to states with the lowest taxes, least comprehensive licensing standards, and fewest regulatory hurdles[42] These varied licensing standards can produce a "race to the bottom" among states.[43] That is, to attract gambling companies, states may relax licensing standards so that they are more attractive than competing states. This is not a phenomenon limited to the gaming world.[44]

42 *See* discussion of State Model #2, *supra*.

43 *Race to the Bottom*, Cambridge Dictionary, https://dictionary.cambridge.org/us/dictionary/english/race-to-the-bottom.

44 For an example of a race to bottom in the cruise ship industry, *see Elizabeth Becker, Destination Nowhere: The Dark Side of the Cruise Industry*, The Saturday Evening Post, Nov./Dec. 2013, http://www.saturdayeveningpost.com/2014/04/17/

States often vie to attract or retain businesses by offering weakened environmental rules, property tax abatements, and lowered wage scales for workers.[45] Although business competition is a hallmark of a capitalistic system,[46] the success of regulated gambling depends upon integrity and public perceptions of integrity. Overly aggressive competition among states may undermine these critical objectives.

- Ineffectiveness of Ensuring Sports Integrity. Effective standards of sports integrity would be challenging to implement.

State Model #4: Liquidity Created by Interstate Agreements. This approach would share most of the characteristics of #3, but it would be based on a compact model. That is, operators could accept wagers from patrons in states that had entered an agreement with other states.

Benefits might include:

- Liquidity. Because it is based on the model used for internet poker and certain lottery products (like Powerball), there is some familiarity with how it would operate. Even though the four states that have legalized poker have reached an agreement to share liquidity, this has not made the activity especially lucrative. Greater liquidity, where states with a significant combined population participate in the compact process, is likely necessary. As more states decide to legalize poker this liquidity may develop. However, the slow rollout prevented poker sites from offering the products that the public wanted. National efforts to engage fans of poker through television and other media were not attached with opportunities to play and increase skill.
- Effectiveness of Wagering Integrity. States would have primary responsibility for regulating the operators in their state. The individual states would also have the power to enter or not enter compacts with other states. States

---

HEALTH-AND-FAMILY/TRAVEL/THE-DARK-SIDE-OF-THE-CRUISE-SHIP-INDUSTRY.HTML.

45 Natalie Wong, *Amazon's HQ2 Deadline: Now the Real Competition Begins*, FORBES, Oct. 19, 2017, https://www.bloomberg.com/news/articles/2017-10-19/amazon-s-hq2-deadline-now-the-real-competition-begins.

46 Nicolas Meisel, GOVERNANCE CULTURE AND DEVELOPMENT: A DIFFERENT PERSPECTIVE ON CORPORATE GOVERNANCE 41 (Organization for Economic Co-operation and Development 2004).

would have the discretion not to allow operators from a state where regulatory oversight is lacking. This prevents race to the bottom concerns where operators would otherwise be attracted to the states with the lowest taxes and least regulation. Moreover, compacts could be worked out between states according to the specific values and interests of the state.

- Barriers to Entry. Because an operator would not need a license in every state, barriers to entry would be lower than Model #1 that only permits intrastate wagering.

Drawbacks might include (in addition to those noted in #3):

- Speed to Market and Political Viability. Compacts would need to reconcile difficult issues of regulation, taxation, licensing, and revenue sharing. These differences may prevent or delay the implementation of a multistate system. As an example, though Nevada authorized internet poker in 2013, and New Jersey authorized internet poker in 2010, the states did not agree to a compact until 2017. Moreover, a larger state, like California, which has significant liquidity on an intrastate basis, may be hesitant to open its market to operators from smaller states.

Category 2—Federal Regulatory Approaches

Federal Model #1: Exclusive Federal Jurisdiction.

One plausible model of regulation would have the federal government as the regulator of sports wagering. A federal law would set out the terms of licensing and regulation, and direct a federal agency or entity to administer the law, promulgate and enforce regulations, and coordinate regulation with states.

Under this approach, states would choose to opt in, or not. That is, no state would be required to offer sports betting.[47] A state choosing to participate, however, would be subject to the federal statutory regime.

Benefits might include:

- Lower Barriers to Entry. Compliance costs for companies would likely be lower compared to a non-uniform system.

---

47 States that do not permit commercial or tribal gambling are: Arkansas, Georgia, Hawaii, Kentucky, New Hampshire, South Carolina, Tennessee, Utah, Vermont, and Virginia. *2016 State of the States*, AMERICAN GAMING ASSOCIATION, https://www.americangaming.org/sites/default/files/2016%20State%20of%20the%20States_FINAL.pdf ; Gambling has always been the purview of the states as PASPA is "the only federal law in history" regulating states' regulation of gambling. I. Nelson Rose, *Betting on Sports Betting*, 18 GAMING L. REV. AND ECON. 956 (2014).

For example, licensing of companies and principals would be a one-time experience (at least initially), rather than the serial approach that most state-based models would produce. Similarly, the burdensomeness of varying state audit requirements would be eliminated. A single template for audit and accounting would streamline the process and reduce costs,[48] and business planning would be enhanced by a uniform and straightforward federal taxing structure. A system could be created for sharing tax revenues with states. Reduced entry barriers would allow for companies to get to market quickly. Also, having to satisfy only one set of regulatory requirements would promote the emergence of non-traditional gambling companies; this would spur competition and innovation.

- Increased Liquidity. Having a unified network of the opting-in states would promote liquidity. Companies would have a single market in which all gaming proceeds would be pooled.
- Fan Engagement. A national liquid market with fan diversity and low barriers to entry is the best incubator for innovative products that are likely to produce the highest degree of fan engagement.
- Effectiveness of Ensuring Sports Integrity. The consistency of standards and enforcement from a federal system of regulation would implicate several aspects of a sports betting structure and help to serve important public policy objectives. Increasingly, the integrity of contests held in the US is not just a matter of regulating bettors in the US. Illegal sports gambling markets in Asia have a connection to contest manipulation, and though their influence may not have affected US betting markets, that could change.[49] International cooperation is essential to address match fixing of contests held inside and outside the US. A federal system that would facilitate the collection of data so that

---

48 A patchwork of regulations and taxes greatly complicates business for companies as evidenced by the current experience of daily fantasy sports companies. *See* Dustin Gouker, *Fantasy Sports Industry 'Deeply Concerned' With $50K Fee in Virginia Law*, LEGAL SPORTS REPORT, Mar. 8, 2016, https://www.legalsportsreport.com/8915/fsta-pushes-back-on-dfs-fees/.

49 Declan Hill et. al., *The Status of Sports Wagering*, 18 GAMING L. REV. AND ECON. 14 (Feb. 2014).

threats to game integrity could be quickly identified and acted upon by federal law enforcement offers efficiencies that state regulation could not achieve. This may be among the reasons the major sports leagues in the US seem to favor a centralized system of regulation.[50]

- Likewise, states are at a disadvantage in developing laws and regulations that would curb insiders from acting on information not available to the betting public. While states could share information on suspected betting irregularities by insiders, a centralized regulatory system would likely be more effective in detecting such activity. This has been one of the strengths of the manner in which securities are regulated at the federal level.[51]
- The Securities Exchange Commission was created by the Securities Exchange Act of 1934 "to restore investor confidence in our capital markets by providing investors and the markets with more reliable information and clear rules of honest dealing."[52] Prior to the establishment of the SEC, regulating the honesty of the securities markets was left to state governments through the creation of state regulatory schemes known as "Blue Sky" laws. These proved ineffective as stock promoters complied only with the laws of the states with the least regulation or the most

---

50 Adam Silver, *Legalize and Regulate Sports Betting*, Nov. 13, 2014, NY Times, https://www.nytimes.com/2014/11/14/opinion/nba-commissioner-adam-silver-legalize-sports-betting.html. "Congress should adopt a federal framework that allows states to authorize betting on professional sports, subject to strict regulatory requirements and technological safeguards. . . Without a comprehensive federal solution, state measures such as New Jersey's recent initiative will be both unlawful and bad public policy."

51 The United States Government regulates securities primarily through the Securities Act of 1933. Securities Act of 1933 73 P.L. 22 The Securities Act has two basic objectives: (1) "[R]equire that investors receive financial and other significant information concerning securities being offered for public sale;" and (2) "[P]rohibit deceit misrepresentations, and other fraud in the sale of securities." See *What We Do*, U.S. Securities and Exchange Commission, https://www.sec.gov/Article/whatwedo.html#laws.; States also have authority to regulate securities within their state. These laws, known as "Blue Sky Laws", are often modeled on their federal analog. Because of the overlapping and duplicative nature of many of these state laws, some have called for total or field preemption, of state regulation of securities. *See* Rutherford Campbell Jr., *The Case for Federal Pre-Emption of State Blue Sky Laws*, The Heritage Foundation, Feb. 28, 2017, http://www.heritage.org/markets-and-finance/report/the-case-federal-pre-emption-state-blue-sky-laws.

52 15 U.S.C. 78(a) (2012); *See also Creation of the SEC*, U.S. Securities and Exchange Commission, https://www.sec.gov/Article/whatwedo.html (last visited Jan. 8, 2018).

corruption and used that as a basis for offering the stocks on a national basis.[53]

- Securities regulation and sports wagering have striking similarities. Both deal with the regulation of exchanges involving contracts where the purchaser/bettor is attempting to earn profits based on a future contingent event. In both markets, the government intercedes to protect the honesty of those contracts. Because the security markets, like the sports markets, exist on a national (and international) level, state regulation alone is inadequate.
- States were unwilling to concede power to regulate the securities markets until after the stock market crash of 1929. While the SEC has faced criticism for both overregulation and under regulation, no serious discussion exists that it is not a better system than what previously existed under state control, or that it should be dissolved. Ultimately, a centralized system has significant advantages.

Drawbacks might include:

- Effectiveness of Ensuring Wagering Integrity. While there is a prominent federal role in areas such as securities regulation and civilian aviation, Congress has no real expertise in establishing gaming regulatory regimes. The most recent effort to address sports betting—the Unlawful Internet Gambling Enforcement Act of 2006—is a deeply flawed law.[54]
- No likely or appropriate federal entity exists where the regulatory locus would reside. A lack of experience and expertise for establishing a regulatory regime could impair achievement of the positives listed above. The "learning curve" for the new regulatory entity could lead to slow implementation which would frustrate potential market entrants.
- However, some federal agencies can serve as models.

53 See Mark J. Astarita, *Introduction to State Securities (Blue Sky) Laws*, SEC LAW, http://www.seclaw.com/introduction-to-state-securities-laws/ (last visited Jan. 8, 2018).

54 Unlawful Gambling Enforcement Act of 2006 31 U.S.C. § 5361-5367 (2012). "[P]rohibits gambling businesses from knowingly accepting payments in connection with the participation of another person in a bet or wager that involves the use of the Internet and that is unlawful under any federal or state law." The criticism of UIEGA has been deep and wide: *See* Nelson Rose, *Viewpoint: The Unlawful Internet Gambling Enforcement Act of 2006 Analyzed*, 10 GAMING L. REV. 537, 538 (2006); Nelson Rose, *Congress Makes Sausages*, 11 GAMING L. REV. 1 (2007).

Agencies such as the U.S. Securities and Exchange Commission (SEC) and Federal Aviation Adminsitration discharge traditional administrative regulatory functions like licensing, enforcement, testing, and audits. As discussed above, the SEC may be the closest parallel both in mission and history.

- Finally, especially with the creation of a new regulatory body, there is a tendency to over-regulate. That is, the new entity might fulfill the standard view of the federal government as a bloated bureaucracy which stifles innovation and competition by imposing burdensome regulations.
- Speed to Market. Nothing about a model of federal regulation supports an idea that market entry could be handled more expeditiously than with a state system.
- Political Viability. The current dysfunction of Congress inspires little confidence that it can establish a workable system, especially since decentralization of government functions is accelerating.[55] Moreover, states will strongly object to being taken out of the regulation of sports betting and emphasize that regulation of gambling is typically left to the states. The state of Nevada, with its mature sports betting market, would not quietly accept being displaced

55 A common way that the federal government has decentralized government functions is in the form of block grants. Block grants are when the federal government provides a state with a sum of money with only general guidance on how the grant is to be administered. States are then free to fill in the gaps in regulation as they see fit, so long as they do not run afoul of the general directions provided by the federal government. Proponents of block grants claim that they allow states to tailor the regulation and provisioning of government funds based on local conditions and needs, whereas critics of block grants contend that unspecific direction from the federal government allows states to sabotage a programs that officials in the state may oppose for political reasons. Shefali Luthra, *Everything You Need to Know About Block Grants—The Heart of GOP'S Medicaid Plans*, KAISER HEALTH NEWS, Jan. 24, 2017, https://khn.org/news/block-grants-medicaid-faq/; The biggest block grant that states receive from the federal government is Temporary Assistance for Needy Families (TANF). In 2015, the federal government spent $16.5 billion in TANF block grants. Office of Family Assistance, *State TANF Spending in FY 2015 Fact Sheet*, US DEPT. OF HEALTH & HUMAN SERVICES, Aug. 15, 2016, https://www.acf.hhs.gov/ofa/resource/state-tanf-spending-2015-factsheet; True to the concerns of some critics of block grants, the Center on Budget and Policy Priorities found that states spend only half of their TANF money on "core welfare reform areas." Liz Schott and Ife Floyd, *How States Use Funds Under the TANF Block Grant*, CENTER ON BUDGET AND POLICY PRIORITIES, Jan. 5, 2017, https://www.cbpp.org/research/family-income-support/how-states-use-funds-under-the-tanf-block-grant.

by a federal system of regulation.

Federal Model #2: Mixed Federal and State Authority.

A variation on the first model would still require federal legislation. It would essentially assign responsibility for sports integrity to the federal government and wagering integrity to the state government. States opting in would be required to demonstrate compliance with a template of regulation established by federal law. States would be in charge of wagering integrity through regulation in their state and would be empowered to tailor that regulation in some ways provided for in the legislation.

Benefits might include:

- Effectiveness of Ensuring Wagering Integrity. States would retain their traditional authority of regulation of gaming, but within a federally-established framework that would still feature uniformity on matters such as licensing, and audit and accounting rules. Also, the ability of a state to tailor its gambling laws in some way respects the different values states attach to gambling and eschews a "one size fits all" approach.
- Effectiveness of Ensuring Sports Integrity. The threats to sports integrity have a genesis in international commerce and need to be addressed through both national and international efforts.
- Having a central agency that is the point of contact for intelligence and can build the national and global expertise necessary to investigate and prosecute threats to sports integrity is important. A small state regulatory agency would not have the experience, knowledge base, information, or jurisdiction to investigate and prosecute international sports corruption. For example, it would have been difficult or impossible for state agencies to develop the case involving the FIFA bribery charges. It took the resources and expertise of the FBI and federal prosecutors to handle this.
- Uniform standards defining permissible conduct, such as insider trading rules, are important to sports integrity. If states have different rules regarding what is permissible, persons wanting to skirt more restrictive regulations need only find the state with the lowest standards. This will frustrate national efforts to police sports integrity.

- Speed to Market. No significant federal bureaucracy would need to be created. The federal entity to which states would certify compliance could have a smaller footprint within an existing federal agency.

Drawbacks might include:

- Effectiveness of Ensuring Wagering Integrity. The federal body with responsibility for ensuring state compliance would have to develop expertise on how different states wanted to adjust gambling laws in their states according to local preference. This would create a federal bureaucracy without the benefits of uniformity on matters such as permitted bet types.
- Barriers to Entry. The economies achieved by a national uniform system of licensing and regulation would be lost, thus increasing costs to operating companies
- Political Viability. This approach would certainly be more acceptable to states than a system that displaces their regulation with a federal system. But a model like this still requires federal legislation, a daunting prospect given the current political climate.

ISSUES THAT WOULD NEED TO BE ADDRESSED IN ANY MODEL OF REGULATION

Some issues would in varying degrees require the attention of policymakers regardless of the model that is implemented. A few of these issues are noted.

Would the Consent of the Leagues Need to Be Obtained for Their Games to be Offered for Wagering?

One of the biggest stumbling blocks to the expansion of sports betting beyond Nevada has been the opposition of the major sports leagues.[56] The opposition has persisted even as the major sports

56 Mike Wilkening, *Goodell: NFL's Opposition to Legalized Sports Gambling Isn't Changing*, NBC Sports, Jan. 31, 2014, http://profootballtalk.nbcsports.com/2014/01/31/goodell-nfls-opposition-to-legalized-sports-gambling-isnt-changing/; Brent Schrotenboer, *NFL's Gambling Policy Appears Consistently Inconsistent*, USA Today, June 11, 2017, https://www.usatoday.com/story/sports/nfl/2017/06/11/gambling-las-vegas-casino-naming-rights-advertising/102634272/; Ryan Lovelace, *Chris Christie Blasts NFL Over Sports Gambling: 'The Hypocrisy is Just So Overwhelming'*, Wash. Examiner, Oct. 25, 2017, http://www.washingtonexaminer.com/chris-christie-blasts-nfl-over-sports-gambling-the-hypocrisy-is-just-so-overwhelming/article/2638588.

leagues have given support to, and have had relationships with, fantasy sports operators whose daily games have some of the characteristics of sports betting.[57]

The hostility toward sports betting appeared to weaken in 2014 when NBA Commissioner Adam Silver wrote an op-ed piece in the New York Times suggesting that sports betting needed to "be brought out of the underground and into the sunlight where it can be appropriately monitored and regulated."[58] Despite this sentiment, the NBA continued to challenge New Jersey's plan to offer regulated sports betting and did not offer a proposal to change PASPA. More recently, Silver said he thought the laws on sports betting would be changing in "the next few years in the United States."[59]

After the Supreme Court accepted review of the New Jersey case in June 2017, Major League Baseball Commissioner Rob Manfred seemed to acknowledge the coming of sports betting. He told the Baseball Writers' Association of America, that, "If there's going to be a change in the regulatory structure ... we needed to be in a position to meaningfully engage and shape, try to shape what the new regulatory scheme looks like."[60] This comment came after Manfred had earlier commented that baseball was "reexamining [its] stance on gambling."[61]

Although NHL Commissioner Gary Bettman curiously asserted that the "game doesn't lend itself to gambling in the way football and basketball do,"[62] the presence of a new NHL franchise in Las Vegas would likely dilute whatever opposition that league has.[63]

---

57 Numerous teams in the major sports in the US have partnership and sponsorship agreements with the daily fantasy sports companies DraftKings and FanDuel. For a complete list of these arrangements LEGAL SPORTS REPORT thttps://www.legalsportsreport.com/dfs-sponsorship-tracker/

58 Silver, *supra* note 50.

59 Kyle Boone, *NBA Commissioner Optimistic Sports Betting Will Be Legalized 'in the Next Few Years'*, CBS SPORTS, July 19, 2017, https://www.cbssports.com/nba/news/nba-commissioner-optimistic-sports-betting-will-be-legalized-in-the-next-few-years/.

60 The Canadian Press, *Manfred: MLB Open to More Aggressively Managing Change*, TSN, July 11, 2017, http://www.tsn.ca/manfred-mlb-open-to-more-aggressively-managing-change-1.802126.

61 Daniel Roberts, *MLB Commissioner: 'We are Re-Examining Our Stance on Gambling'*, YAHOO, Feb. 8, 2017, https://finance.yahoo.com/news/baseball-commissioner-we-are-reexamining-our-stance-on-gambling-170536801.html.

62 Greg Wyshynski, *Gary Bettman's Sports Gambling Flip-Flop?*, YAHOO, Sept. 9, 2016, https://sports.yahoo.com/news/gary-bettmans-sports-gambling-flip-flop-162345685.html.

63 Despite claims by the Las Vegas Golden Knights' owner that betting on the team would have limited availability at Las Vegas sportsbooks, wagering on the team is

It is the intransigence of the NFL that has seemed to be the biggest obstacle to sports betting. Commissioner Goodell has been steadfast in expressing opposition to expanded sports betting. This is usually couched in terms of concerns regarding game integrity. Even Goodell, however, has acknowledged the moving of the Oakland Raiders to Las Vegas raises issues about continued opposition to sports betting.[64]

A theme expressed by both Commissioners Silver and Manfred was that sports betting increased fan engagement with the sport. This is no doubt the case with the NFL (and NHL) as well. The term "fan engagement" is a euphemism for increased revenue for the leagues.

Ultimately, if a federal system of sports betting were established, the legislation would likely not allow the leagues to withhold consent for their games to be the object of wagers. On the other hand, if the system of sports betting was state-based, this option would seem to be available. However, this presents a problem.

One of the criticisms of the manner in which the leagues have opposed sports betting while supporting daily fantasy sports is that the leagues are picking the forms of sports betting that they gain from financially while opposing those they do not.[65] Leagues would be vulnerable to the same criticism if they could selectively withhold consent for sportsbooks to offer their games to the public. The leagues might have a stronger case if they focused on not wanting particular types of bets to be allowed. For example, MLB could plausibly argue that allowing in-game betting on a proposition like, "Will the next pitch be a strike," presents a significant risk of "spot-fixing" and can affect the integrity of the game. Ultimately, legislation establishing a sports betting regulatory regime should address this issue explicitly.

Would Sports Betting be "Monetized" for the Leagues?

From the perspective of the major sports leagues in the US,

---

available at every sportsbook. Dustin Gouker, *Las Vegas NHL Owner: 'You Won't Be Able To Bet On The Golden Knights' At Some Casinos*, Legal Sports Report, Aug. 17, 2017, https://www.legalsportsreport.com/15110/betting-on-las-vegas-golden-knights/; David Purdum, *Betting on Golden Knights Available at Every Sportsbook in Las Vegas*, ESPN, Oct. 10, 2017, http://www.espn.com/chalk/story/_/id/20977517/betting-vegas-golden-knights-available-every-sportsbook-las-vegas.

64 Mike Florio, *How Can NFL Reconcile Loving Las Vegas and Loathing Betting Lines?*, NBC Sports, Mar. 25, 2017, http://profootballtalk.nbcsports.com/2017/03/25/how-can-nfl-reconcile-loving-las-vegas-and-loathing-betting-lines/.

65 Ken Belson, *As It Embraces Las Vegas, NFL is Awash in Gambling Contradictions*, NY Times, Apr. 18, 2017, https://www.nytimes.com/2017/04/18/sports/football/as-it-embraces-las-vegas-nfl-is-awash-in-gambling-contradictions.html.

the opposition to expanded regulated gambling may relate to one fundamental question: what is in it for us? The path forward for legalized sports betting may in some respects depend upon the support or at least acquiescence of the leagues. For this support to be gained, a means of compensating the leagues for the use of their games as the source of betting may need to be established.[66]

One model for doing this would be to put a tax on all sports bets made. For example, a one-cent tax on sports bets could be imposed. Half of the money would be distributed to the leagues and players associations. The other half-cent would be directed to a federally administered fund that would compensate amateur and professional athletes for catastrophic injury.[67] This type of approach would serve two functions: first, it would likely provide the leagues considerable fresh revenue. Most of the betting is currently occurring illegally with the leagues gaining nothing. The betting tax revenues come at the expense of no other lawful activity.

The other benefit to this approach is that it would allow the leagues to present themselves as advancing a good cause. For example, it would offer the NFL the opportunity to support sports betting as a way of advancing societal interests and holding itself out as a good public citizen. Providing compensation to injured athletes might help assuage concerns about the safety of contact sports like football.[68]

Without question, the formula for establishing such a system would be problematic and likely contentious. Administrative costs relating to collecting the tax and distributing the proceeds might be significant. Nevertheless, if leagues were ready to put their weight behind broadly legal sports betting contingent on this being worked out, there would be incentives for all interested parties to reach an agreement.[69]

In 2018, Indiana considered a proposal for sports betting that

---

66 Andrew Brandt, *The NFL Has a Gambling Problem*, Sports illustrated, Nov. 5, 2015, https://www.si.com/mmqb/2015/11/05/nfl-gambling-daily-fantasy-dfs-draftkings-fanduel-goodell.

67 See Anthony Cabot, *The Absence of a Comprehensive Federal Policy Toward Internet and Sports Wagering and a Proposal for Change*, 17 Villanova Sports & Ent. L.J. 271, 306-307 (2010).

68 Shannon Ho, '*Bad for Your Brain': CTE Reports, Concussions Deter Parents from Youth Football*, NBC Chicago, July 28, 2017, http://www.nbcchicago.com/news/health/CTE-Reports-Impact-Future-of-Youth-Football-436639243.html.

69 David Lariviere, *Legalization of Sports Betting Would Be Huge Revenue Producer for Leagues, Expert Says*, Forbes, Sept. 19, 2014, https://www.forbes.com/sites/davidlariviere/2014/09/19/legalization-of-sports-betting-would-be-huge-revenue-producer-for-leagues-expert-says/#551040b02d1c.

included a 1% "integrity tax" being imposed on the handle that would go to the leagues. Some estimates are that leagues could gain as much as $2 billion/year if such a tax were imposed on a national basis.[70] Criticisms of an "integrity tax" emphasize that a tax on handle cuts already thin margins for regulated sportsbooks by approximately 20% and that it is uncertain why leagues would have such high costs for monitoring integrity in a regulated market.[71]

As sports betting markets mature and introduce more betting products, proposals for monetizing the betting activity to benefit the leagues will increase. For example, sports betting could include betting exchanges where bettors offer or take positions on sports events. This peer-to-peer model allows buyers and sellers to be matched up on opposite sides of betting propositions. The betting platform operates similar to a stock exchange, charging a commission fee on the transactions conducted. Exchange wagering platforms in the US originated in horse racing, with New Jersey one of the first states to authorize such markets.[72]

To a significant extent, the exchange wagering model of sports betting resembles traditional securities markets. The federal government predominantly regulates these financial markets.[73] This

---

70 Dustin Gouker, *New Version Of Indiana Sports Betting Bill Includes Hefty 'Integrity Fee' Paid To Sports Leagues,* Legal Sports Report, Jan. 8, 2018, https://www.legalsportsreport.com/17400/indiana-sports-betting-integrity-fee/

71 *Id.*

72 Pioneered by Paddy Power Betfair, now the world's largest publicly traded online gambling company, exchange wagering is a high-tech manner of gaming aimed at enticing younger gamblers into the market. The European company is hoping to use the internet to tap into the $3.5 billion wagered on horse racing online in 2015. Joe Drape, *High-Tech Wagering See Gateway Into America: The Horse Track*, NY Times, July 29, 2016, https://www.nytimes.com/2016/07/30/sports/horse-racing/betfair-exchange-wagering-gambling-horse-racing.html.

73 Equities regulation falls within the purview of numerous organizations. Federal government regulation is undertaken by the Securities and Exchange Commission's Division of Trading and Markets. Among their responsibilities is to "regulate the major securities market participants, including broker-dealers, self-regulatory organizations…and transfer agents." *Trading and Markets*, US Securities and Exchange Commission, https://www.sec.gov/page/tmsectionlanding; The Financial Industry Regulatory Authority (FINRA) is a non-profit organizations authorized by the federal government to regulate equities markets. FINRA regulates the markets by writing and enforcing rules for brokers, examining firms for compliance with rules, and encouraging transparency. *About FINRA*, Financial Industry Regulatory Authority, https://www.finra.org/about.; Other regulatory activities in the equities market are undertaken by the individual stock exchanges, such as the New York Stock Exchange.

may be a factor that would tilt the preferred regulatory model for sports betting exchanges toward a federal rather than state orientation. The diversity of betting offerings in exchange wagering may also be attractive to the sports leagues because the market offerings would not necessarily be tied to point spreads. However, the leagues could still profit from the betting exchanges through a surcharge on the transactions processed through the exchange. This is an approach used in other countries where sports betting is widely permitted.

4

Sports Integrity

Sports integrity is "respect for the core value of fair and open competition in the game or event in question."[1] This includes expectations that participants abide by rules designed to ensure that athletes or teams perform to the best of their abilities and do not have an unfair advantage over opponents. Cheating, gamesmanship, and corruption are the opposite of sportsmanship. As two ethics professors framed it: the sportsmanship model safeguards healthy competition that cultivates "personal honor, virtue, and character," and "contributes to a community of respect and trust between competitors and in society."[2] The ultimate goal of sportsmanship is "to pursue victory with honor by giving one's best effort."[3] At a meeting held at the 2015 Super Bowl, NFL Commissioner Roger Goodell responded to an incident regarding a football team's intentional deflation of footballs (called Deflategate) to gain an unfair advantage in a playoff game. He stated: "I am not going to do anything to compromise the integrity of the league."[4]

Concerns about sports integrity for the governing bodies of professional sports probably have their roots in both economics and ethics. The United States sports industries are valuable businesses: in 2017 the NFL's collective market cap of its 32 teams was estimated to be about $80 billion on annual revenues of about $13.2 billion,

1 Ashutosh Misra, Jack Anderson & Jason Saunders, *Safeguarding Sports Integrity Against Crime and Corruption: An Australian Perspective*. In MATCH-FIXING IN INTERNATIONAL SPORTS, EXISTING PROCESS, LAW ENFORCEMENT AND PREVENTATIVE STRATEGIES 138 (M. R. Haberfield & Dale Sheehan eds., 2013 ed. 2013).

2 Kirk Hanson & Matt Savage, *What Role Does Ethics Play in Sports?*, Aug. 2012, MARKKULA CENTER FOR APPLIED ETHICS, http://www.scu.edu/ethics/publications/submitted/sports-ethics.html.

3 *Id.*

4 Frank Schwab, *Roger Goodell Wraps up 'Tough Year' By Addressing Key NFL Issues*, Jan. 30, 2015, YAHOO SPORTS, http://sports.yahoo.com/blogs/nfl-shutdown-corner/roger-goodell-says-no-judgments-made-in-deflate-gate-controversy-183735200.html.

with broadcasting deals making up about 57% of those revenues.[5] According to NFL Commissioner Roger Goodell, the league aspires to have annual revenue of $25 billion by 2027.[6] The NFL is not the only league with substantial money at stake. In 2017, the thirty teams in Major League Baseball had a combined market cap of about $46.2 billion on aggregate revenues of $9.03 billion.[7] The NBA was not far behind, with a combined market cap for its 30 teams of about $41 billion on revenues of $5.9 billion.[8]

A breakdown of sports integrity can have a devastating economic impact on these multibillion-dollar sports industries. Besides broadcasting and fan attendance, other adverse economic impacts from compromised sports integrity might include loss of sponsorships and merchandising.[9] If the public believes that a sport offers games or events whose integrity is compromised, the public would likely lose interest in that sport or sports league.[10] In contrast, as fan interest increases so does commercial success, private economic investment, and the prospects for public funding of capital investments, like stadiums.[11]

Economic realities can create conflicts of interest related to sports integrity. This conflict arises when corrupt activities threaten the integrity of the game but imposing harsh sanctions might impact fans' willingness to spend money on a sport where they question the legitimacy of the games' results. A sport's governing body may want to cover up or downplay incidents of corruption or cheating for fear that transparency may bring fan rebuke. As an example of

---

5 Kurt Badenhausen, *The Dallas Cowboys Head the NFL'S Most Valuable Teams at $4.8 Billion,* Sept. 18, 2017, FORBES, https://www.forbes.com/sites/kurtbadenhausen/2017/09/18/the-dallas-cowboys-head-the-nfls-most-valuable-teams-at-4-8-billion/#654cc586243f.

6 *Id.*

7 Mike Ozanian, *Baseball Team Values 2017,* Apr. 11, 2017, FORBES, https://www.forbes.com/sites/mikeozanian/2017/04/11/baseball-team-values-2017/#264c24742451.

8 Kurt Badenhausen, *The Knicks and Lakers Top the NBA's Most Valuable Teams 2017,* Feb. 15, 2017, FORBES, https://www.forbes.com/sites/kurtbadenhausen/2017/02/15/the-knicks-and-lakers-head-the-nbas-most-valuable-teams-2017/#101410c07966.

9 *See* Schwab, *supra,* note 4.

10 L. Rebeggiani, & F. Rebeggiani, *Which factors favor betting related cheating in sports? Some insights from political economy.* In In MATCH-FIXING IN INTERNATIONAL SPORTS, EXISTING PROCESS, LAW ENFORCEMENT AND PREVENTATIVE STRATEGIES 138 (M. R. Haberfield & Dale Sheehan eds., 2013 ed. 2013). As one commentator noted: "The perception of integrity must be present for the sports enthusiast to believe that the outcome of a sporting competition is genuine." Richard H. McLaren, *Corruption: Its Impact on Fair Play,* 19 MARQ. SPORTS L. REV., 2008 at 15.

11 *Id.*

this tension, look to Deflategate itself. The ultimate punishment was a four-game suspension for the winning team's quarterback (for failure to cooperate with investigators) that he served during the following season, a team fine of $1 million, and loss of two draft picks.[12] The accused team won the league championship (along with the attendant financial benefits), and the quarterback still earns an annual average of $20.5 million.[13]

This chapter explores these standards for sports integrity and their origins, the implications of sports wagering on sports integrity, and how the sports' governing bodies, the government, and betting interests can achieve economic and ethical goals relating to sports integrity.

SPORTS WAGERING AND SPORTS INTEGRITY

Historically, sports' governing bodies, religious and moral leaders, and many elected politicians have viewed sports wagering as inconsistent with societal values, including those relating to sports integrity. A former NFL Commissioner, Paul Tagliabue, asserted that sports wagering threatened the values of sports integrity:

> Sports gambling threatens the character of team sports. Our games embody our very finest traditions and values. They stand for clean, healthy competition. They stand for teamwork. And they stand for success through preparation and honest effort. With legalized sports gambling, our games instead will come to represent the fast buck, the quick fix, the desire to get something for nothing. The spread of legalized sports gambling would change forever—and for the worse—what our games stand for and the way they are perceived.[14]

Much of the media have shared this position. In 1986, Sports Illustrated noted that, "as fans cheer their bets rather than their favorite teams, dark clouds of cynicism and suspicion hang over

---

12 ESPN, *Deflategate Timeline: After 544 Days, Tom Brady Gives In*, July 15, 2016, http://www.espn.com/blog/new-england-patriots/post/_/id/4782561/timeline-of-events-for-deflategate-tom-brady; While a controversy ensued as to whether the team intentionally deflate the balls ensued, after the matter went to court, a justice on the panel before the US Court of Appeals for the Second Circuit noted in oral argument that ""the evidence of ball tampering is compelling, if not overwhelming." *See also*, Ben Volin, *Brady's Lawyer Feels Pressure from Judges*, March 3, 2016, BOSTON GLOBE, https://www.bostonglobe.com/2016/03/03/tom-brady-deflategate-appeal/TnrgVNVYDpa6n4VtBBJr2I/story.html.

13 Vincent Frank, *How Tom Brady's Career Earnings Compare to Other Quarterbacks Playing This Sunday*, Jan. 20, 2017, FORBES, https://www.forbes.com/sites/vincentfrank/2017/01/20/how-tom-bradys-career-earnings-compare-to-other-quarterbacks-playing-this-sunday/#6c7a92c46020.

14 S. REP. NO. 102-248, at 5 (1992).

games, and the possibility of fixes is always in the air."[15] This popular position convinced key politicians to seek an unprecedented intrusion into the rights of states to determine gambling policy for its residents. Historically, federal policy toward all gambling—including sports wagering—had been relatively simple. Rather than preempting the state laws, federal gambling laws were designed to aid states in the enforcement of their gambling laws.[16] For example, under most federal laws, a gambling business is illegal only if it violates a state or local law.[17] When Congress adopted the Federal Wire Act in 1961, it made clear its respect for the rights of individual states to sanction gambling within their borders.[18]

According to former U.S. Senator Bill Bradley (D-New Jersey), "Legalized sports betting would teach young people how to gamble."[19] Bradley believed that children attracted to sports would soon associate sports with gambling, rather than with personal achievement or sportsmanship.[20] Bradley claimed that, "legalizing sports gambling would encourage young people to participate in sports to win money. They would no longer love the game for the purity of the experience."[21] Bradley's views were echoed by critics who made moral and religious claims that gambling influences the general public's values and priorities.[22] According to this perspective, people may interact with others differently in a community with gambling as opposed to a community without gambling. Gambling's emphasis on luck and wealth may negatively affect community interactions. As a result, undesirable attributes in the community may emerge; residents may

---

15 Richard O. Davies & Richard G. Abram, BETTING THE LINE: SPORTS WAGERING IN AMERICAN LIFE 145, (Ohio State Univ. Press, 2001).

16 Anthony Cabot, *The Absence of a Comprehensive Federal Policy Toward Internet and Sports Wagering and A Proposal for Change,* 17 VILL. SPORTS & ENT. L.J. 271 (2010).

17 The "purpose" of the Wire Act "is succinctly stated in Report No. 588 of the Senate Judiciary Committee of the 87th Congress, on July 24, 1961, as "* * * to assist the several States in the enforcement of their laws pertaining to gambling and to aid in the suppression of organized gambling activities by restricting the use of wire communication facilities." United States v. Yaquinta, 204 F. Supp. 276 (N.D. W. Va. 1962).

18 *See* H.R. REP. NO. 967 (Congress did not intend to criminalize acts that neither states nor Congress desired to be treated as criminal).

19 Bill Bradley, *The Professional and Amateur Sports Protection Act-Policy Concerns Behind Senate Bill 474,* 2 SETON HALL J. SPORT L.5, 6 (1992)

20 *Id.*at 7.

21 *Id.*

22 William R. Eadington, *The Casino Gaming Industry: A Study of Political Economy,* 474 THE ANNALS OF THE AMERICAN ACADEMY OF POLITICAL AND SOCIAL SCIENCE, 1984 at 23-35.

determine that they are better off being lucky than working hard, for instance, and that wealth is the most desirable outcome.[23] Underlying some negative attitudes toward gambling is the fear of any activities that are hedonistic and the idea that pleasure for pleasure's sake is wrong or deviant.[24]

Bradley and others were also concerned that the proliferation of legal sports wagering might harm both the integrity of sports through competition manipulation,[25] and affect the fans' perception of that integrity.[26] For example, a player might miss an easy opportunity to score at the end of a game that did not necessarily affect the game's outcome. Nevertheless, the missed shot altered the final score and could impact who won certain wagers based on the point-spread. Bradley argued that fans might question whether the player was fixing the game, rather than attributing the miss to fatigue or other legitimate factors. Bradley summarized his position by stating that, "Sports gambling ... would irreparably harm amateur and

23 *Id.*

24 Vicki Abt, James F. Smith, & Eugene Christiansen, (1985). The Business of Risk: Commercial Gambling in Mainstream (Univ Press of Kansas, 1985); Bo J. Bernhard, (2007). *Sociological Perspectives on the Pathological Gambling Entry in the Diagnostic and Statistical Manual of Mental Disorders*, 51 American Behavioral Scientist, at 8-32. Moral objections have been particularly harsh when addressing those who gamble excessively or problematically, as moralists see these individuals as posing unique risks to communities. Bo J. Bernhard, Robert Futrell, & Andrew Harper, *Shots from the Pulpit: An Ethnographic Content Analysis of United States Anti-Gambling Social Movement Documents from 1816-2010*. 14 UNLV Gaming Research & Review Journal 15-32 (2010). Retrieved from http://digitalscholarship.unlv.edu/grrj/vol14/iss2/2. For example, the "Social Principles" of the United Methodist Church its reflect stated positions on gambling:

> Gambling is a menace to society, deadly to the best interests of moral, social, economic, and spiritual life, and destructive of good government. As an act of faith and love, Christians should abstain from gambling and should strive to minister to those victimized by the practice.
>
> The United Methodist Church, *Gambling*, (2010) Retrieved from http://www.umc.org/what-we-believe/gambling.

25 While match-fixing is the common term, it fails to adequately describe all the methods of competition manipulation that not only involves the "fixing" who wins or loses the match, but includes point shaving and spot-fixing. Moreover, not all sports are matches, which is a more appropriate term for head to head competitions. *See*, International Olympic Committee, Interpol, *Handbook on Protecting Sport from Competition Manipulation*, May 2016 [hereinafter IOC], Retrieved from https://www.interpol.int/News-and-media/Publications2/Leaflets-and-brochures/Joint-report-INTERPOL-IOC-Handbook-on-Protecting-Sport-from-Competition-Manipulation.

26 Donald L. Barlett & James B. Steele, Throwing the game: *Why Congress Isn't Closing a Loophole That Fosters Gambling on College Sports—And Corrupts Them*, Time, Sept. 25, 2000, http://content.time.com/time/magazine/article/0,9171,998009,00.html.

professional sports by fostering suspicion that individual plays and final scores of games may have been influenced by factors other than honest athletic competition."[27] According to Bradley and others, legal state-sponsored sports wagering was the most objectionable form of wagering because it created the perception of government approval. As Bradley stated, sports wagering puts the "imprimatur of the state on this activity."[28]

With Bradley's support, in 1992 Congress passed the Professional and Amateur Sports Protection Act (PASPA), which preempted state gambling laws regarding sports wagering, and prohibited states from licensing or authorizing sports wagering. No other form of gambling, however, was prohibited.[29] According to the Senate Judiciary Committee Report, the bill served "an important public purpose, to stop the spread of state-sponsored sports gambling."[30]

THE INTERRELATIONSHIP OF SPORTS WAGERING AND SPORTS

Despite some moral and religious opposition, wagering and sports have historically been socially and economically interrelated. As early as the first century B.C., friendly wagers on the outcome of popular sporting events such as chariot races, gladiator fights, and Olympic sports such as running, jumping, javelin-throwing, wrestling, and boxing were both common and lawful in ancient Rome.[31] The reason for this is simple: many humans enjoy the experience of gambling. The late David Spinier, a noted journalist, wrote, "Money is the fuel of gambling; it drives it, as petrol powers a car, but the pleasure of driving a car is not about petroleum. It's about speed, style, movement. Fuel is merely what makes the car run. In that sense, the real motives behind gambling are to be sought elsewhere."[32] In other words, some players are willing to pay for the experience that gambling brings them because they gain enjoyment from simply making a wager.

27 Complaint, Nat'l Coll. Athletic Ass'n v. Christie, 3:12-cv04947-MAS-LHG (D.N.J. Aug. 7, 2012).

28 Bradley, *supra* note 19, at 5.

29 137 CONG. REC. S2256-04 (1991).

30 S. REP. NO. 102-248, at 4 (1991), *as reprinted in* 1992 U.S.C.C.A.N. 3553.

31 Suzanne B. Faris, *Changing Public Policy and the Evolution of Roman Civil and Criminal Law on Gambling*, 3 UNLV GAMING L.J. 199, 200 (2012).

32 David Spanier, THE HAND I PLAYED: A POKER MEMOIR 50 (University of Nevada Press, 2001).

Other bettors may have motives relating to their love of sports and team or player identity, and still others gamble to seek pleasure or avoid pain. Social scientists have identified even more reasons why people like the gambling experience, such as socialization/learning, challenge, escape, and winning.[33] Sports wagering can also intensify social interactions because gamblers are part of the strong connection that a community has with its sports teams. Also significant are the symbolic or social motives,[34] where gambling happens "within social boundaries that create a social organization and symbolic meaning system."[35] Within this social world, people come to feel comfort, security, companionship, and belonging.[36]

Changing Attitudes Toward Sports Wagering

Public View

The impact of religious and moral leaders and elected politicians who view sports wagering as fundamentally inconsistent with societal values has declined since the passage of PASPA. According to a Gallup/CNN/USA Today poll, public attitudes toward sports wagering have shifted dramatically. In the early 1990s, about 56% of American disapproved of legal sports wagering.[37] By 2017, almost the

---

33 Choong-Ki Lee, Yong-Ki Lee, Bo Jason Bernhard, and Yoo-Shik Yoond, *Segmenting Casino Gamblers By Motivation: A Cluster Analysis of Korean Gamblers*, 27 Tourism Management 856-866 (2006).

34 June Cotte, *Chances, Trances, and Lots of Electronic Gaming: Gambling Motives and Consumption Experiences*, 29 Journal of Leisure Research 380 (1997); John A. Tarras, A.J. Singh, and Omar Moufakkir. *The Profile and Motivations of Elderly Women Gamblers*, 5 UNLV Gaming Research & Review Journal 3 (2012); Ipkin Anthony Wong, & Mark Scott Rosenbaum, *Beyond Hardcore Gambling: Understanding Why Mainland Chinese Visit Casinos in Macau*, Journal of Hospitality & Tourism Research, Feb. 2012, at 32-51; Ki-Joon Back, Choong-Ki Lee, & Randy Stinchfield. *Gambling Motivation and Passion: A Comparison Study of Recreational and Pathological Gamblers*, 27 Journal of Gambling Studies 355-370 (2011).

35 Vicki Abt, James F. Smith, & Martin C. McGurrin, *Ritual, Risk, and Reward: A Role Analysis of Race Track and Casino Encounters*. Journal of Gambling Behavior, 1985, at 64-75.

36 *Id.*

37 Rick Maese & Emily Guskin, *Poll: For First Time, Majority of Americans Approve of Legalized Sports Betting*, Wash. Post, Sept. 26, 2017, https://www.washingtonpost.com/sports/poll-for-first-time-majority-of-americans-approve-of-legalizing-sports-betting/2017/09/26/a18b97ca-a226-11e7-b14f-f41773cd5a14_story.html?tid=ss_tw&utm_term=.3f79b057b619.

same percentage (56%) believe that sports wagering should be legal.[38] A different poll, sanctioned by an industry group, the American Gaming Association, showed even greater public acceptance, with 61% of those who rarely watch football supporting legalized wagering. These respondents were joined in that view by over a majority of those who regularly attend religious service.[39]

America's changing attitudes toward gambling are based on many factors. Gambling of any form was rarer in 1991. Today, all states except Hawaii and Utah have some form of legal gambling. Casinos can now be found in 80% of all states, while only two states, Nevada and New Jersey, had casinos in 1988.[40] The public has become accustomed to gambling in their own backyards and is less apprehensive of its impact. Moreover, U.S. society's approach to those who gamble (and especially those who gamble excessively) has also become more sympathetic and research-based.[41]

Major Sports Leagues' View

Changes in public attitudes, however, do not necessarily result in changes to public policy or laws. The pending Supreme Court case described in Chapter 2 could result in the states having a path to permitting sports wagering without congressional action. Absent that, however, change would need to occur through repeal or modification of PASPA.[42] In that case, it is likely the major sports leagues would have a significant influence on any federal legislation.

There are three basic approaches that the sports governing bodies might take to legislative proposals to expand legal sports wagering. The first is to oppose sports wagering in the Congress and in the courts, which has been their historical position.[43] Even if PASPA

---

38 *Id.*

39 The Mellman Group, Re: Executive Summary of Our Recent Super Bowl Polling, Feb. 2, 2016, http://docs.house.gov/meetings/IF/IF17/20160511/104902/HHRG-114-IF17-20160511-SD002.pdf.

40 Christopher Palmeri, *Local Casinos Are a Losing Bet*, BLOOMBERG BUSINESSWEEK, Apr. 3, 2014, https://www.bloomberg.com/news/articles/2014-04-03/casinos-close-as-revenue-falls-in-gambling-saturated-u-dot-s.

41 Bo J. Bernhard, *Sociological Speculations on Treating Problem Gamblers: A Clinical Sociological Imagination Via A Bio-Psycho-Social-Sociological Model*, AMERICAN BEHAVIORAL SCIENTIST, Sept. 2007, at 122-138.

42 See Chapter 2 discussion of New Jersey's challenge to PASPA and pending decision by Supreme Court.

43 *See* Brett Smiler, *Where Major Sports Leagues Stand on Gambling Legislation in the U.S.*, SPORTS HANDLE, Aug. 19, 2017, https://sportshandle.com/gambling-legislation-laws-united-states-leagues-commissioners/.

is found constitutionally wanting, the sports leagues could mount a legislative campaign to modify its provisions to prohibit sports wagering consistent with the Supreme Court decision.

The second possible response is to concede that sports wagering is inevitable and that regulating the activity to achieve policy goals related to both wagering and sports integrity is preferable to leaving the market to illegal, unregulated markets. This appears to be the direction of the major sports leagues. For example, NBA Commissioner Adam Silver noted, "One of the reasons I've been pushing to legalize sports betting is not because that I'm necessarily an advocate of sports betting, it's because all the research shows that it's a multi-hundred-billion-dollar business just in the United States right now."[44] Rob Manfred, the commissioner of Major League Baseball, similarly stated:

> Sports betting happens, ...Whether it's legalized here or not, it's happening out there. So I think the question for sports is really, 'Are we better off in a world where we have a nice, strong, uniform, federal regulation of gambling that protects the integrity of sports, provides sports with the tools to ensure that there is integrity in the competition ... or are we better off closing our eyes to that and letting it go on as illegal gambling'? And that's a debatable point.[45]

A regulated wagering market provides greater tools to protect fans who already are heavily engaged in sports betting. Despite its illegality in most of the United States, bettors make up half of the NFL viewer base and 41% of sports viewers in general.[46] Silver noted that illegal sports wagering is rampant, legal gambling is a "popular and accepted form of entertainment," sports fans want a safe and legal option to wager, and regulated wagering is successful outside the United States.[47] Silver stated that, "Congress should adopt a federal framework that allows states to authorize betting on professional sports, subject to strict regulatory requirements and technological safeguards."[48]

---

44 Will Green, *NBA Supports Sports Betting Regulation, But Will Continue to Refrain from Direct Legislative Lobbying*, Legal Sports Report, Aug. 5, 2016, https://www.legalsportsreport.com/10918/nba-sports-betting-federal-framework-wont-advocate-for-law/.

45 Matt Synder, *Commissioner Manfred Admits MLB is Revisiting Its View on Sports Betting*, CBS Sports, Feb. 8, 2017, http://www.cbssports.com/mlb/news/commissioner-manfred-admits-mlb-is-revisiting-its-view-on-sports-betting/.

46 Daniel Roberts, *Yahoo: Study Reveals Why TV Networks Should Support Sports Betting*, Am. Gaming Ass'n, Sept. 15, 2016, http://tinyurl.com/guzjxkk.

47 Adam Silver, *Legalize and Regulate Sports Betting*, NY Times, Nov. 13, 2014, https://www.nytimes.com/2014/11/14/opinion/nba-commissioner-adam-silver-legalize-sports-betting.html?mcubz=0.

48 *Id.*

A third possible response of the leagues is to lead the efforts for regulated wagering and embrace sports wagering from a profit and fan engagement perspective. The leagues understand that having a wagering option to sporting events stimulates public interest by giving the fan an additional personal stake in a game's outcome.[49] MLB Commissioner Rob Manfred noted that sports wagering is a "form of fan engagement" and "can fuel the popularity."[50] Studies bear this out. One study found that fans who wagered were 86% more likely to watch a game; 74% of the fans would more closely follow teams or players, and 75% had greater enjoyment of the game.[51]

Another study showed that persons who made wagers on games watched almost 20 more games in a season than non-bettors.[52] With greater spectator interest comes higher attendance, fans devoting more time and money to following the sport, more sponsorships, and increased television revenues.[53] Studies have supported the view that legal wagering increases attendance, enhances broadcast and media demands,[54] improves revenues from ticket sales, and boosts revenues from granting rights to provide gambling services on the event premises.[55] Clearly, with the proliferation of sports wagering across the world, money received from sports wagering represents "one of the fastest growing revenue streams for sports organizations, second only to broadcasting rights."[56]

While the positions of MLB and the NBA are evident, the most powerful league, the National Football League (NFL), has been conspicuous in its silence. The NFL has historically been the most steadfast opponent of sports wagering, though there are some indications it has softened its position. The NFL, like the other major leagues, liberalized rules regarding sports sponsorships.[57] Moreover,

---

49 David Forrest, Ian McHale, & Kevin McAuley. *'Say It Ain't So': Betting-Related Malpractice in Sport*, INT'L J. OF SPORT FIN., 2008, at 156.

50 Synder, *supra* note 45.

51 The Mellman Group, *supra* note 39.

52 Roberts, *supra* note 46.

53 Leanna O'Leary, *Price-Fixing Between Horizontal Competitors in the English Super League*, 3-4 THE INT'L SPORTS L.J. 2008, at 77.

54 David Forrest & Robert Simmons, *Sport and Gambling*, 19 OXFORD REV. OF ECON. POL'Y 598-611 (2003).

55 *Id.*

56 Presentation, Council of Europe Convention on the Manipulation of Sports Competitions (Macolin Convention), Council of Europe, Magglingen/Macolin, Switzerland, 2014, http://conventions.coe.int/Treaty/EN/Treaties/Html/215.htm (last visited Mar. 15, 2015).

57 Anita M. Moorman, *Sport Lotteries: The Professional Sports Leagues Take on the State of Delaware, Again!* 19 SPORT MARKETING Q. 107-109 (2010), Retrieved from

the NFL has shown little resistance to the placement of sportsbooks near sports venues, including those in and around Wembley Stadium in London, where sports betting is legal and where the NFL has held regular season games. Reconciling the NFL's anti-gambling stance with its approval of the relocation of the Oakland Raiders to Las Vegas is also difficult. Nevertheless, the NFL has continued to enforce other more arcane prohibitions like preventing an arm wrestling contest involving NFL players from being held at a Las Vegas casino, and prohibiting former Dallas Cowboys quarterback Tony Romo and other NFL players from appearing at a fantasy football convention at a Las Vegas convention center connected to a casino.[58]

The evolving attitudes of the major sports leagues toward legalized sports betting are not necessarily a green light going forward. For example, Commissioner Manfred noted that, "it's incumbent upon us to make sure we understand what the facts are, what kind of legalized gambling are you talking about, how would it be regulated, what are the threats to the integrity of the sport. And make sure the institution is in a position to deal with whatever roads come down the road."[59]

MAJOR THREATS TO SPORTS INTEGRITY

Before discussing the threat that sports wagering presents to sports integrity, it is important to understand the three leading methods of disrupting on-field integrity, *illegal performance enhancement*, *sabotage*, and *competition manipulation*.[60]

Illegal Performance Enhancement

Doping

Illegal chemical performance enhancement, also called doping, involves the use of prohibited substances like stimulants, steroids,

---

http://ezproxy.library.unlv.edu/login?url=http://search.proquest.com/docview/527956675?accountid=3611.

58 David Purdum, *Participants in Arm Wrestling Event in Vegas Could Face NFL Fines*, ESPN, Apr. 10, 2017, http://www.espn.com/nfl/story/_/id/19118471/nfl-look-pro-football-arm-wrestling-championship-possible-violations.

59 Dustin Gouker, *MLB Commish On Sports Betting: Baseball Has Done 'Research On How Gambling Relates To Fan Engagement'*, Legal Sports Report, Feb. 24, 2017. https://www.legalsportsreport.com/13153/mlb-research-sports-betting/.

60 Ian Preston & Stefan Szymanski, *Cheating in Contests*. 19 Oxford Rev. of Econ. Pol'y 612-624 (2003), Retrieved from http://oxrep.oxfordjournals.org/content/19/4/612.full.pdf+html?sid=adc1b713-9593-4d55-84b1-39759640399e.

hormones, and narcotics, or prohibited actions such as oxygen enhancement.[61] Doping impacts sports integrity because athletes can obtain an unfair artificial advantage in sporting events that is not based on natural abilities or hard work. Rather, the performance is a function of how the pharmaceuticals increase their strength, speed, endurance, mental acuity, or recovery time.[62] The public often associates steroids with performance enhancement because of the high-profile cases involving prominent baseball players such as Mark McGuire, Barry Bonds, and Roger Clemens.[63] Steroids are artificial derivatives of the naturally produced hormone testosterone that promote the growth of muscle, thereby improving strength and performance.[64] Steroids were discovered in the 1930s, and Adolph Hitler may have endorsed their use to improve the performance of German athletes in the 1936 Olympic Games.[65] More mainstream use occurred in the mid-1950s among weightlifters internationally, before its rising popularity in the National Football League beginning in the 1970s.[66] A subsequent study indicated that steroid use increased offensive performance in baseball by an average of 12%, a significant statistic in a highly competitive environment.[67]

---

61 David A. Baron, David M. Martin, & Samir Abol Magd, *Doping in Sports and Its Spread to At-Risk Populations: An International Review*, 6 WORLD PSYCHIATRY 118 (2007), Retrieved from http://www.ncbi.nlm.nih.gov/pmc/articles/PMC2219897/; A. Gaudard, E Varlet-Marie, F. Bressolle, & M. Audran, *Drugs For Increasing Oxygen Transport and Their Potential Use in Doping*, 33 SPORTS MED. 187-212 (2003), Retrieved from http://link.springer.com/article/10.2165%2F00007256-200333030-00003.

62 Roberta Furst Wolf, *Conflicting Anti-Doping Laws in Professional Sports: Collective Bargaining Agreements v. State Law.* 34 SEATTLE UNIV. L. REV. (2010) (citing *Steroids in Sports: Cheating the System and Gambling Your Health, Steroids in Sports: Hearing Before the Subcomm. on Commerce, Trade, & Consumer Prot. and the Subcomm. on Health of the Comm. on Energy & Comm.*, 109th Cong. 4 (2005) [hereinafter Steroids in Sports: Cheating the System and Gambling Your Health], at 2-4 (testimony of Rep. Stearns); 12 (testimony of Rep. Upton); 98, 100, 108-09 (testimony of Francis Coonelly, Senior V.P. and Gen. Counsel--Labor, MLB); 123 (testimony of Sandra Worth, Nat'l Athletic Trainers Ass'n).

63 Fox News, *Mark McGwire Admits Using Steroids*, Jan. 11, 2010, http://www.foxnews.com/us/2010/01/11/mark-mcgwire-admits-using-steroids; Mark Fainaru-Wada & Lance Williams. GAME OF SHADOWS: BARRY BONDS, BALCO, AND THE STEROIDS SCANDAL THAT ROCKED PROFESSIONAL SPORTS. (Penguin, 2006); Daniel Healey, *Fall of the Rocket: Steroids in Baseball and The Case Against Roger Clemens.* 19 MARQ. SPORTS L. REV., 2008 at 289.

64 Dan Peterson, *How Do Steroids Work?*, LIVESCIENCE, Feb. 19, 2009, https://www.livescience.com/3349-steroids-work.html.

65 Charles E. Yesalis, Stephen P. Courson & James Wright, HISTORY OF ANABOLIC STEROID USE IN SPORT AND EXERCISE § 2.32 (1993).

66 *Id.*

67 Brian Schmotzer, Jeff Switchenko, & Patrick D. Kilgo. *Did Steroid Use Enhance the Performance of the Mitchell Batters? The Effect of Alleged Performance Enhancing Drug*

Doping has consequences.[68] Fans can become cynical about the natural abilities of athletes in the competition and as a result, may lose interest in the sport or the league.[69] As an example, professional road cycling suffered a tarnished reputation in 2011 after the public disclosure of extensive doping by the sport's biggest star Lance Armstrong, as well as other cyclists. In the three years immediately following the scandals, the sport suffered a 22% decline in television viewership in major markets like the United Kingdom, Netherlands, Australia, and the United States.[70]

Efforts to ban doping have extensive support. The campaign to prohibit the use of steroids has its origins in legislative action, international rules, and the sports leagues' integrity rules. In 1990 Congress passed the Anabolic Steroids Control Act of 1990 that classified steroids as a Class III scheduled drug under the Controlled Substances Act (CSA). Class III drugs are those with "high abuse potential, moderate to low physical dependence, and high psychologic dependence potential, with acceptable medical uses."[71] As a classified drug, physicians can lawfully prescribe steroids only to treat disease or other medical illness.[72] Likewise, the international athletic community has long had concerns about performance-enhancing drugs. The International Amateur

---

Use on Offensive Performance from 1995 to 2007, J. of Quantitative Analysis in Sports July 18, 2008, at 1-14.

68 Besides the impact on fans and the sport, the introduction of performance-enhancing drugs impacts players' health, such as increased incidence of cancer and heart and liver disease. *Id.* citing *Sports: Cheating the System and Gambling Your Health* at 2, 4 (testimony of Rep. Stearns), 5 (testimony of Rep. Waxman), 6-7 (testimony of Rep. Deal), 8 (testimony of Rep. Brown), 11 (testimony of Rep. Schakowsky), 15 (testimony of Rep. Norwood), 18-19 (testimony of Rep. Ryun), 31-32 (testimony of Linn Goldberg, Prof. of Medicine, Div. of Health Promotion & Sports Medicine, Or. Health & Science Univ.), 37 (testimony of Robert Kanaby, Exec. Dir., Nat'l Fed'n of State High Sch. Assns.), 67-68 (testimony of Ralph Hale, Chair. of the Board, U.S. Anti-Doping Agency). Moreover, vulnerable young athletes who want to emulate the success of professional athletes may view drugs as a necessary means to an end. *Id.* citing *Sports: Cheating the System and Gambling Your Health* at 5 (testimony of Rep. Waxman). Performance enhancing drug use among minors is particularly problematic because of their unsupervised use and impact on developing bodies. *Id.*

69 McLaren, *supra* note 10.

70 The Economics of Professional Road Cycling (Daam Van Reeth, Daniel Joseph Larson, eds., 2016).

71 *Schedule III*, McGraw-Hill Concise Dictionary of Modern Medicine (2002), Retrieved June 13, 2017 from http://medical-dictionary.thefreedictionary.com/Schedule+III.

72 Jeffrey Hedges, *The Anabolic Steroids Act: Bad Medicine for the Elderly*, 5 Elder L.J. 293, 295-97 (1997).

Athletic Federation had rules against the use of stimulants as early as 1928 and the International Olympic Committee (IOC) developed reliable testing for steroids in the 1970s.[73] The IOC, like the amateur and professional sports governing bodies in the United States, maintains a list of banned drugs. For example, anabolic agents, growth hormones, Beta-2 agonists, hormone and metabolic modulators, and diuretics and similar masking agents are prohibited. Banned methods include manipulation of blood and blood components, chemical and physical manipulation, and gene doping. Likewise, stimulants, narcotics, cannabinoids, and glucocorticoids are not permitted during competitions.[74] In the United States, each sports league maintains its own rules and procedures relating to testing and sanctions for prohibited drug use.[75] These policies and penalties are frequently part of the collective bargaining agreements between the governing bodies and the players' associations.[76] The National Collegiate Athletic Association (NCAA) does not negotiate with its student-athletes, and its member schools simply adopt and impose its standards "to safeguard the integrity of athletic competition[s]" and "to protect the health and safety of its athletes."[77]

Non-Drug Related Performance Enhancement

Non-drug related performance enhancement often concerns the use of illegally altered equipment.[78] The opposite of sabotage,

73 Darryl C. Wilson, *Let Them Do Drugs-A Commentary on Random Efforts at Shot Blocking in the Sports Drug Game.* 8 FLA. COASTAL L. REV. 53 (2006).

74 Christina Stiehl, *All the Drugs Banned at the Olympics, and What They* Do, THRILLIST, Aug. 5, 2016, https://www.thrillist.com/health/nation/illegal-drug-facts-rio-olympics-2016-international-olympic-committee.

75 Roberta Furst Wolf, *Conflicting Anti-Doping Laws in Professional Sports: Collective Bargaining Agreements v. State Law*, 34 SEATTLE UNIV. L. REV. 1605 (2010).

76 *See e.g.*, National Football League, *Policy and Program on Substances of Abuse 2015*, https://nflpaweb.blob.core.windows.net/media/Default/PDFs/Player%20 Development/2015%20Policy%20and%20Program%20on%20Substances%20of%20 Abuse.pdf (last visited Jan. 27, 2018); *Major League Baseball's Joint Drug Prevention and Treatment Program*, http://mlb.mlb.com/pa/pdf/jda.pdf. (last visited Jan. 27 2018), *NBA & NBAPA Anti-Drug Program Article XXXIII of Collective Bargaining Agreement*, http://performancetrainingsystems.net/Resources/NBAPA%20Drug%20Policy.pdf (last visited Jan. 27 2018).

77 Brian Lee, *Drug Testing and the Confused Athlete: A Look at the Differing Athletic Drug Testing Programs in High School, College and the Olympics.* 3 FLA. COASTAL L. REV. 91, 98 (2001).

78 See an interesting physical analysis of cheating by altering equipment, Alan M. Nathan, Lloyd V. Smith, Warren L. Faber, & Daniel A. Russell, *Corked Bats, Juiced Balls, and Humidors: The Physics of Cheating in Baseball*, 76 AM. J. OF PHYSICS 575-580 (2011),

this form of cheating increases one's output inconsistent with the rules of the game.[79] Cheating by illegally improving or altering one's equipment is common in baseball. Corking bats is the process by which a cylindrical cavity is drilled axially in the bat's barrel and the wood is replaced with cork or other lighter material.[80] The lighter bat increases swing speed and can increase the distance that a batted ball can travel.[81] Major League Baseball has had several incidents of corked bats, including when all-star Sammy Sosa used a corked bat in a regulation game in 2003. In another example of altering equipment, Hall of Fame pitcher Gaylord Perry and others notoriously scuffed or applied foreign substances to the baseball to accentuate the ball's movement and making it harder to hit.[82] Major League Baseball has outlawed this form of cheating since 1920.

As noted earlier, American professional football experienced a scandal involving altered equipment in "Deflategate." New England Patriots star quarterback Tom Brady was allegedly at least aware that the Patriots offense used footballs in a 2015 divisional championship game that were deflated to a level below the air pressure required by league rules.[83] A deflated football allegedly gives the offense an advantage because the quarterback can achieve a better grip on the ball and receivers can more easily catch a softer ball, particularly in cold or rainy weather.[84] The league levied a four-game suspension on Brady because he failed to cooperate by destroying his cellphone.[85]

Boxing also has a history of infractions involving equipment modification to gain an advantage. Perhaps the most infamous involved a featherweight named Antonio Margarito who was suspended for a year after his trainer was found to have put plaster

---

Retrieved from http://baseball.physics.illinois.edu/AJP-June2011.pdf.

79 Luis Garicano & Ignacio Palacios-Huerta, *Sabotage in Tournaments: Making the Beautiful Game a Bit Less Beautiful* (Sept. 2005), available at https://papers.ssrn.com/sol3/papers.cfm?abstract_id=831964.

80 Nathan, et.al, *supra* note 78.

81 *Id.*

82 Anthony McCarron, *Doctoring is in: Tricking Up Baseballs is Tradition as Old as the Game*, NY Daily News, Apr. 12, 2014, http://www.nydailynews.com/sports/baseball/doctoring-tricking-baseballs-tradition-old-game-article-1.1754822.

83 Don Van Natta Jr. & Seth Wickersham, *Spygate to Deflategate: Inside What Split the NFL and Patriots Apart*, ESPN, Sept. 7, 2015, http://www.espn.com/espn/otl/story/_/id/13533995/split-nfl-new-england-patriots-apart.

84 Tony Manfred, *Why Using Deflated Footballs Gave the Patriots A Huge Advantage*, Business Insider, Jan. 21, 2015, http://www.businessinsider.com/advantage-of-deflated-footballs-2015-1.

85 Van Natta Jr. & Wickersham, *supra* note 83.

of Paris in his hand wrapping before a WBA-sanctioned world title fight in Los Angeles. The substance was designed to harden and make the fighter's punches more powerful.[86] In a rare case where the perpetrators were successfully prosecuted for criminal offenses, a trainer for a journeyman boxer named Luis Resto cut out the padding of his boxing gloves before a fight in New York City. Both the trainer and fighter were convicted and given prison sentences for assault, conspiracy, and possession of a deadly weapon.[87]

Doping and Non-Drug Related Performance Enhancement and Sports Wagering

Doping and non-drug related performance enhancement is rarely done to gain an advantage in a wagering transaction. Instead, the motivation is the athlete's desire to obtain sports glory or monetary rewards by competing at a higher level. Therefore, while controlling performance-enhancing drugs is critical for sports integrity, they have a much different impact on wagering integrity. Bettors are not so interested in which drugs are permitted, or if carbohydrate loading, vitamin supplements or other methods improve performance. Sophisticated bettors want the sports governing bodies to have consistent rules on drug use and proper enforcement of those rules. Sports bettors try to predict the performance of a team based on the skill levels of the athletes involved. Predicting performance is difficult if a factor that has to be considered is whether the athlete may or may not be using illegal performance-enhancing drugs that impact the outcomes of a particular competition. Accomplishing a more predictable environment for sports betting requires that sports governing bodies have rules on permitted and prohibited pharmaceuticals, supplements or methods, and transparency, dedication, and consistency in the enforcement of those rules.

Whether illegal performance enhancement or competition manipulation poses the most significant threat to sports integrity is an open question. Then IOC president, Jacques Rogge stated in 2011 that "[W]e have made doping a top priority, now there is a new danger

---

86 Justin Tate, *The 13 Most Shocking Scandals in Boxing History*, BLEACHER REPORT, Dec. 6, 2011, http://bleacherreport.com/articles/965780-13-most-shocking-scandals-in-boxing-history.

87 Steve Silverman, *Boxing's 4 Most Infamous Cheaters of All Time*, BLEACHER REPORT, Aug. 17, 2012, http://bleacherreport.com/articles/1302130-boxings-4-most-infamous-cheaters-of-all-time.

coming up that almost all countries have been affected by and that is corruption, competition manipulation, and illegal gambling."[88]

Sabotage (and Cheating)

A dictionary definition of sabotage is to damage or destroy equipment, weapons or buildings to prevent the success of an enemy or competitor.[89] In the case of sports, a team or athlete engages in sabotage by taking actions to reduce the performance of one of the teams or an athlete in a way that is inconsistent with the rules of the game.[90] Sabotage is particularly useful against those who are the most competitive.[91] Sabotage in sports can take many forms: (a) altering the equipment used in the game to the disadvantage of one team; (b) illegally restraining or assaulting competitors; (c) stealing the other team's playbook, strategy or plays; (d) intentionally injuring or sickening an opponent; (e) attempting to provoke illegal responses from competitors (e.g. by goading); (f) trying to persuade the referee that opponents have engaged in prohibited acts (e.g. flopping to make it appear that an opponent's physical conduct was a foul); and (g) deceiving the referee as to what has occurred in the game.[92]

No sabotage was perhaps more blatant than when the husband of Tonya Harding, a competitive figure skater, hired a thug to intentionally (and ultimately successfully) injure Nancy Kerrigan shortly before the United States Figure Skating championship in 1994. Harding went on to win the competition but, after investigation, was stripped of her medal and banned for life for hindering the inquiry.

While major US professional sports have been relatively free of the recent incidents surrounding match fixing and point shaving, incidences of sabotage (and cheating) are ample and reveal that corrupt behavior is possible at the highest levels of professional sports. For example, "Spygate" involved an employee of the New England Patriots, one of the NFL's most successful teams, who was caught videotaping the opposing team's defensive signals in the opening game of the

---

88 Associated Press, *Jacque Rogge: Corruption Next Fight*, ESPN, July 14, 2011, http://espn.go.com/olympics/story/_/id/6768358/jacques-rogge-says-match-fixing-gambling-big-fights-sports.

89 *See e.g.*, *Sabotage*, The Free Dictionary, https://www.thefreedictionary.com/sabotage.

90 Preston et. al, *supra* note 60 at 612-624.

91 Subhasish M. Chowdhury & Oliver Gürtler, *Sabotage in Contests: A Survey*, May 19, 2015, available at https://www.uea.ac.uk/documents/166500/0/CBESS+15-09.pdf/290ecd5b-a280-4619-8d0b-714b5ba6858b.

92 Preston et. al, *supra* note 60 at 612-624.

2007 season. If the Patriots could record, memorize, and reveal the opposing team's defensive signals, they could alter their offensive play calling accordingly. Spygate resulted in the League fining the Patriots head coach $500,000, and fining the team $250,000. The team also forfeited a first-round pick. Surprisingly, the league handed down the punishment four days after league security uncovered the incident and before investigators even completed a field investigation at the team headquarters. The subsequent investigation showed that this cheating by the Patriots was an advanced institutionalized system that was core to the team's game strategy. The investigation found that the Patriots were involved in similar conduct in 40 games from 2000 to 2007. One team executive that lost to the Patriots claimed the league "didn't want anybody to know that [its] gold franchise had won Super Bowls by cheating."[93]

Major League Baseball also is notorious for incidents of sabotage and cheating.[94] An example is stealing the signs that the catcher transmits through hand signals to the pitcher to indicate what pitch should be thrown. The information is then relayed to the batter who now has a tremendous advantage in adjusting his swing to the pitch thrown. Sign stealing has been present "since the beginning of time," says the late Hall of Fame manager George Lee "Sparky" Anderson. Somewhat surprisingly, however, Anderson added, "And it should be." [95] As one reporter noted: "If baseball is a business, cheating is almost an accepted business practice: It's generally abided as long as it stops once it's detected."[96]

As recent as September 2017, during the height of a tight division race, the Boston Red Sox were accused of stealing signs from the New York Yankees. They did this by reviewing the video feed from their video replay room and then informing an athletic trainer in the dugout by electronic communications who, in turn, tipped the batters as to the pitcher's strategy. The MLB Commissioner fined Boston an undisclosed amount and warned that future violation could result in the loss of draft choices. That baseball has, for so long, accepted

---

93 Van Natta Jr. & Wickersham, *supra* note 83.

94 Garrett Broshuis, *Restoring Integrity to America's Pastime: Moving Towards a More Normative Approach to Cheating in Baseball* 14 TEXAS REV. OF ENT. AND SPORTS L. (2012) Available at SSRN: https://ssrn.com/abstract=2194553 or http://dx.doi.org/10.2139/ssrn.2194553.

95 Jason Turbow & Michael Duca, '*Everyone Cheats in Baseball*', THE WEEK, Mar. 19, 2010, http://theweek.com/articles/495902/everyone-cheats-baseball.

96 *Id.*

certain forms of sabotage and cheating, including sign stealing, corked bats, and spitballs, as minor infractions that are part of the game is somewhat bewildering. These actions are clearly contrary to the fundamental principles of sportsmanship that ensure healthy competition, cultivate "personal honor, virtue, and character," and "contribute to a community of respect and trust between competitors and in society."[97]

Sabotage is relatively common in sports other than baseball. In horse racing, jockeys use various techniques such as intentionally bumping into other horses. In an extreme case, a jockey stole another jockey's whip during a race.[98] Incidents of sabotage in boxing are common because as the number of athletes involved in the competition decreases the impact of sabotage will be greater on the outcome. When the event only has two competitors, like boxing, "any reduction in the opponent's probability of success leads to a one-for-one increase in one's own probability of success."[99] An example of sabotage was when Sonny Liston allegedly used a banned substance on the surface of his gloves to irritate the eyes of the opponent Muhammad Ali in their 1964 heavyweight title fight. This act of sabotage was designed to hinder Ali's performance.[100]

Sabotage incidents related to obtaining an advantage in sports wagering exist but are rare. One example occurred in 1999 when Malaysian gamblers bribed a security guard to intentionally cause the floodlights used in nighttime soccer to fail when the score was tied because an abandonment of the game at that point would be favorable to wagers that the gamblers had placed.[101] Likewise, in 2010, organized crime figures attempting to fix a game intimidated an Italian goalkeeper into taking the unusual step of sabotaging several of his teammates by spiking their drinks to damage their performance in the game.[102] Several players fell ill, and the police uncovered the

---

97 Lawal Yazid Ibrahim, *Integrity Issues in Competitive Sports*, 3 J. of Sports and Physical Educ. 67-72 (Sept.-Oct. 2016), available at http://www.iosrjournals.org/iosr-jspe/papers/Vol3-Issue5/L03056772.pdf.

98 Alasdair Brown, & Subhasish M. Chowdhury, *The Hidden Perils of Affirmative Action: Sabotage in Handicap Contests*, 133 J. of Econ. Behav. & Org. 273-284 (2017).

99 Preston et. al, *supra* note 60 at 612-624.

100 Chowdhury et. al, *supra* note 91.

101 *Man Guilty of Floodlight Plot*, BBC News, Aug. 30, 1999, http://news.bbc.co.uk/2/hi/uk_news/426092.stm; The same group successfully used the same technique in at least two prior matches. *UK Football Guard 'Bribed for* Sabotage', BBC News, Aug. 17, 1999, http://news.bbc.co.uk/2/hi/uk_news/422742.stm.

102 Sheila Norman-Culp, *Soccer Faces Epic Fight Against Match-Fixing*, Associated

scheme after one player was involved in a post-game automobile accident.[103]

Competition Manipulation

The corruption issue most often associated with sports wagering is competition manipulation—intentionally losing or playing to a predetermined result by unethically manipulating the results.[104]

Competition manipulation is as old as organized sports themselves. Incidences of athletes being bribed date to as early as the 388 BC Olympic Games.[105] Competition manipulation in professional soccer dates to the early 1900s.[106] In the United States, the "Black Sox" baseball scandal of 1919 is an icon of sports corruption. Eight members of the Chicago White Sox, including its greatest star, Shoeless Joe Jackson, were criminally charged with purposely losing the World Series. A court subsequently acquitted all eight players, but the new baseball Commissioner and former judge, Kenesaw Mountain Landis, immediately banned all eight players from professional baseball for life. While neither the courts nor subsequent legislative hearings ever revealed the corruptor behind the fix, common folklore was that a prominent member of a New York organized crime syndicate was the mastermind.[107] Moreover, for many years, Landis had to fight the influence of illegal gamblers. To help clean up baseball, he issued four

---

PRESS, Feb. 12, 2013, https://www.yahoo.com/news/soccer-faces-epic-fight-against-match-fixing-105803366--sow.html; Kevin Carpenter, *Match-Fixing—The Biggest Threat to Sport in the 21st Century?*, 2 INTERNACIONAL SPORTS L. REV. 13-23 (2012).

103 Norman-Culp, *supra* note 102.

104 Karen L. Jones, *The Applicability of the United Nations Convention Against Corruption to the Area of Sports Corruption (Match-Fixing)*, 3 THE INT'L SPORTS L.J. 57 (2012). Retrieved from https://www.questia.com/library/journal/1G1-352250314/the-applicability-of-the-united-nations-convention. The Council of Europe in its Convention on the Manipulation of Sports Competitions (or Macolin Convention) defines match-fixing as "an intentional arrangement, act or omission aimed at an improper alteration of the result or the course of a sports competition in order to remove all or part of the unpredictable nature of the aforementioned sports competition with a view to obtaining an undue advantage for oneself or for others". Council of Europe Convention on the Manipulation of Sports Competitions, Sept. 18, 2014, www.coe.int/en/web/ conventions/full-list/-/conventions/treaty/215.

105 HANDBOOK ON THE ECONOMICS OF SPORT 784-94 (Wladimir Andreff & Stefan Szymanski, eds., 2007).

106 *See* Adam Crafton, *Inside the Sensational Match-Fixing Scandal Involving Manchester United and Liverpool*, MAILONLINE (Feb. 8, 2013), http://www.dailymail.co.uk/sport/football/article-2275060/Manchester-United-Liverpool-incredible-match-fixing-scandal-1915.html.

107 Victoria Vanderveer,. *Arnold Rothstein and the 1919 World Series Fix*, HBOWATCH.COM, Archived from the original *on Sept.* 29, 2007.

more lifetime suspensions relating to illegal gambling or the bribing of players during his 24-year tenure.[108]

Competition manipulation often involves an athlete or group of athletes intentionally losing (or tying) a game, popularly called match fixing, taking a dive, or throwing the game. Match fixing can also include intentionally withdrawing from a game without sufficient reason (e.g., faking an injury) to allow a competitor to win a match or proceed to a further round by default. Athletes can engage in competition manipulation either on their own accord or in collaboration with their opponent. "Tanking" is a form of competition manipulation where a team (or athlete) intentionally underperforms without complicity of its opponent to obtain a competitive advantage such as a higher position in a future draft or a better seed in later rounds of a tournament.[109] Collaborative competition manipulation involves opponents agreeing to reach a desired conclusion. [110]

---

108 The Black Sox episode in sports history has inspired considerable scholarly and popular attention. *See* Field of Dreams (Universal Studios 1989) (an Iowa farmer hears a heavenly voice tell him, "If you build it, he will come." He interprets this message as an instruction to build a baseball field on his farm, upon which appear the spirits of Shoeless Joe Jackson and the other seven Chicago White Sox players banned from the game for throwing the 1919 World Series; W.P. Kinsella, Shoeless Joe (Mariner Books 1999) (1982) (movie based on this book); David L.Fleitz, Shoeless: The Life and Times of Joe Jackson (McFarland & Company March 2001) (a scholarly book examining arguments for and against his innocence. A theme of the book highlights that Jackson was a wise businessman whose love of money was stronger than his love of the game.); Donald Gropman & Alan M. Dershowitz, Say It Ain't So Joe!: The True Story of Shoeless Joe Jackson (Citadel 2nd Ed. 1999). (lays out evidence supporting Jackson's innocence); Kenneth Ratajczak, The Wrong Man Out (Author House 2008). (A compilation of historical facts. The last chapter includes a mock trial in which the reader is encouraged to be a juror. The author encourages readers who think Shoeless Joe is innocent to e-mail Major League Baseball and urge his reinstatement.); Eliot Asinof, Eight Men Out (Holt Paperbacks, May 1, 2000) (historical examination of the motives, backgrounds, and conditions of the players that made fixing the 1919 World Series possible); Daniel A. Nathan, *Arnold Rothstein Rigged the 1919 World Series. Or Did He?*, 2004 Legal Aff. 52, (March/April 2004) (discussion of the scandal and who might have been the mastermind behind it); James R. Devine, *Baseball's Labor Wars in Historical Context: The 1919 Chicago White Sox as a Case-Study in Owner-Player Relations*, 5 Marq. Sports L.J. 1 (1994) (analysis of why the players might have thrown the game from a labor perspective i.e. it was the only avenue they had to air their grievances regarding shared ownership and operation of the game with the owners). For a through discussion of how the Black Sox scandal brought public awareness to sports corruption, and was one of the origins of the federal Sports Bribery Act, discussed infra, *see* John T. Holden & Ryan M. Rodenberg, *The Sports Bribery Act: A Law and Economics Approach*, 42 N. Ky. L. Rev. 453 (2015).

109 *Match fixing*, http://dictionary.sensagent.com/Match%20fixing/en-en/.

110 *Id.*

Competition manipulation, however, is broader than the simply predetermining the winner or loser of the competition. Another prominent form involves manipulating the result without impacting who wins the competition, or fixing a smaller part of the contest that is not designed to impact the result. These actions are referred to as "point shaving," and "spot-fixing." Point shaving is when an athlete acts to control the game's final margin to assure that the corruptor wins point-spread bets. Rather than attempting to lose the game, the team, athlete, or another person tries to manipulate the score to gain an advantage in a sports wager. In the United States, point shaving has greatest application to football and basketball wagering because point spread betting is popular on sports that are high scoring and often have clear favorites.

Spot-fixing is when an athlete or other person predetermines the outcome of a specific aspect of a game, unrelated to the result, to allow the corruptor to win a proposition or in-game wager. This can include winning a proposition or portion of the competition but losing the game, losing a proposition or part of the competition, conceding a goal or score, or conceding a penalty. For example, some bookmakers will accept wagers on individual events within the game, such as whether the next pitch in baseball will be a ball or strike. A pitcher can manipulate that event by intentionally throwing a ball. One of the earliest reports of spot-fixing was in 1994, when former England footballer Matthew Le Tissier conspired with friends to place wagers whether the first throw-in would be before the first minute mark of the game; Le Tissier attempted to intentionally kick the ball out of bounds in the opening seconds of a match.[111]

Non-Betting Related Match Fixing

Match fixing is not always related to fixing games to win sports wagers. Non-betting-related competition manipulation that involves intentionally losing a game is almost as prevalent in some sports as betting-related competition manipulation is.[112] For example, of known incidents of competition manipulation in soccer between 2000 and 2010, over 42% were not related to betting.[113]

111 *Football Legend Matthew Le Tissier Admits His Part in Attempted £10,000 Betting Scam*, DAILY MAIL, Sept. 3, 2009, http://www.dailymail.co.uk/news/article-1210882/Football-legend-Matthew-Le-Tissier-admits-10-000-Premier-League-betting-scam.html.

112 *Id.*

113 Samantha Gorse & Simon Chadwick *The Prevalence of Corruption in International Sport*. Coventry, UK: Centre for the International Business of Sport, Coventry

Most non-betting related competition manipulation is done to obtain future position or advantage.[114] One non-betting reason to game-fix is to tank a contest to avoid having to face a stronger opponent later in a tournament or a playoff.[115] This could be present in tournaments where losing a preliminary or seeding game may place the team in a seed or bracket that provides greater opportunity to win the tournament.[116] To ensure losing a game, the competitor or team does not act with any third-party corruptor or need the cooperation of the proponent. It merely loses (tanks) the game. A team can initially rest its star players late in a regular season knowing that they will likely lose games.

The 2012 Olympics saw an extreme case of attempted non-betting related competition manipulation involving badminton teams from South Korea, China, and Indonesia.[117] The structure of seeding in the tournament allowed those teams already qualified for the next round of competition to determine the team they would play in the next round, depending on whether the particular team had won or lost its final game of the previous round. In some cases, the tournament structure motivated the team to lose intentionally because it would result in playing a weaker team in the next round. The 2012 Olympics incident was noteworthy because the teams' efforts to tank the game by dumping serves into the net and missing easy shots was evident to spectators. As a result, the Badminton World Federation suspended eight players from the teams of China, South Korea, and Indonesia.[118] This type of tanking was not limited to badminton. At the same Olympics, the coach of the women's soccer team from Japan allegedly

---

University Business School (2015). Retrieved from http://www.rga.eu.com/data/files/Press2/corruption_report.pdf.

114 Salomeja Zaksaite, *Match-Fixing: The Shifting Interplay Between Tactics, Disciplinary Offence and Crime*, 13 The Int'l Sports L.J. 287-293 (2013)(describing how chess competitors commonly agree to tie games early in long and exhausting tournaments to maintain a mental edge for later matches in the same tournament).

115 Jack Anderson, *Match Fixing and EU Policy in 2014: An Introduction.* (2014). Belfast, UK: Queen's University Belfast. Retrieved from http://papers.ssrn.com/sol3/papers.cfm?abstract_id=2449305.

116 Ed Balsdon, Lesley Fong, Mark A. Thayer, *Corruption in College Basketball? Evidence of Tanking in Post-season Conference Tournaments,* 8 J. of Sports Econ. 19-38 (2007).

117 *Disgraced South Koreans Have Bans Reduced*, Reuters, Aug. 22, 2012, https://www.reuters.com/article/us-olympics-badminton-korea-appeal/disgraced-south-koreans-have-bans-reduced-idUSBRE87L09S20120822.

118 K.C. Johnson & David Wharton, *London Olympics Badminton Scandal: Is it Always Wrong to Lose on Purpose?*, LA Times, Aug. 1, 2012, http://articles.latimes.com/2012/aug/01/sports/la-sp-oly-spirit-of-games-20120802.

instructed the team to intentionally not score against South Africa to gain a more favorable matchup in the subsequent round.[119]

Closely related are match fixes that assure both teams ascend to the next round of the tournament. In the 1982 FIFA World Cup, West Germany and Austria played a game where, if West Germany won by more than one goal, Austria was eliminated. If the game finished in a tie or West Germany won by one goal, however, both teams progressed to the next round to the detriment of a third team, Algeria. This game, called the "Disgrace of Gijón," referring to where it was played, saw West Germany win 1-0 under circumstances that led many to suspect collaborative competition manipulation.[120] The match fix worked to the advantage of West Germany, which ultimately made it to the championship game before losing to Italy.[121]

Besides manipulation to affect the selection of the next opponent or to guarantee advancement, non-betting related competition manipulation may involve how some sports governing bodies handle promotion or relegation of teams to higher or lower divisions based on their records.[122] In European soccer, teams might maintain league status, be promoted to higher leagues, or be relegated to lower leagues based on final season standings. In these cases, they may bargain with another competitor or team to let them win to secure or improve their delegation in future competitions. This barter may not be for cash or other direct compensation but an understanding that the favor might be reciprocated in the future.[123] This type of bartering can also occur in a sport like cycling where stages of a larger competition can be the subject of a bartered result that allows one team to win the stage and the other team to win the overall event.[124] One study involving an Italian soccer league found an incentive for team owners to fix

---

119 *Id.*

120 Rob Smyth, *World Cup: 25 Stunning Moments...No. 3: West Germany 1-0 Austria in 1982*, THE GUARDIAN, Feb. 25, 2014, https://www.theguardian.com/football/blog/2014/feb/25/world-cup-25-stunning-moments-no3-germany-austria-1982-rob-smyth.

121 Raul Caruso, *The Basic Economics of Match Fixing in Sport Tournaments.* 39 ECON. ANALYSIS AND POL'Y 355-377 (2009).

122 Remote Gambling Association, *Sport Betting: Commercial and Integrity Issues*, (2010). Retrieved from http://www.eu-ssa.org/wp-content/uploads/Sports-Betting-Report-FINAL.pdf.

123 Wladimir Andreff, *Corruption in Sport*; Terri Byers, *Contemporary Issues in Sport Management: A Critical Introduction*, SAGE, 2016.

124 *Id.*; *See also*, Raul Caruso (2008), *Spontaneous Match-Fixing in Sport: Cooperation in Contests*, in: THREATS TO SPORTS AND SPORTS PARTICIPATION 63-82 (P. Rodriguez, S. Késenne & J. Garcia, eds., Ediciones de la Universidad de Oviedo).

certain matches to affect the league's final standings.[125] Competition manipulation to retain rank and wages also has also been found in sumo wrestling, where wrestlers needed a certain number of victories to maintain or increase their status.[126]

Another motivation for non-betting manipulation is to reach a better position to acquire future players. In some sports, like the NBA, the draft order for amateur athletes is determined, in part, by the reverse order of teams' win/loss record.[127] Professional teams in American football, baseball, and hockey also have an incentive to tank late-season games to get a better position in the drafts of amateur athletes.[128] For this reason the NBA, where the addition of a single athlete like LeBron James can have a transformative impact, has been criticized for not taking more action to prevent teams from attempting to lose games to obtain a better draft placement.[129] Until recently, the NBA response has been timid. An NBA executive in 2008 brushed the issue aside by stating, "If we ever found a team was intentionally losing games, we would take the strongest possible action in response." He added, however, "a team that decides to change the playing time of its players after being eliminated from playoff contention is a very different story and something that occurs in our league, and others, for reasons that are entirely legitimate."[130] NBA Commissioner Adam Silver, however, has indicated that preventing tanking will have greater priority:

> We are gonna have to react and change incentives a bit. I do think it's

125 Tito Boeri & Battista Severgnini, *The Italian Job: Match Rigging, Career Concerns and Media Concentration in Serie A,* Bonn, DE: The Institute for the Study of Labor (IZA), (Oct. 2008). Retrieved from http://repec.iza.org/dp3745.pdf.

126 Mark Duggan & Steven D. Levitt, *Winning Isn't Everything: Corruption in Sumo Wrestling*. 92 Am. Econ. Rev. 1594-1605 (2000). Retrieved from http://pricetheory.uchicago.edu/levitt/Papers/DugganLevitt2002.pdf.

127 Filip Bondy, *NBA Should Revert to Unweighted Draft: 1985 Patrick Ewing Lottery Was Fairest of Them All*, NY Daily News, May 11, 2015, retrieved from http://www.nydailynews.com/sports/basketball/bondy-1985-patrick-ewing-nba-lottery-fairest-article-1.2218006.

128 Andreff & Byers, *supra* note 123.

129 Dieter Kurtenbach, *A 3-Step Process to Fix the NBA's Tanking Problem*, Fox Sports, Apr. 10, 2017, https://www.foxsports.com/nba/story/a-3-step-process-to-fix-the-nbas-tanking-problem-041017; Jody Avirgan, *How to Stop NBA Tanking: Tie Your Fate to Another Team's Record*, FiveThirtyEight, May 13, 2015, https://fivethirtyeight.com/datalab/how-to-stop-nba-tanking-tie-your-fate-to-another-teams-record/.

130 Howard Beck, *Funny Thing Happens to Knicks on the Way to the Lottery*, NY Times, March 27, 2008, http://www.nytimes.com/2008/03/27/sports/basketball/27knicks.html?mcubz=0.

> frustrating. I was talking to my European soccer men a few minutes ago, I'm not saying we are gonna do it in the NBA, but they have the best incentives of all because teams actually get relegated from the league. Think of the consequences there, they lose their television money, they lose their big-ticket revenue by not playing the top teams. So teams have every incentive not to fall to the bottom.[131]

Competition Manipulation for Betting Purposes

Competition manipulation for betting purposes is most associated with a "corruptor" bribing an athlete, athletic support personnel (including coaches, trainers, team officials or staff, agents, managers, and medical personnel), or a referee (the "targets" or "corrupted") to manipulate the game results. Corruptors are criminals that seek to exploit weaknesses in the enforcement of criminal prohibitions for commercial gain.[132] Corruptors use the pre-determined results to place wagers with the bookmaker knowing that the bet will pay off as the result of the fixed game.

Detail as to the steps in competition manipulation for wagering purposes provides context for how regulation can minimize risk. The first step is the **introduction**, which requires an opportunity to communicate directly or indirectly with the competitors or referees to initiate the bribe or blackmail.[133] Corruptors often create a barrier between themselves and the targets by using intermediaries, sometimes called "runners," to contact the targets.[134] The runners often have a trusted position with the team or the players because they are former players known to the players and team officials.[135] The runners' status as former players provides them with access to hotels, practice facilities, team events, and locker rooms not accorded most persons. This helps them to avoid suspicion.[136] The runner operates between the fixers and the targets mostly through secondary hubs

131 Bruno Manrique, *Adam Silver 'frustrated' with Teams Tanking, Will Look into Changing Incentives to Keep League Competitive*, CLUTCH POINTS, Apr. 14, 2017, https://clutchpoints.com/adam-silver-frustrated-tanking-incentives/.

132 Steve Cornelius, *South African Measures to Combat Match Fixing and Corruption in Sport*, 3 INT'L SPORTS L. J. 68 (2007).

133 Declan Hill, THE FIX: SOCCER AND ORGANIZED CRIME (McClelland & Stewart, Toronto, 2008); Declan Hill, *How Gambling Fixers Fix Football Matches*, 9 EUR. SPORT MGMT. Q. 411-32 (2009).

134 Hill "The Fix", *supra* note 133.

135 *Id., See also*, Irfan Demir, & Kutluer Karademir. *Catching Sports Cheaters: An Example of Successful Police Operations.* IN MATCH-FIXING IN INTERNATIONAL SPORTS 331-348 (Springer International Publishing, 2013).

136 Hill "The Fix", *supra* note 133.

called "project managers," often influential players on the team.[137] The opening approach by the runner to the targets is to establish a personal relationship.[138] For this reason, the runner often targets younger athletes who may welcome the attention and mentoring of a former player.

The second step is the **setup**, where the runner learns the weaknesses of players and reports these to the corruptor, who determines the best way to approach the player with an offer.[139] The first approaches may be for "minor" manipulations such as spot-fixing,[140] which is the "act of deliberately engineering an outcome within a sporting contest without attempting to alter the outcome of the contest itself."[141] In cricket, for example, the corrupted pitcher (called the bowler) can intentionally throw an illegal pitch called a "no-ball." The corruptor can profit by wagering that an agreed delivery will be a "no ball." While the no-ball will result in one-run being added to the tally of the batting team,[142] in a high scoring sport like cricket, it is unlikely to impact the outcome. The initial offers made by the corruptors are typically positive and may include money, expensive gifts (i.e., watches, cars, and vacations), introductions to women, and on some occasions, promises to transfer to a more prestigious club or more playing time.[143] In very corrupt leagues, the runners may directly offer cash bribes. In leagues with low corruption, more elaborate schemes are needed, such as learning and then exploiting players' or other persons' weaknesses.[144] Here, runners may target underpaid players or those with gambling problems by offering competition manipulation as a way to pay accumulated gambling debts.[145]Ultimately, the runners— armed with the offer—need to convince the target to accept it. If the target agrees, then the ensuing approaches may escalate to match fixing or point shaving. If the target refuses, the runner may resort to negative offers include blackmail,

137 Demir et. al, *supra* note 135.

138 IOC, *supra* note 25.

139 Demir et al., *supra* note 135.

140 IOC, *supra* note 25.

141 *Spot Fixing*, Collins English Dictionary.

142 *Understanding the No-Ball Law*, BBC, http://news.bbc.co.uk/sport2/hi/cricket/rules_and_equipment/4172990.stm (last visited Jan. 27, 2018).

143 D. Forrest, *Corruption of football by match-fixers*, Football Perspectives, Aug. 13, 2012, retrieved from http://footballperspectives.org/corruption-football-match-fixers.

144 Hill "The Fix", *supra* note 133.

145 Anderson, *supra* note 115.

duress,[146] or intimidating physical violence.[147]

The third step is the **fix**, where the corruptor analyzes the wagering markets and determines the best approach to achieving maximum profits on the wager of a game with a predetermined outcome. This includes minimizing the risk of detection.[148] The corruptor may attempt to avoid detection by placing multiple wagers in different markets through different entities or agents.[149] The agents who place wagers for the corruptor are known as "beards," "mules," or "runners."[150] When a sportsbook conducts wagering electronically in an unregulated environment, the corruptor can hide his identity by having hundreds of agents, all in impoverished areas and working for low wages, make a torrent of bets both before the game and, where in-game wagering is offered, during the game.[151] Not all agents, however, work for corruptors, as some hide the identity of the bettor for other reasons. These reasons include wanting to avoid reporting the transaction under anti-money laundering rules, or having the book refuse the wager where they would do so if they knew the identity of the actual bettor.

The fourth step is the **performance**, where the competitor (or referee) executes the acts in the sporting event necessary for the corruptor to realize his goals, i.e., win the wagers.[152] This may mean to tank the game, take a fall, to underperform, or in the case of the referee to make or not make calls in an undetectable way to achieve the desired result.

The last step is the **payoff**, which is the payment or a series of payments to the corrupted person. This may be in addition to upfront money given when the corrupt offer is accepted.[153]

Beneficiaries of Competition Manipulation

Competition manipulation principally benefits two groups: (1) the corrupted, such as athletes, athletic support personnel and referees who take bribes or other benefits and agree to influence a game's outcome;[154] and (2) the corruptors who arrange or collaborators who

146 K. Hudson & R. Findley, *Corruption: Agreeing to Match Fixing Under Duress: Analysis*, 8 WORLD SPORTS L. ADVOC. 14-16 (2010).

147 Demir et al., *supra* note 135.

148 Hill "The Fix", *supra* note 133.

149 *Id.*

150 *Id.*

151 Associated Press, *The Beautiful Game? Match-Fixing Leaves Ugly Mark on Soccer*, NY DAILY NEWS, Feb. 14, 2013, http://www.nydailynews.com/sports/more-sports/beautiful-game-match-fixing-leaves-ugly-mark-soccer-article-1.1262098.

152 Hill "The Fix," *supra* note 133.

153 *Id.*

154 Serguei Cheloukhine, *Match Fixing in Soccer: Organization, Structure and Policing: A*

know of the fix and can manipulate or cheat betting markets.

Like other criminals, successful corruptors seek opportunities where they can make significant profits with minimal risk. They are drawn to competition manipulation because they can operate on an international basis with virtual anonymity, and can easily recruit the corrupted because of lax criminal laws, limited law enforcement efforts or experience, and corrupt or inept sports governing bodies.[155] The corruptor can place wagers on corrupt competitions and be guaranteed a winning wager.[156]

Foreign markets have dealt with the involvement of illegal bookmakers in competition manipulation.[157] Spot fixing controversies in India's high profile cricket league, IPL, suggest that underground bookmakers were involved in fixing.[158] Corrupt bookmakers can engage in competition manipulation to improve profits. A bookmaker with knowledge of the results can manipulate prices to favor the bribed team or athlete.[159] Bettors who are aware of the fix will seek to wager on the bribed team.[160] As the corruptor has assurances from the bribed team that these bets will lose, the corruptor has increased his profit far above what honest bookmaking can make by offering the wagering on the same game.[161] More commonly, the favored team is the target, "because then the reduction in the probability of the bribed team's win is proportionately greater, so much so that almost all bettors, including the most pessimistic ones, can be induced to bet on the bribed team."[162]

Criminals can also use competition manipulations to improve the efficiency of money laundering, which is the process by which criminals disguise money that they receive from criminal activities to make it appear that they generated it by lawful means. This is

---

Russian Perspective, in MATCH-FIXING IN INTERNATIONAL SPORTS, EXISTING PROCESS, LAW ENFORCEMENT AND PREVENTATIVE STRATEGIES 113-132 (M. R. Haberfield & D. Sheehan eds. 2013).

155 IOC, *supra* note 25.

156 Rebeggiani, *supra* note 10.

157 When reviewing the American sports wagering industry, the primary factor that would impact the willingness of bookmakers to engage in match fixing is whether the bookmaker is operating in an illegal or unregulated environment. Preston et. al, *supra* note 60 at 612-624.

158 Ed Hawkins, '*Fixing? Its People Like Us Doing It*', ESPNCRICINFO, May 22, 2013, http://www.espncricinfo.com/magazine/content/story/637034.html.

159 Parimal Kanti Bag & Bibhas Saha. *Corrupt Bookmaking in a Fixed Odds Illegal Betting Market*, 127 THE ECON. J. 624-652 (2017).

160 *Id.*

161 *Id.*

162 *Id.*

done to prevent law enforcement from tracing the money to its illicit sources.[163]

Money laundering involves three steps. The first is placement, which involves changing the form of the funds into a less suspicious, more easily manipulated form. Placement is the most well-known phase of money laundering. Criminals like drug dealers tend to accumulate their money in smaller denominations from the sale of drugs to customers. These funds tend to be bulky and awkward to transport. Therefore, methods need to be devised to convert the smaller bills into larger bills, bank checks, money orders, traveler's checks, or some other form of a cash equivalent.[164]

The next step is to layer the funds. Layering is the method by which criminals distance the criminal activity from the converted funds. The idea is to provide a series of financial transactions that inhibit the ability of law enforcement to track the money back to its source. Criminals can use wagering at sportsbooks to give the appearance that money earned from illegal activities was won by wagering on sporting events.[165]

---

163 Anthony Cabot & Joseph Kelly, *Internet, Casinos and Money Laundering*, 2 J. OF MONEY LAUNDERING CONTROL 134-147 (1998), available at https://doi.org/10.1108/eb027180.

164 Using internet sportsbooks for "placement" is difficult. Internet sportsbooks are not set up to accept cash. Instead, they must use an intermediary to obtain money from the bettor. Some unternet sportsbooks, however, facilitate placement by using runners that will physically pick up cash from customers and the internet sportsbook will credit their accounts with the amount received. This is a significant advantage to the criminal who can then wager conservatively and withdraw the funds in either larger denominations or through check, wire transfer or another method. Properly regulated sportsbooks are poor venues for placement because they have requirements for reporting all major cash transactions to the government and must return cash deposits in the same currency denominations as received by the player.

165 A more likely scenario for the use of sportsbooks to launder money is in the layering process. A value of involving sportsbooks is that the funds can be disguised as winnings. For example, a drug dealer could set up multiple accounts with the sportsbook in an unregulated environment. A drug dealer can guarantee an equal amount of winnings and losings by betting both sides of an event and paying the "vig" on the losing wagers. Some accounts result in the drug dealer "losing" all the deposited funds, while other accounts result in the drug dealer "winning." Even paying a 5% vig on the losing wagers provides the drug dealer with an inexpensive way to layer funds. The drug dealer can then transfer funds from the winning accounts to an internet bank in the "layering" process. To anyone investigating the trail, the funds appear to be internet sportsbook winnings. In a regulated environment, sportsbooks prevent layering through "suspicious activity reporting," and "knowing the customer." Organized crime that uses wagering to launder money can regain their money back after it has been laundered by merely betting both sides of each proposition and paying the vig or commission. Criminal-controlled sportsbooks can earn more than 100% return by being the house and-

The last step is integration, which involves transferring the layered funds from the foreign country into a mainstream financial world through a transaction that has a legitimate commercial purpose.

Victims of Competition Manipulation

Bettors

Bettors who are unaware of the fix and bet the losing side of the fixed game are direct financial victims because they have no chance to win.

Sportsbooks

Honest sportsbooks that accept wagers on a fixed contest face the prospect of an unbalanced pool because of the addition of wagers placed by corruptors. In this case, every dollar that they accept from persons with knowledge of the fix is a dollar lost. In some cases, however, the sportsbook may adjust the odds or lines to encourage wagers on the presumptive losing wager in order to balance the money coming from the corruptors. When this occurs, the sportsbook faces the prospect of being middled or sided.[166] These books also may suffer the future loss of business when bettors refuse to place further bets because they fear the results may be fixed.[167]

The Sport's Governing Body, Sponsors, and Related Industries

A sports league hit with significant competition manipulation scandals is likely to experience a decline in revenues when sponsors withdraw their support and fans do not buy tickets. Fans lose interest in a sport if they do not believe the games are fair and the outcomes are

---

betting strategically into their pools. If these same criminals are engaged in competition manipulation, they can influence the betting markets to place wagers on the losing side of wagers by offering better point spreads or odds on these wagers. Likewise, criminals that engage in competition manipulation can earn extraordinary returns while laundering money merely by wagering more heavily on the rigged competitions.

166 For example, suppose New England is a 10-point favorite over Cleveland. A corruptor has convinced a player on New England to assure that the Patriots wins by fewer than 10 points. The corruptor will then bet heavily on Cleveland. If this moves the line, the sportsbook makes New England an 8-point favorite to encourage wagering on New England to balance the book. If New England were to win by 9 points, the book will lose wagers placed by the corruptor and all the bets placed on New England at 8 points.

167 Helmut Dietl & Christian Weingärtner, *Betting Scandals and Attenuated Property Rights – How Betting Related Match Fixing Can Be Prevented in the Future*, Feb. 2012, https://ideas.repec.org/p/iso/wpaper/0154.html.

predetermined rather than based on the abilities of the competitors.[168] Anecdotal evidence of the decline of fan interest occurred with professional soccer leagues in China, Singapore, Malaysia, and Italy.[169] In the latter case, the 2006/2007 Italian Serie A season saw about a 20% decrease in the number of spectators the year after a competition manipulation scandal.[170]

Likewise, sponsorship money is important to the success of most professional sports. The sponsor may have wasted advertising dollars or incurred brand damage as the result of a betting scandal. Sponsors protect their brands and often withdraw their sponsorship if the league or sport fails to maintain a scandal-free reputation. For example, in 2015, Pepsi Cola terminated a multimillion-dollar sponsorship agreement with the Indian Premier League (IPL) because of competition manipulation scandals.[171] Likewise, a Chinese soccer league failed after Pirelli withdrew its support following a competition manipulation scandal.[172]

Sports governing bodies also incur direct costs from competition manipulation including the cost of preventative measures, investigations, and in some cases compensating the disadvantaged team.[173] In one incident, a German soccer team was paid by the league after the discovery that a referee manipulated the game.[174]

Competition manipulation can impact other sectors such as broadcasters and merchandisers. Diminished fan interest in a sport inhibits successful commercialization and lowers the prospects for private investment."[175] Public funding for sports, including new stadiums, also is more difficult to acquire after a major competition

---

168 Adam Hosmer-Henner, *Preventing Game Fixing: Sportsbooks as Information Markets*, 14 GAMING L. REV. & ECON. 31-38 (2010).

169 Hill "The Fix," *supra* note 133.

170 *Weltfussball*, Serie A 2005/2006. (2011) Retrieved from http://www.weltfussball.de/zuschauer/ita-serie-a-2005-2006/1/.

171 *The Challenges of Betting*, SPORTSRADAR SECURITY SERVICES, http://www.sportmalta.org.mt/wp-content/uploads/2016/03/3_marcello-presilla-1.pdf (last visited Feb. 1, 2018).

172 David Forrest, *Match Fixing: An Economics Perspective*, in *Match-Fixing in International Sports* in MATCH-FIXING IN INTERNATIONAL SPORTS, EXISTING PROCESS, LAW ENFORCEMENT AND PREVENTATIVE STRATEGIES 177-197 (M. R. Haberfield & D. Sheehan eds. 2013).

173 *DFB Verlangt 1, 8 Millionen Euro Von Hoyzer*, SÜDDEUTSCHE ZEITUNG, Retrieved from http://www.sueddeutsche.de/sport/manipulierte-spiele-dfbverlangt-millionen-euro-von-hoyzer-1.728303

174 *Id.*

175 Rebeggiani, *supra* note 10.

manipulation scandal; claims that sports emphasizes admirable values such as fair competition, sportsmanship, and community pride lose credibility.[176]

Non-corrupt Players

Competition manipulation can damage non-corrupt players in different ways. The general damage to the reputation of the league or sport impacts the interest in and commercialization of the sport. This could result in lower salaries and the value of endorsements for the athletes. Moreover, non-corrupt teammates of corrupt players can be unfairly associated with the scandal and incur a more direct impact on their careers and endorsements.

PREREQUISITES FOR COMPETITION MANIPULATION

The transaction between the corruptor and the corrupted athlete concerning competition manipulation is nothing more than a contract, albeit an illegal contract. The corruptor makes an offer to the target, such as paying a monetary bribe if the athlete agrees to shave points off his team's total. The targeted athlete can accept or reject the bribe. If he accepts the bribe, he is promising to deliver specific results consistent with the terms of the contract, such as keeping his team's margin of victory to below an agreed point spread.

Attempts at curtailing illegal competition manipulation contracts should focus on the conditions that deter the prospective corruptor from making a bribe or the target from accepting it. Before making a bribe, the corruptor will consider the opportunities, potential benefits, and risks associated with engaging in competition manipulation. The corruptor needs to:

- Have access to liquid betting market(s) that can handle the level of wagering necessary to ensure the sporting event's manipulation will be financially beneficial.
- Place wagering into these markets with minimal risk of detection by law enforcement or the sport's governing bodies.[177]
- Have minimal risk that the target will report the approach.[178]

---

176 *Id.*

177 If the fixer is also a bookmaker operating in an unregulated market, they can more easily create the wagers necessary to profit and avoid detection.

178 Jack Anderson, *Match Fixing and Money Laundering* (2014), https://papers.ssrn.com/sol3/papers.cfm?abstract_id=2424755.

- Extend an offer (reward) consistent with maintaining the profitability of the competition manipulation that the target would find attractive despite the potential consequences of detection (risks).
- Have access to the target to convey the bribe and coordinate the competition manipulation
- Have reasonable certainty that the target can produce the desired results.[179]

The following discussion explores these conditions in greater detail.

Condition One: Access to Liquid Betting Market(s) That Can Handle the Level of Wagering Necessary to Ensure the Competition Manipulation Will Be Financially Beneficial

Having the ability to corrupt athletes is worthless unless the corruptor can place wagers of the type and size necessary to earn significant returns on their money. Corruptors need access to a betting market(s) that can handle these high levels of wagering.

Over the past twenty years, the internet has created large, easily accessible betting markets. Sports wagering lends itself well to online platforms because bettors no longer need to place a bet locally with a legal book, or place a bet with a local illegal bookie over the phone or at a neighborhood bar or deli.[180] Internet sports wagering offers many advantages to the bettor including convenience, lower risk of being caught where wagering is illegal, more bet types, more games offered, and the ability to shop different sportsbooks for better odds. The convenience is important. In real time, a person physically in the United States or elsewhere can access a sportsbook in an unregulated or under-regulated country by computer or smartphone and place a wager on an almost endless variety of global sporting events.[181]

Many illegal operators establish their internet operations in Asia and in countries that have little oversight and a favorable tax structure.[182] A bettor almost anywhere in the world may have the

---

179 *Id.*

180 Ryan M. Rodenberg & Anastasios Kaburakis, *Legal and Corruption Issues in Sports Gambling*, 23 J. OF LEGAL ASPECTS OF SPORT 8, 29 (2013).

181 *Protecting the Integrity of Sport Competition-The Last Bet for Modern Sport*, SPORT INTEGRITY RESEARCH PROGRAMME, 2012-2014 at 9.

182 Emine Bozkurt, *Match Fixing and Fraud in Sport: Putting the Pieces Together* (Sept. 17, 2012) available at http://www.europarl.europa.eu/document/activities/

option of up to 8,000 operators that offer sports bets, about 80% of which are in unregulated or under-regulated countries with low tax rates.[183] For Americans, popular online bookmakers operate in Costa Rica, Antigua, and Curaçao.[184] For much of the rest of the world, Asian sportsbooks are the most popular markets. Estimates of the size of the handle in the illegal Asian sports betting market are as high as $1 trillion, with Interpol putting the estimate at $500 billion.[185]

Distinguishing between the handle and gross gaming win is essential in understanding the size of all sports betting markets, legal and illegal. The handle refers to the total amount of all wagers placed by bettors. In contrast, gross gaming win is the amount retained by the bookmakers after paying out all winning wagers. Estimates put the handle of the global wagering market between $3 and $8 trillion.[186] The unregulated sports wagering sector contributes far larger amounts than the regulated industry to these figures.[187] In 2017, the gross win for legal sports wagering was about $70 billion; the gross win in the illegal markets was between 2.5 and 6.5 times greater.[188]

---

cont/201209/20120925ATT52303/20120925ATT52303EN.pdf.

183 Protecting the Integrity of Sport Competition, *supra* note 181.

184 James Glanz, Agustin Armendariz, & Walt Bogdanich, *The Offshore Game of Online Sports Betting*, NY Times, Oct. 25, 2015, https://www.nytimes.com/2015/10/26/us/pinnacle-sports-online-sports-betting.html?mcubz=0; Walt Bogdanich, James Glanz, & Agustin Armendariz, *Cash Drops and Keystrokes: The Dark Reality of Sports Betting and Daily Fantasy Games*, NY Times, Oct. 15, 2015, https://www.nytimes.com/interactive/2015/10/15/us/sports-betting-daily-fantasy-games-fanduel-draftkings.html.

185 Declan Hill, *Jumping into Fixing*, 18 Trends in Organized Crime 212 (2015).

186 *Global Sports Gambling Worth "Up to $3 Trillion"*, Daily Mail, Apr. 15, 2015, http://www.dailymail.co.uk/wires/afp/article-3040540/Global-sports-gambling-worth-3-trillion.html. The exact size of the illegal sports wagering industry in the United States is unknown. Eilers Research estimated the market handle (total amount wagered) at $160.3 billion, using the United Kingdom as a benchmark and then adjusting for other variables. *Daily Fantasy Sports: The Future of U.S. Sports Wagering?*, Eilers Research, Oct. 16, 2014, Retrieved from http://eilersresearch.com/services/market-research/. In countries where sports wagering is legal, the market share averages 13.8% of all revenues from legal gambling but is as high as 39.1% in the United Kingdom and 16% in Australia.

If the U.S. underground market is 14% of the total legal gambling market, then its gross gaming revenue would be about $14 billion, and its handle would be nearly $280 billion. Jordan Weissmann, *Big Bucks or Bogus Betting Baloney?*, Slate, Nov. 21, 2014, http://www.slate.com/articles/business/moneybox/2014/11/adam_silver_says_there_s_400_billion_per_year_of_illegal_sports_betting.html. In contrast, the legal sports wagering markets have a handle of about $4.5 billion with a net win of a little over $260 million.

187 Remote Gambling Association, *supra* note 122.

188 The world's gross gaming win from all legal sports wagering was estimated to be $58 billion in 2012, with a handle that would be about $1.2 trillion. *Global Sports Betting: The*

The large handle for Asian bookmakers helps them distribute fixed costs more efficiently. Some of these savings accrue to the benefit of the bettors because the illegal operators offer better betting odds in order to be competitive. [189] The Asian bookmakers maintain a house advantage of about 3% compared to the 5-10% provided by American and European bookmakers. Besides better odds, bettor and corruptors are attracted to Asian and other unregulated bookmakers because they can offer more bet types and higher bet limits.[190]

In the US, the legal and illegal markets are much smaller. The exact size of the illegal sports wagering industry in the United States is unknown. No studies support the figures often quoted $400 billion handle in the underground market.[191] Regardless of methodology or accuracy, however, the market is undeniably significant. One commentator noted: "Ultimately, we do not need to know the exact dollar amount that Americans wager each year…Even if it were simply $100 billion rather than $400 billion, it would still be a huge market."[192] In contrast, the legal sports wagering markets have a handle of about $4.5 billion with a net win of a little over $260 million.[193]

A major reason why American sports may have avoided many of the recent international scandals involving competition manipulation is our betting markets are somewhat detached from some of the world's largest wagering markets. Our most popular sports for wagering, American football, basketball, and baseball, have limited wagering volume outside the United States. About 65% of all wagering on the world markets is on soccer, followed by cricket and tennis at about 12% each.[194] Wagering on the National Basketball Association, however, was introduced in Asia about a decade ago,[195] and is increasing in popularity. Moreover, for the professional sports leagues, globalization

---

State of Play, GLOBAL BETTING AND GAMING CONSULTANTS, June 17, 2013, Retrieved from http://www.gbgc.com/global-sports-betting-the-state-of-play/ Legal sports wagering grew by an average of 5.4% per year between 2001 and 2014. Elliott R. Morss, *Gambling - Asia and the U.S. are 2 Different Worlds*, Apr. 15, 2014, Retrieved from http://seekingalpha.com/article/2143343-gambling-asia-and-the-u-s-are-2-different-worlds.

189 *Id.*

190 Rebeggiani, *supra* note 10.

191 Weissmann, *supra* note 186.

192 Weissmann, *supra* note 186.

193 *See* Chapter 1.

194 *Football Betting—The Global Gambling Industry Worth Billions*, BBC SPORT, Oct. 3, 2013, http://www.bbc.com/sport/football/24354124; Daily Mail, *supra* note 186.

195 Associated Press, *World Cup Highlights Asia's Illegal Betting Boom*, USA TODAY, June 18, 2014, https://www.usatoday.com/story/sports/soccer/2014/06/18/world-cup-highlights-asias-illegal-betting-boom/10726143/.

is highly desirable. Along with Major League Baseball and NBA,[196] the NFL has actively sought to extend its audience outside of the United States and into regions with a high penetration of sports wagering.[197] Most significantly, the NFL has expressed interest in expanding its offerings into Europe, where sports wagering is the most popular form of gambling. In 2013, Commissioner Goodell stated that:

> Right now, our focus is on the U.K. since the European fans can get here. We want to build on our success here, and whether it leads to a permanent franchise or not, then we can see. What happens here will dictate that.[198]

Even though American sports are not especially popular in most illegal global markets, they are gaining in popularity, and have wagering volume far greater than Nevada's legal market. As the volume of sporting bets increases globally so does the opportunity for competition manipulation. There are several reasons for this.[199]

First, more liquidity in betting markets allows corruptors to bet larger volumes and increase the profitability of competition manipulation.[200] Second, corruptors can realize greater returns with increased liquidity because they can wager more without causing the line to change or odds to change to their disadvantage.[201] Third, high betting volume in the liquid markets masks irregular betting patterns.[202] Fourth, larger markets allow sportsbooks to offer more bet types, which in turn, gives the corruptor more opportunities to spot-fix,[203] an activity which is harder to detect and offers more manageable ways to bribe athletes. Fifth, as the betting volume increases on minor games with lower paid or otherwise vulnerable

---

196 Sam Riches, *Basketball and Globalization*, The New Yorker, Oct. 7, 2013, http://www.newyorker.com/business/currency/basketball-and-globalization.

197 *Goodell Wants Teams in London and L.A., in No Particular Order*, Sporting News, Oct. 26, 2013, http://www.sportingnews.com/nfl/story/2013-10-26/roger-goodell-franchises-london-los-angeles-la-globalization-nfl-commissioner.

198 *Id.*

199 Forrest et. al, *supra* note 49.

200 *Id.*; Rebeggiani, *supra* note 10.

201 Forrest et. al, *supra* note 49.

202 *Id.*

203 Spot-fixing is when an athlete or other person predetermines the outcome of a specific aspect of a game, unrelated to the result, to allow the corruptor to win a proposition or in-game wager. For example, some bookmakers will accept wagers on individual events within the game, such as whether the next pitch in baseball will be a ball or strike. A pitcher can manipulate that event by intentionally throwing a ball. Still another form includes intentionally withdrawing from a game without sufficient reason (e.g., faking an injury) to allow a competitor to win a match or proceed to a further round by default.

athletes, they can profit from the fix and can more easily, and cheaply, bribe the participants.[204]

Condition Two: Ability to Place Wagering Into These Markets with an Acceptably Minimal Risk of Detection by Law Enforcement or the Sport's Governing Bodies

Even with the existence of large wagering markets, the corruptor needs to place the wagers on the fixed events without detection by law enforcement (who can prosecute the corruptor), the sports governing authorities (who can discipline the athletes and alert law enforcement), and the legitimate bookmakers or their regulators (who can void the bets and alert law enforcement). Risk of detection and criminal prosecution is a significant factor in whether a player, referee, or anyone else is likely to accept a bribe to fix a game.[205] As detection becomes more probable, competition manipulation declines.[206]

Two significant factors impact the likelihood of detection.[207] The first is the difficulty that law enforcement encounters when investigating competition manipulation. Before the internet, countries had much greater control over sports wagering because wagering typically occurred within the borders of a single country by persons acting as bookies or agents interacting directly with the bettors. In that case, the government could enforce proscriptions on the sports wagering contracts through its exclusive power to compel conformity to rules by force within its borders.[208] When US states had difficulty in the 1950s controlling illegal sports wagering operations that crossed state borders, they sought federal assistance because the bookmaking operations were still within US national borders. Congress passed the Federal Wire Act, the Travel Act, and the Illegal Gambling Business

---

204 Forrest et. al, *supra* note 49.

205 Forrest, *supra* note 172.

206 Forrest et. al, *supra* note 54 at 598-611.

207 Other factors that impact the likelihood of detection are the existence of wagering markets where the bookmakers are unlikely to reveal information regarding irregular betting patterns, and wagering markets that do not share information on betting patterns. These factors are more likely to be present in jurisdictions with illegal sportsbooks than regulated jurisdictions.

208 According to German social theorist, Max Weber, "state is a human community that (successfully) claims the monopoly of the legitimate use of physical force within a given territory." Max Weber, *Politics as a Vocation*, in FROM MAX WEBER: ESSAYS IN SOCIOLOGY 77 (H. H. Gerth & C. Wright Mills eds. & trans., Oxford Univ. Press 1967); Max Weber, THE THEORY OF SOCIAL AND ECONOMIC ORGANIZATION 154 (1964).

Act, which gave the Federal Bureau of Investigation and federal authorities jurisdiction to investigate and prosecute these operations.

Attempting to enforce US laws on foreign internet operators, however, is difficult even with the cooperation of international law enforcement. Global illegal and unregulated wagering markets frustrate investigations that detect and sanction competition manipulation. Police need evidence to successfully prosecute offenders, including: (i) documentation of the wager; (ii) video or observation evidence of the match showing the fix; (iii) telecommunications data; (iv) witness testimony; and (v) expert analytical evidence.[209] Most of these evidentiary needs are difficult to satisfy when the corrupt activity occurs across multiple borders. The corruptors understand the challenges facing law enforcement and exploit them by deliberately establishing complicated and clandestine structures with multiple layers of protected criminals in corrupt countries. [210] Moreover, even if the countries were not corrupt, the lack of international cooperation is further frustrated by different legal structures, languages, and law enforcement cultures and priorities.[211] For example, the corruptor may keep his bankroll in separate accounts in multiple countries, open and fund accounts with bookmakers in several other countries,[212] and place wagers on an event that occurs in still another country.[213]

A series of cases in the last 20 years involving European soccer illustrates the global-reach of Asian criminal organizations that leverage the enormous liquidity of unregulated Asian internet sports wagering markets to fix matches internationally.[214] The international criminal nature of sports corruption is evident in soccer, which has global popularity. In 2009, German police uncovered competition manipulation across multiple European countries in a scandal known as the Bochum Competition Manipulation. Police suspected that the

---

209 Ben Gunn & Jeff Rees, *Environmental Review of Integrity in Professional Tennis* at 10, May 2008, available at http://www.sportingintelligence.com/wp-content/uploads/2011/01/Integrity-in-tennis.pdf.

210 Duggan & Levitt, *supra* note 126.

211 Thomas Feltes, *Match Fixing in Western Europe*, in Match-Fixing in International Sports, Existing Process, Law Enforcement and Preventative Strategies 15 (M. R. Haberfield & D. Sheehan eds. 2013).

212 Forrest et. al, *supra* note 49.

213 *Id.*

214 Pascal Boniface et. al, *Sports Betting and Corruption: How to Preserve the Integrity of Sport,* Feb. 13, 2013, Retrieved from http://www.sportaccord.com/media/news/others/publication-of-an-international-study-sports-betting-and-corruption-how-to-preserve-sports-integrity-0-15908/?sphrase_id=173.

criminal network involved over 200 persons that allegedly fixed over 300 soccer matches in ten countries: Germany, Belgium, Switzerland, Turkey, Slovenia, Hungary, Croatia, Austria, Bosnia, and Canada.[215] Singapore-based financers, backed by Chinese organized crime, paid bribes of up to €100,000 that enabled them to make wagers in the millions of Euros.[216] The trail of money from the wagers and the bribes involved 11 countries: Malaysia, China, Isle of Man, Singapore, Russia, Turkey, Malta, Austria, Germany, the Netherlands, and Slovenia.[217] Four years later, EUROPOL, the European Union's Law Enforcement Agency, claimed that an 18 month investigation uncovered an Asian crime syndicate, working with European criminal networks, that fixed more than 680 matches over three years in 15 countries, involving 425 match officials, club officials, players, and criminals under suspicion.[218]

Increasing the likelihood of detection is a high priority for law enforcement in investigating and prosecuting competition manipulation. The same is true for the sport governing authorities that seek to prevent, investigate, and sanction sports corruption.

Without having a set of effective laws, and the motivation to enforce those laws, wagering-related sports corruption will go undetected. The focus of federal criminal laws must be on detecting and prosecuting both competition manipulation and illegal wagering that fosters such sports corruption. Both federal and most state governments have basic criminal code provisions regarding competition manipulation, but the laws are not comprehensive.

One example of a US law addressing this problem is the federal Sports Bribery Act (18 U.S.C. § 224), passed in 1964, which provides:

> Bribery in sporting contests
>
> (a) Whoever carries into effect, attempts to carry into effect, or conspires with any other person to carry into effect any scheme in commerce to influence, in any way, by bribery any sporting contest, with knowledge that the purpose of such scheme is to influence by bribery that contest, shall be fined under this title, or imprisoned not more than 5 years, or both.
>
> (b) This section shall not be construed as indicating an intent on the part of Congress to occupy the field in which this section operates to the exclusion of a law of any State, territory, Commonwealth, or

---

215 IOC, *supra* note 25.

216 *Id.*

217 *Id.*

218 Sara Hefny, *Europol Investigation of Match Fixing in Soccer Reveals Widespread Corruption*, 29 INT'L ENFORCEMENT L. REP. 117 (2013).

possession of the United States, and no law of any State, territory, Commonwealth, or possession of the United States, which would be valid in the absence of the section shall be declared invalid, and no local authorities shall be deprived of any jurisdiction over any offense over which they would have jurisdiction in the absence of this section.

(c) As used in this section-

(1) The term "scheme in commerce" means any scheme effectuated in whole or in part through the use in interstate or foreign commerce of any facility for transportation or communication;

(2) The term "sporting contest" means any contest in any sport, between individual contestants or teams of contestants (without regard to the amateur or professional status of the contestants therein), the occurrence of which is publicly announced before its occurrence;

(3) The term "person" means any individual and any partnership, corporation, association, or other entity.

The federal law set out above, like most state laws, does not cover all potential issues that can arise. For example, no reference is made to insider trading, or where an athlete is not bribed but engages in competition manipulation to make money in the wagering markets. Neither this federal law nor any state laws are sufficiently comprehensive to cover modern global competition manipulation.

The commitment of the federal government to enforcement of the laws related to illegal wagering and sports corruption is not robust. Both sets of crimes have lower priority than other offenses. According to one source, the Federal Bureau of Investigation stopped actively pursuing leads for competition manipulation investigations in the mid-1980s.[219] Recent competition manipulation scandals that the FBI has pursued, he claimed, such as that involving NBA referee Tim Donaghy, and the competition manipulations involving the University of San Diego, University of Toledo, Northwestern University, and Boston College resulted from leads generated in other cases.[220]

This state of affairs is consistent with the low priority that law enforcement has recently placed on gambling-related crimes generally. US law enforcement efforts to deal with illegal gambling have declined dramatically in the past fifty years. In 1960, U.S. law enforcement agencies made almost 123,000 arrests for unlawful

219 Brian Tuohy, *How to Fix an NFL Game*, Vice Sports, Oct. 24, 2014, https://sports.vice.com/en_us/article/kbv9ge/how-to-fix-an-nfl-game.

220 *Id.*

gambling. According to the FBI, 11,951 state and federal law enforcement agencies made only 6,024 arrests for illegal gambling in 2013.[221] Equally telling, the percentage of gambling arrests is down 37.6% since 2009.[222] That amounts to about 2.1 arrests per 100,000 inhabitants.[223] In the Northeast and West, the rates are less than one arrest per 100,000 residents. A given resident in those regions is about three times more likely to be arrested for murder than for gambling.[224] Practically speaking, outside of occasional high-profile arrests,[225] the enforcement of gambling laws is exceedingly rare – and becoming even more so – in the United States.

Many reasons may contribute to this non-enforcement. First, federal laws and prosecutorial policies have become increasingly confusing and contradictory.[226] Therefore, prosecutors may be less eager to test the laws for fear of creating dangerous precedents. Second, the penalties that the courts assess against those who violate sports betting laws are often low, and rarely justify law enforcement's time or expense. Relatedly, there is a perception among some prosecutors that the pursuit of these cases does not put a dent in the underground economy. Third, improvements in technology, such as the internet, have made it harder to detect and prosecute offenders.[227] Attempting to apprehend and prosecute gambling operators in foreign countries is a challenge. Fourth, the public may not perceive sports gambling as a serious crime or even as a crime at all. In the United States, wagering on fantasy sports is widespread. Office pools on sporting events, such as the NCAA basketball tournament and the NFL's Super Bowl, flourish.[228] Governors and mayors have frequently marked

221 Federal Bureau of Investigation. *Estimated Number of Arrests*, Washington, DC: Federal Bureau of Investigation. (2013). Retrieved from http://www.fbi.gov/about-us/cjis/ucr/crime-in-the-u.s/2013/crime-in-the-u.s.-2013/tables/table-29/table_29_estimated_number_of_arrests_united_states_2013.xls.

222 *Id.*

223 *Id.*

224 *Id.*

225 In 2011, various law enforcement agencies announced charges against 10 off-shore books that accepted US players. Ryan M. Rodenberg and Anastasios Kaburakis, *Legal and Corruption Issues in Sports Gambling*, 23 J. OF LEGAL ASPECTS OF SPORT 8-35 (2013).

226 Anthony N. Cabot & Louis V. Csoka, *The Games People Play: Is it Time for a New Legal Approach to Prize Games?* 4 NEV. L.J., 197 (2004). Retrieved from http://scholars.law.unlv.edu/cgi/viewcontent.cgi?article=1286&context=nlj.

227 *See* text accompanying footnotes 207 -213, *supra*.

228 *March Madness: How to Win Your Office Pool*, THE FISCAL TIMES, Mar. 14, 2013, http://www.thefiscaltimes.com/Articles/2013/03/14/March-Madness-How-to-Win-Your-Office-Pool.

championship games by "friendly" bets between themselves.[229] Even former President Obama and Canadian Prime Minister Harper publicized a wager of a case of beer on the outcome of the men's and women's hockey games at the 2014 Winter Olympics – online, via Twitter, no less.[230] The media has contributed to the public perception that gambling on sports is an enjoyable and legal pastime. The National Gambling Impact Study Commission in the United States claimed that because point spreads are available in major U.S. newspapers, the public does not understand that sports wagering is illegal.[231] Since most states have laws against sports wagering, law enforcement is in the uncomfortable position of enforcing laws unpopular among the public.

Because of these attitudes of law enforcement in the US, it is important that sports governing bodies emphasize preventing, investigating, and not sanctioning sports corruption. The commitment of those bodies is essential for both detecting competition manipulation as well as increasing the likelihood that the targeted athlete will report approaches that will lead to the initiation of a criminal investigation. This is discussed below.

Condition Three: The Risk and Consequences That the Target Will Report the Approach

After being approached with a bribe, athletes will assess their risks of not reporting an approach by a corruptor. Whether the athlete reports it may depend on the reputation of the league for corruption, and the governing bodies' commitment to internal rules and enforcement. Corruptors target leagues or sports where the

229 *Kentucky, Wisconsin Governors Bet Bourbon to Root Beer, Cheese*, Channel 3000, Apr. 3, 2015, Retrieved from http://www.channel3000.com/news/kentucky-wisconsin-governors-bet-bourbon-to-root-beer-cheese/32178412.

Hunter Schwarz, *The Annual Super Bowl Governors Bet Has More Governors Than Ever Since New England Isn't a State*. Wash. Post, Jan. 29, 2015, http://www.washingtonpost.com/blogs/govbeat / wp/2015/ 01/29/the-annual-super-bowl-governors-bet-has-more-governors-than-ever-since-new-england-isnt-a-state/.

230 Luke Fox, *Harper Wins 48 Beers from Obama on Hockey Bet*, Sportsnet, Feb. 21, 2014, http://www.sportsnet.ca/olympics/harper-obama-make-tasty-usa-canada-hockey-bet/.

231 National Gambling Impact Study Commission, *Final Report*, 2-14 (1999) Available at http://govinfo.library.unt.edu/ngisc/reports/2.pdf; *See generally*, Adam Weidner, *Sports Gambling in the Cyberspace Era* Chapman L. Rev., http://www.chapmanlawreview.com/archives/923 (accessed March 31, 2017).

governing bodies do not have integrity rules, have rules but fail to enforce them, or the league itself is enmeshed in corruption. This allows the corruptor to target and pursue athletes and others with bribe offers by representing that such activity is unlikely to be detected and is not out of character for the sport.[232]

When faced with the prospect of sports bribery, the targeted player, athletic support personnel, referee, or other person must decide whether to accept the bribe or to report the approach. For persons with high ethical standards, the decision not to accept the bribe may be easy regardless of the potential rewards. But even an ethical athlete may be hesitant to report an approach if it would isolate him from teammates or colleagues, or if the league would target the athlete as a threat to the public's perception of the integrity of the sport. In this case, if the athlete is not breaking any laws or league rules by not reporting the approach, the athlete may logically decide simply to remain quiet.

Condition Four: The Corruptor Must Extend an Offer (Reward) Consistent with Maintaining the Profitability of The Competition Manipulation That the Target Would Find Attractive Despite the Potential Consequences of Detection (Risks).

An athlete or other target without incorruptible ethics may consider the risk versus reward of accepting a bribe. As risk decreases and reward increases, the venality of the target increases.

Potential Rewards

The prospective reward is typically the amount of the bribe offered by the corruptor. Corruptors must find a target, such as an athlete or a referee, capable of manipulating a competition and have that person agree to the corrupt action by offering something of value, typically money. Whether the target will find the bribe to be attractive may depend on several factors, including the amount of the bribe compared to the athlete's salary, and how the athlete perceives his risk of detection and its consequences.

Corruptors usually seek as targets those who need money, are greedy, naïve, lack confidence, have low self-esteem, or are subject to blackmail, coercion, or threats of violence.[233] Of these factors, financial insecurity plays the most substantial role in the venality

232 Ashutosh et. al, *supra* note 1 at 135-155.

233 Preston et. al, *supra* note 60 at 612-624.

of players, referees, athletic support personnel, and others. Athletes whose salaries are commensurate with their actual economic value to the sport's economic success are less likely to engage in competition manipulation.[234] In contrast, the venality of athletes increases if they: (1) are underpaid or low-paid; (2) compete with and against other athletes who are paid considerably more; (3) have not received their salaries timely; or (4) have gambling problems and need to pay off accumulated gambling debts. Players on a team or in a competition who are paid substantially less than their peers can be good targets for corruptors.[235] This may include players at the start of their careers earning less than more established players, and older players who have reached the end of their earnings potential.[236]

Where players are unpaid or underpaid, the incentives for competition manipulation do not have to be significant. Poor compensation is common in some sports, particularly in certain areas. For example, between 2007 and 2009, team members on the Zimbabwe National Team were paid $4500 or less to lose international games intentionally.[237] Similarly, Eastern Europe soccer, where over 40% of players do not receive salaries, and half of the players fail to receive timely bonuses, has faced issues. FIFA claimed that 55% of all soccer players that corruptors targeted were not paid their salaries on time.[238] As a domestic example, the 1919 Black Sox scandal involved a sports team that had been intentionally underpaying its players for many years.[239] Other players may simply be living beyond their means or have a gambling problem.[240]

Not all corrupt athletes are underpaid. In 1968, Denny McLain was the winningest pitcher in baseball, and the only pitcher in the last 50 years to have won over 30 games. He was a highly compensated player and made more in endorsements than he did playing professionally. He was also regularly performing as a musician in

234 Stefan Szymanski, *The Assessment: The Economics of Sport*, 19 OXFORD REV. OF ECON. POL'Y 467-77 (2003).

235 Anderson, *supra* note 115.

236 *Id.*

237 Kevin Carpenter, *Global Match-Fixing and the United States' Role in Upholding Sporting Integrity*, 2 BERKELEY J. ENT. & SPORTS L. 214 (2013) Available at: http://scholarship.law.berkeley.edu/bjesl/vol2/iss1/11.

238 FIFPro Black Book Eastern Europe (2012) available at http://www.fifpro.org/images/documents-pdf/BLACK-BOOK.pdf.

239 Carpenter, *supra* note 102.

240 IOC, *supra* note 25.

Las Vegas. To the sporting world's surprise, Sports Illustrated broke the story in February 1970 that McLain was an investor in an illegal bookmaking operation.[241] As a result, then MLB Commissioner Bowie Kuhn suspended McLain for roughly the first half of the 1970 season. McLain continued his high-risk lifestyle after his playing days ended, and eventually was twice sent to prison. The first time was in 1984 for loan-sharking, extortion, and cocaine trafficking, although that conviction was later overturned. The second time was in 1996 when McLain was convicted of embezzlement, mail fraud, and conspiracy related to the theft of money from his packing company's employees' pension fund. This conviction put him in jail for another six years.[242] Players like McLain may have an inherent desire to challenge rules and authority.[243] Still others may harbor resentment regarding their careers such as feeling that they did not receive the recognition or reward that they deserved. This is a feeling used to rationalize a decision to become part of competition manipulation.[244]

If positive bribes do not work, corruptors may use negative offers. Blackmail may be used when the target has addictive behaviors like taking illegal drugs, or is engaging in activity such as alcohol abuse, homosexual activity, prostitution, or spousal abuse that could damage the athlete's reputation or their future earnings, sponsorships, or endorsements. Another negative offer includes the threat of physical violence against players or their families, including death threats. According to one report, almost 40 percent of the eastern European players who reported being asked to fix a game also said they had been victims of violence. In a stunning 2009 situation, Zimbabwe soccer officials allegedly used a gun in the locker room to threaten harm to their own national team players unless they intentionally lost matches.[245]

Potential Risks

Risk has many components including: (a) the difficulty or probability the player can deliver the intended result;[246] (b) the chances of being

241 *Denny McLain & the Mob*, SPORTS ILLUSTRATED, Feb. 23, 1970.

242 Mark Armour, *Denny McLain*, SOCIETY FOR AMERICAN BASEBALL RESEARCH, http://sabr.org/bioproj/person/6bddedd4 (last revised July 1, 2015).

243 W. Steve Albrecht, Keith R. Howe, & Marshall B. Romney, *Deterring Fraud: The Internal Auditor's Perspective*, (Inst. of Internal Auditors, 1st ed., 1984).

244 IOC, *supra* note 25.

245 Norman-Culp, *supra* note 102.

246 Forrest, *supra* note 172.

exposed;[247] (c) the risk of sanctions if exposed; (d) the nature and impact of penalties imposed; and (e) the other consequences of exposure such as loss of sports glory. The difficulty or probability the player can deliver the intended result is discussed later in this chapter, but an athlete is less likely to accept a bribe if the result is difficult to achieve.

Risks such as loss of sports glory are inherent in the games themselves. Reputational damage related to public disclosure of involvement in competition manipulation brands an athlete as a cheater. The loss of sports glory, where athletes define themselves and their legacy by their success in the field, comes with any efforts by an athlete not to perform at their best but is primarily tied to losing. An athlete is more likely to agree to accept a bribe where his actions have no impact on his standing as an athlete. For example, losing an inconsequential game has a negligible effect on sports glory compared to championship game.[248]

The other risks are dependent on the efforts of law enforcement and the sport's governing body to adequately regulate competition manipulation. Like law enforcement efforts, previously discussed, a sports governing body's success in preventing competition manipulation is dependent on the sport's governing body having a comprehensive code of conduct, and robust enforcement of that code.

Codes of Conduct and Penalties

Governing bodies for all three major American sports have their own separate codes of conduct. In each case, the codes of conduct are included in and enforced through the collective bargaining agreements between the sport's governing body and the players union/association, and between the governing body and the referee's union/association. The significant provisions also are frequently included in the model player agreements.[249] Codes of conduct typically cover wagering, accepting or soliciting bribes, and insider information.

Prohibiting Wagering on Games

The codes of conduct for all three major American sports have similar provisions banning players from wagering on games within their respective leagues. MLB has separate penalties if the players

247 The chances of being exposed may depend on other factors including the government's and the sports governing body's commitment to preventing corruption through a comprehensive code of conduct, robust enforcement, and fair but stern penalties.

248 Rebeggiani, *supra* note 10.

249 The key provisions in the codes of conduct, collective bargaining agreements and model player contracts are quite similar.

bet on their own games as opposed to a game in which they were not participating. The former carries a lifetime ban while the latter has a one-year suspension. The NBA does not distinguish between betting on one's own games as opposed to other games, but gives the commissioner "the power in his sole discretion to suspend the Player indefinitely or to expel him as a player for any Team." The same holds for the NFL where the commissioner can "suspend [a] [p]layer for a period certain or indefinitely; and . . . terminate [his] contract" for betting on an NFL game.[250]

Prohibitions Against Sports Bribery

All the major leagues prohibit sports bribery. The NFL prohibits accepting "a bribe or agree[ing] to throw or fix" an NFL game, while the NBA and MLB have more comprehensive prohibitions. The NBA forbids offering, agreeing, conspiring, aiding or attempting to cause any game of basketball to have a result otherwise than on its merits.[251] The MLB is even more comprehensive and states that players shall not:

> promise or agree to lose, or to attempt to lose, or to fail to give his best efforts towards the winning of any baseball game with which he is or may be in any way concerned; or who shall intentionally fail to give his best efforts towards the winning of any such baseball game, or who shall solicit or attempt to induce any player or person connected with a club to lose, or attempt to lose, or to fail to give his best efforts towards the winning of any baseball game with which such other player or person is or may be in any way connected.[252]

Prohibitions Against Soliciting

MLB prohibits players from giving gifts or soliciting umpires or opposing teams or their players to make decisions that impact game outcome or decisions.[253]

Prohibitions Against Insider Trading or Use of Inside Information

Insider information is anything related "to the participation in, the likely or actual performance in or outcome of an event or in-play activity within an event, which is known by an individual as a result of

250 *NBA Collective Bargaining Agreement* – 2017, GITHUB PAGES, Retrieved from https://atlhawksfanatic.github.io/NBA-CBA/ (last visited Jan. 31, 2018).

251 Constitution and By-Laws of The National Basketball Association May 29, 2012, PRAWFSBLAWG, http://prawfsblawg.blogs.com/files/221035054-nba-constitution-and-by-laws.pdf (last visited Jan. 31, 2018).

252 MLB Rule 21: Misconduct, TICKET RETRIEVER.COM, https://www.ticketretriever.com/article-baseball-misconduct-rule.html (last visited November 03, 2017).

253 http://www.mlbplayers.com/pdf9/4923509.pdf

their role in connection with that event and which is not in the public domain."[254] Insider information is a complicated code of conduct issue because players can give information unknowingly and without ill intent. Restrictions on insider trading are hard to administer because insiders, such as teammates, locker room personnel, and others, may not think that seemingly trivial information has any tactical value to bettors.[255] For example, disclosing game strategies or prospective line-up changes may seem innocuous but they provide gamblers with invaluable betting information.[256]

Nevertheless, sports' governing bodies should have concise and understandable prohibitions against athletes, athletic support personnel, and league and team employees from disseminating any information. Financial markets have long had prohibitions against and significant penalties for insider trading.[257] While serving as models, these provisions are criminal statutes with narrower definitions than the leagues should consider for disciplinary actions. For example, the SEC definition of insider trading provides, "Illegal insider trading refers generally to buying or selling a security, in breach of a fiduciary duty or other relationship of trust and confidence, while in possession of material, nonpublic information about the security."[258] Sports' governing bodies, on the other hand, should have wider reaching prohibitions beyond the release of information for reward and should include "careless or reckless release of information, for example via social media."[259]

Only the NBA has specific prohibitions against the use of insider information by any of its employees. Its code of conduct provides:

> Non-public information concerning the NBA's business (or those of its business partners) that any employee becomes aware of should not be discussed with anyone outside of the NBA, including members of an employee's immediate family. ("Non-public information" is generally information concerning the NBA (or its business partners) that has not been the subject of any press release or otherwise disseminated to the public at large.) . . . It is the policy of the NBA that no employee

254 Gambling Commission, *Misuse of Inside Information: Policy Position Paper*, March 2014, Birmingham, UK: Gambling Commission. Retrieved from http://www.gamblingcommission.gov.uk/PDF/Misuse-of-inside-information.pdf. In contrast to insider information, public domain information "has been published, is on public record or is accessible by an interested member of the public."

255 Anderson, *supra* note 115.

256 Misra et. al, *supra* note 1.

257 Rebeggiani, *supra* note 10.

258 U.S. Securities and Exchange Commission, *Insider Trading*, https://www.sec.gov/fast-answers/answersinsiderhtm.html (last visited Jan. 31, 2018).

259 Gambling Commission, *supra* note 254.

> may use for personal gain, or the gain of others, confidential or non-public information obtained from any source connected in any way with the NBA. Such information could concern, for example, . . . the health of a player, or the identity of the referees at a particular game. Confidential NBA information may be used only for the benefit of the NBA. When in doubt, employees should assume that the information is confidential.[260]

General Morals Clauses

All the major leagues have general morals clauses that apply to players and capture other aspects of involvement in competition manipulation.[261] Major League Baseball has a general provision in its Collective Bargaining Agreement that allows the league to discipline a player for "conduct that is materially detrimental or materially prejudicial to the best interests of Baseball including, but not limited to, engaging in conduct in violation of federal, state or local law."[262] Likewise, the NBA uniform player's contract provides players cannot do anything "materially detrimental or materially prejudicial to the best interests of the Team or the League." The NFL Player Contract allows for discipline to be imposed for actions that work to "the detriment [of] the League and professional football [due to] impairment of public confidence in the honest and orderly conduct of NFL games or the integrity and good character of NFL players."[263]

Robust Enforcement of Integrity Rules by the US Sports Governing Bodies

Either by design or through lack of transparency, the structure, enforcement mechanisms, and priority that each of the major US sports governing bodies place on competition manipulation is difficult to determine. The National Football League is illustrative of this. The League has an elaborate security network designed to protect it from scandal and corruption.[264] While not evident to the public, the network involves multiple layers of security.[265] The top-level headquarters in its New York

---

260 NBA LEGAL COMPLIANCE POLICY AND CODE OF CONDUCT § II.C.

261 Misra et. al, *supra* note 1.

262 http://www.mlbplayers.com/pdf9/4923509.pdf

263 *Integrity of Game Sample Clauses*, LAW INSIDER, https://www.lawinsider.com/clause/integrity-of-game (accessed November 03, 2017).

264 Kent Babb & Adam Goldman, *NFL's Elaborate Security Network is Supposed to Protect League from Trouble*, WASH. POST, Sept. 13, 2014 Retrieved from http://www.washingtonpost.com/sports/redskins/ nfls-elaborate-security-network-is-supposed-to-protect-league-from-trouble/2014/09/13/795949aa-3b4a-11e4-8601-97ba88884ffd_story.html.

265 *Id.*

office has about a dozen employees, mostly former law enforcement officers.[266] This includes a chief security officer who was Pennsylvania's state police commissioner, and a lead investigator who was the assistant director of the FBI.[267] The previous three security directors were former FBI executives.[268] Each NFL team has a contractor and an investigator that acts as liaison between the teams and the Commissioner's office.[269] The league also has representatives in Las Vegas and Honolulu, cities with numerous nightlife venues which players frequent when they visit.[270] These consultants give players practical advice on what and whom to avoid in a city, with the goal of deterring scams and trouble.[271] The consultants serve as a form of risk management to prevent, detect, and respond to player needs and incidents.[272]

Professional sports governing bodies also have partnered with data companies. The NFL, NBA, NHL, and the NCAA have agreements with Switzerland-based Sportradar, the parent company of Betradar, a major global sports betting industry player. Major League Baseball has an agreement with London-based Genius Sports.[273] The Pac-12 conference uses CG Analytics, a subsidiary of CG Gaming, a Nevada sports betting company.[274]

Sanctions for Violation of Integrity Rules by the US Sports Governing Bodies

Governing bodies can impose sanctions for competition manipulation. Contractual penalties can include fines and expulsion from league activities. The governing bodies can also forward incriminating information to authorities for possible criminal punishment and incarceration.[275] A powerful deterrent to athletes concerned about their legacy is reputational damage.[276] As one commentator noted, "Simply being accused of competition manipulation, even if ultimately found not guilty, can see a sports person viewed suspiciously for the rest

266 *Id.*
267 *Id.*
268 *Id.*
269 *Id.*
270 *Id.*
271 *Id.*
272 *Id.*
273 David Purdum & Ryan Rodenberg, *Future of Sports Betting: The Pitfalls*, ESPN, Nov. 1, 2016, http://www.espn.com/chalk/story/_/id/17910253/the-future-sports-betting-go-wrong.
274 *Id.*
275 Carpenter, *supra* note 102.
276 *Id.*

of their career by fellow professionals, fans and journalists, and can ultimately ruin a person's career."[277] Reputation damage to those unfairly accused, such as loss of employment, endorsements, and reputation, can also occur.[278] Therefore, policy approaches must balance the need for transparency in the investigation and prosecution of offenders with the potential damage that false accusations may have on the careers of athletes and others.[279]

Condition Five: Corruptors Must Have Access to The Target to Convey the Bribe and Coordinate the Competition Manipulation

Corruptors need access to the athletes and others they seek to corrupt for two purposes: first, to convey bribes through an "approach" which occurs before the sporting event; and second, to coordinate placing wagers with the athlete altering his performance, which happens slightly before or simultaneous with the sporting event. Disrupting these communications can make match fixing more difficult. As described earlier, gaining access to athletes and referees to cultivate a relationship as a precursor to making a bribe often is not a significant barrier as athletes often have considerable interaction with former players (who may be acting for corruptors) and the public.[280]

Before the Competition

The ability of corruptors to have access to targeted athletes, referees, and other targets depends on the rules and individual commitment of the sport's governing body to policing its sport. Some governing bodies have rules against specific associations. For example, the NFL is unique among the major sports for having a specific prohibition against athletes knowingly associating with gamblers or gambling activity. The NBA has work rules for referees that prohibit associating with persons involved in illegal gambling or professional gamblers.[281]

During the Competition

The most direct method of communication occurs shortly before the sporting event when the corruptor transmits instructions to

277 *Id.*

278 *Id.*

279 *Id.*

280 *Id.*

281 Lawrence B. Pedowitz, REPORT TO THE BOARD OF GOVERNORS OF THE NATIONAL BASKETBALL ASSOCIATION, Oct. 1, 2008, https://www.nba.com/media/PedowitzReport.pdf.

the athlete based on the bets the corruptor wants to and can make. Governing bodies can disrupt these communications by prohibiting non-team personnel from having access to dressing rooms and by monitoring or banning the athlete's use of mobile telephones in the locker rooms or on the premises of the sporting event venue.[282] The NBA has experimented with such restrictions by preventing access to non-public areas of an arena by non-team personnel during playoff games only. The Pedowitz Report that reviewed the Donaghy scandal for the NBA went further and recommended that league "should set and enforce uniform, League-wide regulations regarding access to non-public areas of arenas."[283] Major League Soccer (MLS) is the only league in the United States that has a policy banning the use of cellphones and other devices inside locker rooms.[284] This prohibition includes sixty minutes before and then through the duration of the game.[285]

Condition Six: Have Reasonable Certainty That the Target Can Produce the Desired Results

A successful competition manipulation requires that the result of the game or a portion of it be pre-arranged.[286] The corruptor has to assess the vulnerability of the bet type, the nature of the sport involved, and the status of the game in judging the likelihood of success. These factors are described in greater detail below.

Vulnerability of Bet Types

Policymakers, regulators, and leagues will want to know the vulnerability of different wager types so that they can craft potential solutions that hinder the athlete's ability to manipulate the competition to achieve the desired result necessary.

Money Line

A money line wager requires the corrupted athlete to intentionally lose the game. This is a tricky proposition in most competitions for the following reasons:

- *Bribes need to be substantial.* In high profile sports where athletes are well paid, the corruptor will have difficulty

---

282 Gunn & Rees, *supra* note 209.

283 Pedowitz, *supra* note 281.

284 Carpenter, *supra* note 102.

285 *Id.*

286 Forrest et. al, *supra* note 54 at 598-611.

making an offer attractive enough for an athlete to lose a game.

- *Losing impacts sports glory.* Athletes also will have a more significant concern regarding sports glory when they are on the losing side of games.
- *Likelihood of success is difficult.* In many team sports, no one athlete has enough power to assure a loss. Even corrupting players in key positions like the quarterback in football or the pitcher in baseball poses risks because the coach or manager can make substitutions. For example, fixing a National Football League game on a money line wager is probably impossible. This is because the corruptor needs assurances that a sizeable number of persons are part of a conspiracy to bring about the intended result.
- *Detection is high.* Competition manipulation based on the game result is complex because corruptors must simultaneously control both the targets and the betting market.[287] Leagues, regulators, and sportsbooks closely monitor wagering on game results. Corruptors are concerned that authorities can detect competition manipulation through enforcement, or by reviewing wagering data to determine if betting patterns are irregular and worthy of investigation.[288]

Money line wagering is attractive in some sports, however, and presents challenges for detection because high liquidity in betting markets allows for the placing of large wagers without affecting the lines or otherwise being flagged as irregular.

Point Spread

Point spread wagering is attractive to corruptors:

- *Point spread corruption allows athletes to retain sports glory.* Point spread betting also offers the opportunity to allow the athletes to both win the game and achieve the recognition accorded while underperforming to the benefit of the corruptor.[289] Because of this, spread betting is prohibited in some countries because of concerns it promotes competition manipulation.[290]

---

287 Demir et al., *supra* note 135.

288 *Id.*

289 Forrest et. al, *supra* note 54 at 598-611.

290 Andreff & Byers, *supra* note 123.

- *Likelihood of success depends on the sport.* In games involving point spread wagering, the degree to which a corruptor can achieve the desired result can vary according to the sport involved. Shaving points in football, where nearly two dozen athletes are actively participating on the field, is more challenging than in other team sports, but it is not impossible.[291] In team sports with fewer players, or individual sports, the result is more likely as it requires fewer conspirators. For example, the starting and backup point guards on a basketball team together can have a greater influence on the final score than any two NFL players.
- *Point spread wagering is popular in some major sports.* Point spread wagering is popular in football, basketball, and soccer. This creates high liquidity in betting markets allowing corruptors to place large wagers without impacting the lines or otherwise being identified as irregular.

Partial game wagering

Factors that make partial game wagering attractive to corruptors include:

- *Corruption based on partial game results allows athletes to retain sports glory.* Partial game wagering is more susceptible to competition manipulation because players do not have to lose the game, glory, or the opportunity to advance in the competition. For example, David Savic, a tennis player, was banned for life after offering $30,000 to an opponent if he would allow Savic to win the first set only, with Savic agreeing to allow the opponent to win the match.[292]
- Prop bets and In-Game Wagering
- Many proposition bets appear to be open to manipulation since the incidents to which they relate are usually easier to arrange than the outcome.[293] Frequently, these are under the control of one or a few people.[294]

Sportsbooks have the technology to offer in-game or in-running

291 Daniel Bernard, *The NFL's Stance on Gambling: A Calculated Contradiction*, 4 UNLV GAMING L.J., 273 (2013). Retrieved from http://scholars.law.unlv.edu/glj/vol4/iss2/9/.

292 Anderson, *supra* note 115.

293 Forrest, *supra* note 49.

294 *Id.*

wagering that permit bettors to bet on every play in a game. Examples of such wagers are, "will the next play be a run or a pass," "will the next play result in a turnover," or "will the next play result in a score?" In-game wagering allows athletes to engage in a form of competition manipulation known as "spot-fixing." Spot-fixing is the "manipulation of minor contingencies, which have little or no effect on the outcome of the game,"[295] and is most likely in events where individual players (or referees) can exert significant if not absolute control over individual plays.[296] For example, if the corruptor wants to wager on whether the third pitch of the first inning will be a ball or strike and the compromised competitor is the pitcher, then the likelihood this can be accomplished undetected is relatively high.

South Korea provides examples of spot-fixing in baseball. In late 2016, South Korean police brought charges against 21 people including two pitchers for deliberately allowing walks in certain innings.[297] A cricket manipulation case in 2010 also involved spot-fixing when Pakistani players in a match against England deliberately bowled "no-balls" at predetermined points so that the corruptors could win in-game wagers placed on that outcome.[298] The corruptors, in that case, were convicted and received prison time.[299] Many sportsbooks accept wagers on the first player in a soccer match to commit a major penalty,[300] that is, being issued a red card requiring the athlete to take no further part in the competition (called being "sent off"). Anecdotal evidence from recent soccer cases in the United Kingdom involved players accepting money to commit actions that would cause them to be "sent off." Early warning systems are less effective against spot-fixing.[301] This increases the risk that athletes or referees may engage

---

295 Forrest, *supra* note 172.

296 Anderson, *supra* note 115.

297 *21 people accused of baseball match-fixing schemes in South Korea*, SPORTS ILLUSTRATED, Nov. 7, 2016, https://www.si.com/2016/11/07/ap-bbi-south-korea-match-fixing.

298 Matt Scott, *Cricketers Betrayed Sport Out of Greed, Court Told*, THE GUARDIAN, Oct. 5, 2011, Retrieved from http://www.theguardian.com/sport/2011/oct/05/cricketers-led-by-greed.

299 Tito Boeri & Battista Severgninic, *Match Rigging and the Career Concerns of Referees*, 18 LABOUR ECONOMICS 349-59 (June 2011).

300 This could include illicitly preventing a direct goal-scoring opportunity, deliberately injuring an opponent or starting a fight to get their target sent off. Café Futebol, *Data Says That Sometimes A Red Card is Worth It*, BUSINESS INSIDER, June 30, 2014, http://www.businessinsider.com/sometimes-a-red-card-is-worth-it-2014-6.

301 IOC, *supra* note 25.

in spot-fixing for their benefit without a corruptor intervening.[302] As a result, France only permits bets on final results or on specified phases of the game and prohibits "micro" outcomes.[303] Germany also prohibits in-game wagering.[304]

Proponents maintain that spot-fixing, at least for now, poses less risk from competition manipulation by organized crime due to the lack of a sufficient level of liquidity.[305] The risk of individual fraud is more significant than the risk of organized crime, however, especially since an individual alone can easily manipulate an action during a game.[306] Moreover, as liquidity increases so does the viability of spot-fixing.[307] However, as one commentator noted, "The growth of online betting gambling platforms and exchanges, and the widening of traditional sports betting markets has, in parallel, increased the vulnerability of sport to the spot-fix and to the spread-bet."[308]

Parlay Cards

Corruptors are very unlikely to use parlay cards as the wager for competition manipulation. In a three-team parlay, the corruptor needs to assure wins in all three games or else bet four separate wagers to cover all possibilities that assure a win, with significantly lower returns than if the corruptor bets the single game that was fixed.

Betting Exchanges

Betting exchanges pose unique problems for competition manipulation. One commentator likened betting exchanges to synthetic products available on financial markets that are outside the control of regulators and permit manipulation of the betting based on "simple match-fixing rumours or match-fixing attempts."[309] Another critic noted that exchanges create and spread "problematic betting types" such as a wager on "an event not to happen, which could more

302 *Id.*

303 Ben Van Rompuy, *Limitations on the Sports Betting Offer to Combat Match Fixing: Experiences from Europe*, 18 Gaming L. Rev. & Econ. 989-93 (2014).

304 *Id.*

305 *See* Asser Institute, Centre for European and International Law, *The Odds of Match Fixing: Facts & Figures On The Integrity Risk Of Certain Sports Bets*, Jan. 2015, available at: www.asser.nl/media/2422/the-odds-of-matchfixing-report2015.pdf.

306 International Centre for Sport Security (ICSS), *Protecting the Integrity of Sport Competition: The Last Bet for Modern Sport*, (May 2014) Retrieved from http://www.theicss.org/wp-content/themes/icss-corp/pdf/SIF14/Sorbonne-ICSS%20Report%20Executive%20Summary_WEB.pdf.

307 Forrest, *supra* note 172.

308 Anderson, *supra* note 115.

309 Carpenter, *supra* note 102.

easily be fixed."[310] He noted that the losses born as the result of a fixed match fall on the bettors that took the losing side of the proposition in a betting exchange, as opposed to the bookmaker in traditional wagering.[311] Therefore, the betting exchange lacks the motivation to police the wagers that it posts on behalf of corruptors.[312] France and Greece prohibit betting exchanges.[313]

Negative Wagers

Negative wagers involve betting on the occurrence of negative events such as whether a player or a team will incur penalties, and whether a player will foul out or be disqualified.[314] A single player can often control these events. A negative bet spot-fixing scandal in England illustrates the vulnerability of lower division European soccer. In that case, the 13 players involved were alleged to have intentionally received penalties, either yellow or red cards.[315] A European Parliament Resolution on Online Gambling (September 2013) promoted a ban on wagering on "negative events."[316] France prohibits "negative wagers."

A bet on whether an athlete will be injured, if allowed, would be a negative wager. The more likely situation is when a bettor (or a corruptor) wins a wager because a person sustains an injury. Faking injuries has cast a shadow on professional tennis for many years. If a player withdraws from a tennis match, his or her opponent is awarded the victory, and many sportsbooks pay off the wagers on the winning tennis player.[317] A tennis player wanting to fix a match needs merely to fake an injury. Researchers have concluded that such activity is widespread in tennis, particularly in less prestigious tournaments.[318] A proposed solution is to return the wagers (push) if a player exits the match because of injury. Some books follow this

---

310 Rebeggiani, *supra* note 10.

311 *Id.*

312 *Id.*

313 Rompuy, *supra* note 303.

314 *Id.*

315 *Seven Footballers Arrested in Spot-fixing Investigation*, BBC NEWS ONLINE, 3 April 2014, http://www.bbc.co.uk/news/uk-26869337.

316 *Article 53 of European Parliament Resolution of 10 September 2013 on Online Gambling in the Internal Market*, EUROPEAN PARLIAMENT, http://www.europarl.europa.eu/sides/getDoc.do?pubRef=-//EP//TEXT+TA+P7-TA-2013-0348+0+DOC+XML+V0//EN.

317 Steve Doughty, *Does Procession of Injured Players Show Match-Fixing is Rife in Tennis?*, DAILY MAIL, Mar. 28, 2012, http://www.dailymail.co.uk/news/article-2121877/Does-procession-injured-players-match-fixing-rife-tennis.html.

318 *Id.*

policy. An unintended consequence, however, is for the corruptor to back underdogs where they have inside information that the favorite is not 100% healthy, and then to pay the underdog to play his or her best until they see they cannot win. They would then fake an injury.[319]

Non-Athletic Wagers

Another type of ban could be against wagering concerning events that are not based on athletic performance, such as the flip of the coin in football or the game attendance figures.

Difficulty of Achieving the Contracted Result Based on The Sport

Determining the vulnerability of individual sports to competition manipulation for wagering purposes helps craft potential public policy goals and their legislative implementation. Several factors go into assessing the vulnerability of different sports to competition manipulation, including: (a) whether athletes and others are highly compensated; (b) the presence of asymmetrical rewards both in terms of compensation differences between competitors and differences in rewards between participants in various games; (c) bet liquidity on the sport/bet type; (d) difficulty of fixing based on the number of participants; (e) difficulty of fixing considering the available bet types and nature of the contest (e.g., point shaving is easier in high-scoring games);[320] and (f) whether the wager can be fixed without having to lose the game.

The four major American professional team sports--football, basketball, baseball, and hockey--have not encountered the level of competition manipulation related to sports wagering that other countries or other major international sports have. In the more international sports of soccer and cricket, however, there have been over the past few years numerous scandals even at the highest levels of competition.[321] In the past 50 years, not a single documented case of a player fixing games for betting purposes exists in any of the four major American professional team sports. The only major scandal in that time involved point shaving by an NBA referee.[322]

---

319 Leo Schlink, *Tennis Match-Fixing: How Nikolay Davydenko and Martin Vassallo Arguello Raised Still Unanswered Questions*, Herald Sun, Jan. 18, 2016, http://www.heraldsun.com.au/sport/tennis/tennis-matchfixing-how-nikolay-davydenko-and-martin-vassallo-arguello-raised-still-unanswered-questions/news-story/0183b1248c9d698e7d29517dffab2d9b.

320 Forrest, *supra* note 49.

321 Carpenter, *supra* note 102.

322 *See* notes 379-385 *infra* and accompanying text.

A significant reason for the absence of significant scandal with the NFL, MLB, and NBA is the high salaries and other benefits afforded professional athletes at this level. The minimum salary for a first-year NBA player is $562,493 for the 2017 season.[323] In the NFL, the rookie base salary is $450,000; the base salary of Major League Baseball is $507,500; and the base salary of the National Hockey League is $575,000.[324] Some star athletes in these sports earn more than $10 million each year. These minimum and star salaries are significantly higher than the average family income in America of about $75,000.[325] Consequently, the risk of corrupt players in these sports is minimal. As the previously described case of Denny McLain illustrates, however, exceptions exist.

Other sports are more prone to corruption because of both low earnings by all but a few competitors and a vast difference between the salaries of the top earners and the typical athletes. As noted below, professional boxing is particularly problematic.

A Review of The Vulnerability of Sports That Americans Are Likely to Bet On.

Football

Because of the number of players actively participating on the field, competition manipulation and point shaving in football is more challenging than in other team sports, but it is not impossible.[326] According to Lem Barker, a well-known gambler, a corruptor needs at least three players, a quarterback, an offensive lineman, and a defensive back, to control the outcome of a football game.[327] Corrupting highly scrutinized games would be practically impossible. As one bookmaker noted: "It would be easier to bribe the president of the United States and the entire Senate and Congress than to fix a Super Bowl."[328]

Except for key positions (such as a kicker or quarterback), few

---

323 NBA Minimum Salary, BASKETBALL INSIDERS, http://www.basketballinsiders.com/nba-salaries/nba-minimum-salary/ (last visited Jan. 31, 2018).

324 Aaron Kasinitz, *What Are the NFL, MLB, NBA, and Others' Rookie Minimum Salaries?*, PENNLIVE, July 27, 2016, http://www.pennlive.com/sports/index.ssf/2016/07/nfl_mlb_nba_rookie_salary.html.

325 Matthew Frankel, *Here's the Average American Household Income: How Do You Compare?*, USA TODAY, Nov. 24, 2016, https://www.usatoday.com/story/money/personalfinance/2016/11/24/average-american-household-income/93002252/.

326 Bernard, *supra* note 291.

327 Tuohy, *supra* note 219.

328 Art Manteris & Rick Talley. SUPERBOOKIE: INSIDE LAS VEGAS SPORTS GAMBLING 153 (Contemporary Books 1991).

players have opportunities to control the result. For example, if an offensive lineman intentionally plays poorly, a coach may replace him, or another player may assist in blocking his opponent. Often, the person with the greatest opportunity to affect the game, the quarterback, is the highest-paid player on the team. This reduces the financial incentive to fix a game.[329] Joe Namath, a Hall of Fame quarterback, once accused of fixing a game where he threw five interceptions, stated in his autobiography:

> Hell, you'd have to be an idiot to make it that obvious. If you want to throw a game, you don't have to allow a single pass to be intercepted. You just screw up one or two handoffs, and the running back can't handle them, and he fumbles the ball, and he takes the blame. Then maybe you throw a critical third-down pass a little low, and you let the punter come in and give the ball to the other team. You don't give it away yourself.[330]

Basketball

Several factors make basketball attractive for point shaving: (1) higher scoring games provide for a higher final point differential that provides a greater opportunity to permit the other team to score, or to suppress one's own team from scoring to achieve the result desired by the corruptor while still assuring that the corrupted athlete's team wins the event; (2) relatively few points scored in a single possession allows players to better manage point shaving; (3) fewer players are needed to assure a particular result; and (4) more regular season games reduces scrutiny and chances of detection.[331] NCAA basketball has had more incidents of major domestic betting scandals than any other team sport at any level. These scandals include the University of San Diego 2010,[332] University of Toledo 2004-2006,[333] Arizona

---

329 Bernard, *supra* note 291.

330 Joe Willie Namath, & Dick Schaap. *I Can't Wait Until Tomorrow...:'cause I Get Better-looking Every Day*, (Random House, 1969).

331 George Diemer & Mike Leeds, *Point Shaving in NCAA Basketball: Corrupt Behavior or Statistical Artifact*? No. 1009. Dep. of Econ., Temple Univ., 2010.

332 *Three Plead Guilty in Fixing Case*, ESPN, Aug. 23, 2012, http://www.espn.com/mens-college-basketball/story/_/id/8295478/three-plead-guilty-san-diego-toreros-fixing-scheme. The point shaving scheme involved the team's leading scorer and a former assistant coach. Matt Norlander, *NCAA: No More Punishment for San Diego in Game-Fixing Case*, CBS Sports, Aug. 14, 2013, https://www.cbssports.com/college-basketball/news/ncaa-no-more-punishment-for-san-diego-in-game-fixing-case/.

333 *See* Nicholas Piotrowicz, *Bribery Case Ends with Pleas*, The Blade, Dec. 10, 2014, http://www.bcsn.tv/news_article/show/456049.

State University 1994,[334] Northwestern University 1994-95,[335] Tulane University 1985,[336] Boston College 1978-79,[337] and The City College of New York (and six other colleges - New York University, Long Island University, Manhattan College, Bradley University, University of Kentucky and University of Toledo), 1951.[338] The actual amount of game fixing in NCAA basketball is of considerable debate. One researcher in 2006 estimated that six percent of all games played involved point shaving.[339] This study, however, has been heavily criticized.[340] Nevertheless, the greater number of point shaving scandals in NCAA basketball shows that basketball is more vulnerable to competition manipulation.

The number and nature of the differences in known competition manipulation incidents involving the NBA and NCAA shows that vulnerability increases when unpaid athletes are involved in high-profile sports that are susceptible to point shaving. The NCAA is in a precarious position. The proposition that the athletes at major universities are students first and the events are for the sake of healthy competition is naive. Athletes are highly recruited and often admitted to a university solely because of their athletic abilities. While these athletes can, if so inclined, pursue an education at no or reduced tuition, they are not paid. One study found that almost three out of every four student-athletes on revenue sports teams feel exploited by their school.[341] These athletes harbor resentment toward their schools

---

334 *Point-Shaving Scandal Hits Arizona State*, LA TIMES, Dec. 6, 1997, http://articles.latimes.com/1997/dec/06/sports/sp-61336.

335 Matt O'Connor, *Lee Blames Point-shaving At Nu On 'Stress, Anxiety'*, CHICAGO TRIBUNE, Dec. 24, 1998, http://articles.chicagotribune.com/1998-12-24/sports/9812240030_1_campus-bookie-kenneth-dion-lee-kevin-pendergast.

336 *2 More At Tulane Charged in Fix*, NY TIMES, Mar. 28, 1985, http://www.nytimes.com/1985/03/28/sports/2-more-at-tulane-charged-in-fix.html.

337 Bob Horle, *When 'Goodfellas' Collided With BC Basketball*, BOSTON GLOBE, Mar. 16, 2014, https://www.bostonglobe.com/sports/2014/03/15/and-goodfellas-sports-scandal-and-its-lingering-toll/nvlXKiXCYsGpUqBUtg9BRN/story.html.

338 Joe Goldstein, *Explosion: 1951 Scandals Threaten College Hoops*, ESPN CLASSIC, Nov. 19, 2003, https://espn.go.com/classic/s/basketball_scandals_explosion.html.

339 Justin Wolfers, *Point Shaving: Corruption in NCAA* Basketball, 280 AEA PAPERS & PROCEEDINGS 279, 283 (2006).

340 Richard Borghesi, *Widespread Corruption in Sports Gambling: Fact or Fiction?* SOUTHERN ECON. J. 1063-1069 (2008) (concluding that line shading, not point shaving, "would produce the observed underperformance of strong favorites relative to market expectations."); Dan Bernhardt & Steven Heston. *Point Shaving in College Basketball: A Cautionary Tale for Forensic Economics.* 48 ECON. INQUIRY 14-25 (2010).

341 Derek Van Rheenen, *Exploitation in the American Academy: College Athletes and Self-Perceptions of Value*, 2 THE INT'L J. OF SPORT AND SOC'Y 11-26 (2011).

and can more easily rationalize accepting a bribe to shave points in a system where their talents and efforts generate little for them, but significant income for their schools or other commercial interests.[342] Moreover, very few college athletes have reasonable expectations of playing professionally. Only 1.1% of male college basketball players progress to a professional league of any sort, including foreign and secondary leagues. The number is 1.5% of football players, 9.1% of baseball, and 5.6% of hockey players.[343] Therefore, for most college athletes, banishment from the sport for point shaving has no impact on a future professional sports career.[344]

Baseball

Virtually all wagering on baseball is on Major League Baseball. The absence of wagering liquidity makes both minor league baseball and NCAA baseball unattractive to corruptors. Also, like the NBA and NFL, MLB has highly compensated players, making corruption less likely. Because baseball is such a low scoring game, most wagering action is on a money line or run totals. Therefore, competition manipulation involving athletes is typically confined to intentionally losing the game, which is more unlikely than point shaving because it requires the athlete or athletes to forgo both the sports glory and suffer the career impact of losing.

Baseball presents an opportunity for competition manipulation because a single player, the pitcher, has a significant impact on the outcome of the game. Using only the pitcher to attempt to fix a game presents a risk, however. The only pitcher that the corruptor knows will play in a game is the starting pitcher. A corrupt starting pitcher could intentionally throw pitches that are more hittable by the opposing team. This could lead to more runs by the opponent. The pitcher, however, is being scrutinized by the catcher, the pitching coach, and the manager. If the pitcher can disguise that he is intentionally making poor pitches, he is nevertheless pitching poorly and subject to being replaced by another pitcher.

Baseball is, however, vulnerable to spot-fixing. Here a pitcher only needs to agree to throw a ball or strike, a wild pitch, or hit a batter at an agreed point in time for the corruptor to win an in-game wager.

---

342 Forrest, *supra* note 172.

343 Estimated Probability of Competing in Professional Athletics, NCAA, http://www.ncaa.org/about/resources/research/estimated-probability-competing-professional-athletics (last visited Feb. 1, 2018).

344 Forrest, *supra* note 172.

Another vulnerability in baseball is the home plate umpire. In a relatively low-scoring contest such as baseball, an umpire can decide or materially change the outcome of a game.[345] A home plate umpire can alter the course of a game significantly by how he calls balls and strikes. Favoring the pitchers on both teams by expanding the strike zone will help keep the score low and favor those who bet that the combined score would be under the line set by the sportsbooks.

Other (more vulnerable) Sports

Boxing

Boxing is vulnerable to match fixing and has a long and sordid history of match-fixing in the United States. Organized crime control of the International Boxing Club resulted in widespread competition manipulation in boxing during the late 1950s.[346] More recently, Nevada has had incidents of competition manipulation. For example, the undercard to the 2000 WBA heavyweight fight between Evander Holyfield and John Ruiz in Las Vegas featured heavyweights Thomas Williams versus Richie "the Bull" Melito, Jr. The fight, however, was fixed. Williams received $10,000 and an automobile for throwing the fight. Williams and the manager were found guilty in federal court.[347] The Las Vegas fight was one of the several competition manipulation incidents involving Melito, whose promoter was trying to pad Melito's record and rankings in hopes of attracting a higher paying championship fight.[348] This was far from a unique circumstance, as allegations of dozens of other competition manipulation incidents in the past 20 years continue to shadow boxing.[349]

Boxing and match fixing are so intertwined that the sport developed terminology for intentionally losing by a feigned knockout: *taking a dive*.[350] Boxing has all the attributes necessary for match

---

345 Ashutosh et. al, *supra* note 1 at 135-155.

346 Kevin Mitchell, *Jacobs Beach: The Mob, the Garden, and the Golden Age of Boxing*, (Wallingford, UK: Yellow Jersey Press, 2009).

347 Jace Radke, *Promoter, Boxer Found Guilty of Rigging Fight*, LAS VEGAS SUN, Nov. 9, 2004, https://lasvegassun.com/news/2004/nov/09/promoter-boxer-found-guilty-of-rigging-fight/.

348 Michael J. Goodman & William C. Rempel, *Boxing Probe Details Alleged Fight-Fixing*, LA TIMES, Feb. 2, 2004, http://articles.latimes.com/2004/feb/02/sports/sp-boxing2/4.

349 *Id.*; *See also*, Charles Farrell, *Why I Fixed Fights*, DEADSPIN, Apr. 16, 2014, http://deadspin.com/why-i-fixed-fights-1535114232.

350 While intentionally losing a contest often involves ties to gambling, this is not always the case. Match fixing can occur where the competition structure gives a team or athlete incentives to lose to achieve a greater benefit. As an example, a study of the sumo

fixing. First, the typical compensation for most boxers is meager. An average professional boxer may make $200 per round for a four-round preliminary fight. Of this $800, he may pay $160 to his manager and $80 to his corner man. If he fights 12 times in a year, his pay after expenses is only $6620 a year.[351] Second, the rewards for boxers are asymmetrical. Even putting aside outliers like the 2017 Mayweather-McGregor fight, the top boxers can make several million per fight. For example, in a 164-pound fight between Canelo Alvarez and Julio Cesar Chavez Jr. in May 2017, Alvarez earned $5 million, and Chavez earned $3 million.[352] Third, as a two-person competition, the corruptor only needs to target one of the two competitors. As one match-fixer noted:

> It is surprisingly easy to fix a fight in boxing. You will go into a gym and you'll find a trainer or a manager, someone whose reputation is that of providing what they call in boxing business opponents. Opponents are guys whose livelihood is dependent on their losing on cue. And what you do is you don't say things that are indictable. That's really what it comes down to. You don't want to criminalize yourself if you can avoid it. And you'll say, I have a fighter who needs to get some work. And work is the operative word here. It means that you don't want him to do anything that's going to be too strenuous and that's going to risk his losing. And you're probably talking about a knockout. And you'll say, OK, I've got a guy who's a good fighter but he's not in shape. He hasn't been in the gym much, you know, he's got a job. He's probably good for four rounds. OK, so at this point what you've done is you've fixed the fight and you fixed the duration.[353]

Fourth, boxing does not have a single or stable governing body to protect either the boxers or prevent corruption. Rather, the sport has multiple sanctioning bodies, some of which have a poor reputation for integrity. For example, a court sentenced the president of one of the governing bodies, the International Boxing Federation (IBF), to 22 months in prison for accepting bribes to adjust boxers' rankings.[354] Promoters need the boxers in a match to

---

wrestling industry in 2000 showed that wrestlers threw certain matches in tournaments to allow competitors to gain enough victories to sustain their rankings and resulting higher wages.

351 Tony Guerra, *Salaries of Pro Boxers*, Chron, http://work.chron.com/salaries-pro-boxers-30165.html (last visited Feb. 1, 2018).

352 Brandon Wise, *Canelo Alvarez vs. Chavez Jr. Purse: Boxers to Earn a Combined $8 Million to Show*, CBS Sports, May 6, 2017, https://www.cbssports.com/boxing/news/canelo-alvarez-chavez-jr-purse-boxers-to-earn-a-combined-8-million-to-show/.

353 *The Fix is in*, NPR, http://www.npr.org/2014/06/13/321664970/the-fix-is-in.

354 Paul Magno, *Lowered Expectations: The Modus Operandi of the International Boxing Federation*, The Boxing Trib., June 22, 2011, http://theboxingtribune.com/2011/06/22/

have a high rating in order for the fight to be sanctioned as a world championship and to attract fans. Moreover, boxing commissions, which often consist of political appointees with limited knowledge or expertise, regulate fights on a state level. Therefore, detection is limited.

Fifth, boxing often has significant liquidity in the illegal markets that makes it possible for the corruptors to realize profits.

Tennis

Tennis is particularly vulnerable to competition manipulation because its most popular event, singles matches, can be manipulated by a single player with little risk of detection. As former US Davis Cup caption, Patrick McEnroe noted: "Tennis is a very easy game to manipulate … I can throw a match and you'd never know. A trained eye can figure it out."[355]

Coupling the ease of manipulation with a significant number of poorly compensated players playing in major competitions promotes match fixing. Tennis pays highly ranked players a disproportionately higher amount of tournament prize money than lower ranked players in the same tournaments.[356] The bottom of the top hundred players in the world struggles to earn a living.[357] Thus, lower ranked players with little or no chance of earning a substantial income have a greater incentive to engage in competition manipulation. As a recent example, in June 2017, Australian tennis player Isaac Frost, the 651st ranked player, was charged with competition manipulation in a match at the Challenger Tournament in Traralgon, Victoria. The Victoria police's sporting integrity intelligence unit determined that a "number of people received information that the match would allegedly be fixed and subsequently placed bets through various betting agencies."[358]

Soccer

Soccer is not an easy sport to fix. As one observer noted, a corrupt player needs:

---

lowered-expectations-the-modus-operandi-of-the-international-boxing-federation/.

355 Joe Drape, *Talk of Efforts to Fix Matches Rattles Pro Tennis*, NY TIMES, Nov. 25, 2007, http://www.nytimes.com/2007/11/25/sports/tennis/25tennis.html.

356 *Id.*

357 Miguel Morales, *How the 92nd-Ranked Tennis Player in the World Earns a Comfortable Living*, FORBES, Aug. 26, 2013, https://www.forbes.com/sites/miguelmorales/2013/08/26/aces-into-assets-how-michael-russell-has-made-a-profitable-career-in-the-demanding-world-of-pro-tennis/#6f4621547548.

358 Isaac Robinson, *Australian Tennis Pro Charged with Match-Fixing and Drug Offences*, ESPN, June 14, 2017, http://cdn.espn.go.com/tennis/story/_/id/19631471/australian-tennis-pro-charged-.

> at least three to five other players to help fix the match. In soccer, fixes normally include five to seven players. A successful fix, however, must at minimum include the goalkeeper, a defender, and a striker. For goalkeepers, the key strategy to throw a game is simple: leave his area as much as possible. A corrupt goalkeeper may rush out of his net and allow the forward to step around him and score. Another tactic used by goalkeepers is to drop the ball or pat it loose in a crowded penalty area. Defenders must also be involved, as one mistake by a defender can easily lead to a goal. One tactic used by defenders includes placing the ball too far away for the goalkeeper to clear or gather it, but near enough to the opposing forward for him to run in and score a goal. Forwards must also be involved in the fix in order for the fix to be successful. If forwards score too many goals, the fix becomes obvious. As a result, fixers have various strategies for forwards to follow, including dribbling the ball straight at the opponent's players thereby allowing them to take away the ball, and missing goal opportunities by either kicking directly at the goalkeeper or missing the goal altogether.[359]

Despite these difficulties, several notable soccer matches have either been fixed, or raised suspicions that they were fixed. In 2006, an Asian corruptor associated with a betting syndicate enabled the fixing of two games with the participation of members of the Ghana national team in matches against Italy and Brazil. In the latter, Ghana allegedly allowed Brazil to score three goals to allow the corruptors to be paid on wagers that Brazil would win by more than two goals.[360] A significant issue plaguing soccer is that even notable games played at the international level feature players with much different earnings. Players from developing countries, like Ghana, are much more receptive to bribes than their better paid European counterparts. The bribe to the Ghana captain in the 2006 World Cup scandal was a mere $20,000, which was then distributed to other players.[361]

Corruptors also target soccer referees because they have considerable influence to impact the results due to scoring typically being low.[362] Single decisions by a referee such as calling a penalty, offside, or giving a red card have considerable influence over the result. Anecdotal evidence of corrupt soccer referees is abundant. For

---

359 McLaren, *supra* note 10.

360 Katarzyna Kordas, *Dropping the Ball: How Can FIFA Address the Match-Fixing Problem Facing Professional Football*, 23 Sports L.J. 107 (2016).

361 Declan Hill, *Match-Fixing: How 2006 World Cup Fell Prey to Organised Crime*, Telegraph, Oct. 25, 2008, http://www.telegraph.co.uk/sport/football/3260610/Match-fixing-How-2006-World-Cup-fell-prey-to-organised-crime-Football.html.

362 Norman-Culp, *supra* note 102.

example, a referee allegedly attempted to fix a 2010 World Cup game between Guatemala and South Africa.[363] Also, the size of the bribes to referees is often modest. In the 2004 German scandals, a referee involved in 23 incidents of competition manipulation was paid a total of about $120,000.[364]

Difficulty of Achieving the Contract Result Based on the Nature of the Game

Circumstances can increase the risk that certain games are more vulnerable to competition manipulation. For example, two teams playing a game at the end of a season may involve one team which has already qualified for post-season competition, and another team which needs a positive result to do so. This creates an asymmetry that may promote competition manipulation.[365] As one group of researchers noted, "A match fixing attempt will be more probable if winning begot great amounts of benefits to one of the contestants (team or individual player) and little or no benefits to the other."[366]

These situations present a different risk profile for competition manipulation than a high-profile championship event that, on the one hand, is much more scrutinized and difficult to fix, but on the other hand offers the liquidity for a much higher return if manipulation is successful.

Corruptors concentrate on less scrutinized games that do not have competitive consequences, often called "dead rubbers," where athletes perceive lower risks in agreeing to be part of the competition manipulation.[367] Examples include where both teams either qualified for a postseason championship series or both were eliminated from winning the championship, or where one team has already qualified for the next level, and the other team has already been eliminated. In one case, a France court found handball star Nikola Karabatic guilty of fraud for his part in a competition manipulation scheme in which Team Montpellier, which had already won the French title, purposely lost to Team Cesson. The inquiry spread to seven players and nine others who were involved in either the game or wagering on the game. The game in question involved wagering handle of €103,000

363 *See*, Declan Hill & Jeré Longman, *Fixed Soccer Matches Cast Shadow over World Cup*, NY TIMES, May 31, 2014, http://www.nytimes.com/2014/06/01/sports/soccer/fixed-matches-cast-shadow-over-world-cup.html?_r=1.

364 Kordas, *supra* note 360.

365 Preston et. al, *supra* note 60 at 612-624.

366 *Id.*

367 Ashutosh et. al, *supra* note 1 at 135-155.

when similar games only attracted a few thousand Euros.[368]

Some European regulators have prohibited wagering on inconsequential games that have no impact on "promotion, relegation, or the decision as to which team qualified for a European competition."[369]

Some Other Considerations

When the Corrupted Is Not an Athlete.

Corrupting Referees and Judges

Among non-athletes, referees are among the most vulnerable to corruption because they are among the lowest-paid participants – at least in comparison with the athletes.[370] The targeting of referees by illegal gambling conspirators is a long-standing feature of competition manipulation.[371] In European soccer, team managers for Juventus Turin, a professional soccer team in the Italian Serie A league, conspired with referees during the 2004 season to attempt to fix the outcome of matches.[372] Similar scandals plagued Spanish, Portuguese, and German soccer in 2004 and Brazilian Soccer in 2005.[373]

Besides being the lowest paid person on the field, a referee has considerable power over both the game results and specific events in the game, such as calling penalties or other critical decisions (such as balls and strikes in baseball or offside in soccer).[374] Most decisions that a referee can make in major games like awarding penalties or disqualifying players from further play, however, are important events which are highly scrutinized.[375] Nevertheless, even in major games a referee can have significant influence over the flow of the game and can impact matters such as whether the game is low or high scoring.[376] Corruptors can often pay lower bribes to a lower-paid

---

368 *French Handball Star Karabatic Found Guilty of Match-Fixing*, RFI, http://en.rfi.fr/sports/20150711-french-handball-player-found-guilty-match-fixing. None of those persons found guilty in the incident, however, were sentenced to jail.

369 Rompuy, *supra* note 303.

370 Ashutosh et. al, *supra* note 1 at 135-155.

371 *Id.*

372 Rangan Basu, *Calciopoli 2006: The Match-Fixing Scandal That Got Juventus Relegated*, Sportskeeda, Oct. 30, 2015, https://www.sportskeeda.com/football/calciopoli-2006-match-fixing-scandal-juventus-relegated.

373 Andreff & Byers, *supra* note 123.

374 *Id.*

375 Forrest, *supra* note 172.

376 Ashutosh et. al, *supra* note 1 at 135-155.

referee to obtain cooperation.[377] In some instances, the corruptors do not need to use financial bribery but simply impede the referee's career advancement by using friendly team managers to threaten negative publicity or evaluations.[378]

In the United States, the only major allegation of competition manipulation in the past 50 years involved an NBA referee. The Federal Bureau of Investigation (FBI) in 2007 established that a 13-year veteran referee, Tim Donaghy, had placed wagers on 16 NBA games that he officiated during the 2006-2007 season, and at least twice as many in prior seasons.[379] Moreover, Donaghy had disclosed non-public information on games, including player injuries and the referees assigned to specific games, to his associates who bet on the games.[380] Donaghy bet on 16 NBA games that he refereed in the 2006-2007 season, and at least 30 in the three prior seasons.[381] While Donaghy was arrested and subsequently pled guilty to federal charges resulting from his placing wagers on games that he officiated, he claimed that he never intentionally made incorrect calls. He did concede that the bets may have "compromised his objectivity" as a referee. He also alleged that having non-public "insider information" such as relationships between players, coaches, and referees benefitted his wagering. Regardless of whether Donaghy did or did not intentionally make incorrect calls, the incident nevertheless shows both the vulnerability of referees and that a corrupt referee either "subconsciously" or intentionally can have a significant impact on the final score."[382] Donaghy ultimately pled guilty to conspiracies to commit wire fraud by denying the NBA the intangible right to its employee's honest services and to transmitting wagering information.[383] Donaghy was sentenced to 15 months in prison, followed by three years of supervised release.[384] The government also charged Donaghy's co-conspirators with conspiracy to commit wire

---

377 *Id.*

378 Boeri & Severgninic, *supra* note 299.

379 United States v. Donaghy, 570 F. Supp. 2d 411 (E.D.N.Y. 2008); United States v. Battista & Martino, 570 F. Supp. 2d 411 (E.D.N.Y. 2008).

380 Donaghy, 570 F. Supp. 2d at 411; Pedowitz, *supra* note 284.

381 McLaren, *supra* note 10.

382 Ryan Rodenberg, Brian Tuohy, Rick Borghesi, Katarina Pijetlovic, & Sean Patrick Griffin. *Corruption and Manipulation in Sports: Interdisciplinary Perspectives*, 17 GAMING L. REV. & ECON. 175-87 (2013).

383 Donaghy, 570 F. Supp. 2d at 411.

384 *'Integrity in Sport: Understanding and Preventing Match-Fixing'* at 43, SPORTACCORD, Nov. 2011.

fraud and conspiracy to transmit wagering information.[385]

The Donaghy case was not the first suspicious case involving an NBA referee. Some 40 years earlier, Las Vegas bookmakers tracked unusual betting patterns by a bettor who went from a $500 bettor to a $5000 bettor and was consistently winning the higher amount.[386] The bookmakers analyzed the NBA games on which the bettor was placing the larger wagers and the common link appeared to be a specific referee.[387] They reported this to the NBA.[388] The referee was soon no longer officiating NBA games, but nothing further came of the matter.[389]

Sports with Judges

In professional sports such as boxing where judges determine the outcome if the match goes the maximum number of rounds, the judges hold an absolute impact on the result. Where three judges are used, this would only require the complicity of two individuals. The power of judges to impact decisions is perhaps most prominent in the Olympics, where controversial decisions have impacted boxing and figure skating competitions. Of note, the 1988 Seoul Olympics saw the suspension of three judges that awarded a gold medal to a South Korean boxer in the middleweight division despite his opponent earning the most outstanding boxer award for the games.[390] In March 1999, match fixing allegations surrounded boxing promoter Don King after the judges issued a controversial draw in a fight between Evander Holyfield and Lennox Lewis that ensured a lucrative rematch.[391] Likewise, in the 2002 Winter Olympics, The International Olympic Committee decided to award gold medals to the figure skating team that placed second after the controversial scoring decision that ultimately led to the ban of one judge.[392]

Because of these types of controversies, the French regulators have refused to allow wagering on judge-scored events including

---

385 United States v. Battista & Martino, 570 F. Supp. 2d 411 (E.D.N.Y. 2008).

386 Manteris & Talley, *supra* note 328.

387 *Id.*

388 *Id.*

389 *Id.*

390 Jean-Loup Chappelet, *The Olympic Fight Against Match-Fixing*, 18 SPORT IN SOC'Y 1260-72 (2015).

391 Nishant Gokhale, *Fixing the Fixers: The Justification of Criminal Liability for Match-Fixing*. 2 NUJS L. REV. 319 (2009).

392 Chappelet, *supra* note 390.

gymnastics, figure skating, and animal training.[393]

Corrupting Others

While the most likely people to fix games are players and the referees on the field, others can be the target of corruptors. Coaches can influence results by the range of decisions during the game, including starting line-ups, player substitutions, play selection, and the like.[394] Likewise, medical and training staff can use their position to sabotage the performance of players by various means including the incorrect use of medicine and medical procedures.[395]

393 Rompuy, *supra* note 303.

394 Forrest, *supra* note 172.

395 *Id.*

5

Wagering Integrity

Not unlike the concern that sports governing bodies have regarding the integrity of sporting events, the gaming industry and state governments have similar concerns relating to the integrity of the gaming transactions. Most states have a declared public policy related to gambling. Nevada, which has exemptions for legal gambling, has an illustrative statement that reads:

> The continued growth and success of gaming is dependent upon public confidence and trust that licensed gaming … [is] conducted **honestly and competitively . . . and that gaming is free from criminal and corruptive elements.**[1] [Bolded emphasis added]

Governments that permit regulated gambling have a self-interest to assure its integrity. Some states, like Nevada and Mississippi, use gambling as an economic engine. For example, Nevada resorts employ 327,000 workers, or 28% of the state's labor force. Nevada's government thus has a vested interest in protecting its economic partnership in the gaming industry. Other states legalized casino gambling to raise taxes. Any of the various state policy goals related to legal wagering will be frustrated if the public perceives that a wagering system cannot be trusted.[2] Regulation is the vehicle by which the industry can establish an industry that the public and bettors trust, has access to capital, helps fund government through taxes, or creates jobs.[3]

Consistent with the government's interest, most gambling operators realize the government can more easily earn the public trust through regulation. Convincing gamblers that the industry is honest and free of criminals through self-regulation is difficult. Therefore,

---

1 Nev. Rev. Stat. § 463.0129.

2 Luca Rebeggiani & Fatma Rebeggiani. *Which Factors Favor Betting Related Cheating in Sports? Some Insights from Political Economy*. In Match-Fixing in International Sports 157-176. (Springer International Publishing 2013).

3 Another goal that often accompanies the protection of the industry is the protection of the state's principal interest in tax revenues. This is accomplished by stringent accounting, auditing, and reporting requirements.

most operators will willingly subject themselves to losses of freedom, increases in regulatory risk, and increases in operating expenses as the cost of maintaining the desired public perception.

MAJOR TENETS OF WAGERING INTEGRITY

Four major tenets of wagering integrity drive the public's and bettors' trust:

- The games must be honest,
- The games must be fair,
- The patrons' deposits and winnings must be secure, and
- To a much lesser extent, the government must have impartial procedures to resolve disputes with patrons fairly and according to law.[4]

Governments have developed an elaborate system of regulatory controls governing gambling transactions generally—and sports wagering specifically—that seek to satisfy the basic tenets of wagering integrity. These systems include, among other things, a rigorous licensing process, mandated operational and internal controls, costly accounting and reporting systems, and disciplinary procedures that could lead to severe fines or license revocation for not following the rules. The government also can mandate specific technical, accounting, and reporting standards that each sports wagering system must comply with. Moreover, a wagering system may be required to undergo rigorous testing by a government or independent laboratory before a licensed sportsbook can use it.

The implementation of wagering regulation has two significant steps. The first is the adoption of laws and regulations designed to meet policy goals. States that have mature casino industries have a significant number of laws, regulations, standards, and other controls. For example, the State Gaming Control Act in Nevada is 155 pages long. Nevada gaming regulations encompass an additional 270 pages. Minimum internal controls that detail casino and sportsbook procedures in Nevada are about 300 pages.

The second step is to create a system to enforce the laws and regulations. This process is labor intensive. The Nevada regulators employ over 400 persons, with most being field positions including enforcement (119), investigations (95), and audit (91). This Chapter covers how governments create and enforce laws and regulations designed to protect wagering integrity.

---

4 Anthony N. Cabot & Ngai Pindell, REGULATING LAND BASED CASINOS: POLICIES, PROCEDURES, AND ECONOMICS 112 (UNLV Gaming Press 2014).

Honesty

Honesty in the context of wagering means that the underlying event that determines whether the bettor wins or loses the wager is determined by a random event in the case of a chance contest, or by fair and open competition in the case of a skill event. The antithesis of honesty is where the bettor is cheated or defrauded.

Sports and casino wagering share similar aspects. All wagers are contracts[5]; the price (amount won or lost) is honored according to the terms of the contract when the bettor and a gambling operator, whether a casino or sportsbook, enter it. A distinctive part of all wagering contracts is that the promise of performance is based on a future contingent event (e.g., the outcome of the casino game or the sports competition) that is not under the control of the sportsbook or bettor. Whether the sportsbook must fulfill its promise to pay the bettor is dependent on the terms of the bet and the outcome of that future contingent event, namely, the sporting event.

The difference between casino wagering contracts and sports wagering contracts is that the regulators tightly control the regulation of future contingent events in casino contracts (typically a random event) in a closed casino environment where the regulators have police powers. Given the importance of honesty to the gaming industry, governments that regulate casino gaming implement multi-faceted regulatory measures to assure the honesty of the games. These measures typically feature: (1) licensing of manufacturers and operators of the games; (2) technical standards for all games and gaming devices before being offered to the public; (3) extensive testing of all games and gaming devices before being offered to the public; (4) field observation and review of games and gaming devices in operation in the field; (5) periodic audit and review of games and gaming devices to ensure that they are operating within expected

5 A contract is a promise or a set of promises that the law will enforce. The wager typically is an adhesion contract, or a "take-it-or-leave-it" contract, between the sportsbook and its bettors. *See generally*, Restatement (Second) Of Contracts § 1 (1978); E. Allan Farnsworth, Contracts 312 (2d ed. 1990). An adhesion contract is non-negotiable. *See generally*, Restatement (Second) Of Contracts § 1 (1978); E. Allan Farnsworth, Contracts 312 (2d ed. 1990). The sportsbook defines the terms of the contract (house rules and the posted odds) and allows bettors to wager on the game as-is, with no possibility of changing the rules. The nature of sports wagering necessitates such adhesion contracts. Sportsbooks are in the business to make money. Therefore, the sportsbooks typically only enter into contracts in which they have a statistical advantage. Once the bettor offers to make a wager and the sportsbook accepts it, then a contract is formed.

range for honest games; and (6) internal control requirements that assist in assuring the games are conducted honestly. Many, if not most, of the efforts behind casino regulation focus on the honesty of the casino games. As a result, the occurrence of incidents where a casino in a regulated jurisdiction has been found to cheat the players is rare.

For the most part, the bettor and the sportsbooks in sports wagering contracts are left to their own devices to decide whether the sports events are honest.[6] Neither the sportsbooks nor their state regulators control the honesty of the underlying sporting event that determines a winning or losing wager.[7] The sportsbook is merely making individual wagers with several bettors on the same uncertain event. Both the bettor and sportsbook can be the victim of cheating or fraud and must rely on the efforts of others, such as the government or sport's governing body, to ensure the honesty of the sporting

---

6 Licensed sportsbooks in Nevada could accept wagers on minor league soccer games in Bulgaria or any other professional sporting event if it so desired, provided that "their outcomes are reported in newspapers of general circulation or in official, public records maintained by the appropriate league or other governing body, or unless the pertinent sports events are televised live at the book and a book employee other than a betting ticket writer monitors the telecast, records the occurrence of the pertinent events and contingencies simultaneously with their occurrence, and records the time of their occurrence." NEV. GAMING COMM. Reg. 22.060(4) This verification is a very loose standard and a relic of a bygone era when the number of newspapers of general circulation was limited because of the cost of production. In a world of international sports, globally thousands of newspapers of general circulation report on sporting events and the sportsbooks do not rely on newspapers for accurate reporting of results. If the games that a sportsbook posts are corrupt, the bettors that wagered on a team that had no chance of winning are defrauded. A better regulatory standard would be to identify those competitive events properly governed by a legitimate and trusted governing body and permit wagering only on those events. For example, Nevada has more comprehensive regulations regarding which bets can be posted on amateur sporting events by limiting them to "Olympic sporting or athletic events sanctioned by the International Olympic Committee . . . and [c]ollegiate sporting or athletic events." NEV. GAMING COMM. Reg. 22.120.

7 Theoretically, a sportsbook could be the corrupt influencer in a point shaving situation. A sportsbook could be the perpetrator if it made the line more favorable than any competitor to encourage wagering on the underdog knowing that the favorite was going to make the margin of victory under its published line. Many reasons militate against this situation. First, the licensed sportsbook undergoes a major background investigation. Any propensity for cheating likely would be uncovered. Second, any substantial deviation from the competitive line among the 160 sportsbooks in Nevada would be easily detected. Third, the sportsbooks are only a small percentage of the overall sportsbook revenues and the likelihood that a sportsbook would jeopardize its license with such a scheme is very small. Fourth, the audit and review of the sportsbook records by the state or outside audits, especially in corporate-owned sportsbooks that face an additional level of regulation at the federal level, could flag such indiscretions.

event. Unlike casino games, Nevada regulators have no direct role in assuring that the sporting events are not rigged against the bettor, and neither exercise authority over nor supervise most of the sporting events upon which the licensed sportsbooks offer wagering to the public. If the sportsbook decides to accept wagers on such events, it is taking a risk because the sportsbook must pay non-complicit bettors the full amount of the winning wager even where the event was fixed.

A sportsbook that has any reason to believe that a contest is corrupt has little recourse except to cease taking wagers on that game. For example, many European sports betting operations refuse to accept wagers on certain minor division soccer leagues because of their history of corrupt competitions. Also, sportsbooks typically attempt to minimize their exposure to dishonest sporting events by balancing patron wagers on each possible outcome so that it limits losses based on the results of a given sporting event.

Sports bettors also face risk when sportsbooks are left to self-determine the honesty of sporting events upon which they accept wagers. Bettors may wager on the wrong side of a fixed competition and have no chance of winning their bet.[8]

Efforts to ensure the honesty of the sporting event are consistent with the economic best interests of both the state and the sportsbook operator since both can be victims – the sportsbook directly, and the state indirectly through lower tax revenues. Despite this, Nevada regulators have done little to coordinate efforts with sports' governing authorities to ensure the honesty of the underlying sporting events.[9]

---

8 Despite not having any influence over the sporting event that is the contingent event in the wagering contract, sportsbooks can still cheat or defraud the patron in other ways. For example, the book could short pay bettors on wagers. In 2016, CG Technology, a sportsbook manager at seven Las Vegas casinos, was fined $1.5 million and required to establish an escrow account to pay bettors who were shorted in the calculation of player winnings for certain types of parlay bets. https://www.reviewjournal.com/business/casinos-gaming/cg-technology-agrees-to-pay-1-5-million-fine-and-pay-bettors-who-were-shorted/.

9 Nevada has higher standards for non-sports wagers (like betting on the outcome of a poker tournament), than for sports wagering. Regarding non-sports wagering the Nevada regulators take a more active role. Before authorizing wagering on such events, the sportsbook wishing to accept wagers must show:

> (1) The event could be effectively supervised; (2) The outcome of the event would be verifiable; (3) The outcome of the event would be generated by a reliable and independent process; (4) The outcome of the event would be unlikely to be affected by any wager placed; (5) The event could be conducted in compliance with any applicable

Fairness

Fairness of the game is the second principle of wagering integrity.[10] Fairness can concern: (1) whether the advantage the sportsbooks have over the bettors is reasonable; (2) ensuring that other bettors do not have an advantage because they have inside information; and (3) not allowing sportsbooks to rescind wagers after they are made without cause.

Rate Setting

Another distinctive aspect of most wagering contracts is that the sportsbooks maintain a house advantage over the bettor to secure the economic viability of the sportsbook business. House advantage, explained in Chapter One, represents how much, in terms of percentage of the money wagered, the book can expect to retain in the long run if all bets were placed randomly. For example, if the player must bet $11 to win $10, and all bets were random, the house would have about a 5% advantage. The house advantage reflects the price that a player pays for the opportunity to enter a wagering contract with a licensed sportsbook.[11] In competitive markets, the price that bettors must pay to bet on sports is regulated by market forces. With 86 licensed sportsbooks, the Nevada market has low house advantages. This is necessary because many bettors are price conscious and will select the sportsbook offering the best odds. For this reason, Nevada does not regulate the house advantage that the sportsbooks maintain on wagers. In the even more competitive illegal internet sports wagering markets, the house advantage is lower than the legal Nevada sportsbooks.[12]

> laws; and (6) The granting of the request for approval would be consistent with the public policy of the state. NEV. GAMING COMM. REG. 22.120(2)(c).

For these standards to be adequate, however, the regulators need to have a significant knowledge base regarding the activity being wagered on to adequately determine whether it is supervised competently, is not easily corrupted, and whether an independent service reliably reports the event outcome.

10 Cabot & Pindell, *supra* note 4 at 37.

11 *Id.* at 382.

12 Offshore books will often have lower house advantages on money line wagers and may give rebates to large bettors that will further reduce the house advantage. The offshore books can do this for many reasons. First, they have greater volumes on the same or lower fixed and variable costs than the Nevada sportsbooks. For example, the cost of a sportsbook system is about the same whether you handle $100 million as a Nevada sportsbook or $1 billion as an offshore book. Moreover, offshore books do not have high regulatory costs and have reduced costs related to brick and mortar facilities

The government, however, could regulate house advantage to assure fairness to the player.[13] For example, if sports wagering were lawful in the United States and states could grant exclusive or limited numbers of sports wagering licenses and prohibit others from offering competitive services in their state, sportsbooks with monopoly or oligopoly power could maximize revenues by setting prices at a rate higher than what would be competitive or fair. In this case, the government, much as it does with the regulation of public utilities, could regulate rates to assure the house advantages are fair.

Insider Information

Another factor that influences the fairness of sports wagering, but not sports integrity, is when bettors use insider information to the detriment of other bettors. Nevada provides minimal regulation of insider information. Nevada regulations only provide that a book cannot accept a wager on a collegiate sport or athletic event which the sportsbook knows or reasonably should know, is being placed by, or on behalf of a coach or participant in that collegiate event.[14] Rather than trying to prevent insider trading, however, this regulation appears to be directed at the appearance of impropriety that might be created when college coaches or athletes bet on their own sporting events. Nevada has no similar prohibitions regarding professional sports.

Effective prevention of insider trading requires coordination between sports' governing bodies and the betting operators. The regulators, sportsbooks, and sports' governing bodies should prohibit players, athletic support personnel (including coaches, trainers, team officials or staff, agents, managers, and medical personnel), and referees from wagering.[15] As noted in Chapter Four, governing bodies should supplement this by having rules prohibiting misuse of insider information. Operators can assist by enforcing the governing bodies' rules regarding the player, athletic support personnel, or

---

and labor costs.

13 *See* Doug Grant, Inc. v. Greate Bay Casino Corp., 3 F. Supp. 2d 518, 539 (D.N.J. 1998)(upholding the rights of state of New Jersey to permit casinos, for example, to "(1) 'shuffle-at-will', (2) limit a player to playing and wagering on one hand at a table, (3) selectively limit the betting limit for a given player at a table, (4) count cards themselves to determine when the cards in the shoe should be reshuffled and (5) identify card counters and share this information with other casinos."

14 NEV. GAMING COMM. REG. 22.120(1)(b).

15 Steve Donoughue & Fabian Adams-Sandiford, *Improving the Integrity of Sports Betting*, GAMBLING CONSULTANT (Nov. 2010). http://www.gamblingconsultant.co.uk/articles/improving-the-integrity-of-sports-betting.

referee wagering. They can also file suspicious activity reports with the governing bodies for suspected violations of thier rules, and have policies regarding their employees' use of insider information.[16]

Rescinding Wagers

By entering into a wagering contract with a sportsbook, bettors rightfully expect that the sportsbook will honor that contract and will not rescind without significant cause. In Nevada, books cannot unilaterally rescind a wager without written permission from regulators.[17] This prohibition resulted from an incident where a book made a mistake on its parlay cards. After discovering the mistake, the book quit accepting the parlay cards and informed patrons it would not honor wagers made before it discovered the mistake. This angered bettors who were only given their wagers back.[18] Regulators retain the discretion to allow a sportsbook to rescind wagers when just cause exists. Examples of this might include where the sportsbook learns that the wager was placed in violation of state or federal law, was placed by an athlete or agent in violation of league rules, or involved a corrupt competition.

Securing Patron Winnings and Deposits

The third principle of wagering integrity is that patrons are secure in their winnings and deposits.[19] Like other businesses, a sportsbook can fail but still be liable to bettors for deposits, future bets, and winnings. Unregulated sports wagering poses the threat that the book may abscond with players' deposits. This occurred in 2006 when the Costa Rican site, BetOn Sports, closed, and patrons were left without their winnings or account balances.[20]

Regulators should require sportsbooks to maintain a minimum level of cash reserves or a minimum net worth to assure that they can pay all winning wagers and refund all of a bettor's deposits. Nevada adopted regulations requiring its sportsbooks to maintain minimum reserves after the sudden closure of two sportsbooks in

---

16 *Id.*

17 NEV. GAMING COMM. REG. 22.115.

18 Richard N. Velotta, *CG Technology Agrees to Pay $1.5 Million Fine and Pay Bettors Who Were Shorted*, LAS VEGAS REVIEW JOURNAL, July 21, 2016, https://www.reviewjournal.com/business/casinos-gaming/cg-technology-agrees-to-pay-1-5-million-fine-and-pay-bettors-who-were-shorted/.

19 Cabot & Pindell, *supra* note 4 at 36.

20 James Banks, *Online Gambling and Crime: A Sure Bet?*, THE ETHICOMP J. (2012) http://shura.shu.ac.uk/6903/1/Banks_online_gambling.pdf.

Las Vegas in the 1980s. In 1985, Gary Austin's Race and Sportsbook, an independent sportsbook on the Las Vegas Strip, closed without paying more than $1 million in winnings and deposits to bettors, most of whom had telephone accounts.[21] Austin later moved to Costa Rica and resumed bookmaking, albeit over the internet. In another case, Santa Sportsbook in Las Vegas closed its doors and filed for bankruptcy while owing bettors over $500,000.[22]

Nevada sportsbooks must comply with Gaming Commission Regulation 22.040, which governs reserve requirements. The actual amount of the reserve must exceed the sum of the amount held on account for patrons, plus amounts for wagers whose outcomes have not been decided, plus the amounts owed but unpaid by the sportsbook on winning wagers.[23] The reserve must be: (a) in a bond, cash or cash equivalent; (b) if cash or cash equivalent, held by a federally-insured financial institution; and (c) monitored monthly by an independent certified public accountant.[24] The chairman of the Gaming Commission must approve the agreement between the book and the financial institution or insurance carrier.[25] Regulators enforce these reserve and net worth standards by auditing the sportsbooks' operations and fining sportsbooks that fail to meet the standards.

Resolution of Patron Disputes

The fourth principle of wagering integrity is that a process exists to resolve patron disputes impartially, with all parties having the right to present evidence and arguments. Disputes occasionally arise when the sportsbook and bettor disagree either about the terms of the

---

21 Ronald Koziol, *Bookies' Closing Could Deal Out Telephone Wagers*, CHICAGO TRIBUNE, Mar. 11, 1986, http://articles.chicagotribune.com/1986-03-11/news/8601180593_1_santa-anita-bookmakers-nevada-gaming-control-board.

22 *Id.* Shortly after closing, the book filed for bankruptcy and patrons having money on deposit did not receive a refund. Several patrons filed lawsuits against Nevada gaming authorities claiming negligent regulation of the book. The patrons argued that the state had regulations to protect their deposits and those regulations created a special duty to them. The Nevada Supreme Court ultimately ruled for the gaming authorities. Epstein v. State, 103 Nev. 802 (1987). The court did not believe that the state should function as an insurer of the patrons' deposits. In addition, the court found that Nevada gaming authorities took every reasonable step within their budget to maintain a fair gaming industry.

23 NEV. GAMING COMM. REG. 22.040(1).

24 NEV. GAMING COMM. REG. 5.225 (20)(a)(b)(c).

25 NEV. GAMING COMM. REG. 5.225 (20)(d)(5).

contract or about the result of the event that determines the outcome.

These disputes can be handled either by an administrative procedure through the regulatory agency, or through the courts. Nevada has a transparent administrative process for resolution of patron disputes. When a patron has a dispute with a sportsbook involving the payment of alleged winnings and the sportsbook cannot resolve it to the patron's satisfaction, the sportsbook has certain statutory obligations. If the patron claims entitlement of less than $500, the sportsbook must inform the patron of the right to ask the regulators to investigate the dispute.[26] If the amount in dispute is $500 or more, the sportsbook must immediately notify the Nevada Gaming Control Board.[27] An enforcement agent will investigate the matter and issue a written determination resolving the dispute within 45 days.[28] Within 20 days after receipt of the agent's decision, the aggrieved party may request a hearing before the Board to reconsider the decision.[29] If either the patron or the sportsbook is not satisfied with the decision, it may file a petition for reconsideration.[30] The regulatory hearing provides all traditional notions of procedural due process, including the right to call and examine witnesses, introduce evidence, cross-examine any witnesses, impeach any witnesses, and offer rebuttal evidence.[31] The Nevada Gaming Control Board has subpoena powers.

After the regulatory hearing, a party may appeal the decision to the Gaming Control Board. The party seeking review of the decision of an administrative law judge acting on behalf of the GCB has the burden of proof to show a basis for modifying or reversing the decision.[32] The decision of the regulators is then subject to limited

---

26 NEV. REV. STAT. § 463.362(2)(b).

27 NEV. REV. STAT. § 463.362(2)(a).

28 NEV. REV. STAT. § 463.362(3).

29 NEV. REV. STAT. § 463.363(1).

30 NEV. GAMING COMM. REG. 7A.030.

31 NEV. GAMING COMM. REG. 7A covers the hearing process.

32 NEV. REV. STAT. § 463.364. At the hearing, the party seeking reconsideration may make an opening statement stating the nature of the case and why the hearing examiner should grant a decision in his or her favor. The other party may then state why the agent's decision should be upheld or may reserve the right to make this statement until after the petitioner puts on his or her case. Both parties then present their evidence. The hearing officer does not need to follow technical rules of evidence. The regulators may consider any evidence that a reasonable person would in the conduct of serious affairs. NEV. GAMING COMM. Reg. 7A.070.The photographs and written statements acquired through investigation may help the sportsbook's presentation to the regulators. After all evidence is presented, the parties may give closing arguments. After the hearing, the

judicial review whether it favors the patron or the sportsbook.[33]

GOALS OTHER THAN MAINTAINING WAGERING INTEGRITY

Prohibiting Organized Crime Involvement

Depending on the state's public policy in permitting wagering, other government goals may play a part in sports wagering regulation. For example, some states may have concerns regarding the involvement of organized crime. These concerns can be significant because: (1) criminals have already shown a propensity to violate the law and exploit other citizens; (2) the perception of criminal involvement may dissuade bettors from trusting the system; (3) proceeds from legal wagering may be used to fund illegal ventures; and (4) the legislature and public may decide to ban wagering based on the perception of benefit to criminal figures.

Protecting State Tax Revenues

Another common policy goal of regulated gambling is to create a source of tax revenues. If this objective is important to the state, a goal of regulation is assuring that the sportsbook accounts for all revenue and pays its tax assessed on revenue.[34] This includes confirming that:

- Sportsbooks cannot skim money before counting it for tax purposes.
- No cheating occurs in the processing of the wagers, such as past posting (writing a wager after the outcome of the event is known).
- Employees cannot void tickets after the results of the event are known.
- Employees do not overpay tickets.
- Employees do not write tickets with incorrect odds to the advantage or disadvantage of the patron.

---

hearing examiner must recommend whether to sustain, modify, or reverse the agent's determination. This recommendation must contain findings of fact and a determination of the issues presented. The regulators must consider the recommendation and the record before deciding. The regulators may affirm or reverse the decision or remand the case for the taking of additional evidence.

33 Judicial review is available in the district court for the county where the dispute arose. NEV. REV. STAT. § 463.3662(1).Filing of a petition must occur within 20 days of the issuance of the regulators' decision. NEV. REV. STAT. § 463.3662.

34 Cabot & Pindell, *supra* note 4, at 305.

- Employees do not commit similar actions inconsistent with the internal controls, regulations, or the law.

Skimming

Governments often tax sportsbooks based on gross revenues, i.e., the difference between all amounts received as winnings less all amounts paid out as losses. Dishonest owners can avoid paying "gross revenue" taxes (and income tax) if they can remove winnings before counting and reporting it. This is "skimming," a form of tax evasion. Formerly, if sportsbooks wanted to attempt to skim, they could maintain two separate set of books, much like they did to evade the 10% Federal Excise Tax. Until fairly recently, the accounting, cash counting, and reporting were done by hand; this facilitated dishonest operators who could falsify records and reports to understate revenues.

New technology makes skimming extremely difficult. Licensed third-party vendors design computerized sportsbook systems that are built to technical standards mandated by the regulators. These systems automatically produce detailed revenue reports and auditable trails. The systems are subject to significant independent review, testing, and approval by regulators. Licensees have ongoing obligations to keep their software up to date and to report to regulators any deficiency, material risk, or errors they discover.

Government auditing and accounting controls also help maintain the integrity of a tax system. Auditing in the sportsbook industry involves accounting for cash and count transactions that occur in the business. A sportsbook must implement accounting controls and procedures to prevent or detect errors or irregularities. These mechanisms are buttressed by technology approvals of the sportsbook management systems, surveillance systems, intelligence gathering, whistleblower procedures, and covert observation of the book operations.

Another method of skimming is to exaggerate losses. This could be done by entering wagers for confederates that are much more favorable than the odds offered to the public. These wagers can be legitimately entered into the system and appear as regular transactions except that over time the operator, through the confederate, will realize significant revenue that he records as losses because wagers entered have a significant advantage over the house. Nevada attempts to solve this potential problem by requiring that all propositions be entered into the sportsbook system and displayed at the book or audibly announced at the sportsbook.[35]

Protecting Vulnerable Persons

The National Council on Problem Gambling (NCPG) has a useful definition of "problem gambling":

> Problem gambling is gambling behavior which causes disruptions in any major area of life: psychological, physical, social or vocational. The term "Problem Gambling" includes, but is not limited to, the condition known as "Pathological", or "Compulsive" Gambling, a progressive addiction characterized by increasing preoccupation with gambling, a need to bet more money more frequently, restlessness or irritability when attempting to stop, "chasing" losses, and loss of control manifested by continuation of the gambling behavior in spite of mounting, serious, negative consequences.[36]

Public health issues dictate additional policy goals designed to minimize the impact of problem gambling including:

- Preventing gambling-related problems in individuals and groups at risk of gambling addiction;
- Promoting informed and balanced attitudes, behaviors and policies towards gambling and gamblers both by individuals and by communities, and;
- Protecting vulnerable groups from gambling-related harm.[37]

A myriad of laws and regulations exist in countries that permit sports betting and casino wagering that are designed to address problem gambling. Examples include:

- Creating a comprehensive problem gambling program that includes training, prevention, education, research, and treatment
- Prohibiting entry to the sportsbook for those below 18 or 21 years
- Restricting locations of sportsbooks
- Limiting hours of operation
- Allowing self and third-party exclusion
- Displaying information on problem gambling, help services, rules governing wagering, and odds of winning
- Restricting advertising of casino and casino gambling

---

35 Nev. Gaming Comm. Reg. 22.060.7.

36 National Council on Problem Gambling, http://www.ncpgambling.org (last visited Nov. 20, 2017).

37 David Korn, Roger Gibbins, & Jason Azmeier, *Framing Public Policy Towards a Public Health Paradigm for Gambling*, 19 J. of Gambling Studies 246 (Summer 2003).

- Restricting the extension of gaming credit
- Having maximum bets or loss limits
- Prohibiting acceptance of credit or debit cards; no ATMs allowed within the sportsbook.
- Allowing bettors to set loss limits.

While problem gambling protection focuses on the concerns above, public policy also can seek to protect the player (and related parties) from other potential harms including risks to player data and privacy.

TOOLS TO ACHIEVE GOVERNMENT GOALS

Licensing

Licensing is the process by which government decides whom it will allow to enter or associate with the sports wagering industry. The government has an interest in assuring that persons who threaten any aspect of wagering (or sports) integrity or other policy goals are not involved in its sportsbook industry. Persons who can do direct harm are those who skim funds without paying taxes, are likely to cheat patrons, or are so incompetent that the government will lose tax revenues through employee or patron theft or poor management. Foremost among policy goals is protecting patrons from dishonest acts by operators. If one operator cheats by underpaying patrons on winning wagers, the public may believe or fear that the entire industry is dishonest. Organized crime figures can do indirect harm to the government's economic interest because their mere presence so taints the industry that legislators may consider making gaming illegal. Similarly, existing and prospective patrons may be dissuaded from coming to the sportsbooks.

In many respects, gaming licensing is not unique. In various professions, the government imposes licensing requirements to protect the public.[38] A primary reason is to shield the public from abuse. This occurs where the person being licensed holds a position of trust, and the public is in a vulnerable position. For example, few persons can assess the competency of a medical doctor. Therefore, patients must rely on the state's licensing of physicians as a guarantee

---

38 *In re* Cason, 294 S.E.2d 520, 523 (Ga. 1982) (*citing* Penobscot Bar v. Kimball, 64 Me. 140, 146 (1875)); David Forrest & Robert Simmons, *Sport and Gambling*, 19 OXFORD REV. OF ECON. POL'Y 598 (2003).

of minimum competency.

Regulators also may want to exclude unfit persons before they get their license because policing is difficult once they are admitted.[39] Another reason is to protect the public image. Again, by excluding unfit individuals before they can act dishonestly or unethically, public trust is enhanced.[40]

Licensing also has a significant advantage in protecting the image of the industry. A sportsbook industry can suffer credibility problems if the media exposes a licensee as having criminal ties, regardless of whether the licensee otherwise complies with all regulations and acts ethically. Pre-licensing examinations can readily expose areas that could create image problems that affect the broader industry.

A significant criticism of pre-licensing inquiry is that it is flawed when its purpose is to predict the future behavior of an individual.[41] Commentators have expressed doubt as to the accuracy of such predictions.[42] Attempting to predict future behavior assumes that people have fundamental character traits that govern their conduct. The validity of this assumption is questionable.[43] Critics assert that character assessments have little predictive value because conduct is contextual, and "the situational nature of moral conduct makes predictions of behavior uncertain under any circumstances."[44] As one commentator has said, "a half century of behavioral research underscores the variability and contextual nature of moral behavior: A single incident or a small number of acts committed in dissimilar social settings affords no basis for reliable generalizations."[45]

Nevertheless, social scientists can predict behavior in groups. For example, they can use statistics to predict that some recovering alcoholics will relapse, but that prediction cannot be extended to an individual alcoholic with any reliability.[46] Regulators may decide that persons who by past actions put themselves into high-risk categories should not be licensed, even if the regulators cannot predict if a

39 Deborah L. Rhode, *Moral Character as a Professional Credential*, 94 YALE L.J. 491, 509 (1985).

40 *Id.*

41 Banks McDowell, *The Usefulness of "Good Moral Character,* 33 WASHBURN L .J. 323, 327 (1992); *See also* In re Mostman, 765 P.2d 448, 454, (Cal. 1989); *In re* Bowen, 447 P.2d 658, 660 (1968)).

42 Rhode, *supra* note 39 at 559; McDowell, *supra* note 41 at 327.

43 Rhode, *supra* note 39 at 556.

44 *Id.* at 559.

45 *Id.* at 560.

46 *Id.*

particular applicant is likely to create problems. Therefore, despite the criticism, all established governments that allow gambling impose some form of licensing.

Differences between licensing systems are based on five factors: breadth, level of review, depth, criteria, and standards of the licensing process.

Breadth means the extent to which a government requires persons or entities associated with the sportsbook industry to obtain a license.

Level of review refers to the intensity of the investigative process. A low-level review might include simple checks with law enforcement agencies to learn whether the applicant has an arrest record. A high-level review may require specially trained agents to conduct a complete and independent review of the applicant, including both background and financial information. This investigation may be more intense than that required by a government for the highest security clearances.

The depth of licensing means the extent to which government requires persons within a licensable entity to undergo individual investigation. For example, some jurisdictions may require only the sportsbook operator to obtain a license, while others may require cashiers to do so.

Criteria are those matters that the government considers in granting licenses. These can include good moral character, honesty, lack of association with criminals, financial ability, and business experience. Some jurisdictions set forth specific criteria.

Standards are the minimum attributes that applicants should meet to qualify for licensing. These refer to how rigid the regulators will be in applying the criteria. For example, under the same set of facts, an applicant may obtain a license in one jurisdiction, but not another. This is because the one jurisdiction requires the applicant to meet a higher standard of conduct.

Breadth

The breadth of licensing concerns how governments attempt to prevent unsuitable persons from exercising authority and influence over any aspect of sportsbook operations that could impact wagering integrity. The purpose of the breadth criterion is to prevent unsuitable persons from attempting to influence operations through control of some goods or services critical to the sportsbook, or gaining influence through the ability to control labor unions.[47]

One example of the operation of breadth involved the wire services that provided race results in the 1930s. Benjamin "Bugsy" Siegel was a member of the New York Crime Syndicate "Murder, Inc." A major activity of that organization was monopoly control over the wire services. For a racebook to operate, it needs information from the track on such matters as post positions, starting times, track odds, the order of finish, and track pay-outs. The Syndicate realized that if it could control this information, it could extract high fees from legal and illegal bookmakers that relied on the information for their livelihood. Creating a monopoly was not a significant problem for the Syndicate. Following World War II, a new war of sorts broke out, known as the "great wire-service war." People were killed, including the owner of the largest wire service. After the bleeding stopped, a few wire services remained, but all under the control of Siegel and the Syndicate. This situation created problems for Nevada. Las Vegas and Reno racebooks were paying monopoly prices for the track information and were being extorted for small interests in their operations. Although the Syndicate had few or any economists who set prices, it had a rough method of deciding fees, that is, to set the fees at the highest rate possible without putting the books out of business. The disseminator could also discriminate against certain racebooks by charging different rates or refusing to supply information. These events eventually led to Nevada's requirement that services that provide the results of races must obtain a license.

Typical regulatory systems involve "tiered" licensing. Tiered licensing involves categorizing every group of individuals or entities that are associated with the sportsbook industry into two or more tiers. Each tier is then subject to a different level of licensing scrutiny. For example, regulators may decide to extend the breadth of licensing to both owners and sportsbook employees. The level of review, however, might be different. Owners may have to undergo a thorough investigation that requires the regulators to spend months reviewing all aspects of the owner's life, while the review of the sportsbook employees is a check of their police records.

Operators

Operators are the persons or business entities that contract for or otherwise have the right to conduct gaming at a sportsbook. It is

47 Lester B. Snyder, *Regulation of Legalized Gambling, An Inside View*, 12 Conn. L. Rev. 665, 714 (1980).

understandable that operators should be required to obtain a license. Operators deal directly with the patron, create and post the wager, and have responsibility for accounting. In Nevada, a person may not own or operate a sports pool without obtaining the highest level of gaming license. The applicant must meet the rigorous standards for such a license.[48]

Owners

Owners are persons who hold the rights to conduct business on the premises by having an interest in the real property and buildings. An owner's interest can be perpetual, through owning the property and buildings, or temporary, through holding a lease on the property. Owners may either operate the sportsbook or hire an operator to run the sportsbook on their behalf. An owner may assign the right to conduct business by leasing the property to another party. In this instance, the person reduces his status to a landlord, which is discussed below.

While owners who are not also operators do not have direct contact with the public, they may have considerable influence over the operators and often share in sportsbook profits.

Persons Entitled to Profits

Analyzing how to treat persons entitled to profits for licensing purposes varies little from that of owners. The only difference between the two groups is their basis for entitlement to profits. Owners receive profits by having an interest in real property and buildings, and by retaining an operator to conduct business on the premises. Persons entitled to profits are those who provide other property or services in exchange for some of the profits. This can include providing furniture, fixtures or equipment, financing, management, or marketing services.

Creditors

A sportsbook may have many types of creditors. Lenders of money usually are the largest. Other creditors can include suppliers of gaming and non-gaming equipment, financial institutions, and others who provide furniture, fixtures, equipment leases, and vendors that sell on credit. The government may even be a creditor if it is owed taxes.

Another type of "lender" potentially subject to regulatory scrutiny is a person who buys a debt security, such as a bond, issued by a

---

48 NEV. GAMING COMM. REG. 22.020.

sportsbook company. Debt securities may include bonds, debentures, and other interests or instruments. A debenture is a bond issued by the sportsbook company to evidence the debt owed. Debentures entitle the holder to rights, including the payment of interest. Some debentures or bonds are convertible into stock. In other words, a convertible debenture holder can change his status from a debt holder to an equity investor.

Three considerations surround the degree of regulatory scrutiny accorded creditors. First, creditors that lend money or provide financing expect a return on their money commensurate with the costs and risks involved in the transaction. Second, as the amount lent or financed increases, so does the creditor's vested interest in the success of the business. Third, unsuitable persons may use the guise of being lenders or creditors to extract money at excessive interest rates from the sportsbook operations. Regulation must balance the first consideration against the latter two.

Information Services

Information services fall into three categories:

- Oddsmakers that provide line, point spread, or odds or advice, or consultation that sportsbooks consider in setting its line, point spread, or odds; or advice or prediction regarding the outcome of competition or events within the competition.[49]
- Services that provide the results of competitions or events within the competitions.
- Services that aggregate the current odds from multiple sportsbooks and provide them to sportsbooks to assist in managing risk.

Odds makers raise regulatory concerns because they can intentionally misprice a line, point spread, or odds or advice, and then bet through a third party to the disadvantage of their client sportsbooks. For this reason, Nevada requires oddsmakers to obtain a full license.

Services that provide the results of competitions present a regulatory concern because of the potential for delaying the result to allow persons to past post. This occurs where a bettor places a wager on a winning proposition after acquiring knowledge of the outcome of the competition or an event within a competition.[50] The converse

49 NEV. REV. STAT. § 463.01642 & NEV. REV. STAT. § 463.160(1)(b).

50 CAL. PENAL CODE § 337(u) provides a definition and punishment for past posting in

of past posting is where a bettor cancels or withdraws a wager on a losing proposition after acquiring knowledge of the outcome of the competition or an event within a competition. Both have occurred in the context of sports and horse race wagering.

The 1973 American caper film, *The Sting*, set in September 1936 featured a scheme involving past posting on horse races. In 1936, race books operated by receiving race results from a wire service (often owned by organized crime families). The wire service sent the results electronically over telegraph wires, and the race book received them over a rudimentary device that printed the results on a paper tape. As the race book did not have access to any other immediate reporting of the results, it had to rely on the wire service's results as both accurate and simultaneous. If the wire service or an employee of the wire service could delay the results, a co-conspirator might be able to place a wager on the race after it was over but before the results were transmitted. These types of past posting schemes became more difficult with the widespread broadcasting of events. Past posting can still occur if the perpetrators have access to the betting systems and can place wagers after betting on the event is supposed to have closed.[51]

For sporting event results, a sportsbook receives the information that they use to determine the results from a third-party company like Sportradar. Sportsbooks now have closed betting on final results before the start of the competition, so the notion of the historical past posting depicted in *The Sting* is now practically impossible. Moreover, because most sporting events are simulcasted, if the sports information service delayed the results, the problem would be immediately apparent to the sportsbook by comparing the live feed to the sports wagering system.

Vulnerabilities to past-posting, however, still exist. To conduct in-game wagering, the betting companies require data scouts, who are charged with logging play-by-play information in real time at the location of the sporting event.[52] Past-posting becomes feasible where the data scout delays the inputting of information for a few seconds

the context of casino games but the concept is identical for sports wagering.

51 Joe Drape, *Horse Racing; Ways to Keep Schemers from Beating the System*, NY TIMES, Oct. 22, 2003, http://www.nytimes.com/2003/10/22/sports/horse-racing-ways-to-keep-schemers-from-beating-the-system.html?mcubz=0.

52 Ryan Rodenberg & Jack Kerr, *Fake News, Manipulated Data and the Future of Betting Fraud*, ESPN, June 28, 2017, http://www.espn.com/chalk/story/_/id/19752031/future-sports-betting-fake-news-manipulated-data-future-betting-fraud.

to allow the placing of a wager after the outcome. Because human actors enter the information, it may be difficult to determine whether a delay is intentional or merely inadvertent due to distraction, human error, or otherwise.

A scandal of this nature occurred in tennis in 2016. The International Tennis Federation entered an agreement with a data company called Sportradar to provide live results from ITF events. Sportradar also sold this information to betting operations for in-play wagering.[53] According to news reports, ITF umpires had "to immediately update the scoreboard after each point using their official IBM tablets. This score is then transmitted around the world to live-score sites and bookmakers, allowing the latter to update their prices as the match proceeds."[54] Some corrupt umpires, however, delayed entering the results for up to a minute to allow bettors to past post their in-game wagers. This practice even acquired a name, "courtsiding."[55]

These vulnerabilities are serious enough that government should consider whether to require services that provide results—particularly for in-game wagering—to obtain some level of licensure.

Services that aggregate the current odds from multiple sportsbooks and provide them to sportsbooks to assist in managing risk present the fewest regulatory concerns. Conceivably they could misrepresent the current odds at the various books to entice the sportsbook to misprice its odds, but the information that it accumulates is readily available from the source, and their service merely accumulates and redistributes it. Altering the information would be subject to simple verification and would be easily detectable.

Manufacturers of Sportsbook Equipment

While sportsbook equipment cannot impact the outcome of the underlying sporting event, the system does determine the amount of the payouts and the necessary reports for tax and regulatory purposes. The requirement that the sportsbook equipment be designed according to regulatory standards and then be tested helps assure proper payout and accounting. If regulators are not confident that these procedures are adequate to mitigate the risk of noncompliance

53 Sean Ingle, *Revealed: Tennis Umpires Secretly Banned Over Gambling Scam*, THE GUARDIAN, Feb. 9, 2016, https://www.theguardian.com/sport/2016/feb/09/revealed-tennis-umpires-secretly-banned-gambling-scam.

54 *Id.*

55 *Id.*

to an acceptable level, they may decide to require the manufacturer to obtain some level of licensing.

Call Centers

Players not placing wagers in person may need to contact the sportsbooks for assistance in establishing an account or in the placing of wagers. While computer systems can frequently handle these services, personal intervention may be required if the automated system does not adequately respond to the questions posed. Sportsbooks may outsource call centers to an independent third party that provides its service to multiple sportsbooks. This is particularly cost effective for small sportsbooks because they do not have to incur the fixed costs such as computer and telecommunications equipment, and rent for a dedicated call center. Nevada considers call centers worthy of licensure because they interface with the bettors and write the tickets for wagers.[56] Moreover, employees of a call center who are "receiving and transmitting wagering instructions" and "any employee supervising this function" are gaming employees and must register.[57]

Depth

When a government requires a license to engage in an occupation related to gaming, the entity that must apply and obtain the license often is not an individual. The depth of licensing refers to which persons associated with the applicant/entity must file an application and obtain a license.

A sportsbook typically has four levels of employees. The lowest level of employee is the writer, so called because writers once hand wrote the wagering tickets for patrons. In the modern book, the writers accept money from the bettor and place it in their register. They then enter the requested wager into a sports wagering system on their computer terminals. Once entered, the terminal produces a ticket, and the writer gives the ticket to the patron for verification and proof of his wager. The manufacturer of the system must register with the gaming authorities.

A writer has minimal opportunity to undertake actions that present significant regulatory concern. Like cashiers at a bank, they process all transactions through computerized systems that provide safeguards and checks and balances. For example, a ticket writer could not write a wager for a friend for free without substantial

56 NEV. GAMING COMM. REG. 22.032.

57 NEV. GAMING COMM. REG. 22.037.

risk of detection. This would put their bank out of balance, and subsequent investigation of the reasons for this imbalance would lead to discovering their action.

The second level of employee is the supervisor, who is responsible for the performance and protection of ticket writers. As part of the licensing process, a sportsbook must designate one or more employees with supervisory authority. One supervisor must be on the premises of the sportsbook whenever wagering occurs, and report to the sportsbook manager.

Supervisors can discover and exploit vulnerabilities in the systems and procedures at a sportsbook. For example, in 2012, the Palms Casino Resort was defrauded of more than $800,000 by a scheme devised by some of its sportsbook employees.[58] The employees schemed with a sports bettor to accept invalid horse racing wagers from him, pay out winning bets, and refund losing bets from 2006 and 2007.[59] The Chief of Enforcement for the Nevada regulators said this kind of activity is infrequent because the "'scheme can only work if you have employees involved.'"[60] The regulators participated with Homeland Security agents to investigate the operation and uncover it. The supervisor received one year in prison, the administor and the writer each received three years of probation, and the bettor received three years of probation. The court ordered all of them to share in the restitution of $232,231 to the Palms.[61]

The third level of employees are odds makers. These employees are becoming increasingly important to sportsbook operators as they offer more types of wagers. The odds makers are responsible for reviewing and adjusting odds derived from algorithms that calculate odds for in-game wagers, or odds on propositions. Some larger sportsbooks offer bettors the opportunity to propose wagers. The operators will calculate and offer wagering odds on those propositions based on the odds maker's calculations. Larger Nevada operators like William Hill employ over a dozen odds makers in their operations.[62]

---

58 Jeff German, *Former Palms Employee Sentenced in Betting Scheme*, Las Vegas Review-Journal, Oct. 20, 2014, http://www.reviewjournal.com/news/las-vegas/former-palms-employee-sentenced-betting-scheme.

59 *Id.*

60 Jeff German, *Former Palms Employees Indicted in Race and Sportsbook Scheme*, Las Vegas Review-Journal Aug. 23, 2012, http://www.reviewjournal.com/sports/betting/former-palms-employees-indicted-race-and-sports-book-scheme.

61 *Id.*

62 Presentation of Dan Schwartz, William Hill at SportsBettingUSA Conference (Nov. 16, 2017).

These odds makers are in sensitive positions because they can harm the book maker and the state by posting odds favorable to the bettor if they are not properly supervised.

The fourth level is the sportsbook manager. The manager's responsibilities are to correct errors and enforce rules, policies, and procedures within the sportsbook. The sportsbook manager is responsible for the overall operation of the sportsbook, including approving wagers over specific amounts, risk management (such as making line movements), and compliance with laws and regulations.

In light of their relative importance to operations and the potential damage that they can cause if they engage in dishonest acts, sportsbook managers should receive the highest level of licensing scrutiny. The case involving a sportsbook manager at Cantor Gaming working with illegal gambling sites as described in this Chapter demonstrates these vulnerabilities.

The position posing the next highest risk are supervisors, who play a critical role in policing the action that a sportsbook accepts and whose failure to undertake these responsibilities can present serious threats to their sportsbook.

Nevada requires all sportsbook employees to undergo a state-conducted background check and obtain a gaming work registration, although this is a low-level review for writers and supervisors.[63]

Criteria

A key aspect of any licensing scheme is to review the suitability of the individual applicants seeking a license regardless of whether they are owners, operators, or employees. To do so, regulators must apply criteria that the government deems essential in determining their suitability. Criteria can be of a fixed or discretionary nature. Fixed criteria are quantifiable ones that an applicant either meets or not. Fixed criteria can include whether a person has been convicted of a felony (South Dakota)[64] or whether an applicant has been convicted of any crime involving gambling, prostitution, or sale of alcohol to a minor (Mississippi).[65]

Discretionary criteria are minimum qualifications not subject to quantification. They are based on the discretion of the gaming regulators. For example, Great Britain requires a showing an

63 NEV. REV. STAT. § 463.0157.

64 S.D. CODIFIED LAWS § 42-7B-33(3) (2011).

65 MISS. CODE ANN. § 75-76-67(3) (West 2013).

applicant is likely to act consistently with the licensing objectives.[66] Great Britain's requirement follows the most common discretionary criteria, those involving good character, associations, management capabilities, and financial abilities.

Good Character or Good Moral Character

Gaming statutes and regulations often require regulators to consider "good moral character" as a factor in screening applicants for professional and other vocational licenses involving a high degree of public trust. In Indiana, gaming commissioners will examine the applicant's "good moral character."[67] Besides gaming, good moral character is a common criterion in considering whether to grant a professional license, such as accounting, law, or medicine. Despite its frequent use, the term has limited practical utility because it is difficult to define and apply. The major problem with using "good moral character" as a criterion is the inherent subjectivity involved when judging another's character.[68]

Judicial attempts in the United States to give concrete meaning to the term "good moral character" are unhelpful. One case that attempted to define the term is *Konigsberg v. State Bar of California*.[69] There, the State Bar denied an applicant's admission because of "questionable moral character," based on the applicant having made certain political statements.[70] The Court, discussing the definition of "good moral character," stated that:

> The term, by itself, is unusually ambiguous. It can be defined in an almost unlimited number of ways for any definition will necessarily reflect the attitudes, experiences, and prejudices of the definer. Such a vague qualification, which is easily adapted to fit personal views and predilections, can be a dangerous instrument for arbitrary and discriminatory denial. . . .[71]

Ultimately, what is good or bad depends on the individual

---

66 UK Gambling Act 2005, c. 19 Part 5 Section 70§ 70(2)(b).

67 INDIANA GAMING COMMISSION, *Occupational Licensing*, http://www.in.gov/igc/2344.htm (last visited Nov. 20, 2017).

68 Rhode, *supra* note 39 at 529.

69 353 U.S. 252 (1957). Other courts have struggled with the same ambiguities. The Arizona Supreme Court, ten years after *Konigsberg*, conceded that "the concept of good moral character escapes definition in the abstract," and held that each case must be judged on its own merits in an *ad hoc* determination. *In re* Klahr, 433 P.2d 977, 979 (Ariz. 1967). The conclusion that the individual has good moral character and therefore is fit, is a subjective opinion only reached by comparing the individual to one's personal concept of what is moral or immoral.

70 *Konigsberg*, *id.* at 258-59.

71 *Id.* at 262-63.

perceptions of the person making the judgment. The United States Supreme Court has articulated this concern.[72] In *Schware v. Board of Bar Examiners of State of New Mexico*, an applicant for admission as a lawyer was rejected for questionable moral character because of his membership in the Communist Party.[73] The Court reversed, stating that:

> [A] state can require high standards of qualification, such as good moral character or proficiency in its law, before it admits an applicant to the Bar, but any qualification must have a rational connection with the applicant's fitness or capacity to practice law.[74]

While a common criterion for licensure, "good moral character" is an inherently vague benchmark which functions as a total grant of discretion to regulators. Though courts have tried to narrow the definition of "good moral character," they have been mostly unsuccessful.

Integrity, Honesty, and Truthfulness

Integrity, honesty, and truthfulness are commonly used in gaming licensing as criteria to assess an applicant's suitability. In New Jersey, the commission will grant a casino license only if the company is under the control of persons of integrity.[75] Under New Jersey law, besides character, the commission reviews the applicant's honesty and integrity by considering personal, professional, and business associations, history of criminal convictions, history of civil litigation, credit history, bankruptcies, and personal and professional references.[76]

While related, the concepts of integrity, honesty, and truthfulness have different meanings. Truthfulness means to tell the truth and is only one component of honesty. One can be truthful, but dishonest. It is dishonest to use some truths and not disclose other truths to create a false impression.[77] A person arrested by state police can truthfully state that city police had never arrested him. If, however, he responded to a question about his criminal record by stating, "I have never been arrested by the city police," it would be truthful but dishonest. Regulators want full disclosure by applicants and licensees. This means telling the truth and conveying accurate impressions.

---

72 Schware v. Bd. of Bar Exam'rs of State of N.M., 353 U.S. 232 (1957).

73 *Id.* at 238.

74 *Id.* at 239.

75 N. J. STAT. ANN. § 5:12-85 (West 2011).

76 N. J. STAT. ANN. § 5:12-89 (West 2011).

77 Wiggins v. Texas, 778 S.W.2d 877, 889 (Tex. App. 1989).

Therefore, "honesty" as a criterion is preferable to truthfulness.

How useful is "honesty" as a criterion? Shakespeare wrote, in Hamlet, "Ay sir, to be honest, as this world goes, is to be one man picked out of ten thousand."[78] Thomas Fuller conveyed a similar thought, "He that resolves to deal with none but honest men must leave off dealing."[79] The sentiment that both men convey is that no matter how committed to honesty a person may be, few people can claim complete honesty in all their dealings.[80] Moreover, lies can be altruistic rather than self-serving by supporting another person or not wanting to offend them.[81]

When regulators apply the "honesty" criterion, two general rules emerge. First, the honesty criterion usually should be considered in a business, as opposed to a personal, context. This is justified because the purpose of licensing is to predict the conduct of an applicant in a business relationship as a gaming licensee. Second, honesty in business conduct becomes more relevant with the importance of the transaction. It may be of minor materiality that an applicant, to cut short a telemarketing call, lied by telling the salesman he recently bought the product being offered. The materiality increases dramatically if the applicant misrepresents the value of inventory to convince a lender to loan money to his business. The crime of perjury, as an example, required that the false statement "must be in some point material to the question in dispute; for if it only be in some trifling collateral circumstance, to which no regard is paid, it is not punishable."[82]

While conceptually a person with "integrity" generally exhibits "honest" behavior, honesty is nothing more than a component of integrity. According to one court, the word integrity means "soundness of moral principle and character, as shown by one's dealing with others in the making and performance of contracts. . ."[83] As one commentator noted:

---

78 William Shakespeare, Hamlet act 2, sc.2.

79 Thomas Fuller, Gnomologia: Adages and Proverbs; Wise Sentences and Witty Sayings, Ancient and Modern, Foreign and British 93 (1st ed. 1732), *available at* http://books.google.com/books?id=3y8JAAAAQAAJ&pg=PP1#v=onepage&q&f=false.

80 Bella M. DePaulo & Deborah A. Kashy, *Everyday Lies in Close and Casual Relationships*, 74 J. of Personality and Soc. Psychol. 63 (1998).

81 *Id.*

82 United States v. Wells, 519 U.S. 482 (1997)(quoting Sir William Blackstone, Commentaries on the Laws of England Vol. 4, 137 (1769), and citing 1 W. Hawkins, Pleas of the Crown, ch. 27, § 8, p. 433 (Curwood ed. 1824)).

83 *In re* Bauquier's Estate, 26 P. 178 aff'd, 26 P. 532 (Cal. 1891).

> At a minimum, persons of integrity are individuals whose practices are consistent with their principles, even in the face of strong countervailing pressures. Yet the term also implies something more than steadfastness. Fanatics may be loyal to their values, but we do not praise them for integrity. What earns our praise is a willingness to adhere to values that reflect some reasoned deliberation, based on logical assessment of relevant evidence and competing views. Some theorists would add a requirement that the values themselves must satisfy certain minimum demands of consistency, generalizability, and respect for others.[84]

Integrity is a complex concept that involves commitments to prioritized, personal moral principles. As another commentator noted, "Integrity does not consist of molding and adapting one's principles to whatever behaviors we and those around us find convenient. Integrity means to take the high road, the road of conforming our behavior to our principles."[85] These principles can include honesty, family, friendship, religion, honor, country, or fairness. Integrity means upholding these commitments for the right reasons in the face of temptation.[86] Persons prioritize these commitments such that it is acceptable to violate some commitments to honor others. For example, most people believe lying (dishonesty) is acceptable to protect another from harm or injustice. For regulators to test a person's integrity, they would have to understand the person's priorities and decide whether the person is consistently faithful to these commitments and their priority. This is an impossible task in a neutral setting but is even more problematic because the regulators' sense of personal priorities might differ from the applicant's.

Integrity might even contravene regulatory policy due to the priority of the applicant's commitments. Suppose an applicant who highly values personal friendship has been friends since childhood with a person of a notorious reputation. The regulators demand that licensees not associate with such persons; however, the applicant's integrity places his commitment to friendship above the dictates of regulation. The applicant, to maintain his integrity, would continue to maintain his friendship even though it is likely to make him unsuitable to hold a gaming license. Therefore, regulators must be adept at defining which commitments are most important to

84 Deborah L. Rhode, *If Integrity Is the Answer, What Is the Question?*, 72 FORDHAM L. REV. 333, 335-36 (2003).

85 David Luban. *Integrity: Its Causes and Cures*, 72 FORDHAM L. REV. 279, 289 (2003).

86 Lynn McFall, *Integrity*, 98 ETHICS 5, 9 (Univ. of Chicago Press, Oct. 1987).

proper regulation, and at testing the person's behavior against those commitments.

The criteria of integrity, honesty, and truthfulness all suffer from some degree of difficulty in application. Honesty, however, is the easiest of the three for regulators to measure and judge in a meaningful way, provided the inquiry is limited to material, business-related behaviors.

Compliance with Law

An applicant's compliance with all laws pertaining to its role with the sportsbook is material in granting a gaming license. One function of the licensing process is to predict whether, if granted a license, the applicant will comply with all gaming laws and regulations. Strict compliance with these laws and regulations is necessary to achieving the policy goals underlying them. Nothing is more predictive of future compliance with business laws and regulations than a review of past compliance in the same context.

Some jurisdictions' laws and regulations have fixed criteria for determining suitability based on legal compliance. A felony conviction or an offense involving gambling may be a disqualifying factor and pose an insurmountable hurdle for convicted applicants.[87] Other jurisdictions follow flexible standards where regulators make qualitative decisions whether the person or company is suitable based on the totality of factors. In these jurisdictions, some instances of noncompliance may be less material than others.

Material violation of laws is a useful licensing criterion because past compliance is a reliable indicator of future compliance. Compliance is much more than whether the company has violated the law. It also relates to whether the company has institutional controls for assuring compliance with all laws, domestic and foreign. This is especially relevant where they have other casinos or do business with other casinos.

Noncompliance with laws in one's personal affairs is a more difficult proposition because many laws are not enforced. For example, should a married applicant be denied a license because he had an affair that violated a state law prohibiting adultery? This violation is less material to a prediction of his conduct as a licensee than if he violated laws dealing with wire fraud. An intentional violation of a law against tax evasion is a valid consideration because it reflects on the person's honesty. Using a violation law against adultery as a predictor

---

87 *See e.g.*, MO. REV. STAT. § 313.810 (2010).

of behavior as a gaming licensee, however, is more problematic because of personal privacy issues. Also, the offender may conduct his business in an honest and honorable manner.

Still, regulators may have some concerns any time an applicant knowingly violates the law because of greed, power, or notoriety, because it shows that some things will motivate him to commit illegal actions. These actions need to be viewed in relation to the severity of the crime and its predictive value as to one's conduct as a licensee.

Manner of Doing Business

Different people have distinct manners of doing business. While some are conciliatory, and successfully resolve most disputes without litigation, others are more adversarial and regularly litigate disputes. The adversarial type may create disputes to delay payment and seek favorable settlement by the threat of suit. In dealing with regulators, the conciliatory type may tend to be cooperative and agree on appropriate behavior while the adversarial type is more likely to challenge the authority of regulators and tie up regulatory resources in court challenges.

Conciliatory types make more obedient gaming licensees. They are more willing to conform their behavior to the expectations of the regulators. By not challenging the regulatory authority through litigation, costs are reduced.

Adversarial types, however, may provide an essential check on regulators. If no licensee challenges regulatory actions that might exceed the regulator's authority, or that might contravene legislative policy, public policy goals might be frustrated, and the legislature may be none the wiser. Citizens in most societies have the right to seek judicial redress of grievances. Prejudicing an applicant for exercising legal rights might appear unjust, and may contravene governmental policy goals.

Adversarial types may, however, abuse the system where they use litigation to silence critics, avoid paying debts, or extort settlements. This requires the regulators to understand the court process and have the ability to identify frivolous litigation and patterns of abuse. Where an applicant abuses the legal system, regulators may justifiably consider this in assessing suitability for a license.

Criminal History and Prior Convictions

Most jurisdictions that regulate gaming activities investigate the applicant's criminal history, background, or records. Given that regulators necessarily must focus on past actions, especially past criminal actions, to predict future behavior, what type of history should disqualify someone from obtaining a license? A jurisdiction may take two approaches.

First, the jurisdiction may use a fixed criterion system where anyone convicted of a felony, a crime involving gambling, or a crime involving "moral turpitude," is ineligible for a gaming license.

The second approach considers a criminal conviction as evidence of the person's unsuitability but maintains flexibility to consider other evidence to decide suitability. Under this view, a criminal conviction often creates a presumption of unsuitability and shifts the burden to the applicant to rebut that presumption by showing rehabilitation.[88] Still, no definitive tests are available to decide whether a person with a history of criminal activities can earn a gaming license. Regulators may consider several facts in assessing whether to deny an application based on prior criminal activities. These include:

- The nature of the crime; criminal activities such as thievery or embezzlement are very significant;
- Seriousness of the crime or the person's involvement;
- Mitigating or extenuating circumstances;
- Proximity in time of the criminal activity;
- Age at time of the criminal activity;
- A pattern or high frequency of criminal activity;
- The applicant's honesty and forthrightness in revealing the past criminal activity to gaming investigators, and
- Relevance of the crime to policy goals related to casino gaming.

Some past crimes committed by an applicant may have no connection to policy goals that inform casino gaming. A person convicted of child molestation 15 years ago is probably unfit to be licensed to operate a child care center, but it does not follow that the same person is not suitable to operate a gaming operation. No rational

88 Maureen M. Carr, *The Effect of Prior Criminal Conduct on the Admission to Practice Law: The Move to More Flexible Admission Standards*, 8 GEO. J. LEGAL ETHICS, 367, 383 (1995). The Georgia Supreme Court stated this rebuttal must be by clear and convincing evidence. *In re* Cason, 249 Ga. 806, 808, 294 S.E.2d 520, 522 (1982). The Court stated that for lawyer fitness purposes, the applicant must reestablish his or her reputation by showing a return to a "useful and constructive place in society." This cannot be evidenced by merely paying a fine or serving time, but must be evidenced by affirmative action, such as community service, occupation, or religion This "test," allows licensing committees considerable leeway in determining eligibility based upon their own subjective attitudes.

connection exists between the two; that a person was convicted of child molestation provides a weak basis for predicting a person's capability of operating an honest casino.

Predicting future behavior using an applicant's criminal history may be an imperfect assessment, but it still may provide the most reliable predictive evidence available to regulators. Both approaches have their costs and benefits. A fixed criterion approach is an easy standard to implement, but may not be a useful predictive tool, notably when the applicant's criminal history and license obligations do not correlate. A nuanced discretionary approach, on the other hand, can address some shortcomings of the fixed criteria test by looking at the circumstances surrounding an applicant's criminal history and the applicant's subsequent conduct, but can be costly and overly subjective.

Sometimes, an applicant may never have been convicted of a crime but still have a history of suspected criminal activity or arrests. Gaming authorities may deny licenses to persons who show an involvement in criminal activities, even if they have never been convicted of a crime.

Associations with Unsuitable Persons

If licensed sportsbooks have associations with notorious persons, the public may believe that the unsuitable persons have an interest in, or influence over, the gaming operations. A person's willingness to associate with disreputable people may also call into question his judgment or propensities toward crime. The problem with the concept of association is definitional. As one court noted, "the word 'associate' is not of uniform meaning but is, rather, vague in its connotation."[89] Do incidental or involuntary contacts with known criminals constitute association? What if the applicant did not know of the other person's unsuitability?

Some courts define association as more than incidental contact with unsuitable persons. In interpreting a regulation prohibiting police officers from "associating" with criminals, one court held that the term means more than "incidental contacts" between police officers and known criminals.[90] The New Jersey Supreme Court held unknowing associations are not a basis for a finding of unsuitability

---

89 Weir v. United States, 92 F.2d 634, 638 (7th Cir. 1937), *cert. denied*, 302 U.S. 761 (1937).

90 Sponick v. City of Detroit Police Dept., 211 N.W.2d 674 (Mich. Ct. App. 1973).

by gaming regulators.[91]

While difficult to define, the concept of unsuitable "associations" should focus on the following:

- The nature and intensity of the relationship. Facts considered include: (1) type of relationship; *i.e.*, business or friendship; (2) knowledge of the second person's unsuitability; (3) whether the relationship was voluntary; (4) frequency or involvement of the relationship; and (5) the applicant's attitude after becoming aware of the gaming authorities' concern with the relationship;
- The influence or control over the applicant by the other person;
- The nature of the concern about the second person and how that concern poses a threat to the public interest; and
- The number of questionable relationships.

An inquiry based on these factors is more likely to avoid the injustices of a "guilt by association" approach while preserving regulators' ability to exclude persons genuinely unsuitable due to their associations.

Conduct During the Investigation

Laws should require applicants to make full and accurate disclosure of all information requested on the forms or by the regulatory agents.[92] The applicant's conduct during the investigation may become relevant to his suitability for many reasons. If the applicant attempts to hide or mischaracterize a past transgression, the regulators may question the applicant's current credibility. If the applicant is not cooperative, the regulators may question whether the applicant will adopt a similar attitude toward compliance after licensing. If the applicant keeps disorganized and incomplete financial and personal records, the regulators may question the applicant's ability to properly account for taxes.

---

91 *In re* Boardwalk Regency Casino License Application, 434 A.2d 1111 (N.J. 1982). The Court stated, however, that after an applicant knows of the unsuitability of an association, failing to dissociate is a knowing association. There, the New Jersey Casino Control Commission decided that the founder of a casino company was unsuitable because of, among other reasons, a recurring and enduring relationship with an individual who allegedly had ties to organized crime. The applicant sought judicial review. In upholding the agency decision, the Court noted it was "not critical of a proposition denouncing guilt adjudication predicated solely on unknowing or otherwise innocent association and is sensitive to the difficulties defending against such a premise." 434 A.2d at 1119.

92 *See, e.g.*, NEV. REV. STAT. § 463.339.

Competency/Management Abilities

Operating a sportsbook takes specialized knowledge and skills. Regulators may have concerns that otherwise honest persons might frustrate governmental goals if the operators lack the capacity properly to manage operations. Incompetence can be just as destructive to a jurisdiction's policy goals as malfeasance. Poor managers may not recognize when dishonest writers cheat a bettor. This may frustrate a primary governmental goal by failing to ensure that operations are honest. Similarly, professional cheaters and dishonest employees can more easily steal from sportsbook operations with poor management. This may frustrate governmental goals of collecting taxes on all revenues derived from gaming operations.

Regulators may scrutinize managerial competency proportionate to the complexity of the organization and sportsbook operation. The tools needed to manage larger facilities with higher limits can be daunting. But in a large diverse public company, regulators rarely expect the chairperson of the board of directors to have operational experience. The more relevant focus is on the management structure established for the gaming operations. Regulators often require applicants to provide organizational charts designating the persons in each position, their responsibilities, and lines of authority. These are then tested against standards of depth, *i.e.,* is there enough management coverage? Are all key management areas covered? Are responsibilities properly segregated? Do the persons have adequate knowledge and experience?

At the lower levels of employees, the government can use occupational certification to address competence and reduce skill deficiencies. This could be beneficial where the skills required to perform a job, such as a writer, are easily identifiable, can be quantified and framed in a license requirement, and can be tested.[93]

Financial Capabilities

Regulators may wish to review the financial capabilities of a sportsbook. This inquiry is directed to assuring that the owner or operator in financial trouble does not turn to dishonest means, or seek cash infusions from unsuitable persons to keep the operations viable.

---

93 FRONTIER ECONOMICS, DEPT. FOR EDUC. & SKILLS, AN ECONOMIC REVIEW AND ANALYSIS OF THE IMPLICATIONS OF OCCUPATIONAL LICENSING (2003), http://webarchive.nationalarchives.gov.uk/20130401151715/https://www.education.gov.uk/publications/eOrderingDownload/RR467.pdf.

The government also may want to protect the rights of sportsbook patrons by assuring the payment of winnings—although reserve requirements more directly accomplish this objective.

A review of financial capability has two major components: assuring current cash on hand, and cash flow and long-term viability. The review assures that the sportsbook has adequate cash on hand and reserves to immediately pay all current expenses including winnings and deposits. The regulators then can test the accuracy of cash-flow projections by comparing the applicant's projections with actual figures that the regulators have compiled on similar sportsbooks within the same area. An under-financed sportsbook may have an unrealistic view of projected net revenues and, therefore, have insufficient funds to carry it through to a stage of profitability.

AUDITING AND ACCOUNTING

After a company has obtained a license, regulators need to have controls over the operations to assure that the licensee is operating according to the highest standards of wagering integrity. A primary tool to accomplish this is by the imposition of accounting controls. Governments may impose any of the following requirements: (1) minimum internal controls; (2) recordkeeping requirements; (3) reporting requirements; and (4) governmental and independent audits.

Government has three principal objectives in setting regulations governing the accounting of sportsbooks. First, accounting regulations can prevent non-licensed persons from sharing in the sportsbook revenues. The regulations can assist gaming regulators in learning the cash flow of sportsbooks. If an unsuitable person is profiting from the sportsbook, regulators may be able to detect it through audits facilitated by revenue trails created by internal controls. This assures that unsuitable persons are not evading the licensing process through "hidden interests."

Second, internal controls provide procedures that protect wagering integrity. For example, requirements that the sportsbook record every wager and corresponding payout can assure that the payouts are honest and accurate, and meet any fairness standard. Moreover, proper recording of unpaid winning wagers, future wagers, and deposits creates an auditable trial to assure that all reserve requirements are met.

Third, depending on its tax rate, the government could have a minor or major interest in assuring that all revenues are properly accounted for so that it can receive all taxes. This prevents "skimming," where the owners receive revenues but do not pay taxes on them. It can also deter employee theft and embezzlement.

Minimum Internal Controls

Internal controls are policies and procedures that are designed to prevent and detect errors or irregularities that may occur in the operation of a business. They are also intended to assist a business to operate effectively and cost-efficiently. Governments can require sportsbooks to adopt and adhere to a comprehensive set of internal procedural operating controls, known as the "Internal Controls System." In a sportsbook environment, internal controls are particularly important due to the inherent risk associated with a business environment that involves cash transactions.

Internal controls are procedures that the sportsbook must follow or implement to maintain the integrity of wagering and help protect and account for its assets. Internal control systems are a method of checks and balances that help ensure wagering integrity. This is done by establishing procedures governing the conduct of wagering, movement and handling of cash and cash equivalents, and the accounting and record trail of all transactions.[94] Nevada has 18 pages of minimum internal controls that specifically regulate sportsbook operations and many more general restrictions that apply to the overall sportsbook operations.

Access Controls

Access controls are physical safeguards. They segregate responsibilities of employees and only allow employees to have access to places or systems relevant to their assigned responsibilities. Given modern computer sports betting management systems, much of this involves access to and limitations on the systems. Before writers can access a betting machine to enable them to write tickets, they must sign in, and the system then creates a record containing the writer's/cashier's identity, the date and time, station number, and that the station was opened/closed. Employees, including supervisors, who

---

94 *Legislating and Regulating Casino Gaming: A View from State Regulators* (Mar. 1, 1999), https://govinfo.library.unt.edu/ngisc/reports/belletire.pdf [hereinafter State Regulators].

write or cash tickets, cannot access the administrative terminal or perform critical functions.[95]

An example of how access controls work is by preventing alterations to wagers to enable past posting. If a sportsbook accepts wagers on which American football team will win after the event has begun, and the favorite team's quarterback breaks his leg during the first play of the game, the chances for the underdog team to win will significantly increase. If the wagering patron could place a wager on the closing line after the event commenced, he would have a signifiant advantage. To prevent this, control procedures should lock out wagers on the closing line after the sporting event begins. The most obvious method of accomplishing this is by using access controls to prevent the sportsbook's ticketing system from processing wagers after a set time, such as the kickoff. Other access controls should prevent a writer from voiding or canceling a losing ticket after the outcome of the event is known without obtaining necessary approvals.[96]

Documentation Controls

Documentation controls require sportsbook employees to make physical records of all transactions. This provides a full audit trail of every transaction. Examples of such requirements are provisions requiring that, "upon accepting a wager, a record of the wager is created in the sports computer system that contains the ticket number, the date and time and terms of the wager,"[97] and, "an original betting ticket that includes the book's name and address is printed and given to the patron."[98] Besides the transaction, a restricted computer system

95 Nevada Gaming Control Board, Minimum Internal Control Standards, Race and Sports, Standard 48.

96 Nevada Gaming Control Board, Minimum Internal Control Standards, Race and Sports, Standard 7. "The race and sports computer system either is incapable of transacting/accepting a wager subsequent to the above cutoff times or produces a report which specifically identifies such wagers." When this occurs, additional Access, Documentation and Personnel Controls must be met. Typically, the voiding of a ticket requires either the signature or access code of a supervisor. This is a Personnel Control. Voided tickets, winning payouts, and a summary of each day's sporting events (including the start time) are usually forwarded to the Accounting Department that audits them as an additional Documentation and Personnel Control. A sportsbook also has controls that relate to the synchronizing of clocks to increase the effectiveness of lock out controls.

97 Nevada Gaming Control Board, Minimum Internal Control Standards, Race and Sports, Standard 11.

98 *Id.*

record is created at the same time as the original betting ticket.[99] The sportsbook employees can access the restricted record for inquiry-only functions (access control).[100] Before paying a ticket/voucher or crediting the winnings to the patron's account, the writer enters the ticket/voucher number in the sports computer system to authorize the payment; or for wagering account bets, after posting the event results. The system will then authorize payment of winning wagers and update the patron's wagering account.[101] After scanning by the writer, the sports computer system brands the ticket/voucher with a paid designation, the amount of payment, and the date. The sports computer system cannot authorize payment on a previously paid ticket/voucher, a voided ticket/voucher, a losing ticket, or an unissued ticket/voucher.[102]

Personnel Controls

Personnel controls are persons watching other persons. For example, a ticket cannot be unilaterally voided by the sportsbook employee who issued the ticket to the patron. Instead, internal controls require all voids to be "signed by the writer/cashier and a supervisor (who did not write the ticket) at the time of the void."[103] Moreover, employees who perform the supervisory function of approving void tickets typically cannot write tickets. The log of any voided tickets is sent to an independent department such as accounting or audit each day for a complete audit of void tickets (using the log and the tickets), of the proper signatures on the ticket, of a void designation on the ticket, of date and time of the void on the ticket, of any indications of past-post voiding, and for other appropriate regulation compliance.[104]

Reporting

Sportsbooks should maintain and provide many layers of reports on their wagering activity. Regulators may require that the books generate reports to track all transactions so that both the sportsbook's internal and external auditors and the regulator's audit division may

99 *Id.*

100 *Id.*

101 Nevada Gaming Control Board, Minimum Internal Control Standards, Race and Sports, Standard 26.

102 Nevada Gaming Control Board, Minimum Internal Control Standards, Race and Sports, Standard 31.

103 Nevada Gaming Control Board, Minimum Internal Control Standards, Race and Sports, Standard 12(c).

104 *Id.*

find and investigate discrepancies.[105]

Each book's computer system should generate multiple end-of-day reports that an employee who is independent of the sportsbook department can perform or observe. Each such report should contain the date, the sportsbook's name, and the title of the report.[106] These reports include a transaction report, a futures report, an unpaid report, a purge report, an unpaid and voucher summary report, a wagering account report and an accrual basis recap report. These reports are summarized below:

- A **transaction report** typically lists the amount of writes, voids, payouts, vouchers issued, and vouchers redeemed, all broken down by each ticket writer.[107] This report details the date and time, event, results/winners, and payout amounts for different wagers.[108]
- A **futures report** typically lists the total amount of wagers placed on previous days for the present day's event, and lists the totals of the amount of wagers placed on previous days and the present day.[109]
- An **unpaid report** contains the details of unexpired winning tickets that have not been paid, and details of unexpired vouchers that patrons have not redeemed.[110]
- A **purge report** contains details of expired winning tickets and vouchers that have not been paid or redeemed, the payout amount, and ending balance of unredeemed vouchers.[111]
- An **unpaid and voucher summary report** lists the beginning balance of unpaid tickets/unredeemed vouchers, previously unredeemed tickets/vouchers that were paid on the present day, new unpaid tickets/ unredeemed vouchers

105 Nevada Gaming Control Board, Minimum Internal Control Standards, Race and Sports, Standard 58.

106 Nevada Gaming Control Board, Minimum Internal Control Standards, Race and Sports, Standard 57.

107 Nevada Gaming Control Board, Minimum Internal Control Standards, Race and Sports, Standard 58(a).

108 Nevada Gaming Control Board, Minimum Internal Control Standards, Race and Sports, Standard 58(b) and (c).

109 Nevada Gaming Control Board, Minimum Internal Control Standards, Race and Sports, Standard 58(e).

110 Nevada Gaming Control Board, Minimum Internal Control Standards, Race and Sports, Standard 58(f).

111 Nevada Gaming Control Board, Minimum Internal Control Standards, Race and Sports, Standard 58(g).

for events that occurred the present day, and the ending balance of unpaid tickets/unredeemed vouchers at the close of the present day.[112]

- A **wagering account report** lists, by writer, each transaction and totals by transaction type, and contains a summary report listing by wagering account the amount of deposits, winnings, voided wagers, wagers, withdrawals and other adjustments.[113] Totals for writes, voids, net write payouts and net win are also listed with the Wagering Account Reports.
- An **accrual basis recap report** summarizes the other reports previously mentioned, taxable revenue (including expired unredeemed vouchers that were included in payout amounts), and book revenue.[114] Exception information includes (1) voids, (2) changes in odds, cut-off times, results, and event data and (3) all supervisory approvals.[115]

The sportsbook should also report statistics. The sportsbook should maintain these for each month and year-to-date indicating the total amount of wagers accepted, total amount of payout on winning wagers, the net amount or taxable win by the sportsbook, and the win-to-write percentage for each sport, and for sports parlay cards.[116] Management personnel independent of the sportsbook should review these reports on at least a monthly basis and investigate any large or unusual statistical fluctuation. Management should undertake these investigations within one month of the month-end statistical report.[117]

Special Reporting – Suspicious Activities

Regulators should rely on the sportsbooks to assist them in ensuring wagering and sports integrity and general enforcement of criminal laws. This can be accomplished in several ways.

---

112 Nevada Gaming Control Board, Minimum Internal Control Standards, Race and Sports, Standard 58(h).

113 Nevada Gaming Control Board, Minimum Internal Control Standards, Race and Sports, Standard 58(i).

114 Nevada Gaming Control Board, Minimum Internal Control Standards, Race and Sports, Standard 58(j).

115 Nevada Gaming Control Board, Minimum Internal Control Standards, Race and Sports, Standard 58(k).

116 Nevada Gaming Control Board, Minimum Internal Control Standards, Race and Sports, Standard 92 and 93.

117 Nevada Gaming Control Board, Minimum Internal Control Standards, Race and Sports, Standard 94.

The first is to require the sportsbook to report any incidents that violate or evade any federal, state, or local law or regulation or code of conduct impacting either sports integrity or wagering integrity. For example, if the sportsbook has reason to believe that a bet was made or attempted to be made on behalf of a referee, player or athletic support personnel, the sportsbook should be required to report the incident as a suspicious activity. Also, after examining the available facts, including the bettor's background, sportsbooks should report any wager for which there is no reasonable explanation or apparent lawful purpose, or that is not the type of wager that the particular patron would normally be expected to place.[118] If a writer has personal knowledge that a person usually places bets for $100, but one day wagers $5,000 and no reasonable explanation exists for the wager, this wager would be considered suspicious. If a patron refuses to provide identification when cashing in a winning ticket of more than $10,000, a suspicious wager report will be filled with identifying information and conveyed to the regulators. There can be other reasons why a patron might refuse to provide identification (e.g., the player does not want a spouse to know about his or her gambling), but if the regulators are building a case against a criminal, suspicious wager reports will supplement the investigation.

A suspicious wager report should be filed promptly within the time set by regulators after the sportsbook initially detects it, but if more time is needed to identify a suspect, the reporting period may be extended.[119] The patron should not be informed that a report has been filed against him.[120]

Second, the sportsbook should immediately report by telephone any suspected violations of the laws governing sports or wagering integrity.

Finally, regulations requiring the licensees to have compliance committees or to report regulatory violations or illegal activities can assist in compliance. Compliance committees also can have responsibilities for vetting and reporting changes in key personnel, vetting significant vendors, and reviewing and reporting material events.[121]

Large Wagers

Closely tied to suspicious activity reporting are requirements that sportsbooks report large wagers. In Nevada, sportsbooks cannot

118 NEV. GAMING COMM. REG. 22.121(1).
119 NEV. GAMING COMM. REG. 22.121(3).
120 NEV. GAMING COMM. REG. 22.121(5).
121 State Regulators, *supra* note 94.

accept large wagers (over $10,000) without obtaining the patron's name, permanent address, and social security number. They also must examine and copy a government-issued identification like a driver's license or passport.[122] The sportsbook needs to maintain records of the amount of each wager over $10,000 and personal identifiers of the patron or his agent, including name, permanent address, social security number, and document number for government-issued identification. These wagers must be logged in a Book Wagering Report and submitted to the regulators every month.

The sportsbooks also need to keep multiple transaction logs that prevent any circumvention of these requirements. They also must log all wagers in excess of $5,000, or in smaller amounts that aggregate in excess of $5,000 that the sportsbook or its employees know are from a player during a designated 24-hour period.[123] Once the aggregate amount hits $5,000, the sportsbook must log a physical description of the patron, the patron's name if known, and identifiers on the wager itself. Before completing a wager that would aggregate over $10,000, the sportsbook must get full identification of the patron.[124] A sportsbook violates the regulations if it or its officers, employees, or agents encourage or instruct the patron in any manner to willfully evade or circumvent the recording and reporting requirements.

Recordkeeping

Documentation control is of little value unless the operator maintains the records. Recordkeeping facilitates the audit process by the government and independent auditors and allows for governmental investigations into the sportsbooks' activities. Sportsbooks may be required to retain all records for a fixed number of years.

Audits

Government audits are a method of assuring proper cash controls. The government must retain a trained and competent staff to conduct the audits with sufficient regularity to be a deterrent to illegal or poor accounting practices. Audit objectives should ensure that the sportsbook: (1) is not paying or allowing unlicensed persons to receive gaming revenues; (2) has adequate internal control procedures; (3) follows internal control procedures for the handling

122 NEV. GAMING COMM. REG. 22.061(1).
123 NEV. GAMING COMM. REG. 22.062(2).
124 NEV. GAMING COMM. REG. 22.062(5).

of cash and transactions; (4) is properly reporting its revenues; and (5) is paying all taxes and fees. An important accounting function of audits is to assure that the sportsbooks are complying with internal controls and regulations. Because the sportsbook industry is primarily a cash business, controls and regulations dealing with cash and cash equivalent accounting predominate over other regulations. Audits can often detect violations of these controls and regulations better than other forms of enforcement.

Government audits often are unannounced and have irregular intervals to prevent licensees from following proper accounting principles only when they expect to be audited. These audits may involve detailed reviews or spot compliance with certain regulations or procedures. The failure of a licensee to allow agents to access records on demand can be deemed an unsuitable method of operation, and can subject the licensee to disciplinary action including restrictions, fines, or potential revocation of licensing.

OPERATING REQUIREMENTS

Governments also can impose operating requirements on sportsbooks. These operating requirements can cover areas related to: (1) protecting sports integrity; (2) protecting wagering integrity; (3) achieving policy goals related to wagering; or (4) achieving policy goals unrelated to wagering.

Examples of operating requirements related to protecting sports integrity can include:

- Prohibiting wagers from athletes, athletic support personnel (including coaches, trainers, team officals or staff, agents, managers, and medical personnel), or referees.
- Prohibiting wagers on events where the sport's governing body requests that books not accept wagers on the team's sports event and the regulators grant that request.[125]
- Prohibiting certain types of wagers such as negative wagers or spot wagers, or on certain types of competitions such as amateur sports, sports with high potential risk of corruption, or on sporting events in leagues with a history of corruption.

Examples of operating requirements related to protecting wagering integrity can include:

125 NEV. GAMING COMM. REG. 22.120.

- Prohibiting book employees from placing any wagers at the book where they work or at an affiliated book.[126]
- Establishing the age and identification of patrons.
- Mandating reserve requirements.
- Establishing procedures for accepting contingent wagers.
- Setting requirements for honoring winning tickets including the obligations to honor tickets when presented.
- Setting requirements for handling disputed ownership of tickets.
- Setting how long the books must honor winning tickets from the date of issuance or the event that determined a win.
- Setting whether, under what conditions, and how books can make layoff wagers.
- Defining under what conditions and how a book can rescind wagers.
- Setting requirements regarding disclosure, display, and contents of house wagering rules.
- Setting requirements for public posting of betting odds and the public's rights to place wagers at the posted odds.
- Establishing permitted methods of wagering, and if remote wagering is permitted, establishing the acceptable communications technologies.
- Determining if account wagering is permitted and, if so, how the sportsbook establishes the accounts and acceptable methods for the patron to fund such accounts.

Operating requirements related to achieving policy goals for wagering in general may include restricting certain activities linked to problem gambling as previously described in this Chapter. There are also examples of operating requirements related to assisting in the prevention and detections of illegal wagering. Nevada prohibits messenger betting to prevent illegal books from laying off wagers. The regulation provides: "No book or agent or employee of a book may accept a wager from a person who the book, agent, or employee knows or reasonably should know is a messenger bettor or is placing the wager in violation of state or federal law."[127]

SURVEILLANCE

Another tool that governments can use to control sportsbook

126 NEV. GAMING COMM. REG. 5.013(3).
127 NEV. GAMING COMM. REG. 22.061(1).

operations is surveillance. Sportsbook surveillance involves covert observations of the sportsbook operations, usually with video cameras. Sportsbook surveillance should be an integral part of the sportsbook plan of internal controls. The purpose of surveillance is to: (1) safeguard the licensee's assets; (2) deter, detect, and prosecute criminal act; and (3) maintain the public trust that licensed gaming is honest and free of criminal elements.[128] Regulations can dictate the number of cameras, their placement, recording capacities, and retention requirements. [129] Surveillance coverage in the sportsbook should, at a minimum, cover the windows, counters, and cash drawers.

Surveillance can provide an independent check on sportsbook operations and a video recording of persons making otherwise anonymous wagers. The surveillance operators can be either government regulators, sportsbook employees, or both. Larger sportsbooks can assign supervision over surveillance independent of operations personnel and management.[130] These sportsbooks may have surveillance rooms that resemble a control center. In front of a sweeping desk are video monitors tied to computer hard drives that store the surveillance videos of the sportsbook.

ENFORCEMENT

Another key component to effective regulation is that gaming regulators enforce the gaming laws. A government that fails to enforce laws can effectively render them meaningless. The regulated may soon realize that they can violate the law with impunity and those with low ethics will do so. In contrast, those with high business probity will be placed at a competitive disadvantage or will not do business in the jurisdiction. Likewise, patrons may lose confidence in the integrity of the industry or be victims of regulatory or criminal violations. Detection and discipline concentrate on the licensee's behavior. Here, the regulators hope to uncover regulatory violations and fine or revoke the license of the violator. A fine is intended to dissuade the violator from committing other regulatory violations. A license revocation assures that he will not.

Regulatory agencies typically have enforcement agents that conduct law enforcement, investigative, and intelligence activities.

---

128 *See* NEV. GAMING COMM. REG. 5.160.

129 State Regulators, *supra* note 94.

130 *Id.*

The law enforcement agent's primary task is to ensure wagering integrity at sportsbooks. Agents should investigate allegations of cheating by the sportsbooks, sportsbook employees or customers, and investigate suspicious activities related to any betting event. They also may investigate player disputes, determine sportsbook compliance with regulations and accepted standards of operation, and review surveillance systems.[131] These agents may also investigate allegations of skimming and hidden interest in sportsbooks by unsuitable persons.[132]

Intelligence agents may collect information on organized crime activities, including match fixing, attempts by illegal bookmakers to use sportsbooks to lay-off illegal wagers from other jurisdictions, or attempts to use the sportsbooks for money laundering.[133] A model for intelligence gathering is the Sports Betting Intelligence Unit (SBIU), an entity acting under the auspices of the UK Gaming Commission. This specialty division "receives information and intelligence relating to potentially criminal breaches of sports betting integrity, or breaches of sports betting rules or codes of conduct."[134]

Prevention Measures

In contrast to detection and discipline, prevention attempts to reduce the likelihood of noncompliance through education and training. Regulatory agents should meet with sportsbook managers to review compliance procedures. Agents may hold industry seminars to review emerging threats to wagering integrity or to provide awareness or training regarding regulatory issues that may have been observed in the industry. This helps to reinforce rules regarding wagering and wagering information.[135] Regulators also can organize summits involving the sportsbooks and sports' governing bodies to facilitate the exchange of information, improve communications, and help to enforce codes of conduct.

The UK created a "Sports Betting Integrity Forum" in 2012 that included representatives from sports' governing bodies, betting operators, sport and betting trade associations, law enforcement, and

131 Nevada Gaming Licenses Overview of the Regulatory Agencies, http://www.gaminglawclass.com/NVGaming2.pdf (last visited Nov. 20, 2017).

132 *Id.*

133 *Id.*

134 Department for Culture, Media & Sport, *Consultation on Updates to Schedule 6 of the Gambling Act 2005* (Nov. 9, 2016), https://www.gov.uk/government/uploads/system/uploads/attachment_data/file/567011/2016-11-09_OFFICIAL-_Schedule_6_consultation_for_publication_closing_8_Dec.pdf.

135 *Id.*

gambling regulators. The purpose of the forum was to collaborate on ideas that could promote the common goals of sports integrity that underlie Britain's Action Plan for enhancing integrity in sport and sports betting. Such meetings can be used to highlight new and existing threats and help coordinate efforts to address them through advanced early warning systems and improved communications. Other goals are researching and developing best preventative measures, promoting governance arrangements, conducting common training and promotion of best practices, supporting awareness, identifying existing weaknesses in processes and creating new solutions, promoting consistent and fair disciplinary frameworks within sports governing bodies, and building other national and international alliances.[136] Such meetings can also be the means by which to plan for special events like the upcoming Olympics in Los Angeles.

Deterrence and Government Participation

Another method of prevention is deterrence. This involves creating a perception on the part of licensees that the regulators will detect future violations of gaming laws. Licensees, however, are more likely to perceive the possibility of detection as a threat where the regulators maintain a strong regulatory presence that permeates all critical aspects of the sportsbook environment. In additon to audits, regulators can help establish a continuing regulatory presence through involvement in surveillance (including remote access to systems), knowledge that the regulators conduct undercover operations, and routine inspections. The presence of an agent of the regulatory body helps oversee operations and uncover irregularities.[137] Nevada regulations provide that a regulatory agent may be present at a licensed sportsbook during all hours of operation with the cost borne by the sportsbook. Moreover, regulatory agents should be given immediate access to all books, records, and to communications from or to the sportsbook.[138] Allowing such access may be a condition of obtaining a license.

Crimes

Ensuring wagering integrity of legalized sportsbook wagers requires an ability for the government to exercise authority to

136 Sports Betting Integrity Forum, *Sports Betting Profiles*, http://www.sbif.uk/images/Documents/SBIF-Sports-Betting-Profiles-External-Final-Version.pdf (last visited Nov. 20, 2017).

137 State Regulators, *supra* note 94.

138 NEV. GAMING COMM. REG. 22.190.

prosecute those who engage in cheating and other egregious activity.[139] The major reason governments decide that certain sportsbook-related activities should be criminal violations is that they involve morally reprehensible conduct that is deserving of criminal penalties. Regulation has inherent limits in disciplining morally objectionable conduct. Regulators typically cannot incarcerate an offender because the limit of their authority is to fine the offender or revoke his or her license.

Another major reason that governments may decide that certain activities should be criminal violations is because it would not otherwise have jurisdiction over the perpetrator. Certainly, a regulatory agency could pass regulations that govern the conduct of sportsbook operators and discipline those operators that fail to comply with them. In most places, however, the regulatory body may not have independent authority to regulate or penalize the conduct of third parties, such as patrons, or to impose civil penalties on their conduct. Therefore, the government may pass criminal statutes that govern the conduct of non-licensees, and provide a basis for enforcement.

A third reason that government may decide that certain activities should constitute criminal violations is because of the sensitivity of the activity. For example, a government may decide that the damage to a sportsbook industry may be significant if the public perceives that the operators are involved in laundering money from illegal activities. In many instances, the sportsbooks may be unknowing participants in the money laundering scheme. To prevent money laundering, the government may not only require the sportsbook to track and report, or prohibit, certain cash transactions but may also decree that violations are criminal. The hope is that the prospects of criminal sanctions may provide a greater deterrence to violations.

Police agencies usually have responsibility for enforcing the criminal laws within their jurisdictions. This often involves concurrent jurisdiction between two or more different police agencies. For example, jurisdiction to enforce the criminal laws in a US city may be shared between the city police, a county sheriff, state police, and some federal agencies, such as the Federal Bureau of Investigation or the Secret Service. In this instance, certain police agencies may have the authority only to enforce certain types of criminal statutes. For example, the FBI may have jurisdiction only if a federal statute is violated.

---

139 State Regulators, *supra* note 94.

One issue that arises is the extent to which agents of a gaming regulatory agency should have authority to enforce criminal gaming statutes. The options range from no authority to exclusive authority. A factor in deciding whether to grant police powers to a regulatory agency is the experience and training of the agents. Most police officers have extensive training in handling investigations and arresting criminal suspects. The rules that govern their conduct are substantially different than those that govern regulatory investigations. Criminal suspects have certain rights, such as protection against unlawful search and seizure or entitlement to Miranda warnings. These rules do not apply to enforcement of civil gaming regulations.

These differences reflect the fact that a gaming regulatory agent may have limited experience in handling a criminal investigation and assuring compliance with all constitutional requirements. Moreover, unlike a civil regulatory investigation where cooperation from the sportsbook is assured, criminal suspects may become unruly or violent. Regulators may not have significant experience in arresting a hostile suspect.

Gaming agents, however, may bring knowledge and experience to criminal investigations that a traditional police force may not have. This may be particularly appropriate where the police force is small and does not have officers dedicated to gaming crimes. For example, gaming agents may be better trained and have greater experience in detecting cheating or other gaming scams. They also may have better sources of intelligence information on criminal suspects that prey on sportsbooks or their patrons, or of the types of cheating operations that they employ.

A compromise between granting no authority and exclusive authority is to give limited concurrent authority to gaming regulators. The limits can be to enforce the criminal gaming laws and to make arrests for other crimes that occur in their presence within the sportsbook environment (such as the simple theft of chips). Concurrent jurisdiction will allow the gaming regulators to work in conjunction with traditional police agencies. This will allow each to bring their respective strengths to the investigation and arrest of criminal suspects.

Cheating and Fraud

Potential activities by operators that should be criminal include cheating, embezzling money in bettor's accounts, defrauding bettors by accepting bets with the intention not to pay winning wagers, participating in competition manipulation, and knowingly allowing minors to gamble. Cheating or engaging in fraudulent activity is the most egregious. While cheating by operators is rare in regulated markets, it is not without precedent. In July 2016, the Nevada Gaming Commission accused sportsbook operator CG Technology of underpaying bettors by more than $700,000 on approximately 20,000 parlay wagers.[140] These wagers have complex methods of determining the actual winning amounts compared to straight bets. Many bettors simply assumed that the calculations were correct. Some bettors, however, recognized the error and informed the gaming regulators, who undertook an investigation. They found, and CG admitted, that the company's software miscalculated payouts, and that after discovering the error CG failed to timely inform either the bettors or the regulators.[141] As a result, the company was fined $1.5 million, and was required to repay the underpayments to bettors. In addition, the Company's CEO was forced to resign.[142] There are no recorded incidents of regulated Nevada sportsbooks being involved in any aspect of competition manipulation.

By Employees

Crimes or frauds by employees involving sports wagering are also uncommon. Because of the computerization of the sports wagering systems, even employees with access to the system should not be able to facilitate past posting, i.e. issuing a winning ticket after the result of the sporting event is certain. In one case, however, a race and sportsbook kept unclaimed winning tickets in a locked box. An employee who had access to the box reviewed the tickets and found those with large payouts. He then had a friend pose as a tourist claiming to have "lost" his portion of the winning ticket. The book verified the ticket in the unclaimed ticket box, and paid the "tourist."

By Bettors and Others

The stealing or claiming of uncashed sports tickets is the most common crime associated with sportsbooks. A bettor who does not use a computer-based account wagering system is given a ticket with his or her wager. As the wager is made with cash, often on an anonymous basis, the ticket is the proof of the transaction and a

140 Velotta, *supra* note 18.
141 *Id.*
142 *Id.*

person in possession of a winning ticket can cash it. A third party may steal the winning tickets and attempt to cash them. In one such case, a postal worker stole the US Mail addressed to sportsbooks where bettors had sent in their winning tickets for redemption.[143]

Other Crimes

By Operators or Employees

In 2013, the former Director of Risk Management and Vice President of Cantor Gaming, Michael Colbert, pled guilty to a single felony charge of conspiracy regarding a nationwide illegal bookmaking ring.[144] Colbert was charged with enterprise corruption, money laundering, and conspiracy charges. Two dozen other people allegedly were involved in the illegal bookmaking and money laundering.[145] Colbert knew that runners (persons who place bets on behalf of another person for compensation) were placing bets at Cantor Gaming's Race and Sports Book at the M Resort in Henderson, Nevada.[146] One of the runners, who was alleged to have placed 4,464 sports wagers worth about $22 million with Cantor Gaming in a 15 month period starting in July 2011, pled guilty to money laundering.[147] According to the complaint, another runner placed 1,612 wagers amounting to $7.9 million.[148] The Board also filed an 18-count complaint alleging that the CEO of CG Technology (formerly known as Cantor Gaming) should have known that his vice president was involved with the illegal betting operation.[149] In 2014, the Board agreed to settle the complaint with a record fine of $5.5 million against the company.[150]

By Bettors

In 2011, Robert Walker, a member of a well-known sports betting

---

143 David Purdum, *U.S. Postal Service Worker Accused of Stealing Mailed-in Sports Betting Tickets*, Betting Talk, May 21, 2014, http://www.bettingtalk.com/las-vegas-sports-book-tickets-stolen-u-s-postal-service/.

144 Christ Sieroty, *Ex-Cantor Gaming Executive Pleads Guilty to Conspiracy Charge*, Las Vegas Review-Journal, Oct. 3, 2013, https://www.reviewjournal.com/business/ex-cantor-gaming-executive-pleads-guilty-to-conspiracy-charge/.

145 *Id.*

146 *Id.*

147 John L. Smith, *Las Vegas Betting Scandal Earns $5.5 Million in Fine but the Boss Walks.* The Daily Beast, Jan. 21, 2014, http://www.thedailybeast.com/articles/2014/01/21/las-vegas-betting-scandal-earns-5-5-million-fine-but-the-boss-walks.html.

148 *Id.*

149 *Id.*

150 *Id.*

business, pled guilty to a misdemeanor count of causing a violation of recordkeeping and procedures.[151] The Golden Nugget Race and Sports Book accepted $72,020 in wagers from Walker within two weeks.[152] Federal laws require accurate information regarding the persons who place wagers of more than $10,000 in one day. Walker admitted that he willfully did not advise the sportsbook that he was placing the bets for ACME Group Trading.[153] This withholding of information caused the Golden Nugget to fail to comply with federal laws.[154] Walker was sentenced to one year of unsupervised probation as part of his plea agreement.[155]

In June 2014, a federal grand jury indicted a bettor and some members of his family for operating a multimillion-dollar illegal bookmaking operation.[156] They also were charged with conspiracy to structure $2.6 million by using casinos and a bank to prevent the Internal Revenue Service from discovering the money.[157] The bookmaking operation allegedly involved offshore sportsbooks.[158] Prosecutors sought to recover $13.2 million in cash and casino chips from the family and gambling enterprise which operated from March 2011 through December 2013.[159] The casinos were used between December 2008 and November 2013 to structure funds to avoid the federal currency reporting laws.[160] "According to the indictment, the bettor tried to conceal $1.4 million at the Mirage, $503,303 at the LVH resort, $199,500 at The Venetian, $183,500 at the South Point and $79,350 at the Fremont. They also are alleged to have structured $256,136 at Bank of America.[161]

In April 2014, two bettors each entered guilty pleas to a single felony count of operating an illegal gambling enterprise.[162] The two

151 Jeff German, *Messenger Betting Case Nets Probation, Fine in Plea Deal*, LAS VEGAS REVIEW-JOURNAL, Feb. 8, 2013, http://www.reviewjournal.com/news/crime-courts/messenger-betting-case-nets-probation-fine-plea-deal.

152 *Id.*

153 *Id.*

154 *Id.*

155 *Id.*

156 Jeff German, *Las Vegas Sports Bettor, Family Indicted in Bookmaking Operation*. LAS VEGAS REVIEW-JOURNAL, June 4, 2014, http://www.reviewjournal.com/news/las-vegas/las-vegas-sports-bettor-family-indicted-bookmaking-operation.

157 *Id.*

158 *Id.*

159 *Id.*

160 *Id.*

161 *Id.*

162 Jeff German, *Las Vegas Sports Bettors Plead Guilty to Illegal Bookmaking*, LAS VEGAS

men were originally charged in 2013 with engaging in illegal chip transfers between their Cantor Gaming accounts at various Strip casinos to avoid filing Currency Transaction Reports.[163] The IRS and state gaming agents raided one of the bettor's homes in 2012 and seized evidence of an illegal bookmaking operation involving offshore betting organizations.[164] Both bettors were alleged to have made more than $1 million in chip transfers to avoid the federal currency filing requirements.[165] It was also alleged that one bettor used fake Social Security numbers when filing Currency Transaction Reports at two licensed Nevada sportsbooks.[166]

REVIEW-JOURNAL, Apr. 2, 2014, http://www.reviewjournal.com/news/2-las-vegas-sports-bettors-plead-guilty-illegal-bookmaking.

163 *Id.*

164 *Id.*

165 *Id.*

166 *Id.*

6

The Emergence of eSports

GENERALLY

The professional sports landscape in the United States has been dominated by the same major sports for a half century. Conventionally, this includes baseball (Major League Baseball), basketball (National Basketball Association), football (National Football League), and hockey (National Hockey League). This stasis in the American sports diet has remained for decades without much challenge, even though recently some commentators have claimed that soccer (Major League Soccer) should be included in the "major" American professional sports leagues.[1] However, American professional sports have not been immune to the technological disruption experienced by other industries in the late twentieth and early twenty-first century. The disruptor in the sports world has been the meteoric rise of an upstart sport: eSports.

As with many topics in the gaming world—especially in the case of eSports and its dynamic growth—circumstances change. This chapter does not aim to be a comprehensive treatment of all the issues implicated by eSports. Rather, the goal is to provide an introduction to eSports basics and shed some light on its lightning fast growth. If eSports continues this rapid growth, everyone, whether interested in sports and gaming or not, will become familiar with what may be America's next major sport.

WHAT IS ESPORTS?

Organized video game competition, known as eSports, illustrates how quickly the world, and gaming world, is evolving. Buoyed by the

1 Nate Silver, *The 'Big Five' in North American Pro Sports*, FIVE THIRTY EIGHT, Apr. 4, 2014, https://fivethirtyeight.com/datalab/theres-a-big-five-in-north-american-pro-sports/.

technological revolution, the popular growth of eSports has enjoyed its own version of Moore's law.[2] This has led to a boon for video gamers, video game developers, media companies, and investors. But this sport, a sport which has more viewers than the World Series or NBA Finals,[3] is still unknown to many people, especially to those who are not "digital natives."[4] So what are eSports?

Esports are "a form of sports where the primary aspects of the sport are facilitated by electronic systems; the input of players and teams as well as the output of the eSports system are mediated by human-computer interfaces."[5] Simply put, eSports is organized competition between individuals, teams, or a combination of both, playing a game in which the winner is determined by the particular outcome of a video game played on a widely available gaming console.

While some may quibble whether competitive video gaming fits within the amorphous definition of a "sport," eSports tournaments are immensely popular—filling stadiums,[6] drawing millions of online and television viewers,[7] and generating multi-million-dollar purses.[8] The eSports name is a derivative of the familiar technological

---

2 Moore's law is the observation by Intel co-founder Gordon Moore that the computing power of integrated circuits roughly doubles every two years. Moore initially predicted that the exponential growth would last a decade but his prediction held steady until at least 2012. *See* Gordon Moore, *Process in Digital Electronics*, IEEE speech 1975, http://www.eng.auburn.edu/~agrawvd/COURSE/E7770_Spr07/READ/Gordon_Moore_1975_Speech.pdf.

3 Nick Schwartz, *More People Watch eSports Than Watch the World Series or NBA Finals*, May 19, 2014, http://ftw.usatoday.com/2014/05/league-of-legends-popularity-world-series-nba

4 Digital natives are persons born during the widespread use of digital technology which facilitates an almost innate understanding of computers and the internet; Oliver Joy, *What Does it Mean to be a Digital Native?*, CNN, Dec. 8, 2012, http://www.cnn.com/2012/12/04/business/digital-native-prensky/index.html

5 Hamari, J., & Sjöblom, M. (2017). What is eSports and why do people watch it? INTERNET RESEARCH, 27(2). DOI: 10.1108/IntR-04-2016-0085, Forthcoming. Available at SSRN: https://ssrn.com/abstract=2686182

6 Paul Armstrong, *46 Million Watched Live eSports Event (10 Million More Than Trump Inauguration Broadcast)*, FORBES, Mar. 16, 2017, https://www.forbes.com/sites/paularmstrongtech/2017/03/16/46-million-watched-live-esports-event-10-million-more-than-trump-inauguration-broadcast/ (noting the record setting live attendance for the Intel Extreme Masters World Championship in Poland).

7 Robert Elder, *The eSports Audience is Escalating Quickly*, BUSINESS INSIDER, Mar. 20, 2017, http://www.businessinsider.com/the-esports-audience-is-escalating-quickly-2017-3 (describing the World Championships in Poland as the "most watched eSports tournament in history, with 46 million unique viewers").

8 Chris Morris, *Largest Prize Pool in eSports History Tops $20 Million*, FORTUNE, July 13, 2017, http://fortune.com/2017/07/13/esports-largest-prize-20-million/.

portmanteau[9] of "electronic sports."

ESPORTS GAMES

While the game in question could be almost any video game with a clear outcome, there are five major types of games: Multiplayer Online Battle Arenas (MOBA), First-Person Shooters, Real Time Strategy games, Collectible Card games, and Sports games.[10] Among these genres, the most popular genres are Multiplayer Online Battle Arenas and First-Person Shooters.

A MOBA is a game where the player controls a single character within a gaming environment and, typically as a member of a team, attempts to defeat an opposing team by utilizing strategy to achieve a particular objective such as destroying the other team's structure. This can be roughly analogized to a digital version of "capture the flag."

The two dominant games within the MOBA genre are Defense of the Ancients (popularly known at Dota 2) and League of Legends (referred to as LoL). Dota 2 is the most lucrative eSports competition in aggregate as well as individually.[11] LoL was the third most lucrative game in eSports in 2016 and the second most popular in terms of number of competitors.[12] The largest tournaments and biggest prize purses are often in tournaments involving multiplayer online battle arenas.[13]

The second most popular category of game is first-person shooters. First-person shooters are games where a player controls a character within a game and the objective is for the character to "kill" the other characters in the game utilizing a variety of weapons, but

---

9 Well known examples include email (electronic mail), e-commerce (electronic commerce), and e-marketing (electronic marketing).

10 Hamari & Sjöblom, *supra* note 5 at 3.

11 Dota 2 was the top game of 2016 doling out over $37 million in prize money spread over 134 tournaments. Additionally, the 2017 International Dota 2 Championships in August 2017 had the largest prize pool in eSports history. *Top Games of 2016*, ESPORTS EARNINGS, https://www.esportsearnings.com/history/2016/games; Morris, *supra* note 8..

12 Top Games of 2016, *supra* note 11 (1465 players competed in 156 LoL tournaments in 2016).

13 The top earning game of 2016 was Dota 2, which awarded $37 million in 134 tournaments, *Top Games of 2016*, ESPORTS EARNINGS, https://www.esportsearnings.com/history/2016/games; League of Legends, often referred to as LoL, was third in earnings in 2016 and second in players and tournaments, *Top Games of 2016*, ESPORTS EARNINGS, https://www.esportsearnings.com/history/2016/games.

typically a gun. The perspective of the player is through the eyes of the character, hence the description as "first-person."[14] The dominate eSports competition within the first-person shooter category is Counter-Strike: Global Offensive.[15] In 2016, CS: GO (common shorthand for the game) awarded the second most prize money in eSports ($17 million),[16]witnessed the most competitors (over 4000), and held the most tournaments (852).[17]

Another popular category of eSports is real-time strategy games. Real-time strategy games require players to devise, implement, and adjust strategy in real time. The strategic environment can take many forms but the most popular form for eSports is war strategy games. The biggest game in this category is Starcraft 2.[18]

Other popular categories of eSports are collectible card games—which is a digital version of the traditional collectible card game (such as Magic: The Gathering), where players collect unique cards that are used within a game to accomplish a certain objective. Hearthstone is among the leaders in this category.[19]

Finally, eSports competitions are simulations of traditional sports such as soccer or football. Soccer and football are played on the most popular titles of the games, such as EA Sports' FIFA soccer series or Madden.[20] Sports games are not among the most popular eSports for dedicated eSports fans but have been used to try to draw in more casual fans as the familiarity with the game (the rules of soccer and football) can open up competitive gaming to a wider audience.[21]

---

14 First-person shooters are games which the player "assumes the field of vision of the protagonist, so that the game camera includes the character's weapon, but the rest of the character model is not seen"; *First-Person Shooter*, DICTIONARY.COM, http://www.dictionary.com/browse/first-person-shooter

15 Hamari & Sjöblom, *supra* note 5.

16 *Top Games of 2016*, ESPORTS EARNINGS, https://www.esportsearnings.com/history/2016/games.

17 *Id.*

18 Hamari & Sjöblom, *supra* note 5.

19 *Id.*

20 *Id.*

21 For example, during the 2017 Super Bowl, ESPN aired the "Super Bowl" of FIFA on its broadcast. *See* Imad Khan, *ESPN to Broadcast eSports During Super Bowl*, ESPN, Feb. 3, 2017, http://www.espn.com/esports/story/_/id/18613645/espn-broadcast-fifa-ultimate-team-electronic-arts-super-bowl.

HISTORY

The growth of eSports emerged from non-descript beginnings. The first known video game competition took place in 1972 at Stanford University.[22] The prize was modest—a one-year subscription to *Rolling Stone* magazine—and the game was *Spacewar*!, one of the earliest and most popular video games.[23]

As video games became more popular, concomitant with the digital revolution of the last two decades of the twentieth century, the number of participants in video game competitions grew by orders of magnitude. Additionally, after early reticence, video game developers joined in on the action. Developers recognized the promotional utility of competitions involving their products. Atari was the first organization to sponsor a large-scale competition with the *Space Invaders* Championship in 1980.[24] A decade later, Nintendo got into the act of tournament promotion, with the Nintendo World Championships. The Nintendo World Championships toured the United States stopping in twenty-nine cities.[25] This culminated with the World Finals held in December at Universal Studios in Hollywood.[26] Nintendo held another tournament named Nintendo PowerFest four years later, this time with their second-generation gaming console, Super Nintendo (SNES).[27]

The technology revolution of the 1980s also spawned another technology that assisted the growth in popularity of video game competition: cable television. The multi-decade dominance of over-the-air broadcast television networks was broken by Ted Turner's

---

22 Owen Good, *Today is the 40th Anniversary of the World's First Known Video Gaming Tournament*, Kotaku, Oct. 19, 2012, https://kotaku.com/5953371/today-is-the-40th-anniversary-of-the-worlds-first-known-video-gaming-tournament.

23 *Id.*

24 *Atari Space Invaders Tournament*, Megalextoria, Apr. 18, 2017, http://www.megalextoria.com/wordpress/index.php/2017/04/18/atari-space-invaders-tournament-1980/.

25 Frank Cifaldi, *The Story of the First Nintendo World Championships*, IGN, May 13, 2015, http://www.ign.com/articles/2015/05/13/the-story-of-the-first-nintendo-world-championships.

26 Chip Carter and Jonathan Carter, *Nintendo's Powerfest '90 is the Video Game Olympics*, Chicago Tribune, Dec. 7, 1990, http://articles.chicagotribune.com/1990-12-07/entertainment/9004110423_1_thor-aackerlund-jeff-falco-video-game-showdown.

27 Darren Murphy, *World's "Only" PowerFest '94 SNES Cartridge Up for Auction*, Engadget, Apr. 27, 2007, https://www.engadget.com/2007/04/27/worlds-only-powerfest-94-snes-cartridge-up-for-auction/.

Atlanta-based WTCG in the late 1970s.[28] Turner soon took his channel national with WTBS beaming it nationwide via satellite.[29] In search of affordable programming for the upstart station, Turner's channel broadcasted one of the first shows to feature video game competitions in *Starcade*.[30] While the show only ran for three seasons, they produced over 130 episodes featuring youthful competitors playing various arcade games.[31]

Network television did not completely ignore the new fad as the 80s variety show *That's Incredible!* featured segments with video game competitions.[32] These televised competitions did not make for the best television—video resolution of the games was substandard (particularly for contemporary viewers), segments were edited for brevity, and the rudimentary nature of the games made it difficult to track the competition. The difficulty in following the competition was compounded by hosts' lack of familiarity with the games.[33] Shortcomings aside, the competitive nature and the use of emerging technological mediums helped expose video games to a younger generation and engender a following which would develop into an industry with almost triple the revenue of the worldwide film industry in three decades.[34]

In its infancy, video game competitions served as a hobby for its competitors, a content-filler for upstart television stations, and a curiosity for the few spectators they did draw. However, beginning in the 1990s, video game competitions began to take on a different role as a bona fide business. While it would take until the second decade of the twenty-first century to draw eight and nine digit revenues, the explosive growth eSports enjoys began its ascent in the late 1990s with organized video game leagues. Among the pioneers in this field were

---

28 Ted Turner: A Cornerstone of TV History, WTCG and WTBS, The Evergreen State College, Apr. 1, 2011, http://blogs.evergreen.edu/rc1nick/.

29 *Id.*

30 Alex Gilyadov, *1980s Gaming Game Show Starcade is Coming Back*, IGN, Jan. 10, 2017, http://www.ign.com/articles/2017/01/10/1980s-gaming-game-show-starcade-is-coming-back.

31 *Id.*

32 John Biggs, *The That's Incredible! Video Game Invitational: This is What We Used to Watch*, TECH CRUNCH, July 29, 2009, https://techcrunch.com/2009/07/29/the-thats-incredible-video-game-invitational-this-is-what-we-used-to-watch/.

33 *Id.*

34 Market Brief – Year in Review 2016, Superdata, https://www.superdataresearch.com/market-data/market-brief-year-in-review/; Ryan Faughnder, *Global Box Office Barely Grew in 2016. Blame it on China*, LA TIMES, Mar. 22, 2017, http://www.latimes.com/business/hollywood/la-fi-ct-mpaa-box-office-20170322-story.html.

Cyberathlete Professional League (CPL) and Professional Gamers League (PGL).[35] However, it was South Korea, not the United States that experienced the first mass popularity of eSports.[36]

South Korea is in many ways ground zero for the professionalization of eSports. While theories vary as to what conditions led to South Korea earning a preeminent spot on the eSports world stage, many point to a low point in recent South Korean history—the Asian financial crisis of the late 1990s.[37] This theory of the chain of events centers on the build-up of telecommunications infrastructure by the South Korean government.[38] With their financial industry cratering due to a continent-wide financial contagion, the South Korean government focused on infrastructure development of telecommunications and improving access to the then-nascent world wide web.[39] This facilitated the rise of South Korean internet cafes which are known as a "PC Bang"—essentially an internet connected gaming room.[40]

Following the popularity and growth of eSports in South Korea, including the famed Korean video game network OGN,[41] American television broadcasters began to dip their toe into the eSports pond before taking a headlong dive. Beginning in 2005, American sports behemoth ESPN teamed up with video game developer EA Sports to produce *Madden Nation*. The show was an effort by the Worldwide Leader in Sports to capitalize on two rising pop culture phenomena, namely, eSports and reality television, that happened to intersect with

---

35 John Gaudiosi, *CPL Founder Angel Munoz Explains Why He Left Esports and Launched Mass Luminosity*, Forbes, Apr. 9, 2013, https://www.forbes.com/sites/johngaudiosi/2013/04/09/cpl-founder-angel-munoz-explains-why-he-left-esports-and-launched-mass-luminosity/#48b2f604648e; Greg Miller, *Out of the Arcade*, LA Times, Nov. 3, 1997, http://articles.latimes.com/1997/nov/03/business/fi-49823.

36 Paul Mozur, *For South Korea, E-Sports is National Pastime*, NY Times, Oct. 19, 2014, https://www.nytimes.com/2014/10/20/technology/league-of-legends-south-korea-epicenter-esports.html?_r=0.

37 *Id.*

38 *Id.*

39 John D. Sutter, *Why Internet Connections Are Fastest in South Korea,* CNN, Mar. 31, 2010, http://www.cnn.com/2010/TECH/03/31/broadband.south.korea/index.html.

40 Martin Pasquier, *Curious About the South Korea Gaming Culture? A Closer Look at the Popularity of Esports Reveals Some Trends,* E27, May 25, 2017, https://e27.co/curious-south-korea-gaming-culture-closer-look-popularity-esports-reveals-trends-20170525/.

41 Kwanghee Woo, *Wait, Overwatch Esports is Actually Popular in Korea?*, Medium, Apr. 15, 2017, https://medium.com/@SaintSnorlax/wait-overwatch-esports-is-actually-popular-in-korea-1c8d7c76186d (crediting OGN for "basically invent[ing] modern esports").

their niche—sports programming.[42] *Madden Nation* enjoyed modest success but only ran until 2008.[43] DirecTV also aired early iterations of video game competition programming,[44] as did CBS.[45] Comcast also joined in on video game programming when they launched the channel G4 in mid-2002.

The launch of the G4 network in April 2002 was one of the earliest, most ambitious efforts at capturing the video game audience. Recognizing the potential value in video gaming, due to the predominance of the demographic most sought-after by advertisers (males 18-34) and the intense loyalty that video gaming arouses, Comcast launched the channel in hopes of cornering the emerging market. At the time, video games did not have a significant presence in broadcasting. Aside from the scattered aforementioned shows, the video game generation did not have programming dedicated to their interests. The only "channels" that were exclusively dedicated to video games were the San Francisco-based Tech TV once-owned by Paul Allen (of Microsoft fame) and the AllGames Network featured on the early streaming channel pseudo.com.[46] The goal of the G4 network was to become the MTV of video games imitating the hip, almost underground feel of the wildly successful music video channel.[47]

When G4 launched, the channel quickly gained a small, but loyal following. Despite their early success, the channel was hampered by its limited distribution with the channel being available to only fifteen million households.[48] Despite their strong and loyal viewer base, the limited distribution of the channel made it unattractive to advertisers and required the channel to take steps that eventually eroded its fan

---

42 *See* Jon Robinson, *Madden Nation*, IGN, Dec. 7, 2005, http://www.ign.com/articles/2005/12/07/madden-nation.

43 David Pincus, *Remembering Stuff ESPN Used to Put on TV*, SB NATION, Jan. 14, 2013, https://www.sbnation.com/2013/1/14/3767596/old-espn-tv-shows.

44 Ryan Kim, *League Beginning for Video Gamers*, SF GATE, June 11, 2007, http://www.sfgate.com/business/article/League-beginning-for-video-gamers-2587547.php.

45 Seth Schiesel, *Video Game Matches to Be Televised on CBS*, NY TIMES, July 28, 2007, http://www.nytimes.com/2007/07/28/arts/television/28vide.html; Justin McElroy, *World Series of Video Games to air on CBS*, June 01, 2007, ENGADGET, https://www.engadget.com/2007/06/01/world-series-of-video-games-to-air-on-cbs/.

46 Rachel Scheier, *The Demise of Dot-Com with Television Silicon Valley's Pseudo Programs Goes from Internet Revolutionary to a Victim of Financial Circumstances*, NY DAILY NEWS, Sept. 25, 2000, http://www.nydailynews.com/archives/money/demise-dot-com-tele-vision-silicon-alley-pseudo-programs-internet-revolutionary-victim-financial-circumstances-article-1.878715.

47 Rob Dean, *Let's Examine the Rise and Fall of the G4 Channel*, AV CLUB, Dec. 3, 2014, http://www.avclub.com/article/lets-examine-rise-and-fall-g4-channel-212541.

48 *Id.*

base. One of these missteps was its acquisition of its erstwhile rival TechTV late 2004.[49] While TechTV and G4 certainly had overlap in content, TechTV was focused on more on the technical aspects of video games and technology whereas G4 focused on the product and experience of playing the video games. The merger between the two channels alienated both fan bases and the marriage lasted only ten months.[50]

As G4 was still searching for a way to grow its audience and increase its advertising revenue and carriage among television providers, the channel began to diversify its content. First, it reoriented to attempt to be more broadly entertainment-oriented encompassing music, movies, and other subjects to appeal to a wider youth audience. This led to a carousel of different slogans and a constant shuffling of programming, further alienating their loyal fan base.[51]

Eventually, in a futile attempt to draw in the coveted young male demographic, G4 began to emulate other channels in the area (such as Spike TV) by presenting programs with more adult content through late night programming with not-so subtle double entendres. Following this departure from their original vision, G4 slowly wilted away after DirecTV dropped their channel in 2010 and a failed rebranding to the Esquire Channel.[52] G4 finally went off the air permanently at the end of 2014.[53]

Despite its quick rise and slow fall, G4 had a significant effect on the mainstreaming of video game culture among the broader popular culture and opened the door to more video game-exclusive programming, including the ascending sport of video game competition.[54]

PLAYERS

Like any traditional sport or competition, eSports has standout players. And those players develop a reputation and a fan base akin to those of athletes in other sports. Due to the decentralized nature

---

49 *Id.*

50 *Id.*

51 *Id.*

52 *Id.*

53 Merrill Barr, *NBC Shutting Down G4 Network on November 30th*, SCREEN RANT, Nov. 17, 2014, http://screenrant.com/g4-tv-network-canceled-2014/.

54 For an excellent history and recap of the rise and fall of the G4 Network, *See* GoodBadFlicks, *The Rise and Fall of G4 TV 4 Gamers*, YOU TUBE, Dec. 2, 2014, https://www.youtube.com/watch?v=ZEBwGOHntro.

of eSports, players have risen to prominence from all corners of the globe. Any canvass of the top competitors in eSports begins with Lee "Faker" Sang-hyeok of South Korea. Sang-hyeok, popularly known by his in-game nickname as "Faker,"is widely considered to be the greatest eSports player of all time.[55] Faker has been referred to as a "God" of League of Legends and some consider him to be the Michael Jordan or Tiger Woods of LoL.[56] Another South Korean eSports prodigy is Byun Hyun-woo. Hyun-woo, who previously went by "GhostKing," is one of the biggest stars in South Korea. Hyun-woo was named ESPN's eSports player of the year for 2016.[57] Hyun-woo enjoyed a big boost to his profile when he won South Korea's most prestigious event in Global StarCraft League. Hyun-woo capped off his year by taking home the StarCraft championship in at the World Championship at BlizzCon in Anaheim, California in 2016.[58]

One of the most popular players on social media is Jarowslaw Jarzabkowski who competes for the team Virtus.pro.[59] Other stand outs in eSports include Saahil Arora, a Dota 2 player who is the highest earning eSports player of all time,[60] and Sumail Hassan, a 17-year-old Pakistani who was named one of the 30 most influential teenagers in the world by Time magazine.[61]

COMPETITIONS

Esports tournaments are often staged much the same way as traditional sporting events. They take place in front of a live (and often raucous) crowd, in an arena or theatre with officials or referees monitoring the action. Large, well-established, popular games often

---

55 *2016 ESPN eSports Awards-Player of the Year*, ESPN, Jan. 10, 2017, http://www.espn.com/esports/story/_/id/18445357/2016-espn-esports-awards-player-year.

56 Mina Kimes, *The Unkillable Demon King*, ESPN THE MAGAZINE, June 10, 2015, http://www.espn.com/espn/feature/story/_/id/13035450/league-legends-prodigy-faker-carries-country-shoulders.

57 ESPN *supra* note 56.

58 *Id.*

59 Christian Kresse, *The Most Famous eSports Pro Players in LoL, Dota 2, and CS: GO: Testimonials and Influencers in eSports*, ESPORTS MARKETING BLOG, Jan. 22, 2016, http://esports-marketing-blog.com/testimonials-esports-pro-players-lol-dota2-csgo/#.WVMUpsaZPpB.

60 *Id.*

61 Time Staff, *The 30 Most Influential Teens of 2016*, TIME, Oct. 19, 2016, http://time.com/4532104/most-influential-teens-2016/; Hassan is also noteworthy because in 2015 he became the youngest person to ever earn one million dollars playing eSports.

have multi-million-dollar prize purses.[62] The largest total prize purse was The International 2016, which was a Dota 2 competition broadcast on ESPN.[63] Previously, the largest eSports purses had been The International 2014 which was later eclipsed by The International 2015.[64] While Dota 2 has perennially had the largest prize purse, the largest non-Dota purse was the 2016 World Championships for LoL which exceeded five million dollars.[65]

ECONOMICS OF eSPORTS

For anyone interested in investing, betting, or acquiring a greater understanding of eSports, a strong, functional understanding of the economic landscape of eSports is critical. The fractured organizational structure simply compounds the learning curve. So, it helps to begin with the basics.

One clear distinction between eSports and other major sports industries is the lack of a monopoly. All four major American professional sports (NFL, MLB, NBA, and NHL) and the major individual sports (PGA, WTA) have an organization that is considered the premiere level of competition. The clear hierarchal structure of these sports breeds a familiarity in popular culture that eSports, for its broad and strong fan base, does not enjoy yet. This can serve as an obstacle for those who may be interested in investing in eSports.

Teams can be organized in a variety of different ways. They can be organized as a corporation, limited liability company (LLC), or as international versions of such entities.[66] The internal organization of the teams can include umbrella parent companies with subsidiaries or affiliates.[67] These "teams-within-a-team" can be separate legal entities

---

62 *See* Eric Van Allen, *Wings Gaming Takes TI6, Wins $9 Million and the Aegis*, ESPN, Aug. 14, 2016, http://www.espn.com/esports/story/_/id/17297168/wings-gaming-takes-ti6-wins-9-million.

63 *Id.*

64 *Top Games of 2016*, eSports Earnings, https://www.esportsearnings.com/history/2016/games.

65 Leo Howell, *2016 League of Legends Worlds Prize Pool at $5.07M With Fan Contributions*, ESPN, Oct. 29, 2016, http://www.espn.com/esports/story/_/id/17919126/2016-league-legends-worlds-prize-pool-507m-fan-contributions.

66 Alex Knapp, *Three Things You Need To Know Before Investing In eSports*, Forbes, Feb. 24, 2017, https://www.forbes.com/sites/alexknapp/2017/02/24/three-things-you-need-to-know-before-investing-in-esports/#53b41c656361.

67 *Id.*

of their own.[68] This allows a potential investor to purchase a stake in one team under an umbrella parent team, or invest in the umbrella team.[69]

The revenue streams accruing to investors, whether debt or equity, can be from streams more traditional to sports investment—such as sponsorship relationships, endorsement deals, and merchandise sales—or from revenue sources more *sui generis* to eSports: revenue from streaming services (Amazon's Twitch among them), prize money from tournaments, and revenue from content creation.[70] Investors will find that more established tournaments and competitions (such as LoL, CS: GO, and Dota 2) will offer larger prize pools, more supple relationships in marketing, and loyal, substantial international fan bases.[71]

Despite the new terrain of investing in eSports, the sport has still drawn many notable investors. Included in the largest investments in eSports has been large media corporations, both old and new. Among the largest initial investors is Amazon who acquired the video game streaming service Twitch for just under $1 billion.[72] While many analysts were confused why Amazon would go as far afield as they did from their core business, the gamble has appeared to pay off as Twitch has 100 million users and assists Amazon in their competition between other tech behemoths like Facebook, Google, and Microsoft—who are all competing to get video game developers to host their games on the competing cloud-based servers.[73] Amazon is not the only tech company to invest heavily in eSports.

In 2017, Facebook signed a deal with ESL, an eSports tournament producer, to create live and on-demand video for the social network.[74] Facebook's goal is to produce thousands of hours of eSports programming in an attempt to cut into Amazon's market share via Twitch.[75] But Facebook is not the only social media company

68 *Id.*

69 *Id.*

70 *Id.*

71 *Id.*

72 Eugene Kim, *Amazon Buys Twitch for $970 Million in Cash*, BUSINESS INSIDER, Aug. 25, 2016, http://www.businessinsider.com/amazon-buys-twitch-2014-8.

73 Matthew Weinberger, *Amazon's $970 Million Purchase of Twitch Makes So Much Sense Now: It's All About the Cloud*, BUSINESS INSIDER, http://www.newsobserver.com/news/politics-government/state-politics/article158476209.html.

74 Robert Elder, *Facebook is Now Financing eSports For Its New Video Tab*, BUSINESS INSIDER, May 19, 2017, http://www.businessinsider.com/facebook-is-now-financing-esports-content-2017-5.

75 Sarah Perez, *Facebook Takes on Twitch with New Live-Streaming Deal for eSports*,

attempting to catch up to Amazon in the eSports content market. Twitter, which has dabbled in streaming other sports,[76]joined forces with ESL and DreamHack to stream eSports competitions.[77] The 2017 deal came on the heels of a successful debut for eSports on Twitter when the social media site streamed the last two rounds of Eleague's CS: GO tournament.[78]

YouTube also got into the eSports streaming game in 2017 when it inked a multi-year deal with Faceit to stream Esports Championship Series (ECS).[79] YouTube's, owned by Google's parent company Alphabet, deal with Faceit illustrates the company's resolve to compete in the eSports marketplace with Amazon.[80]

Investment in eSports programming is not limited to tech giants, as more traditional media companies such as Disney, via ESPN, and Time Warner, through Turner Broadcasting, have also attempted to gain a foothold in broadcasting.[81]

Broadcasting programming is not the only area of eSports which is ripe for investment. Direct investment in teams is also available and some notable "players" have joined in on the action. In 2016, one of the most famous athletes in the world, Shaquille O'Neal, got into the eSports action when an ownership group he was a part of purchased an equity stake in NRG eSports.[82] Other members of the group include former baseball superstar Alex Rodriquez and all-star

---

TechCrunch, May 19, 2017, https://techcrunch.com/2017/05/19/facebook-takes-on-twitch-with-new-livestreaming-deal-for-esports/.

76 Twitter streamed ten Thursday night NFL games during the 2016 NFL season. *See* Jonathan Chew, *Here Are the NFL Games That Will Be Streamed Live on Twitter*, Fortune, Apr. 15, 2016, http://fortune.com/2016/04/15/nfl-twitter-games/.

77 Sarah Perez, *Twitter Will Live Stream 1,500 Hours of eSports, Including Original Content*, TechCrunch, Mar. 2, 2017, https://techcrunch.com/2017/03/02/twitter-will-live-stream-1500-hours-of-esports-including-original-content/.

78 Taylor Cocke, *ELeague to Stream CS: GO Semifinals and Finals on Twitter*, Yahoo Esports, July 28, 2016, https://esports.yahoo.com/eleague-to-stream-csgo-semifinals-and-finals-on-twitter-171919728.html.

79 Anya George Tharakan, *YouTube Makes Its Biggest E-sports Bet with FACEIT Streaming Deal*, Reuters, Mar. 16, 2017, http://www.reuters.com/article/us-alphabet-youtube-faceit-idUSKBN16N257.

80 BI Intelligence, *YouTube Has Made Its Biggest eSports Investment Yet*, Business Insider, Mar. 17, 2017, http://www.businessinsider.com/youtube-has-made-its-biggest-esports-investment-yet-2017-3.

81 Scott Gamm, *Amazon, Disney, Time Warner Competing in eSports Market*, TheStreet, Apr. 19, 2016, https://www.thestreet.com/story/13534830/1/amazon-disney-time-warner-competing-in-esports-market.html.

82 Bob Woods, *Why A-Rod and Shaq Is Betting Big on Their Own eSports Team*, CNBC, Oct. 29, 2016, http://www.cnbc.com/2016/10/28/a-rod-and-shaq-buy-a-stake-in-nrg-esports-team.html.

baseball player Jimmy Rollins.[83] Shaq and company are not the only athletes to enter in to an eSports enterprise.

Among the biggest investors is former NBA player Rick Fox. Fox, an NBA champion and former teammate of Shaq, purchased the team Echo Fox in 2015.[84] Fox was reported to have spent $1 million on his team.[85] Fox even formed a private equity firm in 2017 focused on eSports.[86]

WAGERING ON ESPORTS

As eSports has become more popular and visible, one of its tantalizing aspects is the potential to be a source of wagering. States would surely lick their chops at the prospect of having these competitions be part of a robust gambling market. It would be an understatement to say the eSports betting market is nascent as the first legal wager in the United States was accepted in Las Vegas by William Hill Sports Book in November of 2016.[87] Nevada, obviously the gaming capital of the US, desires to be the "eSports capital of the world,"[88] by getting ahead of any would-be competitors on the gaming side of eSports.

One major difference between the eSports betting market and the sports betting market is gender participation. The eSports betting market has greater female involvement (39% of the betting market) versus the traditional sports betting market (29.2%).[89] The eSports bettors are also younger and began gambling in their twenties.[90]

---

83 *Id.*

84 Dan Gelston, *Former NBA Player Rick Fox Big in eSports Gaming World*, WASH. TIMES, Feb. 9, 2017, http://www.washingtontimes.com/news/2017/feb/9/retired-nba-star-rick-fox-big-in-esports-gaming-wo/.

85 Sean Morrison, *Rick Fox and Investors Form Private Equity Firm With eSports Focus*, ESPN, Apr. 13, 2017, http://www.espn.com/esports/story/_/id/19153058/rick-fox-investors-form-private-equity-firm-esports-focus.

86 *Id.*

87 Eric Van Allen, *Las Vegas Takes First Legal eSports Wagers in U.S. for IEM Oakland*, ESPN, Nov. 21, 2016, http://www.espn.com/esports/story/_/id/18082536/las-vegas-takes-first-legal-esports-wagers-us-iem-oakland; Dustin Gouker, *Place Your eSports Bets in Las Vegas: Downtown Grand, William Hill to Offer First Legal Wagers in US*, eSports Betting Report, Nov. 18, 2016, https://www.esportsbettingreport.com/legal-esports-betting-las-vegas-league-of-legends/.

88 *Id.*

89 Sally M. Gainsbury, et. al., *Game On: Comparison of Demographic Profiles, Consumption Behaviors, and Gambling Site Selection Criteria of eSports and Sports Bettors*, GAMING L. REV., Oct. 2017, 21(8): 575-587, 579-80.

90 *Id.* at 581.

This suggests that gamblers may have just begun wagering,[91] thus obviously being attractive to casinos as "new money" rather than just cannibalizing existing bets. Other attractive traits of eSports bettors are they have higher educational attainment, higher incomes, and they are more frequent gamblers.[92]

The enthusiasm with which Nevada has embraced eSports is illustrated by a bill signed by Nevada Governor Brian Sandoval in May 2017 clarifying that pari-mutuel betting on eSports was also legal under state law.[93] The Nevada legislature passed this proposal at the urging of law students at UNLV despite money line wagering being legal in the state (bets had already been accepted the previous November).[94] Nevada's designs on eSports go beyond allowing wagering on the sport—state officials would also like to host live events which they expect would draw thousands of eSports fans to the city and state.[95]

Whenever gaming regulators consider allowing betting on an activity, the unfamiliarity with the activity causes regulators to proceed cautiously. In Nevada, for example, eSports is covered under gaming regulation 22.120 which governs wagering on "events other than a horse race, greyhound race or athletic event."[96] This designation

---

91 *Id.* at 585.

92 *Id.* at 580.

93 Dejan Zalik, *Nevada Governor Signs Bill Legalizing Wagers on eSports Events*, eSports Betting Report, May 31, 2017, https://www.esportsbettingreport.com/nevada-esports-betting-law/.

94 *Id.*

95 Dustin Gouker, *Can Las Vegas Become the eSports Capital of the World? Nevada Gaming Committee Eyes Future*, Esports Betting Report, Nov. 10, 2016, https://www.esportsbettingreport.com/nevada-gaming-committee-esports-meeting/.

96 Nev. Gaming Comm. § 22.120(2): A request for approval to accept wagers on an event other than a horse race, greyhound race, or an athletic sports event shall be made by book on such forms approved by the chairman, and shall include:

(a) A full description of the event and the manner in which wagers would be placed and winning wagers would be determined.

(b) A full description of any technology which would be utilized to offer the event.

(c) Such other information or documentation which demonstrates that:

(1) The event could be effectively supervised;

(2) The outcome of the event would be verifiable;

(3) The outcome of the event would be generated by a reliable and independent process;

(4) The outcome of the event would be unlikely to be affected by any wager placed;

(5) The event could be conducted in compliance with any applicable laws; and

requires sports books to seek permission from regulators each time they want to offer bets on eSports contests. This has led to Nevada sports books offering wagers on only three events as of September 2017. The Gaming Control Board has recently revised its procedures to allow an entity to seek approval to offer a series of eSports events.[97]

One of the limiting features of eSports that promotes caution by regulators is the absence of an overall governing body. Governing bodies such as the NFL, NASCAR, and other major sports leagues offer a level of integrity that reassures gaming regulators who are asked to approve betting on the events of the groups. There is no universally recognized body for eSports, though the Esports Integrity Coalition (ESIC) has gained some recognition.[98] The ESIC was formed in 2015 by stakeholders in the eSports industry to identify and manage integrity issues in eSports.[99]

Another reason ESIC was established was to address an issue that blunts the enthusiasm of regulators to approve betting on eSports, namely the possibility of cheating and fraud. Shortly after its establishment, ESIC conducted an assessment of the dangers facing eSports and identified four areas in descending order of priority: cheating to win using software, online attacks to disrupt opponent's play, match-fixing, and doping.[100] To give notice to competitors what is legal within the rules and what is not, ESIC has drafted a Code of Conduct,[101] Anti-Corruption Code,[102] and Anti-Doping Policy.[103]

ESIC has published a list of prohibited substances. These substances are completely banned from competitors unless they qualify for a Therapeutic Use Exemption (TUE).[104] Among the substances banned by the EIC are Adderall, Evekeo, ProCentra,

---

(6) The granting of the request for approval would be consistent with the public policy of the state.

97 Richard Velotta, *Nevada Gaming Policy Panel Urges New Rules on eSports*, LAS VEGAS REVIEW-JOURNAL, Nov. 16, 2016, https://www.reviewjournal.com/business/casinos-gaming/nevada-gaming-policy-panel-urges-new-rules-on-e-sports/.

98 *About Us*, ESPORTS INTEGRITY COALITION, http://www.esportsintegrity.com/about-us/ (last visited Aug. 2, 2017).

99 *Id.*

100 *Id.*

101 *Code of Conduct*, ESPORTS INTEGRITY COALITION, http://www.esportsintegrity.com/the-esic-integrity-programme/code-of-conduct/ (last visited Aug. 2, 2017).

102 *Anti-Corruption Code*, ESPORTS INTEGRITY COALITION, http://www.esportsintegrity.com/the-esic-integrity-programme/anti-corruption-code/ (last visited Aug. 2, 2017).

103 *Anti-Doping Policy*, ESPORTS INTEGRITY COALITION, http://www.esportsintegrity.com/the-esic-integrity-programme/anti-doping-code/ (last visited Aug. 2, 2017).

104 *Id.* at Art. 4.

Focalin, and Vyvanse which are all prescription drugs used to treat Attention Deficit Hyperactivity Disorder (ADHD) but assists the competitor in maintaining focus and energy for extended periods of time.[105] In addition to the prohibited substances list, EIC published a "monitoring list" every year to assess the likelihood of misuse of certain substances. For 2016 this included non-stimulant medications for ADHD such as Strattera and Intuniv, and anxiety medications including Zoloft and Norpramin.[106]

In March 2017, the ESIC's purview has grown since the coalition signed a Memorandum of Understanding with the Nevada Gaming Control Board.[107] The MOU allows the NGCB and ESIC to "share information about suspicious bets and other information related to betting fraud and match manipulation in eSports without further formality."[108] The agreement will allow the NGCB to communicate information with the ESIC's panel of partners and regulators to facilitate real-time exchange of critical information about suspicious betting, match manipulation, and other activities which could harm the integrity and reputation of the eSports wagering market.[109] Unusual betting patterns have been identified in match fixing incidents in recent years.[110]

As noted, the fragmented nature of eSports is a hurdle to regulatory confidence. ESIC is simply a voluntary organization which members choose to join and adhere to their rules. Among the members of EIC are ESL (originally Electronic Sports League)[111], Intel, Dreamhack,

---

105 *See Procentra*, WEBMD, http://www.webmd.com/drugs/2/drug-151914/procentra-oral/details (last visited Aug. 1, 2017).

106 *ESIC Prohibited List*, ESPORTS INTEGRITY COALITION, http://www.esportsintegrity.com/the-esic-integrity-programme/esic-prohibited-list/ (last visited Aug. 4, 2017).

107 Rasmus Tillgaard, *The Nevada Gaming Control Board Signs an Information Sharing Memorandum of Understanding with The Esports Integrity Coalition*, ESPORTS INTEGRITY COALITION, Mar. 1, 2017, http://www.esportsintegrity.com/2017/03/01/the-nevada-gaming-control-board-ngcb-signs-an-information-sharing-memorandum-of-understanding-with-the-esports-integrity-coalition-esic-to-promote-integrity-in-esports-wagering-in-nevada-and-to-ai/.

108 *Id.*

109 *Id.*

110 *See* Richard Lewis, *New Evidence Points to Match-Fixing at Highest Level of American Counter-Strike*, DOT ESPORTS, Jan. 16, 2015, https://dotesports.com/counter-strike/match-fixing-counter-strike-ibuypower-netcode-guides-1256.

111 ESL is the largest and oldest professional eSports organization in the world. *See* Jessica Conditt, *Swedish Media House Buys World's Largest eSports Company*, ENGADGET, July 1, 2015, https://www.engadget.com/2015/07/01/esports-mtg-acquires-esl/.

and Sportradar.[112] Some eSports commentators believe that until a central organization or federation can be empowered to effectively regulate the fragmented industry, game developers should take a greater lead in regulations of their games.[113] One can expect that as the eSports industry matures many of these problems will be addressed. Indeed, they will need to be if eSports is going to flourish as a source of wagering.

Wagering on eSports comes in several different forms, both familiar and unfamiliar to those accustomed to wagering on traditional sports. The familiar mode of wagering on eSports is sportsbook betting for eSports. Sportsbook betting on eSports is just like its traditional counterpart—cash betting on competitive outcomes.[114] The most popular sportsbook betting are CS:GO and LoL.[115] Sportsbook betting on eSports has similarities to traditional sports, including a similar audience demographic and the engagement of the fan as an extension of their devotion to a player, team, or game.[116] Because eSports betting is so new, pricing bets is difficult for sportsbooks. A relative dearth of data on the players and competitions is another obstacle for bookmakers.[117]

Another familiar manner of wagering on eSports is fantasy eSports. Fantasy eSports is one of the smallest forms of eSports wagering.[118] Fantasy eSports functions essentially the same way as the traditional fantasy sports. A player chooses a line-up of eSports competitors competing in an event or series of events. The digital line-up of eSports competitors with the most points wins.[119] The popularity of fantasy eSports is attributable in large part to the same reason that traditional fantasy sports are popular. This includes a greater level of engagement players feel with their favorite game or players, "peer to peer wagering," and a broad existing familiarity with

---

112 *Esports Integrity Coalition*, EIC, http://www.esportsintegrity.com (last visited Aug. 5, 2017).

113 Aurangzeb Durrani, *Match-fixing Comes to the World of eSports*, TECHCRUNCH, Apr. 23, 2016, https://techcrunch.com/2016/04/23/match-fixing-comes-to-the-world-of-e-sports/.

114 Chris Grove, *Esports Betting: Overview of The Market and Frequently Asked Questions*, ESPORTS BETTING REPORT, Apr. 25, 2016, https://www.esportsbettingreport.com/guide/.

115 *Id.*

116 *Id.*

117 *Id.*

118 Chris Grove, *Fantasy Esports: Overview And FAQ*, ESPORTS BETTING REPORT, Apr. 24, 2016, https://www.esportsbettingreport.com/fantasy-esports/.

119 *Id.*

the concept of fantasy sports.[120] Fantasy eSports does face challenges originating from the currently small pool of fantasy eSports players, leading to issues with liquidity and competition.[121]

Besides the typical sportsbook betting and fantasy eSports, there is another popular manner of eSports wagering. "Skin betting" is a more exotic form of wagering and is likely unfamiliar to many players who have not engaged in it, even though it was one of the earliest forms of wagering—even prior to Nevada's legalization of money line betting. So what is skin betting?

According to Chris Grove of Narus Advisors, a "skin" is an item that is used to change the appearance of an avatar (character), weapon, or piece of equipment used within a game.[122]A skin has no functional role in a game.[123] It does not increase a character's life, power, or capabilities. It does not allow a player to do anything they could not previously do in the game. It simply alters the appearance of the item or character to which the skin is connected. CS: GO is the main currency used in the skin betting market.[124] A skin was not an original feature of CS:GO but was included in the game as part of the "Arms Deal" update by Valve in August 2013.[125]

Players acquire skins a variety of ways: during gameplay, via promotional giveaway by developer, trading with other players, or purchasing on a marketplace.[126] Since skins hold no intrinsic value, and they do not improve gameplay or a player's abilities within the game, they are much like a casino chip. They hold value because people within the market value them. Once a player receives a skin there are several options: leave the skin in their gamer inventory, use in game to change their weapon or character, trade with other players, sell their skin on Steam[127] for credit (but not cash), or exchange the

---

120 *Id.*

121 *Id.*

122 Chris Grove, *Understanding Skin Gambling*, Narus Advisors, 2016, https://www.esportsbettingreport.com/sites/skins/.

123 *Id.*

124 *Id.*

125 Samit Sarkar, *How Do Counter-Strike: Global Offensive Skins Work?*, Polygon, July 11, 2016, http://www.polygon.com/2016/7/11/12129136/counter-strike-global-offensive-cs-go-skins-explainer.

126 Grove, *supra* note 123.

127 Steam is a gaming platform that distributes PC games. It also offers multiplayer gaming and streaming services. *See* Ben Gilbert, *Everything Valve Does is Because of Steam*, Engadget, Mar. 13, 2015, https://www.engadget.com/2015/03/13/valve-steam/.

skin for cash on third-party sites.[128] Because of concerns about the legality of skins trading Valve, the parent company of Steam, cracked down on skins trading in mid-2016.[129]

Despite the concerns from Valve and other third parties, the illegality of skins betting is undetermined. Primarily this is because it is not clear whether skins have "value." There are no cases that have addressed this question directly related to skins.[130] Courts have addressed similar issues with virtual currency and prizes with social games.[131] The courts ruled in each of these cases that any money paid by the players were for access to play the game and not placing wagers.[132] Some commentators have interpreted this case law as indicating that skins have no legal "value" and thus do not violate gambling statutes.[133]

Wagering on eSports is not limited to the United States. The United Kingdom, a country that has long embraced wagering due in part to the popularity of horse racing, allows eSports betting. The United Kingdom Gambling Commission, the regulatory body responsible for wagering in the UK, released a position paper in early 2017 identifying some of the same concerns with eSports that have been voiced in the US.[134] Among these shared concerns are underage gambling,[135] integrity issues related to cheating,[136]and licensing.[137] "Skins gambling" on eSports shares the same uncertain legal status that it does in the US.[138]

The gaming side of eSports, much like the sport generally, is still in its embryonic stage in the United States. Gamblers are becoming

128 Grove, *supra* note 123 at 2.

129 Chris Grove, *Where eSports Betting Goes Following Valve's Crackdown on Skins Gambling*, ESPORTS BETTING REPORT, July 14, 2016, https://www.esportsbettingreport.com/valve-skin-gambling-crackdown-analysis/.

130 Desiree Martinelli, *Skin Gambling: Have We Found the Millenial Goldmine or Imminent Trouble?*, GAMING LAW REVIEW, Oct. 2017, 21(8): 557-565, 564.

131 *Id.*

132 *Id.*; *See Mason v. Mach. Zone, Inc.*, 851 F.3d 315 (4th Cir. Mar. 17, 2017); *See also Soto v. Sky Union* 159 F. Supp. 3d 871 (N.D. Ill. 2016); *Phillips v. Double Down Interactive,* 173 F. Supp. 3d 731 (N.D. Ill. 2016).

133 Martinelli, *supra* note 131.

134 Gambling Commission, *Virtual currencies, eSports and Social Casino Gaming*, UNITED KINGDOM GAMBLING COMMISSION, Mar. 2017, http://www.gamblingcommission.gov.uk/PDF/Virtual-currencies-eSports-and-social-casino-gaming.pdf.

135 *Id.* at 3.

136 *Id.* at 4.

137 *Id.* at 5.

138 *Id.* at 7.

more familiar with the sport and the growth in betting is projected to shadow the exponential growth in the sport itself.[139] The burgeoning growth should also fuel more interest in the sport itself and vice versa.

CONCLUSION

In this decade, eSports has experienced a meteoric rise in visibility, popularity, and notoriety. For the first time, it is regularly broadcast on American television. The biggest tournaments are offering eight-figure prize pools. Media giants such as ESPN, Amazon, and Facebook have recognized the immense opportunity and have attempted to gain a foothold in the eSports media environment. Athletes and organizations of traditional sports, rather than eschewing the sport as a hobby not deserving of the imprimatur of "real" sports, have dove head first into eSports in hopes of cashing in on its intense fan following. eSports has reached an important time in its history and now—with visibility that could have only been dreamed of twenty years ago—will attempt to show that it is not a "flash in the pan" but an enduring sport worthy of mention alongside the other major American sports. As this growth occurs regulators will likely become more familiar with the contests. This could make eSports a leader in the wagering arena.

---

139 Joss Wood, *New Report: Esports Audience Could Almost Double to 600 Million by 2020, With Big Growth for Esports Betting*, Legal Sports Report, Feb. 22, 2017, https://www.legalsportsreport.com/13132/esports-betting-and-audience-growth-2020/.

7

Recommendations

This chapter contains recommendations that the sports governing bodies, the government, and legal sportsbooks should consider in protecting both sports and wagering integrity. Sports governing bodies have the most direct responsibility, interest, and opportunity to address sports integrity. Cooperation with all stakeholders, however, enhances the likelihood of success. For example, the governing bodies need to take measures to minimize the conditions for a corruptor successfully entering into a contract with a corrupted to fix a competition, and the sports books need to share information indicating irregular betting patterns that can expose competition manipulation.

CONSIDERATIONS FOR THE RESPONSIBILITIES OF SPORTS GOVERNING BODIES TO MINIMIZE WAGERING-RELATED CORRUPTION

The following are practices that the sports governing bodies should consider or augment.

Cooperation Agreements

Sports governing bodies should enter integrity agreements with the sportsbooks to cooperate in monitoring games and to share wagering data and suspicious activities.[1] Bookmakers can assist in exposing a match fix where price movement on an event is significant and irrational. Most regulated sportsbooks are willing to cooperate with the governing bodies because the integrity of the game was essential to their business. Without it, their customers could not

1 *See e.g.*, Emine Bozkurt, *Match Fixing and Fraud in Sport: Putting the Pieces Together*, (2012) *available at* http://sportetcitoyennete.com/en/ressourceseuropeen/pdf/parliament/bozkurt_match_fixing_2012.pdf.

exercise their skills needed to handicap games,[2] and would soon lose interest knowing that the games are not honest. Likewise, books were the financial victims of accepting wagers that they had no chance to win. The legal Nevada bookmakers have long been an important source for uncovering irregular betting patterns that uncovered competition manipulation in several instances.[3] Cooperation agreements also are standard in Europe. For example, Betfair has had agreements with UEFA and the International Federation of Association Football (FIFA) and the ATP Tour for many years.[4]

---

2 Richard O. Davies & Richard G. Abram, BETTING THE LINE: SPORTS WAGERING IN AMERICAN LIFE (Ohio State University Press, 2001).

3 As early as 1946, then NFL Commissioner Bert Bell hired undercover agents to monitor the Las Vegas betting lines for unusual line movements after gamblers attempted to bribe two members of the New York Giants by offering each $2500 and to place a $2000 wager each on their behalves. He also suspended both players for failure to report the offer. During the 1993-1994 NCAA season, Nevada sports books alerted the State Gaming Control Board of suspicious wagers regarding Arizona State University's basketball games. Sun, V. (1999, November 18). 'I was just trying to make an easy buck.' Las Vegas Sun. Retrieved from http://lasvegassun.com/news/1999/nov/18/i-was-just-trying-to-make-an-easy-buck/. Sandoval, G. (1998, January 7). Fixing scheme: Work of the 'devils. Los Angeles Times. Retrieved from http://articles.latimes.com/1998/jan/07/sports/sp-5925/2. The sportsbooks had to move the line several times because of heavy bets against some ASU games. The Board began an investigation and notified the FBI. Two players from the ASU basketball team, Steven Smith and Isaac Burton, had agreed to shave points. Smith was paid $20,000 per game, and he gave Burton $4,300 to intentionally miss some free throws, if needed, to shave points during games. The student bookie who initiated the scheme received a 46-month prison sentence and a $25,000 fine. Smith received a one-year sentence and a $8,000 fine, and Burton received a two-month sentence and $8,000 fine. Gamblers who knew of the point shaving are reported to have bet a total of $506,000 on the fixed games and served time in prison. Teitelbaum, S. H. (2008). Sports heroes, fallen idols. Dexter, MI: Thomson-Shore. In this instance, the legal sports betting apparatus enabled law enforcement to take steps against illegal sports betting and its adverse consequences. In 2004, Las Vegas betting interests alerted the state gaming regulators who, in turn, notified the NCAA of suspicions surrounding point shaving by the University of Toledo's football team and several books would not accept wagers on their games. Mike Fish & George Tanber, *As Summer Ends, Heat is On in Toledo Point-Shaving Case*, ESPN, Sept. 2, 2009, http://www.espn.com/espn/news/story?id=2988714.

4 Richard H. McLaren, "*Corruption: Its Impact on Fair Play.*" 19 MARQ. SPORTS L. REV. 15 (2008); *citing Officials Look into Irregular Betting on Match*, ESPN.com, June 28, 2006, http://sports.espn.go.com/sports/tennis/wimbledon06/news/story? id=2502709. ("At Wimbledon in 2006, Betfair reported irregular betting patterns surrounding a first-round match between British wild card player, Richard Bloomfield, and the higher ranked Carlos Berlocq of Argentina, who had lost in straight sets. Berlocq, who was ranked 170 places higher than Bloomfield, lost 6-1, 6-2, 6-2. Most of the bets placed were on Berlocq to lose. The International Tennis Federation (ITF), which oversees Grand Slam tournaments, investigated the matter but found no illicit wrongdoing." McLaren, Richard H. "Corruption: its impact on fair play.")

An industry-wide comprehensive centralized program should replace informal understandings and individual agreements between the sports governing bodies and the sportsbooks. Some models exist that are worthy of review. The United Kingdom sponsors a program that brings together "representatives from across sport, law enforcement, regulators and betting businesses who work together to implement" a sports betting integrity action plan.[5] Likewise, the Australia sports ministers proposed a model calling for sports controlling bodies to enter integrity agreements with legal sportsbooks to exchange information as part of a broader effort for information exchange and cooperation between governments, major sports leagues, betting operators, and law enforcement.[6]

While enhanced private cooperative efforts are commendable, a statutory requirement of collaboration may be appropriate. For example, in the US, the future federal law could mandate cooperative partnership agreements between the sportsbooks, the sports governing bodies, and government authorities. If such a law established minimum requirements for sharing suspicious activities, cooperating on investigating suspected incidents of competition manipulation, and placement of wagering data into a centralized system, significant reductions in sports corruption might be achieved.

Data Analysis and Early Warning Systems

A key component of stakeholder cooperation is data sharing

In another example, in 2007, Betfair alerted the ATP that it voided bets involving the world's fourth-ranked player because of irregular wagering patterns, including the placing of wagers at many times the typical levels. *Davydenko Faces Betting Inquiry*, BBC SPORT, Aug. 27, 2007, http://news.bbc.co.uk/sport2/hi/tennis/6928635.stm. There were several striking features about these betting patterns. The wagering heavily favored a player that was ranked 83 spots lower than the fourth-ranked player, and this betting pattern continued even after the lower ranked player lost the first set convincingly. Also, a significant amount of money wagered on the underdog came from three Russian accounts. John Barr & William Weinbaum, *Evidence Shows Something Terribly Corrupt in Infamous Match*, ESPN, Feb. 7, 2008, http://www.espn.com/sports/tennis/news/story?id=3235411. The fourth-ranked player eventually retired from the match citing a stress fracture in his foot. Had Betfair not voided the wagers, those who bet on the underdog would have been paid. After an investigation no charges were brought against the tennis players involved despite the unusual betting patterns. Even the International Olympic Committee (IOC) looked to legalized sportsbooks as both an ally in the fight against competition manipulation and as a source of funding for such efforts. *Sport: A Right to Bet?* SPORT BUS. INT'L. MAG, No. 166, April 2011.

5 United Kingdom Gambling Commission, How we work with other authorities, http://www.gamblingcommission.gov.uk/about/Who-we-are-and-what-we-do/How-we-work-with-other-authorities.aspx and *http://www.sbif.uk/images/Documents/FINAL-SBI-Action-Plan-V2.0.pdf (last visited March 4, 2018).*

6 *Id.*

agreements between the sports governing bodies and the sportsbooks.[7] Such agreements intend that the sportsbooks would provide raw wagering data rather than reports only of suspicious activity. The responsible authority would commingle the data from each sportsbook and analyze the cumulative data using advanced algorithms to detect irregular betting patterns.[8] Such data analysis could be the basis for an early warning system to determine if any betting activity is inconsistent with anticipated patterns, or has unusual characteristics for the market or sporting event in question. This might include: (a) a gambler placing unusually high wagers;[9] (b) betting volume being high compared to a typical type or level of game;[10] (c) betting volume abnormally skewing in favor of the underdog;[11] (d) substantial unexplainable changes in odds or lines across multiple bookmakers;[12] (e) several new accounts placing the same wager; or (f) a large number of identical wagers coming from the same region or the same internet address.[13] Also, a forensic review of historical data can uncover "relationships that might be evident from a consideration of thousands of contests and the betting markets even though no individual incident was so exceptional as to justify canceling all transactions."[14]

The sportsbook industry can voluntarily cooperate on early warning systems both as a prophylactic and potentially as a public relations measure. For example, ESSA, a European organization provides an example of an effort by book operators to create a private cooperative early warning system.[15] ESSA is a not for profit organization

---

7 McLaren, *supra* note 4.

8 IOC, Interpol, HANDBOOK ON PROTECTING SPORT FROM COMPETITION MANIPULATION, https://www.interpol.int/News-and-media/Publications2/Leaflets-and-brochures/Joint-report-INTERPOL-IOC-Handbook-on-Protecting-Sport-from-Competition-Manipulation.

9 Scott Ferguson, *Tackling the Match-Fixers*, NEW SCIENTIST, Vol. 221, Issue 2950, at 3-65 (January 4, 2014).

10 David Forrest & Rick Parry, *The Key to Sports Integrity in the United States: Legalized,* REGULATED SPORTS BETTING, Sept. 2016.

11 *Id.*

12 *Id.*

13 *Id.*

14 *Id.*

15 ESSA (Sports Betting Integrity) » About ESSA, http://www.eu-ssa.org/about-essa/ (accessed June 16, 2017).

The ESSA Code of Conduct is based upon the following overriding principles:

- Participation in ESSA's Early Warning System;
- Preventing conflicts of interests;

whose members are licensed land-based and interactive operators.[16] The effectiveness of the system is contingent on sharing data and reporting suspicious activity under memorandums of understanding with more than 400 bookmakers.[17] ESSA has agreements to share information with more than 20 sports federations including FIFA, the IOC, the Tennis Integrity Unit, and government regulators including the UK Gambling Commission, the Alderney Gambling Control Commission, the Malta Lotteries and Gaming Authority, and the Gibraltar Gambling Commissioner.[18]

If legal sports wagering extends beyond Nevada, the value of the

---

- Members must implement adequate internal policies and operational control tools;
- Cooperation with sports regulators, sports federations and public bodies
- Promotion of responsible gaming;
- Protection of minors and of the socially vulnerable;
- Maintain consumer privacy and data protection;
- Enforcement and disciplinary action.

16 ESSA (Sports Betting Integrity) » About ESSA, http://www.eu-ssa.org/about-essa/ (accessed June 16, 2017).

17 Carpenter, *infra* note 49. Its early warning system assembles and identifies irregular betting threats based on traceable wagers provided from the sports operators' database. The 148 alerts in 2013 resulted in 30 suspicious betting reports being filed with the relevant sporting bodies and regulatory authorities. *Sports Betting: Legal, Commercial and Integrity Issues*, REMOTE GAMBLING ASSOCIATION, 61, London (UK): (2010).

18 ESSA describes the operational process as follows: "an ESSA member detects something unusual in a betting pattern on a particular event (Tier 1, ICS). That is then immediately reported and escalated to ESSA's security team and Head Bookmaker and which if substantiated as a potential danger triggers an alert to the whole EESA membership (Tier 2). If such an alert is issued, which occurs through ESSA's Advanced Security Platform (ASP), members are required to respond quickly confirming whether or not similar trends have been seen elsewhere in their markets and, if they have, giving as much detail as possible. On the latter, whilst ESSA members are fully committed to the fight against sports betting corruption and to fully cooperating with all other stakeholders to that end, it should be noted that they are also bound to adhere to certain legal requirements such as data protection legislation. Where evidence emerges that there may be potentially fraudulent activity taking place, e.g. because several members have confirmed an irregular betting pattern, ESSA will:

> i) report that information under the applicable Memorandum of Understanding (MoU) to the relevant sports governing body; and
> ii) advise the member(s) concerned to make a report to their own national regulatory authority...
> The recipient (sports governing body and/or gambling regulator) will [determine] whether the particular alert in question requires action on their part." ESSA (Sports Betting Integrity) » About ESSA, http://www.eu-ssa.org/about-essa/ (accessed June 16, 2017).

data increases as the legal markets replace the illegal markets. Having more data is particularly valuable on American sports like football and baseball where the volume of wagering in the non-US markets is relatively small. To realize the highest effectiveness of this data, however, federal law should require all legal sportsbooks to provide their raw data in real time to a shared data pool for a comprehensive analysis of betting patterns and the most effective early warning system. An independent body could oversee the collection and analysis of the data and consistently evaluate the processes used to assure credibility of the process.[19] The independent body could impose uniform procedures for investigating any irregular betting patterns.[20]

Codes of Conduct for All Players, Referees, and Athletic Support Personnel on the Dangers of Competition Manipulation

As noted in Chapter 4, the sports governing bodies for the sports most popular with bettors all have codes of conduct that address gambling and competition manipulation. While each has essential prohibitions and sanctions, they lack consistency. As the UK Sports Betting Integrity Panel noted in a 2010 report, "It is imperative that sports governing bodies have clear rules in relation to betting and insider information in their sports and for those rules to be communicated in an effective manner which is clearly understood by participants or competitors."[21] Therefore, codes of conduct should have uniform provisions across all sports that prohibit players, referees, and all athletic support personnel (including coaches, trainers, team officials or staff, agents, managers, and medical personnel) from:

- Betting on any contest in which they or their team are participants;[22]
- Seeking or accepting a bribe to fix an event;[23]
- Offering or attempting to offer any bribes to affect an event outcome;[24]

---

19 Thomas Feltes, *Match Fixing in Western Europe*, In MATCH-FIXING IN INTERNATIONAL SPORTS 15-30 (Springer International Publishing, 2013).

20 *Id.*

21 Sports Betting Integrity Panel, *Report of the sports betting integrity panel.* Feb. 2010, London, UK: Author. Retrieved from http://www.sportsbettinggroup.org/docs/reports_sports_betting_integrity_panel.pdf

22 *Global Match-Fixing and the United States*, http://scholarship.law.berkeley.edu/cgi/viewcontent.cgi?article=1034&context (accessed June 27, 2017).

23 Sports Betting Integrity Panel, *supra* note 21.

24 *Id.*

- Soliciting or facilitating anyone to bet on any contest in which they or their team are participants;[25]
- Not performing to the best of their abilities;[26]
- Failing to report any activities in violation of the policies regarding integrity;[27]
- Misusing privileged or insider information.[28]

Beyond provisions that deal with prohibited activities, sports governing bodies may adopt rules and procedures that assist in the investigation and prosecution of wagering-related corruption. These include requiring athletes, athletic support staff, referees, and others to:

- Agree to cooperate with investigators;
- Agree to hold the league and others including witnesses harmless from the potential consequences of the investigation; and
- Waive certain privileges that could prevent the investigators from obtaining all evidence (e.g., privacy rights that prevent access to bank accounts, or doctor-patient privileges that prevent access to evidence of whether the player faked an injury.)[29]

Without clear and significant requirements and penalties, many athletes may prefer to avoid the controversy surrounding reporting fellow competitors or teammates. As sports integrity is so important and detection problematic, the sports governing bodies must rely on the players, athletic support personnel, referees, and others to self-report violations. Affirmative obligations to be forthright and truthful should buttress the requirement that the athlete report violations and cooperate with the investigation. Players, referees, and others should face sanction if they fail to provide truthful, accurate, and complete information and documentation without undue delay.[30] Likewise, punishment is appropriate for any attempt to obstruct or delay the investigation including concealing or tampering with

25 *Id.*

26 *Id.*

27 Robert Williams, *INTERPOL-Led Operation During the FIFA World Cup Raises Questions About Illegal Gambling's Role in International Soccer*, Int'l Enforcement L. Rep., Nov. 2014.

28 Sports Betting Integrity Panel, *supra* note 21.

29 Williams, *supra* note 27.

30 Rules For The Application During In 2016 In Rio De Janeiro https://stillmed.olympic.org/Documents/Commissions_PDFfiles/Ethics/rio2016_rules (accessed October 27, 2017).

evidence, intimidating or retaliating against any witnesses, altering or destroying any relevant documentation or other information,[31] or bribing or unethically attempting to influence the investigators or tribunal.

Sportsbooks should adopt uniform provisions that prevent, detect, and report code of conduct violations. For example, sportsbook rules should be consistent with league codes of conduct as to who can place a wager and who cannot. Can a professional baseball player wager on other sports? Can an employee of a sports team wager on the outcome of a game involving teams other than the team that employs him? Does this extend to all athletic support personnel and employees or just players, coaches, trainers and medical professionals? Sportsbooks and sports leagues should have the same answers to these questions.

A Uniform and Fair Policy on Penalties for Competition Manipulation Whether for Betting or Other Reasons

Sports governing bodies should reinforce codes of conduct related to competition manipulation with a commitment to enforcement and meaningful sanctions.[32] Significant sanctions are essential to the anti-corruption policy."[33] As the court noted in a case involving the Association of Tennis Professionals (ATP), "General prevention... is best achieved by imposing a just (individual) sanction. If the term of ineligibility and the amount of the fine are not reduced, the punishment imposed upon the Appellant places the proportionality of the sanction in question and vitiates the preventive purposes which it intends to achieve."[34]

Sanctions should address: (a) whether the athletes are betting on their events and whether they were betting against their performance; (b) whether the betting was in connection with a corrupt motive; (c) the amount and frequency of the wagering; and (d) the athlete's honesty and cooperation in the investigation.[35]

---

31 *Id.*

32 *Id.*

33 Ashutosh Misra, Jack Anderson, & Jason Saunders. *Safeguarding Sports Integrity Against Crime and Corruption: An Australian Perspective,* in MATCH-FIXING IN INTERNATIONAL SPORTS 135-155 (Springer International Publishing, 2013.)

34 CAS 2007/A/1427 M. V ATP Tour Inc., June 11 2008 at par. 31.

35 The fairmindedness of lifetime bans for merely betting on the sport in which the athlete is a participant is debatable. Major league baseball has separate rules for betting on a game in which the athlete is a participant and those in which the athlete is not. Baseball rules provide that "any player, umpire, or club or league official or employee, who shall bet any sum whatsoever upon any baseball game in connection with which

Sports governing bodies should impose strict sanctions for the most serious violations. The risk of reputational damage should deter athletes concerned with sports glory, and direct monetary risks may dissuade corruptors and the corrupted.[36] Therefore, lifetime bans of athletes involved in competition manipulation should be a universal standard.[37] The imposition of lifetime bans is less to prevent the offending player or referee from engaging in similar conduct in the future as it is to inform all participants of the consequences of engaging in corrupt behavior.[38] More significant penalties for failure to report

the bettor has a duty to perform shall be declared permanently ineligible." *Blacklisted Players*, Baseball Reference, retrieved from https://www.baseball-reference.com/bullpen/ This rule makes no distinction between betting for or against your team. This fate befell Pete Rose, the all-time baseball leader in hits. He agreed to a lifetime ban, permitted under baseball rules, for betting on baseball while the manager of the Cincinnati Reds, although later allegations included that he bet while he was a player and used bookies tied to organized crime. William Weinbau, & T.J. Quinn, *Entries in Long-Hidden Notebook Show Pete Rose Bet on Baseball as Player*, ESPN, June 22, 2015, http://www.espn.com/espn/otl/story/_/id/13114874/notebook-obtained-lines-shows-pete-rose-bet-baseball-player-1986.

Baseball's rule in this regard has advantages. First, the rule is clear. Players and others cannot claim confusion about their responsibilities. Second, it relieves the sport's governing body of having to prove that the player intended to match fix; only that he bet on the game. This is a much easier burden to meet than the investigators having to produce evidence of the player being bribed and then tying the bribe to a wager.

Still, a lifetime ban seems severe for a player who merely bets that his team will win as this is less likely to be tied to a corrupted game. Baseball has a lesser penalty for betting on games where the player or coach is not a participant. This rule provides: "Any player, umpire, or club official or employee, who shall bet any sum whatsoever upon any baseball game in connection with which the bettor has no duty to perform shall be declared ineligible for one year." *Basketball Articles - MLB Rule 21: Misconduct*, https://www.ticketretriever.com/article-baseball-misconduct-rule.html (accessed October 27, 2017). While this appears sufficient for most violations, it does not adequately address more culpable behavior such as betting on insider information or a belief that the game is fixed.

36 Wladimir Andreff, *Corruption in Sport*, Terri Byers. Contemporary Issues in Sport Management: A Critical Introduction, Sage, 2016.

37 Kevin Carpenter, *Global Match-Fixing and the United States' Role in Upholding Sporting Integrity*, 2 Berkeley J. Ent. & Sports L. (2013). Available at: http://scholarship.law.berkeley.edu/bjesl/vol2/iss1/11.

38 This has a long history in US sports including the highest profile lifetime bans of athletes for competition manipulation involving the 1919 Chicago White Sox. As one tribunal noted for tennis, a sport plagued with corruption partially because it is an individual sport, "It is therefore imperative that, once a Player gets caught, the Governing Bodies send out a clear signal to the entire tennis community that such actions are not tolerated. This Panel agrees that any sanction shorter than a lifetime ban would not have the deterrent effect that is required to make players aware that it is simply not worth the risk." Daniel Kollerer v Association of Tennis Professionals, Women's Tennis Association, International Tennis Federation & Grand Slam Committee at para 123,

an approach also are worthy of consideration. Finally, uniform and reciprocal sanctions across jurisdictions are more critical in sports that have an international following. A US basketball player found guilty of competition manipulation and banned from the NBA should not, for example, be able to move to Europe or Asia and participate in their professional leagues.[39] Sports governing bodies need to reach reciprocity agreements with sister bodies across the world to prevent evasion of meaningful sanctions.

Whistleblower Programs

Sports governing bodies should have comprehensive whistleblower programs that use a system of rewards to encourage players and others to report any competition manipulation. At a minimum, the sports governing bodies should have hotlines or other methods that allow athletes, coaches or others, who may have valuable information or suspicions about match fixing or insider trading, to anonymously report these occurrences.[40] The information derived from the hotline is particularly helpful when data analysis can corroborate it.[41] This system could be like the 24/7 "integrity hotline" that FIFA created in 2013.[42]

The whistleblower programs should consider financial and other incentives to persons who provide information leading to the discovery of corrupt acts,[43] or, in working with law enforcement or regulators, the ability to offer immunity or non-prosecution agreements.[44]

Education Programs

Sports governing bodies should develop comprehensive educational programs on the rules concerning wagering and wagering information.[45] Individually tailored educational programs on

---

Mar. 23, 2012.

39 "Twenty-seven nations within the European Union have banded together to fight the "growing threat" of match-fixing." Katarzyna Kordas, *Dropping the Ball: How Can FIFA Address the Match-Fixing Problem Facing Professional Football*, 23 SPORTS L.J. 107 (2016).

40 John T Holden & Ryan M. Rodenberg. *The Sports Bribery Act: A Law and Economics Approach*. 42 N. KY. L. REV. 453 (2015).

41 Mark Duggan & Steven D. Levitt. *Winning Isn't Everything: Corruption in Sumo Wrestling*, No. 7798. NAT'L BUREAU OF ECON. RES., 2000.

42 Williams, *supra* note 27.

43 Holden & Rodenberg, *supra* note 40 at 470.

44 *Id.*

45 *Id.* An emphasis on comprehensive educational programs for US sports needs improvement. Only the NBA has provisions in its collective bargaining agreement that

competition manipulation should "raise awareness about expected codes of conduct, clear definitions of corrupt behaviors, and effective accountability practices."[46] Athletes should be informed of the league rules and the criminal laws regarding competition manipulation including prohibitions on match-fixing, disseminating insider information, gambling, and obligations to report violations. The programs should provide an understanding of how corruptors approach athletes, convince them to be involved with competition manipulation, and then after compromising the player, use blackmail to assure further cooperation in later manipulation.[47] The programs should further highlight the long-term implications on the player's career such as potential income and reputation losses,[48] and possible criminal penalties for offenders.[49] The program and the documents also should include materials and training regarding problem gambling.[50] The governing bodies should require referees, athletic support personnel

mandates educational programs related to sports integrity. It is an excellent starting point that should be emulated across all sports. It provides:

> COLLECTIVE BARGAINING AGREEMENT JANUARY 19, 2017
>
> Section 4. Mandatory Programs. (a) NBA players shall be required to attend and participate in educational and life skills programs designated as "mandatory programs" by the NBA and the Players Association. Such "mandatory programs," which shall be jointly administered by the NBA and the Players Association, shall include a Rookie Transition Program (for rookies only), Team Awareness Meetings (which shall cover, among other things, substance abuse awareness, HIV awareness, and gambling awareness), and such other programs as the NBA and the Players Association shall jointly designate as mandatory. http://nbpa.com/wp-content/uploads/2016/02/2017-NBA-NBPA-Collective-Bargaining-Agreement.pdf
>
> Section 5. Media Training, Business of Basketball and Antigambling Training.
>
> (c) All players shall be required each Season to attend and participate in one (1) anti-gambling training session conducted by their Team and/or the NBA. If a player, without proper and reasonable excuse, fails or refuses to attend an anti-gambling training session, he shall be fined $20,000. http://nbpa.com/wp-content/uploads/2016/02/2017-NBA-NBPA-Collective-Bargaining-Agreement.pdf

46 Tobias Nowy & Christoph Breuer, *Match-Fixing in European Grassroots Football*, Eur. Sport Mgmt. Q., Vol. 17, Iss. 1, 2017.

47 *The Challenges of Betting*, Sportradar, http://www.sportmalta.org.mt/wp-content/uploads/2016/03/3_marcello-presilla-1.pdf

48 Luca Rebeggiani & Fatma Rebeggiani. *Which Factors Favor Betting Related Cheating in Sports? Some Insights from Political Economy*, in Match-Fixing in International Sports 157-176 (Springer International Publishing, 2013).

49 Kevin Carpenter, *Match-Fixing—The Biggest Threat to Sport in the 21st Century?* 2 Internacional Sports L. Rev. 13-23 (2012).

50 *Id.*

(including coaches, trainers, team officials or staff, agents, managers, and medical personnel), and team and league representatives to take similar compulsory and continuing ethics education courses.[51]

Sports governing bodies also should address financial issues affecting players. More specifically, how much have they been paid, what are their post-retirement benefits, and have they been adequately advised regarding their post-retirement lives?[52] As one commentator noted, "It is not that players do not know the correct ethical position in gambling competition manipulation: it is that players have not been paid their salaries, benefits or have received no significant post-retirement education."[53]

A Special Sports Integrity Group

All sports governing bodies should have specially dedicated enforcement arms that have no other responsibilities except to educate, investigate, and enforce rules regarding sports integrity. As noted in chapter 4, the major US sports governing bodies have extensive, although not transparent, enforcement arms that cover issues regarding corruption and some have dedicated compliance officers. Nevertheless, sports integrity groups across all sports upon which the government permits wagering should have dedicated sports integrity enforcement.[54] These units should have considerable authority that is spelled out as part of the collective bargaining or employment agreements with players, athletic support personnel (including coaches, trainers, team officials or staff, agents, managers, and medical personnel), and referees. The investigators should be able to interview players, athletic support personnel, and referees on request and have access to financial, telephone, computer, and other records that are helpful to an investigation. Random financial

51 Farrukh B. Hakeem, *Sports-Related Crime: A Game Theory Approach*, in MATCH-FIXING IN INTERNATIONAL SPORTS, 247-260 (Springer International Publishing, 2013); Feltes, *supra* note 19.

52 Jack Andersen, *Match Fixing and EU Policy in 2014: An Introduction, Risk Assessment, Conflicts of Interest and the Fight Against Betting-Related Match Fixing in the EU*, available at https://papers.ssrn.com/sol3/papers.cfm?abstract_id=2449305.

53 Declan Hill, *Jumping into Fixing*, 18 TRENDS IN ORGANIZED CRIME 212, 226 (2015).

54 An example worthy of study is the Union of European Football Associations (UEFA) which represents 55 national football associations primarily in Europe and conducts competitions including the UEFA European Championship, UEFA Champions League, UEFA Europa League, and UEFA Super Cup, The UEFA has 53 integrity officers that work within each national association, monitors gambling patterns, and undertake intelligence gathering including using informants. *Match Fixing and Fraud in Sport: Putting the Pieces Together* Jun. 27, 2017 <http://www.europarl.europa.eu/document/activities/cont/201209/20120925ATT52303/2>.

audits of players and referees to uncover unreported income may be warranted. For example, in cricket, international players must provide bank and telephone account statements, raising their awareness that suspicious transactions may lead to further inquiry.

Due Diligence Review of Match Organizers and Team Owners

Sports governing bodies should undertake extensive due diligence review of match organizers and team owners to determine their propensity to follow the code of conduct generally, as well as their inclination to engage in corrupt practices. Unvetted persons are particularly problematic in boxing, where promoters have a keen interest in using fights that are lower on a boxing card to inflate a boxer's record to establish the credentials for higher profile boxing matches. With such motivation, a corrupt promoter could attempt to corrupt the outcome of fights that assist in furthering the promoter's best interest.

Greater Transparency

Sports governing bodies should have transparency in their operations and their investigation and enforcement of competition manipulation rules.[55] A sport that is transparent in its operations and subject to rigorous scrutiny is less likely to have competition manipulation.[56] Two reasons support the importance of increased transparency. First, the willingness to cooperate with law enforcement in the prosecution of corruptors and corrupted athletes, athletic support personnel, and referees is a significant deterrent to future misconduct because it increases both detection and perceived risk by potential abusers.[57] Cooperation includes stringent enforcement

55 Sports governing bodies have conflicting interests when it comes to transparency related to competition manipulation, sabotage, or other corrupt practices. They want the public to have the perception that the games are fair and decided on the merits. The public disclosure of an alleged point-shaving scandal would likely damage that perception. Holden & Rodenberg, *supra* note 40. Therefore, sports leagues have a natural inclination to want to "settle disciplinary matters internally whilst trying to limit communication." Institut de Relations Internationales et Stratégiques - IRIS, *Sports Betting and Corruption: How to Preserve the Integrity of Sport*, (2012), available on the internet at: http://www.spordiinfo.ee/est/g22s355 (visited 25-08-2015), p. 51. This position is counter-productive, however, and sports governing bodies should be bound by contract and regulation to transparency and cooperation with the sportsbooks and government police and regulatory agencies.

56 Carpenter, *supra* note 49.

57 Holden & Rodenberg, *supra* note 40.

and swift prosecution of any actor who engages in competition manipulation.[58] Publicizing the names of those who have committed a sports-related crime also increases the risk of loss of sports glory.[59]

Second, transparency in operations makes information equally available to the public and bettors and reduces the value of insider information. The NFL, as an example, requires teams to release an injury report on a specified date each week that lists "significant or noteworthy injuries" and practice participation breakdowns of its players.[60] The league explained that, "Without such a policy, you could envision a potential scenario in which a teammate or team personnel could be approached by a third party to sell inside information about a player's undisclosed injury that could sideline or inhibit his performance."[61] Operational transparency related to allocating and evaluating referees also can reduce corruption.[62]

Review of Asymmetrical Rewards for Winning

Sports governing bodies should review and minimize easy asymmetrical rewards. The ways in which a sports league rewards teams and competitors can affect the propensity of athletes and others to fix the matches.[63] The rewards system for players and teams shapes the way players and teams perceive the value of winning. This has two components. The first is to reduce the number of irrelevant "dead rubber" matches or to at least change the incentives that teams have in playing such games. These are most often the end of season games where at least one of the teams is not motivated to win except for

58 Hakeem, *supra* note 51.

59 *Id.*

60 While the NFL denies the policy relates to maintaining wagering integrity, it does acknowledge that the policy "curtails the potential for someone to attempt to gain and exploit inside information." Travis Durkee, *Richard Sherman Still Hates Injury Reports, Says They're for Vegas*, SPORTING NEWS, Sept. 21, 2017, http://www.sportingnews.com/nfl/news/richard-sherman-injury-reports-nfl-betting-odds/1l4m4y3f6549y1qcgz5resuj77.

61 *Id.*

62 Tito Boeri, Battista Severgninic, *Match Rigging and the Career Concerns of Referees*, 18 LABOUR ECON. 349-59 (2011). After the Donaghy scandal, the NBA changed its policies by publishing referee assignments each morning for that evening's games. REPORT TO THE BOARD OF GOVERNORS OF THE NATIONAL BASKETBALL ASSOCIATION, Oct. 1, 2008 ("Pedowitz Report") https://www.nba.com/media/PedowitzReport.pdf.

63 Asymmetric rewards play a role in non-betting competition manipulation. This includes competition manipulation by tanking at the season's end to obtain higher draft choices (most American sports), to match fix to maintain status in a league or other level of competition (sumo wrestling or European soccer), or to tank matches to manipulate one's opponents in future rounds of a tournament (Olympic badminton), or in the playoffs.

minimal sports glory.[64] Governments and sports governing bodies may want to address the increased risk by changing the reward structure associated with high-risk competitions. For example, teams or athletes may be granted additional monetary reward for winning late-season games without competitive consequences or penalized for losing through loss of status in drafting, reduced compensation, or otherwise. Performance bonuses for such games would assist in ensuring an uncertain outcome.[65] If neither of these is possible, the sports governing bodies should closely monitor dead rubbers.[66] The second component is to redesign tournaments, draft order, and other artificially imposed nonlinear incentives.[67]

Effective Physical Control Mechanisms

Sports governing bodies should have reasonable access controls that prevent non-critical and non-team personnel from entry into the locker rooms before a competition, or on the sidelines during a game. Unauthorized cell phones and other communication devices should not be allowed in the locker room before and on the field during the game.

Referees

Referees are vulnerable to corruption because they can have a considerable influence on a game and are often the lowest paid persons on the field. Sports governing bodies should affirmatively address officiating to avoid the participation of referees in competition manipulation.

First, sports governing bodies should pay the referees commensurate with their responsibilities to minimize financial incentives to engage in corruption.

---

64 Rebeggiani & Rebeggiani, *supra* note 48.

65 Raul Caruso, *The Basic Economics of Match Fixing in Sport Tournaments*, 39 ECON. ANALYSIS AND POL'Y 355-77 (2009).

66 Rebeggiani & Rebeggiani, *supra* note 48.

67 In 2017, the NBA faced with growing criticism that its draft structure encouraged teams to tank games by resting their starters to improve the prospects for higher draft choices, proposed changes to their system that would result in the teams with the worst records having a lesser chance of locking up the number one pick in the draft. Stanley Kay, *Report: NBA Board of Governors to Vote on Draft Lottery Reform, Rules for Resting Players*, SPORTS ILLUSTRATED, Sept. 15, 2017, https://www.si.com/nba/2017/09/15/draft-lottery-reform-proposal-vote. For example, a team with the worst record in the league now has a 25% chance of obtaining the top draft choice in the draft lottery but under the proposed changes would only have a 14% chance. *Id.* Moreover, the team with the worst record would not face the prospect that they could fall further in the draft than the top four picks. *Id.* Finally, the commissioner would have greater powers to sanction teams that rest their starters. *Id.*

Second, sports governing bodies should attempt to limit the influence of a single referee.[68] This can be done by having multiple referees on each competition, permitting appeals on some decisions to the team of referees or based on instant replays, and consideration of using technology to replace some decisions made by human referees,[69] such as whether a tennis ball was in bounds or a baseball pitch was a ball or strike.

Third, not only should sports governing bodies adopt new technologies that assist in assuring accurate on-field decisions, but these and other technologies should be part of a system to review the on-field performance of the referees and for detecting corrupt practices by players and others after the conclusion of the event.[70] To this end, sports governing bodies should use their specialized integrity unit to consistently review film and use available technologies to determine if players or referees have engaged in any questionable activity. Sports governing bodies should report suspected cases as soon as practical to regulatory authorities entrusted to check movements in the betting market.[71]

Finally, to prevent corruptors from targeting certain referees for corrupt offers, the sports governing bodies should have tight controls over referee assignments. They should not permit access to the process by which they assign referees and should announce assignments at a time close to the competitions.[72] Once the sports governing body makes an assignment, however, they should publicize the decision to avoid bettors from using such assignments as insider information and gaining an advantage over other bettors. Each sports governing body should have a system in place to replace referees and other officials at late notice if it is suspected or known that a referee or official may have a potential bias or be involved in manipulation during an upcoming competition.[73]

Conflicts of Interest

Sports governing bodies should adopt policies that reduce conflict between two competing interests: handling sports integrity in an honest,

68 David Forrest, *Match fixing: An Economics Perspective*, in MATCH-FIXING IN INTERNATIONAL SPORTS 177-197 (Springer International Publishing, 2013).

69 *Id.*

70 Ian Preston & Stefan Szymanski, *Cheating in Contests*, 19 OXFORD REV. OF ECON. POL'Y 612-624 (2003).

71 Rebeggiani & Rebeggiani, *supra* note 48.

72 *Id.*

73 IOC, *supra* note 8.

transparent and comprehensive way, on the one hand, and wanting to keep scandals private to protect their commercial interests in wagering, on the other hand. Areas worthy of discussion include whether sports teams should rely on or accept sponsorship money from sportsbook operators.[74] The sports governing bodies should avoid situations where they must weigh the impact of exposing wagering or sports corruption against the financial benefits received from sportsbooks sponsorships. This can be particularly acute where the activity by the sportsbook would justify disassociation. For example, regulators accused a licensed Nevada sportsbook of knowingly underpaying bettors on parlay cards. This incident illustrates the conflicts that a sports governing bodies would face if it had allowed sponsorships between that sportsbook and teams or athletes under its governance.

CONSIDERATIONS FOR THE RESPONSIBILITIES OF THE GOVERNMENT TO MINIMIZE WAGERING-RELATED CORRUPTION

Law enforcement needs to use all available tools to combat competition manipulation. Data analysis, referrals from sports governing bodies, sportsbooks, and other law enforcement agencies domestic and international, physical surveillance at both sporting and wagering venues, sports betting information exchange systems under agreements with the sports governing bodies and sportsbooks, and whistleblowers, represent only a partial list of the resources law enforcement will resort to.[75]

The government also plays a vital role by enacting legislation aimed at the prevention and detection of competition manipulation and by adequately regulating a sports betting market. An equally important function of government is to act as the facilitator for cooperation between the government, betting companies, and sport governing bodies.[76] This effort, however, is ineffective unless the government is committed to both a national sports integrity program and participation in international efforts to prevent corruption. Ronald K. Noble, INTERPOL Secretary General, noted in 2012 that governments must be committed to sports integrity because, "Match-fixing is clearly a many-headed dragon that

74 Misra et. al., *supra* note 33.

75 IOC, *supra* note 8.

76 Rebeggiani & Rebeggiani, *supra* note 48.

we must slay with a coordinated national and international effort"[77] State governments are not equipped to play a significant role in this process. In a moment of candor, a former Florida Attorney General conceded that "evolving technology appears to be outstripping the ability of government to regulate gambling activities on the Internet and of law enforcement to enforce such regulations. Thus, resolution of these matters must be addressed at the national, if not international level."[78]

In light of these factors, this section reviews the measures that the federal government should consider in combating sports corruption.

Establish and Fund a National Sports Integrity Program

The federal government should establish a national sports integrity program that oversees and coordinates all aspects of preventing and detecting sports corruption. A single point of contact for critical regulatory roles such as data collection and analysis is essential; submission of data by states for inclusion in a national database is preferable to a system where each state collects and stores its findings. A central authority should analyze all suspicious activity reports to determine if individual incidents show patterns worthy of investigation.

Likewise, state regulatory authorities do not have the resources or jurisdiction to investigate and prosecute national or international corruptors. A National Sports Integrity Program would address the issues set out below by working with all stakeholders, and coordinating police efforts across international borders. To this end, the government should develop sustainable ways to finance a national program to safeguard sports integrity.[79]

Define statutory obligations of the stakeholders

Regulations for Sportsbook Operators

Chapter 5 provides the requirements for oversight of sportsbook operators for wagering integrity purposes. For example, the government, whether at the state or federal level, should create a standard licensing scheme for all key persons in the sports wagering industry to prevent unscrupulous sportsbooks from using their

---

77 R.K. Noble, *No Quick Fix to Fighting Sports Corruption, INTERPOL Chief Tells FIFA Congress*, July 16, 2013, http://www.interpol.int/News-and-media/News-media-releases/2012/PR044.

78 Florida Attorneys General's Office Formal Opinion. AGO 95-70 (Oct. 18, 1995).

79 European Commission Adopts Action Plan on Online Gambling, PRACTICAL LAW COMPANY, November 1, 2012.

position to assist in competition manipulation. Governments, however, would use the same licensing criteria for ensuring that sportsbook operators adhere to the highest levels of wagering integrity, including not cheating the bettors. Because many of the tools for achieving wagering integrity are the same for achieving sports integrity, repetition here is unnecessary.

Other requirements, however, go directly to sports integrity and governments that regulate the sportsbooks only for wagering integrity may not impose these requirements. They include:

Data Sharing - Early warning detection

Two different systems of data sharing are worthy of consideration. As described earlier, the first is that sportsbooks should share wagering information with a government-run or supervised central database to create a national early warning system. The government should define the information and the protocols necessary for the sportsbooks to provide this information. The government should further explore how to use this information in conjunction with other countries to create an international early warning system.

Second, the federal government should create a national database for the collection and cataloging of historical data on sports wagering and integrity. The collection should include data on wagering events, sports integrity warnings and alerts, crimes, and investigations related to sports or wagering corruption.[80] Information that does not compromise current investigations or bettor privacy should be available to scholars, academics, and law enforcement officials.[81] The government should further explore how this information can be shared internationally with other trusted foreign agencies.

Reporting

Nevada sportsbooks have both federal and state requirements to file suspicious activity reports regarding potential criminal activities by patrons. The government should expand these filing requirements to require all sports books to report any suspicion of sports corruption. Britain, which requires licensed sportsbooks to report suspicious activities or breach of a sporting rule to both the regulator and the sports league, can serve as a model.[82] Like in Britain, book operators

80 Hakeem, *supra* note 51.

81 *Id.*

82 Section 15.1 of the Licence Conditions and Codes of Practice (LCCP) requires licensed betting operators to provide the sports governing bodies with information related to a breach of a rule of the sport governing body. Gambling Commission (Apr.

should have an obligation to report irregular gambling patterns or other suspicious activities related to sports corruption to the Special Sports integrity unit and the sports governing bodies.[83] The sportsbooks should share these reports and any augmented reports (such as a report of a suspected violation of league rules) with the sports governing bodies concurrently with reporting to the respective governmental agencies. Bookmakers' systems for identifying suspicious circumstances should be subject to approval in advance and then subject to independent audit.[84]

Know Your Customer Requirements

The government should impose "Know your Customer" (KYC) standards on sportsbooks for all substantial bets. Flexibility and anonymity in the wagering transaction lend themselves to betting conspiracies.[85] KYC will make assist in deterring sports corruption by making detection more likely and aid in the investigation and enforcement of potential violations of the law. KYC has proven effective in spread betting markets where clients must register by reducing incidences of trading on insider information compared to the less regulated fixed-odds betting markets.[86] Government-imposed KYC requirements should include obtaining and examining government identity information, reviewing the bettor identification against lists of persons that present sports integrity risks (e.g., players, officials, referees, convicted corruptors), providing the customer with house rules and other requirements related to wagering, and monitoring of a bettor's transactions against expected behavior.

Define What Bets And Bet Types That Can Be Accepted

The federal government should restrict some wagers that the

2013), http://www.gamblingcommission.gov.uk/Gambling-sectors/Betting/Operating-licence-holders/Information-that-must-be-provided/Reporting-suspicious-bets.aspx. The British regulators also maintain a dedicated confidential tip line. The Gambling Commission's Betting Integrity Decision Making Framework, 1.4, GAMBLING COMMISSION (Oct. 2013), http://www.gamblingcommission.gov.uk/pdf/Betting%20integrity%20decision%20making%20framework.pdf. Between October 2012 and March 2014, the British gambling authorities received 135 cases of suspicious betting activities, with most being reported by the licensed sportsbooks. Of these 135 cases, the gaming authorities are actively investigating 17 cases. *Id.* at 4.220.

83 Bozkurt, *supra* note 1.

84 David Forrest, Ian McHale, & Kevin McAuley. "*Say It Ain't So*": *Betting-Related Malpractice in Sport*, 3 INT'L J. OF SPORT FIN. 156 (2008).

85 Misra et. al., *supra* note 33.

86 David Forrest & Robert Simmons, *Sport and Gambling*, 19 OXFORD REV. OF ECON. POL'Y 598-611 (2003).

sportsbook markets offer to bettors.[87] If the gambling markets only offer wagers that are difficult to fix, then the likelihood of competition manipulation is lower.[88] Whether a type of wager should be regulated may depend on an assessment of how difficult it is to make the wager the subject of a corrupt contract. Two areas require consideration.

The first is whether wagering should be allowed on minor league or minor sports. Many of these concerns do not apply to accepting wagers on major sports like the NFL, NBA, MLB, and NHL. The most conservative approach is to limit wagering to games that are least likely to have integrity issues because the athletes are fairly paid, the scrutiny of the competition is intense, and the sports organization commits to integrity. Consideration, however, needs to be given to prohibiting wagers on games in minor leagues where the teams may not have a sports organization to monitor integrity, and the media does not widely publicize the results.[89]

The second area that warrants attention relates to bet types such as in-game wagering. Corruption with these bets is both easier to accomplish and less likely to be detected than match fixing or point shaving.

Prohibition of specific bets and bet types needs careful consideration, however. If certain bet types are prohibited, or if domestic operators are constrained to offer "unattractive" odds, serious bettors, who are responsible for a disproportionate share of betting volume, may shift their activities to the international market, further enhancing liquidity in the part of the market where regulatory supervision is weak or non-existent.[90]

---

87 Two jurisdictions, Victoria, Australia, and France, give the sports governing bodies the right to determine which events sportsbooks can accept wagers on and the type of wagers that they can accept. *Sports Betting: Legal, Commercial and Integrity Issues*, REMOTE GAMBLING ASSOCIATION 50-51, London (UK): RGA (2010).

88 *Id.*

89 Ben Van Rompuy, *Limitations on the Sports Betting Offer to Combat Match-Fixing: Experiences from Europe*, GAMING L. REV. AND ECON. Volume 18, Number 10, 2014. In the most extreme cases, bookmakers and bettors were conned into wagering on games that were not even played.

90 As two commentators noted:

> New bet types and their inherent cheating potential should be closely supervised; the regulator should be entitled to impose explicit restrictions on some types of bets, to the point of banning them altogether, a measure which should be taken into consideration with some live bets. However, prohibiting bet types always entails the danger of a shift to the grey market (especially to Asian operators). Therefore, a certain limitation of the offerings in combination with a close supervision should be the more effective strategy.

Regulations for sports governing bodies

The government should require sports governing bodies to adhere to minimum standards for sports integrity including education programs, governance, policing, and compliance programs.[91] Moreover, sports governing bodies should have affirmative responsibilities for reporting suspicious activities or irregular betting patterns to the respective government authorities including any sports integrity agency.

Uniform Criminal Laws

Federal law should have a comprehensive definition of what constitutes competition manipulation and other corrupt acts, who faces criminal liability for engaging in competition manipulation or other corrupt acts, and the penalties including fines, prison, and asset forfeiture.[92] Such a detailed scheme of criminalization of fixers and corrupt activities is an essential tool to combat competition manipulation and other corrupt acts.[93] The current federal criminal law is inadequate, however, and states do not have uniform laws.[94] In addition to standards to supervise and control the betting market

---

Forrest & Simmons, *supra* note 86.

For example, a new jurisdiction considering sports wagering must make a policy decision as to whether to permit in-game wagering. Legislators can speculate whether spot wagering is likely to attract competition manipulation through spot fixing. Some may argue that a spot fix is particularly vulnerable because a corrupted baseball pitcher can decide to walk a batter at an agreed point in a game to facilitate a spot fix on an in-game wager. The corrupt pitcher may feel that this can be accomplished with negligible risk of detection. The legislature must decide: Does it prohibit in-game wagers until scientific evidence provides proof that the spot wagering can efficiently be regulated? Or, does it permit in-game wagers until evidence proves that spot fixing poses an unacceptable risk?

91 Nowy & Breuer, *supra* note 46.

92 Bozkurt, *supra* note 1.

93 Andreff & Byers, *supra* note 36. The anti-corruption reform could include a similar convention through the auspices of UNESCO. U.N. EDUC., SCIENTIFIC, & CULTURAL ORG., INTERNATIONAL CONVENTION AGAINST DOPING IN SPORT, art. 1, Oct. 19, 2005, http:// unesdoc.unesco.org/images/0014/001425/142594m.pdf [hereinafter UNESCO Convention].

94 This situation is not uncommon outside the United States. In Europe, only a limited number of member states have specific prohibitions addressing competition manipulation, and violations in these countries often carry low punishments. Bozkurt, *supra* note 1. Some European countries have general offenses of corruption or fraud, while others have more specific criminal laws addressing match-fixing. Feltes, *supra* note 19.

and bookmakers,[95] the United States and foreign countries need to standardize the criminal offenses associated with sports corruption. These should include specific crimes for competition manipulation, insider trading, and sabotage. Sports bribery statutes should cover blackmail and extortion.[96]

Enforce the Laws against Illegal Sports Wagering

The federal government should enforce existing laws against illegal sports betting to redirect bettors from the illegal bookmakers, who have little interest in protecting sports integrity or policing competition manipulation, to regulated sportsbooks. Large operations in Asian often benefit from corruptors and money launders because they increase liquidity and thus profitability. These operations are agnostic as to the source of the funds or the bettor's motivation for using their platforms. Fewer illegal gamblers cut into the profitability for syndicate operators and match-fixers[97] by reducing the size of the unlawful winning pool for fixed matches. Government efforts would not only include prosecuting violators, [98] but also undertaking steps to block illicit sites, prohibiting advertising for illegal sites,[99] and working with a financial institution to stop the flow of funds between unlawful operators and bettors.[100]

---

95 *Id.*

96 Holden & Rodenberg, *supra* note 40.

97 Williams, *supra* note 27.

98 The particulars regarding more effective means to prosecute violators is covered in the next section.

99 The prohibition against advertising of illegal sportsbook sites needs to pass constitutional muster. For a discussion of these issues, see Michael Hoefges & Milagros Rivera-Sanchez, *Vice Advertising under the Supreme Court's Commercial Speech Doctrine: The Shifting* Central Hudson *Analysis*, 22 HASTINGS COMM. & ENT. L.J. 345 (2000); Kathleen E. Burke, *Greater New Orleans v. United States: Broadcasters Have Lady Luck, or at Least the First Amendment, on Their Side*, 35 NEW. ENG. L. REV. 471 (2001); Megan E. Frese, Note, *Rolling the Dice: Are Online Gambling Advertisers "Aiding and Abetting" Criminal Activity or Exercising First Amendment-Protected Commercial Speech?* 15 FORDHAM INTELL. PROP. MEDIA & ENT. L.J. 547 (2005); Kraig P. Grahmann, *Betting on Prohibition: The Federal Government's Approach to Internet Gambling*, 7 NW. J. TECH. & INTELL. PROP. 161 (2009)

100 The government already has ample tools to stop the flow of funds between illegal internet operators and bettors. The Unlawful Internet Gambling Enforcement Act of 2006, 31 U.S. Code § 5361-5367 ("UIGEA") focuses on two of the three parties to the transfer of money, namely, the online gambling site and the financial institutions that helped to fund the bettors' accounts with the internet company. Sections 5363 and 5364 of the law make it a felony for a person (1) engaged in the business of betting or wagering to (2) knowingly accept money (3) in connection with unlawful gambling. Additionally, federal regulators were directed to draft regulations designed to compel

Extraterritorial Jurisdiction and Extradition

Federal anticorruption statutes should provide for extraterritorial jurisdiction and extradition. Liability should attach when a US citizen or a resident of the US is involved in corrupt practices, or when any activity related to the corruption occurred in the US or while playing in a US league, even if the act occurred in a foreign jurisdiction, or if the corrupt act affects a US sports league.

Create a Special Sports Integrity Unit[101]

The federal government should authorize and assign dedicated agents or a unit within a dedicated agency such as the Federal Bureau of Investigation, to work on combating competition manipulation.[102] This Special Integrity Unit could be modeled in part on Great Britain, which has a dedicated Sports Betting Intelligence Unit with powers to both void bets and prosecute offenders.[103]

For several reasons, the Special Integrity Unit preferably should be organized at the federal level. First, investigating and prosecuting competition manipulation is difficult if the police unit investigating has only a state presence. It would be the equivalent of having local police investigate international securities fraud cases. Second, dedicated integrity units require adequate funding that is more likely to be available at the federal level. Third, the unit needs interstate investigative and law enforcement authority, which is only achievable

financial institutions to identify and block illegal gambling transactions. Financial institutions that didn't comply with the regulations are subject to civil penalties.

The provisions of UIGEA apply only to "unlawful Internet gambling," but the law itself does not declare internet gambling to be illegal. The legality of internet gambling is determined by reference to state and federal law, so for there to be a violation of UIGEA there must be a state or federal law that makes internet gambling illegal.

As for the financial institutions, though UIGEA said that financial institutions must identify, code, and block transfers supporting illegal gambling transactions, the implementing regulations that were finally adopted abandoned this requirement. Instead, entities with the closest relationship to the internet gambling business had to exercise due diligence to determine whether the business was engaged in unlawful internet gambling.

Despite the flaws in the law and the uncertainty regarding the obligations of financial institutions, UIGEA gave federal authorities a potent weapon to go after offshore internet companies and cut off their means of funding.

101 Bozkurt, *supra* note 1.

102 *Id.*

103 The Gambling Commission's Betting Integrity Decision Making Framework, 1.4, GAMBLING COMMISSION (Oct. 2013), http://www.gamblingcommission.gov.uk/pdf/Betting%20integrity%20decision%20making%20framework.pdf.

at a national level. State or local units would not have these powers. Fourth, the Special Integrity Unit must work closely with sports governing bodies, betting operations, state regulators, and foreign governments. A single federal agency can more easily accomplish this than through multiple state agencies.

A special sports integrity unit has many advantages. First, a well-trained and educated, specialized task force can concentrate on prosecuting illegal gambling. A Special Integrity Unit is particularly crucial since federal, state, and local governments currently give low priority to policing both illicit sports gambling, sports corruption, and related crimes.

Second, a Special Integrity Unit could acquire a level of expertise in sports corruption that will assist in both investigation and prosecution of sports corruption cases with consistency and uniformity. Moreover, the dedicated unit could coordinate joint investigations with other government agencies including state gaming regulators, the Financial Crimes Enforcement Network, Homeland Security, and others.

Third, the unit could also serve as the agency that initially reviews alerts from the early warning systems and then functions as both the lead investigators and the communications hub for sports governing bodies, book operators, participants, and other interested parties about suspicious matches.[104]

Fourth, the Special Integrity Unit can set up national contact points that bring together all relevant actors, including regulators from each state that are involved in preventing competition manipulation.[105] The Special Integrity Unit could support both the sport's governing bodies' and the sportsbooks' prevention and deterrent efforts by monitoring betting activities of key individuals.[106] The unit also can serve as the vehicle where people can anonymously report suspicious activities or observations.[107]

To increase its effectiveness, the Special Integrity Unit should have specific powers including: (1) police investigation powers including free access to all sportsbook data and employees; (2) the right to interview sportsbook personnel, players, athletic support personnel (including coaches, trainers, team officials or staff, agents, managers, and medical personnel), referees, and league officials; (3)

---

104 Feltes, *supra* note 19.

105 *Id.*

106 *Id.*

107 *Id.*

subpoena power over third parties; (4) police intelligence powers; (5) technology and personnel to conduct data review and analysis; and (6) the power to recommend or bring disciplinary or criminal prosecutions.[108]

Besides enforcement responsibilities, the Special Integrity Unit can have other vital duties. First, they can provide training and education to other governmental agencies, the sports governing bodies, and the sportsbooks regarding corrupt practices, current threats, and best practices. Second, they can identify weaknesses in processes by both the sports governing bodies and the sportsbooks and propose new rules and methods to address these weaknesses.

Cross-Border Cooperation

Currently, because of its tolerance of large illegal markets and its unwillingness to address their existence, the United States (along with Asian, Central American and Caribbean countries) is impeding the creation of a worldwide organization dedicated to the prevention of competition manipulation.[109]

Instead, the federal government should develop new standards for legal and administrative international cooperation.[110] Such cooperative efforts are not without precedent. On a regional scale, Europe has developed conventions for cross-border cooperation designed to reduce illegal accessible liquid markets for sports wagering and help ensure the detection and prosecution of those involved in competition manipulation.[111]

Essential elements of a cross-border agreement should include:

- Entering bilateral and multilateral treaties, where cooperating countries use active communications channels to exchange intelligence and information related to the investigation and prosecution of sports manipulation.[112] The exchange of information between law enforcement agencies in different countries is helpful in the detection and prosecution of sports corruption.[113] Such cooperation

---

108 Sports Betting Integrity Panel, *supra* note 21.

109 Carpenter, *supra* note 49.

110 Feltes, *supra* note 19.

111 Michael Plachta, *A Council of Europe Adopts New Convention on The Manipulation Of Sports Competitions*, 30 INT'L ENFORCEMENT L. REP. 408 (2014).

112 Michael Plachta, *Council of Europe Acts Against Manipulation of Sports Results, Notably Match-Fixing*, 28 INT'L ENFORCEMENT L. REP. 64-66 (2012).

113 Feltes, *supra* note 19.

creates a shared knowledge base regarding the structure of global betting cartels and organized crime networks and their involvement in competition manipulation.[114] For example, Interpol has worked successfully with Asian law enforcement officials in operations in China, Hong Kong, Macao, Malaysia, Singapore and Vietnam that have led to arrests, seizure of money, and the closing of illegal internet gambling sites.[115]

- Defining corrupt betting and competition manipulation as serious crimes.[116]
- Establishing in each country's laws that participating in or aiding and abetting competition manipulation is a criminal offense under its domestic law when committed intentionally.
- Agreeing to close access to illegal remote and land-based sportsbook operators in their jurisdiction.
- Agreeing to assist in blocking the flow of funds between illegal operators and bettors.
- Agreeing to prohibit advertising for illegal operators.
- Agreeing to seize and forfeit funds related to illegal gambling and competition manipulation.
- Withholding "financial support and operating licenses from those athletes or organizations that fail to comply with the terms of the Uniform Anti-Corruption Program."[117]
- Requiring appropriate investigative means, such as monitoring of communications, seizing of material, covert surveillance, control of bank accounts, and other financial investigations in the fight against manipulation of sports results, especially in cases of manipulation of competitions offered for bets.
- Agreeing to collect and preserve evidence including electronic data related to competition manipulation.
- Agreeing to require customer identification (KYC) and monitor sports bets transactions for suspicious activities

114 Id.

115 Williams, *supra* note 27.

116 Id.

117 Miguel A. Ramos, *Game, Set, Match-Fixing: Will International Anti-Doping Initiatives Pave the Way for Similar Reform for Corrupt Betting in Tennis*, 32 HOUS. J. INT'L L. 201, 237 (2009).

to prevent money laundering,[118] and to assist in sports corruption investigations.

The United Nations Convention Against Corruption can serve as a model for addressing sports corruption on a global basis.[119] The Convention addresses "establishment of anti-corruption bodies and enhanced transparency in the financing of election campaigns and political parties." It includes a code of conduct for public officials, requirements for financial disclosure, and procedures for uniform disciplinary actions. A separate chapter stresses creating or extending uniform criminal acts concerning public corruption, establishing clear rules regarding introducing evidence of corruption, and standards for protecting witnesses and whistleblowers.[120] Additional chapters cover international cooperation,[121] asset recovery,[122] technical assistance and information exchange, and mechanisms for implementation.[123]

Consideration Should Be Given To Repealing The Federal Excise Tax On Sports Wagers And Redirecting The Money To Compensate The Leagues For Promoting Sports Integrity

Whether federal law should require sportsbooks to enter a revenue-sharing agreement of some type with the sports governing bodies and the contestants is controversial.

Three reasons support compensating the leagues. First, the teams and contestants have rights in their names and performance, and the sports betting operations are using this information for commercial advantage. Under existing law, the sports betting operations do not have to pay to use the names or performance data because the First Amendment preempts these rights and other intellectual property protections do not attach to the information.[124] Despite not having

---

118 *Id.*

119 Karen L. Jones, *The Applicability of the United Nations Convention against Corruption to the Area of Sports Corruption (Match-Fixing)*, 3-4 THE INT'L SPORTS L.J. 57 (2012). Adherence to the Convention is optional for the United Nations member states, but the guidelines and are intended to strengthen national laws and bring consistency across countries in handling corruption. *Id.*

120 CHAPTER III, ARTICLES 15–44.

121 CHAPTER IV, ARTICLES 43–49.

122 CHAPTER V, ARTICLES 51–59.

123 CHAPTER VI, ARTICLES 60–62.

124 In National Football League v. Governor of Delaware, 435 F. Supp. 1372 (D. Del. 1977), the court found that once the NFL disseminates schedules and scores, it no longer

a legal right to compensation, public policies underlying the right of publicity suggest that compensation to the teams and players that create the opportunity for commercial exploitation of the games for wagering may be worthy of consideration. As some commentators have noted, "Without these events, betting providers would not be able to sell a marketable product. Betting providers share this dependence on the platform sport with other stakeholders of football institutions."[125]

Second, the sportsbooks need the efforts and cooperation of the sports governing bodies and the athletes to assure that the wagering propositions that they offer are resolved based on honest competition. Giving the governing bodies a financial stake in the revenues from wagering on their sports can only enhance this cooperation.[126]

Finally, any failures of the wagering and sports industries to assure the integrity of the game has negative economic consequences to society. Compensating the sports governing bodies to put into place additional structures and procedures can help to reduce the likelihood of these failures.

On the other hand, the sportsbooks have a compelling argument that the margins on sports wagers are small and that any revenue sharing would raise prices and drive consumers to illegal markets where they can get better odds. Moreover, the concept of revenue

---

expects generating revenue. The value of a sporting event is based on the uncertainty of the outcome, Walter Neale, *The Peculiar Economics of Professional Sport*, 78 Q.J. of Econ., 1–14 (1964). So, once the event has occurred, the value of the recording of that event drops to virtually nothing. Stefan Szymanski, *The Assessment: The Economics of Sport*, 19 Oxford Rev. of Econ. Pol'y 467-77 (2003). The same is true of sports wagers where the principal concerns of the player are that the games are honest (not fixed), fair (that they are played according to transparent and evenly informed rules) and they will get paid if they win. In National Basketball Association v. Motorola, 105 F.3d 841 (2d Cir. 1997) the Second Circuit found that basketball games are not subject to copyright protection because they are not original works of authorship. Anastasios Kaburakis, Ryan M. Rodenberg, & John T. Holden, *Inevitable: Sports Gambling, State Regulation, and the Pursuit of Revenue*, (2015). http://www.hblr.org/wp-content/uploads/2015/01/Kaburakis-Rodenberg-Holden-Inevitable.pdf. See also, C.B.C. Distribution and Marketing, Inc. v. Major League Baseball, 505 F.3d 818 (8th Cir. 2007)

125 Betting scandals and attenuated property rights – How betting related match fixing can be prevented in future, Helmut Dietl and Christian Weingärtner, February 2012, Kaburakis, Anastasios, Ryan M. Rodenberg, and John T. Holden. *Inevitable: Sports Gambling, State Regulation, and the Pursuit of Revenue*, (2015).

126 For example, to this end, the head of the International Olympic Committee has proposed that legislation provide that a portion of gambling revenues go back to the sports organizations to help protect the integrity of the sport. Sport: A Right to Bet, *supra* note 4.

sharing is contrary to existing law in the United States where the sportsbooks only need the results of the contest or events within the game (i.e., names, statistics, scores, real-time data) and anyone can use them for free once made public.[127] Therefore, the government should not create rights not recognized by law to benefit an industry.

A potential solution may be to redirect the existing federal excise tax on sports wagers, which was initially designed to dissuade gambling activities, to the sports governing authorities to combat competition manipulation.

The federal excise tax on sports wagers was first imposed in 1951 at a rate of 10% on the gross handle.[128] The legislative history of the law creating the tax was to "facilitate the enforcement of state criminal laws against gambling."[129] If the purpose of the tax was to prevent legitimate, licensed sportsbook operations from operating, it succeeded, as no sportsbook could operate profitably with that tax load.

In 1974, the tax rate was reduced to 2% with the result being that the first casino-based sportsbooks sprang up in Las Vegas. And in 1983, the tax was reduced to its present rate of 0.25%.[130]

Based on figures compiled by the Urban Institute & Brookings Institution Tax Policy Center, approximately $4.2 million in revenue was generated by the sports wagering excise tax in 2015, an infinitesimal portion of the $3.3 trillion of total tax revenue collected by the IRS.[131] However, if sports betting were more widely available, the excise tax revenues could increase dramatically. A total handle of $100 billion in regulated US markets would produce $250 million in excise taxes.

While the federal government might be unwilling to forego all that revenue, a national interest exists in reducing corruption in sports wagering. Directing some of the excise tax revenue to the sports governing bodies can help to curb corruption while still allowing for sportsbooks to be profitable undertakings. This approach has the

---

127 Helmut Dietl and Christian Weingärtner, *Betting Scandals and Attenuated Property Rights—How Betting-Related Match-Fixing Can Be Prevented in Future*, Feb. 2012.

128 David G. Schwartz, CUTTING THE WIRE: GAMING PROHIBITION AND THE INTERNET (UNIVERSITY OF NEVADA PRESS, 2005), 169

129 Note, *The Federal Gambling Tax and the Constitution*, 43 J. of Crim. Law and Criminology 637, 637 (1953).

130 Schwartz, *supra* note 128, at 169

131 Urban Institute & Brookings Institution Tax Policy Center, Federal Excise Tax Revenue, 2015, (available at http://www.taxpolicycenter.org/statistics/federal-excise-tax-revenue)

benefit of not imposing additional costs on sportsbooks which are already paying the excise tax. The excise tax on sports betting was created to discourage betting on sports, a sentiment that has changed considerably over the years. Ultimately, if a system of sports betting with integrity is to exist in the US, compromises from all parties, including the federal government, will be needed.

SPORTSBOOK RESPONSIBILITIES

The obligation of and the regulations imposed on the sportsbooks to maintain wagering integrity is covered in chapter 5. As noted in this section, the sportsbooks also should have specific obligations related to sports integrity. First, the sportsbooks should have a responsibility to share betting data with a government-regulated shared database for purposes of early warning and corruption detection. Second, the sportsbooks should have an obligation to share suspicions of corruption with the sports governing bodies and the government. This would include following standard procedures for contacting sports organizations and public authorities.[132] Third, the sportsbook should have defined obligations to cooperate with sports governing bodies, foreign governments, and sportsbooks in foreign countries regarding sports corruption, including aiding in the sports governing bodies' code of conduct.[133]

132 Bozkurt, *supra* note 1.

133 *Id.*

About the Authors

Anthony Cabot is the Distinguished Fellow of Gaming Law at the Boyd School of Law, where he teaches gaming law. Before joining the Boyd School of Law in March 2018, Professor Cabot practiced gaming law for 37 years and was a former chair of the gaming law practice and executive committee member at Lewis Roca Rothgerber Christie LLP.

Professor Cabot is a prolific author on gaming law. Besides numerous journal articles, he is the founding editor of *The Internet Gambling Report XI* (2009). He has co-authored *The Law of Gambling and Regulated Gaming: Cases and Materials* (2d 2015), *Regulating Internet Gaming: Challenges and Opportunities* (2013), *Practical Casino Math* (2d ed. 2005), *Casino Credit and Collections* (2003), *International Casino Law* (3rd ed. 1999), and *Federal Gaming Law* (1999). He also co-edited Regulating Land-based Casinos, (2d. 2018).

Professor Cabot was editor of the *UNLV Gaming Law Journal*, (2009-2015), Editor in Chief of the *Journal of Gambling and Commercial Gaming Research* (JGCGR), (2013-present), Co-editor of the *Gaming Law Review* (1999-2005) and editorial board (1996-2005, 2017-present), a member of the editorial board of the *Gaming Research & Review Journal*, UNLV International Gaming Institute, (1996-present) and a member of the editorial board of the International Gambling Studies, *(1999-2004).*

Professor Cabot is a founder and past president of the International Masters of Gaming Law, past president of the Nevada Gaming Attorneys Association, and past general counsel to the International Association of Gaming Attorneys.

Professor Cabot is on the Board of Advisors, International Center for Gaming Regulation, University of Nevada, Las Vegas (2015-present), is an appointed member of the Governor's Advisory Committee on Problem Gambling, State Of Nevada, a , Director and Vice President of the Nevada Council on Problem Gambling, (2009-present) and a member of the Gaming Law Advisory Council, University of Nevada, Las Vegas, Boyd College of Law (2009-present). He is an honorary president and serves on the academic council to the Asia Pacific Association for the Study of Gambling and Commercial Gaming, an organization made up of professors from the entire Asian region including Taiwan, Japan, China, Macau, and Australia.

Keith C. Miller is the Ellis and Nelle Levitt Distinguished Professor of Law at Drake University in Des Moines, Iowa. Professor Miller teaches the course on Gaming Law at Drake along with courses in the area of Torts. In addition to numerous law review articles, he is co-author of *The Law of Gambling and Regulated Gaming* (2d edition), the leading casebook on gaming law.

Professor Miller is the Vice-President of Educator Affiliates of the International Masters of Gaming Law (IMGL), a global gambling law network and educational organization, and Vice-Chair of the Gaming Law Committee for the Business Law Section of the American Bar Association. Professor Miller serves on the Editorial Board for *Gaming Law Review*, the leading peer-reviewed gaming law journal, and is a member of the UNLV Gaming Law Journal Advisory Board.

He has spoken on and moderated panels for the IMGL and the ABA, and has conducted symposia and lectured at law schools in France and the US, including being a Visiting Professor at the University of Nevada-Las Vegas Boyd School of Law. Professor Miller also consults on gaming law cases, has been an expert witness in gaming law litigation, and is a frequent resource for media on matters involving gaming law.

Professor Miller received his J.D. from the University of Missouri-Kansas City where he was the Editor-in-Chief of the UMKC Law Review. After practicing law in Kansas City, Missouri, Professor Miller obtained his LL.M. degree from the University of Michigan Law School before beginning his career as an academic lawyer. Professor Miller also served as the NCAA Faculty Representative at Drake University from 1995-2000.

Index

Pages with charts are indicated by "**C**" following the page number, and pages with pictures are indicated by "*illus.*" following the page number.

Also from UNLV Gaming Press

Tales from the Slot Floor: Casino Slot Managers in Their Own Words
David G, Schwartz, editor

Regulating Land-Based Casinos: Policies, Procedures, and Economics
Second Edition
Anthony Cabot & Ngai Pindell, editors

Tales from the Pit: Casino Table Games Managers in Their Own Words
David G, Schwartz, editor

On the Frontline in Macao:
Casino Employees, Informal Learning, & Customer Service
Carlos Siu Lam

Regulating Land-Based Casinos:
Policies, Procedures, and Economics
Anthony Cabot & Ngai Pindell, editors

Regulating Internet Gaming: Challenges and Opportunities
Anthony Cabot & Ngai Pindell, editors

Frontiers in Chance:
Gaming Research Across the Disciplines
David G. Schwartz, editor

The UNLV Gaming Press, a collaboration between the University Libraries, the UNLV Harrah Hotel College, and the UNLV William S. Boyd School of Law, was established in 2012 in order to make available the scholarly output of university-sponsored conferences, historic materials that the university holds, and new work that illuminates the legal, economic, social, and historical dimensions of gambling and gaming in all of its forms.